ILLUSTRATED

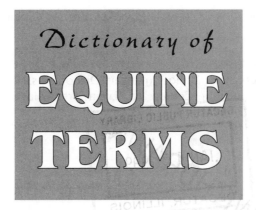

Dictionary of

EQUINE
TERMS

Compiled by
New Horizons Equine Education Center, Inc.

Alpine
PUBLICATIONS

Loveland, Colorado

DICTIONARY OF EQUI

Library of Congress Cataloging-in-Publication Data

Dictionary of equine terms / compiled by New Horizons Equine Education Center.
    p.   cm.
  ISBN 0-931866-88-X
  1. Horses--Dictionaries. 2. Horsemanship-Dictionaries. I. New Horizons Equine Education Center, Inc. (Livermore, Colo.)
SF278.D535 1996
636.1'003--dc20

96-6759
CIP

The contents of the *Illustrated Dictionary of Equine Terms* has been compiled as carefully and accurately as possible. Regional variations in the interpretations or definition of terms may not always be reflected here. Whenever possible, the pronunciation of terms has been provided. Most foreign words are not accompanied by pronunciations. Alpine Publications, Inc. and New Horizons accept no responsibility for the use of information contained herein, either favorable or unfavorable.

This book is available at special quantity discounts for breeders and for club promotions, premiums, or educational use. Write for details.

1 2 3 4 5 6 7 8 9 0

Cover design by Bob Schram, Bookends
Interior Design: Harlene Finn
Typesetting: Lyn Chaffee Book Typography

Printed in the United States of America

Dedication

With deep appreciation to

Vera Bergsten

for having the heart and determination to
begin this important endeavor.

Acknowledgments

Compilation of this vast array of equine terminology required the help of many individuals and much deserved appreciation is extended to each of these people.

Research: Vera Bergsten, Colette May

Project Coordinator: Julianna May

Artists: Pam Froemke, Michele Spalding, Kathy Walker

Editing: Catherine O'Hala

Proofreading: Ute Jung, Laura Hake, Betsy Lynch, Sue Reynolds, Kirsten Woy, Bobette Host, Cherry Hill, Deborah Helmers

Publication Coordinator: Sharon Anderson

In 1986, New Horizons developed the first comprehensive home-study program that now includes over forty courses. This innovative program provides students with a working knowledge in equine science without the hassle and expense of on-campus study. A broad range of subjects is included, such as nutrition, reproduction, anatomy, first aid, breeding, genetics, stable management, psychology, behavior, trailering, and training—to name just a few. The success of this unique program is largely due to the individual feedback the students receive.

In addition, New Horizons Equine Education Center, Inc., now has specialized home education programs for

- The American Quarter Horse Association
- The International Arabian Horse Association
- The Appaloosa Horse Club
- The American Paint Horse Association.

For more information on these programs, contact:

New Horizons Equine Education Center, Inc.
425 Red Mountain Road
Livermore, CO 80536
Phone: (970) 484-9207
Fax: (970) 224-9239

A

abasia (ə bā′ zhe ə) trembling or shaking of the legs; an inability to walk due to some defect in coordination

Abats Le Sultan a Russian game played on horseback; the riders wear fencing masks covered with feathers and carry swords; the object of the game, which involves a number of players, is to cut off the feathers from the mask, the winner being the only one with feathers remaining

Abayyan one of the strains in the purebred Arabian

abdomen (ab′ dō mən) the part of the body (except the back) between the thorax and the pelvis; the belly; contains the stomach, intestines, liver, bladder, kidney, reproductive organs, etc.

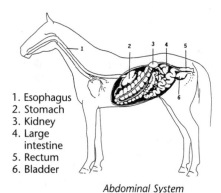

1. Esophagus
2. Stomach
3. Kidney
4. Large intestine
5. Rectum
6. Bladder

Abdominal System

abdominal pain see *colic*

abdominocentesis (ab däm′ i nō sen tē′ sis) withdrawal of fluid through a needle from the abdominal cavity

abduction (ab duk′ shən) moving a limb away from the middle of the body

abnormal (ab nôr′ məl) not typical; unusual

abort (ə bôrt′) to expel a fetus before it is capable of living independently

abortifacient (a bôr′ tə fā shənt) substance that causes abortion

abortion (ə bôr′ shən) the premature expulsion of the fetus; the reasons for abortion are many and varied, but the timing and symptoms may offer clues to the cause

about turn (ə bout′ tʉrn) a dressage movement in which the horse is made to turn or pivot on the forehand or haunches

above the bit evasion of the bit; the horse carries his head too high and is difficult to control

abrasion (ə brā′ zhən) a wound due to the wearing away of the hair and top layer of skin by friction

ABRS Association of British Riding Schools

abrupt transition (ə brupt′ tran zish′ ən) occurs when the rider has given aids too suddenly to move a horse smoothly from one gait into another; balance, rhythm, head carriage may be lost

abscess (ab′ ses) a localized accumulation of pus formed by disintegration of tissues

---

a=fat; ā=ape; ä=car; â=bare; e=ten; ē=even; i=is; ī=bite; ō=go; ô=horn; ōō=tool; ŏŏ=look; u=up; ʉ=fur; ŋ=ring; ə=sofa

absorbent (əb zôr' bənt) **1.** a compound or carrier used to apply topical medications to a horse; medicines that draw out and remove dead tissue from a wound **2.** a material that absorbs or removes various fluids from the body; examples are gauze, cotton, wool

absorption (əb zôrp' shən) the incorporation of substances into or across tissues

Abu' urqub one of the strains in the purebred Arabian

acceptance time the time designated prior to a race or event during which the owner or trainer has to announce whether a particular horse, previously nominated, will indeed be a starter

accept the leg when the horse willingly accepts the light pressure of the rider's legs on his side

accessory carpal bone the disk-shaped bone forming the sharp ridge at the back of the knee

accessory glands (ak ses' ə rē glandz) glands located along the urethra of the male horse that produce fluids to nourish and preserve sperm; includes the prostate gland, the bulbourethral glands (Cowper's gland), and the seminal vesicles

acclimatize (ə klī' mə tīz') to become accustomed to a new climate or management

accommodation (ə käm' ə dā' shən) the automatic adjustment of the lens of the eye for focusing on objects at various distances

account for (ə kount' fôr) when a fox, or other hunted game, is killed or pursued to its den by the hounds

acephalia (ə' se fā lē ə) a lethal condition in which the skull of a foal is not formed on birth; the fetus is always aborted or born dead

acepromazine (ə' se prō mə zēn) the trade name for acetyl promazine; a commonly used tranquilizer

acetabulum (as' ə tab' ōō ləm) the pelvic structure that receives the head of the femur to make the hip joint

acetyl promazine (a' sēt' əl prō mə zēn) also known as ace or acepromazine; a tranquilizer commonly used for horses

acey-deucey (ās' ē dōō' sē) riding with one stirrup leather adjusted longer than the other; done by some jockeys to keep their balance on sharp turns

Achilles' tendon (ə kil' ēz ten' dən) the large tendon at the back of the hind leg, originating from the point of the hock and connecting to the large muscles of the gaskin

acidosis (as' ə dō' sis) a condition of acid accumulation in the body due to disruption of the normal acid-base balance; may be caused by overworking an unfit horse

acid salts (as' id sôlts) salts given to the horse that counteract or negate the buildup of alkaline salts in the horse, which can occur in hot weather or during strenuous exercise

acne (ak' nē) a skin condition caused by bacterial infection; occurs as small lumps or pimples that may break open and exude pus; treatment includes wiping the surface of the skin with an antibacterial agent and cleaning all tack

acorn poisoning (ā′ kôrn poi′ zə niŋ) poisoning due to eating oak leaves or green acorns; causes severe intestinal and kidney damage, and often results in death

acoustic (ə kōōs′ tik) pertaining to sound or to the sense of hearing

acquired gaits (ə kwīrd′ gāts) gaits that a horse must be taught

across the board (ə krôs′ thə bôrd) a combination pari-mutuel (race) ticket on a horse, meaning that you collect a prize if your horse runs first, second, or third

ACTH see *adrenocorticotropic hormone*

acting master (ak′ tiŋ mas′ tər) a person temporarily appointed to organize a hunt until a permanent master is selected

action (ak′ shən) how a horse moves at all gaits; degree of flexion of the joints of the legs during movement; some classes require high, snappy action and others seek easy, ground–covering action

activated charcoal (ak′ tə vā′ tid chär kōl′) substance used to inactivate and bond to ingested toxins to prevent their absorption in the intestinal tract

active immunization (ak′ tiv i myōō nə zā′ shən) acquired immunity due to the presence of antibodies formed by the body in response to an antigen

acuity (ə kyōō′ ə tē) sharp, clear vision

acupuncture (ak′ yoo punk′ chər) an ancient Chinese practice of piercing

parts of the body with needles in an effort to treat disease and relieve pain

acute (ə kyōōt′) a short and relatively severe course of development; opposite of chronic

acute inflammatory response (ə kyōōt in flam′ ə tŏr′ ē ri späns′) swelling due to a recently acquired bruise or injury; can be reduced with cold therapy

adaptability (ə dapt′ ə bil′ ə tē) ability to adjust to new circumstances

adaptation (ad′ əp tā′ shən) changes so behavior will conform to new circumstances

Adayevsky a light type of Russian breed; similar to the Kazakh

Addison's disease (ad′ i səns di zēz′) disease caused by insufficient corticosteroid hormone production by the adrenal gland

adduction (a duk′ shən) moving a limb toward the body

adenocarcinoma (ad′ ən ō kär′ sə nō′ mə) cancer of glandular tissues

adenovirus (ad′ ə nō vī′ rəs) a virus affecting horses and causing upper respiratory symptoms; of little significance except in horses with weakened immune systems

adequate bone (ad′ ə kwit bōn) a term used to indicate that the horse appears to have enough height and/or thickness of bone for his size; generally reflects personal opinion

---

a=f<u>a</u>t; ā=<u>a</u>pe; ä=c<u>a</u>r; â=b<u>a</u>re e=t<u>e</u>n; ē=<u>e</u>ven; i=<u>i</u>s; ī=b<u>i</u>te; ō=g<u>o</u>; ô=h<u>o</u>rn; ōō=t<u>oo</u>l; ŏŏ=l<u>oo</u>k; u=<u>u</u>p; ʉ=f<u>u</u>r; ŋ=ri<u>ng</u>; ə=sof<u>a</u>

adhesion   (ad hē′ zhən) a fibrous attachment abnormally joining two adjacent tissues or organs

adipose   (ad′ ə pōs′) animal fat; tissue that can store fat

adjunct   (aj′ uŋkt) an additional agent or measure used to assist a horse in overcoming a problem

adjuvant   (aj′ ə vənt) an extra substance added to a prescription to increase the effect of the main ingredient

adrenal   (ə drē′ nəl) pertaining to the adrenal glands

adrenal glands   (ə drē′ nəl glandz) two small, flat organs located in front of the kidneys that secrete hormones directly into the bloodstream

adrenalin   (ə dren′ əl in) epinephrine; a hormone secreted by the adrenal gland that acts primarily as a stimulant; synthetic adrenaline may be used to increase the heart's rate and to treat asthma

adrenocorticotropic hormone   (ə drē′ nō kôr′ ti kō trōp′ ic hôr′ mōn) a hormone secreted by the pituitary gland to stimulate corticosteroid secretion by the adrenal glands

ADS   American Driving Society

AERC   see *American Endurance Ride Conference*

aerobe   (er′ ōb) a microorganism that can live and grow in the presence of oxygen

aerobic   (er ō′ bik) requiring air or free oxygen to live and grow

aerophagia   (er′ ə fā′ jē ə) spasmodic swallowing of air followed by the belching of air from the stomach

Aesculus   (es′ kyŏŏ′ ləs) see *buckeye*

afferent   (af′ ər ənt) carrying toward a center

Affirmed   (ə fʉrmd′) the first racehorse to earn $2,000,000

aficionado   (ə fish′ ə nä′ dō) ardent follower, supporter, or enthusiast; a fan

aflatoxicosis   (af′ lə täk′ si cō′ sis) toxins produced by molds growing on feed; can cause severe liver damage

"A" fork   (ā fôrk) a narrow saddle fork with no swell, shaped like the letter A, peaking at the base of the horn; see *Western saddle forks* (illus.)

African horse sickness   (af′ ri kan hôrs sik′ nis) a highly fatal viral infection transmitted by flying insects

afterwale   (af′ tər wāl) the upper ridge of the padded harness collar; see *harness parts B* (illus.)

against the clock   (ə genst′ the kläk) term used in show jumping, a competition, or jump-off, in which the competitor with the fewest faults and the fastest time becomes the winner

agalactia   (ə′ gə lak′ shē ə) inability of the mare to produce milk; can be caused by grazing on fescue pasture during pregnancy

agar gel immunodiffusion test (AGID)   (ā′ gär jel i myŏŏ nō di fyŏŏ zhən test) the technical name for the procedure used for the Coggin's test

age (āj) 1. the number of years since birth 2. the age of many registered horses is computed from January 1 of the year in which the horse is foaled

aged horse (ājd hôrs) a mature horse; in show horses, aged horses are six years and older; also called *senior*

agent (ā' jənt) any substance or technique capable of producing a physical, chemical, or biological effect

agglutination titer (ə glōōt' ən āsh ən tīt' ər) the highest dilution of a serum that causes clumping of bacteria or other particulate antigens

AGID see *agar gel immunodiffusion test*

agility (a jil' ə tē) ability to change direction of the body or its parts rapidly

aging by teeth see *teeth, aging*

agistment (ə' gist mənt) the use of someone else's land and pasture for the grazing of a horse for the payment of a fee, generally on a weekly or monthly basis

agonist (ag' ə nist) a muscle (or group of muscles) that contracts to contribute to the desired movement

agonistic behavior (ag' ə nis' tik bi hāv' yər) combative behavior; a basic behavior pattern; includes aggression, submission, and attempts to escape

agoraphobia (ag' ər ə fō' bē ə) fear of the outside; usually the horse is afraid to leave the barn after being stalled for long periods

AHC see *American Horse Council*

AHSA see *American Horse Shows Association*

AI see *artificial insemination*

aids (āds) signals or cues used by the rider to communicate with the horse; see *artificial aids; natural aids; back aids*

aids, diagonal (dī ag' ə nəl) rein acting on one side; leg pressure being applied to the opposite side

aids, lateral (lat' ər əl) rein and legs acting mainly on the same side

aids, parallel (par' ə lel') right and left aids doing the same thing; for example, both reins making light contact with the bit during a halt; also called *bilateral aids*

aids, unilateral (yōō' nə lat' ər əl) right and left aids doing different things; for example, right leg applying pressure while the left leg holds a neutral position

aiken (āk' ən) jump made of vertical rails and a mound of fir boughs

airs above the ground (ârs ə buv thə ground) any of the high-school movements in which the horse's forelegs or fore- and hind legs are off the ground; includes ballatade, capriole, courbette, croupade, and levade

airs, classical (klas' i kəl) exercises designed to develop and perfect the natural movements of the horse

---

a=fat; ā=ape; ä=car; â=bare; e=ten; ē=even; i=is; ī=bite; ō=go; ô=horn; ōō=tool; ŏŏ=look; u=up; ʉ=fur; ŋ=ring; ə=sofa

airways (âr′ wāz) route of passage of the air into the lungs; including nose, trachea, and bronchi

AJPHA American Junior Paint Horse Association

Akhal-Teké Russian breed known for withstanding severe weather conditions; noted for speed and jumping; lively, stubborn, even rebellious; average height: 14.2–15.2 hands

albert head collar (al′ bert hed′ käl′ ər) a head collar with an adjustable throatlatch that is slotted up into the loops of the front and over the headpiece; it has no metal rings on the cheek pieces; it is less liable to break, because when the horse pulls back he tends to give in because of the pressure at the poll

Albino (al bī′ nō) a horse suffering from albinism, which is the congenital absence of pigment in the skin, hair, and eyes; the eyes and skin are very sensitive to light; although not considered a true breed, they were started in the U.S., originating from Morgan and Arabian crosses; the color may be white, cream, or ivory; they are docile, long lived, and intelligent, with a special ability to learn circus exercises

alfalfa (al fal′ fə) high-protein hay from the legume family

alight (ə līt) to dismount

alimentary canal (al′ ə men′ tər ē kə nal′) the tract in which digestion occurs, that extends the length of the body from the lips to the anus, gastrointestinal

alkaline salts (al′ kə līn′ sôlts) salts given to a horse to offset the buildup of acid salts in the body, which can

occur if unfit or malnourished horses are overworked

alkaloid (al′ ka loid) a bitter, basic organic substance found in plants

alkalosis (al′ kə lō′ sis) disturbance of the acid-base balance resulting in excess base or a deficit of acid or carbon dioxide

All American Futurity (ôl ə mer′ i kən fyōō tōōr′ i tē) a famous race held at Ruidoso Downs for two-year-old Quarter Horses

allantoic fluid (al′ ən to′ ik flōō′ id) yellowish brown fluid originating in the placenta and kidneys that protects the fetus and lubricates the birth canal; expelled on rupture of the placenta

all-around cow horse a horse skilled at carrying out all the duties required of him by a cowboy

All-Around World Champion Cowboy a title achieved by the top money winner who competed in two or more rodeo events

allele (ə lēl′) nonidentical genes that are located at the same physical position on a chromosome

allergen (al′ ər jən) substance capable of inducing an allergy or hypersensitivity

allergic bronchiolitis (ə lʉr′ jik broŋ′ kē ō lī′ tis) inflammation of the smallest divisions of the bronchial tubes, deep in the lungs; caused by allergic reaction to a substance

allergic urticaria (ʉr′ ti kär i ə) see *sand fly*

allergy (al′ ər jē) hypersensitivity to a particular substance (food, pollen, dust, mold, medications, etc.); may cause physical reactions such as sneezing, respiratory problems, or wheals

allotriophagy (ä lot′ rē ō fā jē) eating unnatural material

allowance race (ə lou′ əns rās) a race with both allowances and penalties in regard to the conditions of the race, moneys won, races won, or date the last race or races were won

all the way home see *home*

alopecia (al′ ə pēsh′ ē ə) a lack of hair in areas where normally present

alpha tocopherol (al′ fə tō käf′ ə rôl′) vitamin E

alsike (al′ sīk) a type of clover that is toxic to horses

also-ran (ôl sō ran) any unplaced horse in a race

alter (ôl′ tər) to castrate or geld a horse, rendering him sterile

alternaria (al′ tər när ē ə) genus of fungus that if grown in the lungs causes irritation, inflammation, and allergic reaction

alternative inflammation (al tur′ nə tiv in′ flə mā′ shən) an inflammation in which cell changes caused by bacterial toxins lead to tissue necrosis

Altér-Real (äl tär′ rā äl′) a breed from Portugal; quiet and intelligent; used for saddle horses; used by royalty in the eighteenth century; average height: 15–16.1 hands

alum (al′əm) a white powder with a sweet taste; used for its astringent action in control of diarrhea; mixed with zinc sulfate to control proud flesh

aluminum racing shoe (ə lōō′ mə nəm rās′ iŋ shōō) a lightweight shoe commonly worn by racehorses; the shoe weighs about 5 oz

alveolar periostitis (al vē′ ə lər per′ i äs tīt′ əs) an inflammation of the periosteum of the alveoli due to infection; marked by separation and pain

alveolar ventilation (al vē′ ə lər ven′ tə lā shən) the volume of air that moves in and out of the lung alveoli each minute

alveoli (al vē′ ō lī) tiny air sacs in the lungs where oxygen and carbon dioxide are exchanged

alveoli, dental (al vē′ ō lī den′ təl) socket in the jaw bones in which the teeth are held

amateur (am′ ə chər) a rider older than eighteen who does not get paid for riding

Amateur-Owner (am′ ə chər ō′ ner) class open to horses where the owner or member of the owner's immediate family is the rider

amble (am′ bəl) a slow, four-beat gait in which the horse's hind leg and foreleg on the same side are moved forward together but land separately, without suspension

American Appaloosa Association Appaloosa breed registry

---

a=fat; ā=ape; ä=car; â=bare e=ten; ē=even; i=is; ī=bite; ō=go; ô=horn; ōō=tool; ŏŏ=look; u=up; u=fur; ŋ=ring; ə=sofa

American Association of Owners and Breeders of Peruvian Paso Horses a breed registry; to qualify for registration there must be a stallion report on file and proper paperwork submitted with photos and fee or, if imported, must be registered in Peru or Honduras

American Bashkir Curly a breed noted for a long, curly coat of hair; especially well adapted to extremely cold weather, such as exists in their native home—the eastern slopes of Ural Mountains of Russia; the mane hair and often the tail falls out completely each summer and grows back during the winter; in build, Curlies are medium size and chunky; the breed is noted for small nostrils, a gentle disposition, and heavy milking; many have a natural fox-trot gait; all colors are accepted; the American Bashkir Curly Registry was formed August 14, 1971; horses weighing in excess of 1,350 pounds or having faulty conformation are disqualified from registry

American Belgian Horse a large draft breed known for its docile temperament and powerful action; distinctively taller than other Belgians; height: 17–19 hands

American Buckskin Registry Association color registry for all breeds of buckskins, duns, red duns, and grullos

American Connemara Pony Society a registry for purebred and halfbred Connemaras

American Council of Spotted Asses a registry for spotted donkeys with at least two spots behind the throatlatch and above the legs

American Creme Draft Horse Association a registry for draft horses with cream color, white mane and tail, amber eyes, and pink skin

American Creme Horse a color breed rather than a distinctive type; given breed status in 1970, at which time the American Albino Association, Inc., established a separate American Creme Horse division for their registration

American Dartmoor Pony Association an association developed to preserve, promote, and encourage the breeding and use of Dartmoor Ponies in North America

American Dominant Gray Registry a color registry in which at least one parent must be gray or roan for registration

American Donkey & Mule Society, Inc. an international breed society for donkeys, mules, and hinnies (and all ass hybrids) of all types, sizes, and breeds; founded in 1967

American Endurance Ride Conference (AERC) organized in 1971 to promote endurance riding and keeping trails accessible to horsemen; maintains records of all horses and riders; encourages better horse care and prevention of cruelty to animals

American Exmoor Pony Registry a registry for Exmoors born of registered parents in North America

American Horse Council, Inc. a national trade organization formed to represent all sectors of the U.S. horse industry; formed in 1969; dedicated to the development of the American equine industry, it seeks a fair tax consideration for horse producers (farmers) and develops educational programs and activities; a key function is to advise government officials about legislation affecting horse owners and horse activities

American Horse Shows Association (AHSA) an organization that sanctions over 2,500 shows

American Miniature Horse Association (AMHA) a registry for horses that do not exceed 34 in. in height; both parents must be AMHA registered

American Mule Association a breed registry for mules

American Mustang and Burro Association a registry for wild equine and their offspring adopted through the Bureau of Land Management or any of the recognized placement programs

American Mustang Association a registry for the Mustang, a versatile breed of horse that originated on the Iberian Peninsula

American Paint Horse Association a breed registry in which Paint, Quarter Horse, and Thoroughbred bloodlines with tobiano or overo coat patterns are eligible for registration

American Pinto Arabian Registry a registry that documents the pedigree of Pinto Arabian partbreds, purebreds, and breeding stock

American Quarter Horse Association (AQHA) a registry that documents the pedigree of Quarter Horses, which are best known for their speed and versatility; founded in 1940, more than 3,000,000 horses have been registered with the association

American Quarter Horse Studbook a stud book containing two parts—

the numbered studbook and an appendix in which Thoroughbred crosses may be registered; a horse can move from the appendix to the numbered studbook by a register of merit system

American Quarter Pony Association an association for Quarter Ponies

American Saddlebred a breed originating in Kentucky; height: 15–16.5 hands; long necks; three and five gaited; comfortable, animated ride; sometimes called *American Saddle Horse*

American Saddle Horse see *American Saddlebred*

American Saddle Horse

American Shetland a breed of pony developed in the U.S. from imported European stock for riding and light draft work; capable of pulling loads much heavier than their own weight; weight: approximately 340 lbs

American Shetland Pony Club a registry for Shetlands

American Standardbred a breed created in the U.S. from breeding

---

a=f<u>a</u>t; ā=<u>a</u>pe; ä=c<u>a</u>r; â=b<u>a</u>re; e=t<u>e</u>n; ē=<u>e</u>ven; i=<u>i</u>s; ī=b<u>i</u>te; ō=g<u>o</u>; ô=h<u>o</u>rn; ōō=t<u>oo</u>l; ŏŏ=l<u>oo</u>k; u=<u>u</u>p; ʉ=f<u>u</u>r; ŋ=ri<u>ng</u>; ə=sof<u>a</u>

stock imported from different European countries; used for trotting and pacing races under harness

American studbook Thoroughbred horse registry

American Trotting Horse see *Standardbred*

American Walking Pony Registry a registry for foals of a Welsh Pony/Tennessee Walking Horse cross

American Welara Pony Society a registry for Welsh/Arabian crosses

American Welsh Pony a breed developed in the U.S.; suitable for light draft work and riding; a good mount for children; patient, lively, and intelligent; height: 12.1–14 hands

amino acid (ə mē′ nō as′ id) any of a class of organic compounds containing nitrogen and forming the building blocks of proteins

ammonia poisoning (ə mōn′ yə poi′ zə niŋ) nitrate poisoning

amnion (am′ nē ən) a transparent sac that directly envelops the fetus

amniotic fluid (am′ nē ät ik flōō′ id) colorless liquid surrounding the fetus; contains acids, salts, cells, and mucus

amphetamine (am fet′ ə mēn′) a drug that stimulates the central nervous system, increases blood pressure, and reduces appetite and nasal congestion

anabolic (ə na bäl′ ik) pertaining to any constructive process in which simple substances are converted into living tissue, building muscle and conditioning

anabolic steroid (ster′ oid) hormone that increases muscle mass

anaerobe (an′ er ōb) an organism capable of growing in the complete absence of oxygen

anaerobic (an′ er ō′ bik) able to survive only where there is no oxygen

anal atresia (ā nəl ə′ trē zḫa) blocked anus; foal born with no anal opening, hence no products of digestion may pass; surgical correction is rarely beneficial

analeptic (an′ ə lep′ tik) any drug that stimulates the central nervous system, e.g., caffeine, amphetamines, etc.

analgesic (an′ əl jē′ zik) any drug that temporarily relieves pain without causing unconsciousness

anaphylaxis (an′ ə fə lak′ sis) a severe allergic reaction to a foreign protein or drug that results in a state of shock

anatomy (ə nat′ ə mē) the science of the structure of the animal body and the relation of its parts

ancestor (an′ ses tər) early type of horse from which the horses of today descended

anconite (aŋ′ kō nīt) see *monkshood*

Andalusian (an′ də lōō′ zḫən) a breed originating from Spain with influences from the Barb and many other European and American breeds; characterized by high-stepping movement; color: bay, black, gray, and roan

androgen (an′ drə jən) hormone

that contributes to masculine characteristics

anemia (ə nē' mē ə) a blood condition caused by deficiency of hemoglobin; usually accompanied by reduced number of red blood cells; caused by excessive bleeding, infection, dietary deficiency, or presence of toxins in the body

anesthetic (an' əs thet' ik) a drug or agent that is used to abolish the sensation of pain

anesthetize (an əs' the tīz) to cause a loss of sensation of pain with or without a loss of consciousness

anestrus (an es' trəs) a period of sexual inactivity in the mare where there is absence of observable heat due to season, pregnancy, and other physical and psychological causes

aneurysm (an' yər iz əm) a blood-filled sac formed by an abnormal dilation of the wall of an artery, a vein or the heart

angle of bite the outer angle at which the upper and lower incisors meet

Anglo Arab (aŋ' glō ar' əb) a horse defined by the Arabian horse society as being an animal with a pedigree that shows no other strain of blood other than Thoroughbred and Arabian

Anglo Argentine (aŋ' glō är' jən tēn') a South American cross between the Thoroughbred and the Criollo; a local cow pony

Anglo Persian (aŋ' glō pʉr' zhən) a Persian breed bred by the Shah of Persia as a general-purpose horse; a cross of the Arab and the Persian

angular limb deformity (aŋ' gyə lər lim di fôr' mi tē) abnormal angulation of the leg when viewed from the front or rear; can be due to genetics, trauma, congenital problems, or nutritional imbalances

anhidrosis (an hī drō' sis) an abnormal deficiency of sweat

animal hair bleach (an' ə məl hâr blēch) a substance used to remove yellow stains and discoloration in mane and tail

ankle (aŋ' kəl) 1. fetlock 2. the joint on both the fore- and hind limbs between the cannons and the pasterns 3. a leg marking in which the white extends to and covers the fetlock joint; see *points of the horse* (illus.)

ankle boots a common type of brushing boot; shaped and rounded padded cap of leather or kersey to protect the fetlock joint as well as the tendons and ligaments above it

ankle, marking a white leg marking from the coronet to and including the fetlock; see *markings, leg* (illus.)

ankles, cocked see *cocked ankles*

ankylosis (aŋ' kəl ō sis) immobilization and fusion of a joint due to disease, injury, or surgical procedure

anodynes (an' ə dīnz) medicines or drugs that relieve or eliminate pain

anorexia (an' ə rek' sē ə) loss of or decrease in appetite

---

a=fat; ā=ape; ä=car; â=bare e=ten; ē=even; i=is; ī=bite; ō=go; ô=horn; ōō=tool; ŏŏ=look; u=up; ʉ=fur; ŋ=ring; ə=sofa

anoxia   (an äk′ sē ə) lack of oxygen

anquera   a "rumble seat" or "mother-in-law's seat" attached to the back skirt of a Mexican saddle; enables a passenger to accompany the rider

antagonist   (an′ tag ən ist) a muscle (or group of muscles) that acts opposite of the agonist to control and stabilize movement

antebrachium   (an′ tē brā′ kē əm) the forearm

ante-post betting   (an′ te post bet′ tiŋ) the placing of bets on a race at an agreed price prior to the day of the race

anterior   (an tēr′ ē ər) situated in front of or in the forward part of an organ; toward the head end of the body

anthelmintic   (ant′ hel min′ tik) a drug designed to reduce the number of parasitic eggs in the environment; acts by killing adult parasites and reducing the reproductive capabilities of the parasites that survive; deworming agent

anthrax   (an′ thraks) an infectious disease resulting from the ingestion of the spore *Bacillus anthracis*; leads to acute blood poisoning in the horse and rapid death

antibiotic   (an′ ti bī ät′ ik) chemicals produced from fungi; the chemicals possessing the ability to inhibit or destroy bacteria, fungi, and other infectious organisms

antibiotic-induced diarrhea   (in dōōsd′ dī′ ə rē′ ə) diarrhea that occurs after the use of oral antibiotics, especially tetracyclines, in the horse; the diarrhea is due to a change in the resident bacteria in the intestinal tract

antibody   (an′ ti bäd′ ē) a disease-fighting substance produced by the body in response to the presence of an antigen

antibrushing shoe   see *featheredge shoe*

anticast rollers   see *arch rollers*

anticipation   (an tis′ ə pā′ shən) when the horse is aware of what is about to happen; in the case of a transition, the horse may try to make the transition before the rider's aid

anticoagulant   (an ti kō ag′ yə lənt) any compound that destroys the ability of the blood to clot

antidote   (an′ tə dōt′) a remedy for counteracting a poison

antiferment   (an′ tə fɤr ment) an agent that prevents fermentation

antigen   (an′ tə jən) any substance that the immune system recognizes as foreign and reacts to by producing an antibody

antihistamine   (an′ tə his′ tə mēn) a drug used to suppress a histamine, which is a substance produced by the body in response to injury or allergies

anti-inflammatory   (an tī in′ flam′ ə tōr′ ē) an agent that counteracts or suppresses the inflammatory response

antilug bit   a jointed snaffle with one arm of the mouthpiece shorter and more curved than the other; the short side has a stronger action than the long side and is fitted on the side of the horse that is less responsive

antioxidant (an' tē äk' sə dənt) a substance that inhibits the chemical addition of oxygen to another substance

antiphlogistic (an' tə flə jis' tik) an agent that counteracts fever and inflammation

antiprostaglandin (an' tə präs' tə glan' din) a drug that blocks the action or stops production of prostaglandins, which are inflammation-causing chemicals produced by cells in response to injury

antipruritic (an' ti prōō rit' ik) any substance that relieves or removes any problems of itching and scratching

antipyretic (an' tə pī ret' ik) any fever-reducing drug; increases the rate of heat loss or reduces the rate of heat production

antirearing bit, chifney a bit that has three rings, two for the cheek pieces and one for the lead rein; the upper part of the cheek swivels on the mouthpiece independently of the lower section; used to help control horses that rear

antiseptic (ant' ə sep' tik) an agent used in the treatment of wounds or disease to prevent the growth and development of germs

antiserum (ant' i sir əm) a fluid extracted from blood containing one or more specific antibodies taken from an animal that has been immunized against a specific antigen; injected into other animals to give immediate, though very short-term, protection

antispasmodic (an' ti spaz mäd' ik) an agent that relieves muscle spasms

antisweat sheet (an' ti swet shēt) sheet used to keep a sweating horse warm as he cools down from a workout, thus preventing him from getting a chill

antitoxin (an' ti täk' sin) an antibody that neutralizes toxin of a bacteria

antivenin (an' ti ven' ən) a proteinaceous material used in the treatment of poisoning caused by animal venom

anuria (an yōōr' ē ə) little or no excretion of urine

anus (ā' nəs) the external opening of the rectum

anvil (an' vəl) a heavy steel block with a smooth flat face on which horseshoes are shaped

Anxois a French draft horse with excellent endurance; selectively bred to maintain their type

aorta (ā ôr' tə) the main or "trunk" artery of the arterial system carrying blood away from the heart to be distributed by branch arteries throughout the body

apathy (ap' ə thē) lack of feeling or emotion; indifference

apex (ā' pəks) the point of the frog; toward the toe; see *hoof* (illus.)

APHA see *American Paint Horse Association*

aplasia (ə plā' zhē ə) complete lack of development of a tissue or organ

---

a=f<u>a</u>t; ā=<u>a</u>pe; ä=c<u>a</u>r; â=b<u>a</u>re; e=t<u>e</u>n; ē=<u>e</u>ven; i=<u>i</u>s; ī=b<u>i</u>te; ō=g<u>o</u>; ô=h<u>o</u>rn; ōō=t<u>oo</u>l; ŏŏ=l<u>oo</u>k; u=<u>u</u>p; ʉ=f<u>u</u>r; ŋ=ri<u>ng</u>; ə=sof<u>a</u>

aplastic anemia   (ə plas' tik ə nē' mē ə) lack of red blood cells due to an inability of the bone marrow to produce them

apnea   (ap' nē ə) cessation of breathing

Appaloosa   (ap' ə lōō' sə) an American breed, development is attributed to the Nez Perce Indians in the Oregon, Washington, and Idaho region; agile, docile, athletic, with good stamina; noted for a variety of colorful coat patterns and markings; mottled skin on the nose and genitals; striped hooves and white sclera encircling the eye; most common uses: cow horse, pleasure, stock, saddle, and endurance

Appaloosa Horse Club   a breed registry of more than 500,000 Appaloosas

Appaloosa Sport Horse Association an organization that promotes Appaloosas in Olympic disciplines

appendix   (ə pen' diks) a part of the American Quarter Horse Stud Book

appetite   (ap' ə tīt) the desire of the horse to eat feed and drink water; depressed appetite is usually a symptom of a health problem

appleton   (ap' əl tən) an almost round horn cap the size of a small hen's egg

appointment card   (ə point' mənt kärd) a card sent out to interested parties by the hunt secretary informing them of the time, date, and place of forthcoming meets

appointments   (ə point' məntz) clothing, tack, and equipment used in show riding

apposition   (ap' ə zish' ən) the placing of things in proximity; bringing together the edges of a wound for suturing

apprehensive   (ap' rə hen' siv) anxious or fearful about what may be ahead

apprentice   (ə pren' tis) a jockey in training

apron   (ā' prən) 1. a strong covering worn by farriers to protect the front of the body while shoeing a horse 2. cloth draped across the lap to keep passengers warm and dry while driving 3. a waterproof protective shield of the carriage; see *carriage parts* (illus.)

AQHA   see *American Quarter Horse Association*

AraAppaloosa Foundation Breeders International   a registry of horses bred through the use of foundation Appaloosa lines and spot line Arabians

Arab   (ar' əb) see *Arabian*

Arabian   (ə rā' bē ən) a breed originating in Saudi Arabia; oldest and purest of today's breeds; a general-purpose horse known for their arching necks, flat croups, refined heads, and one less vertebra; common uses: show, pleasure, stock, saddle, racing, and endurance; also called *Arab*

Arabian Horse Registry of America (AHRA)   breed registry for Arabians; a purebred domestic that must be conceived and born in the U.S. or Mexico; a purebred import is eligible based on approved pedigree or importation source and documentation

Arabian

Arabian Sport Horse Association (ASHA) a registry of Arabian Sport Horses

arcade (är kād′) an anatomic structure resembling a series of arches; usually refers to the surface of the jaws that holds the teeth

arch roller (ärch rō′ lər) a device to prevent pressure on the spine by preventing a horse from rolling and becoming cast in the stall; some are hinged at each side of the arch to fit any width of horse

Ardennais (är den′ ās) a breed that originated in France; among the most powerful of all draft breeds

arena (ə rē′ nə) a large, enclosed (by fence or wall) riding area, indoors or outdoors, in which horses are schooled and horse shows may be held

arena markers points used to define patterns and mark areas of an arena; see *dressage ring*

Ariègeois a French breed; black in color with a thick mane and tail; energetic and well suited to farm work, especially in mountainous regions

Aristides (ar′ i stē dez) the first winner of the Kentucky Derby in 1875

arrhythmia (ə rith′ mē ə) any variation from the normal heart beat

arrow grass (ar′ ō gras) a plant poisonous to horses; may reach a height of five feet with green flowers along the upper part of the stalk in the spring; livestock death results from respiratory failure after ingestion

arsenic (ärs′ nik) chemical found in rodenticides, weed killers, and insecticides; poisoning affects the intestinal tract and causes massive diarrhea that can lead to death

arteritis (är′ tə rīt′ əs) inflammation of the arteries, causing edema; can be caused by equine viral arteritis (EVA)

artery (är′ tər ē) a thick-walled muscular vessel through which blood passes from the heart to various organs and parts of the body

arthritis (är thrīt ′is) inflammation of a joint and its adjacent tissues

arthrocentesis (är′ thrō sen tē′ sis) puncture and aspiration of joint fluid

arthrochondritis (är′ thrō kon drī′ tis) inflamed joint cartilage

arthrodesis (är′ thrō dē sis) surgical fusion of a joint

arthroscope (är′ thrō skōp) an instrument that is inserted into a joint for examination and/or surgery

---

a=fat; ā=ape; ä=car; â=bare e=ten; ē=even; i=is; ī=bite; ō=go; ô=horn; ōō=tool; ŏŏ=look; u=up; ʉ=fur; ŋ=ring; ə=sofa

arthroscopy (är′ t̲h̲räs kə pē) examination of the interior of a joint through a needle-size fiber-optic instrument

articulate (är tik′ yə lit) divided into or united by joints

articulation (är tik′ yə lā′ s̲h̲ən) junction between two or more bones; joint

artifact (art′ ə fakt) any artificial structure or feature concerning the anatomy of the horse; e.g., a mark on a radiograph that may indicate bone fracture and or damage

artificial aids (är′ tə fis̲h̲′ əl āds) items such as a crop, whip, spurs, and martingales used to support natural aids; used to help convey instructions to a horse

artificial insemination (in sem′ ə nā s̲h̲ən) depositing collected stallion semen into the vagina or cervix of the mare by artificial means to fertilize an egg

artificial lighting (līt′ iŋ) system used to prolong estrus during the later winter and hasten estrus in the early spring months when mares are most generally more reproductively inactive; system works on the photoreceptivity principle of the mare; also used to promote shedding and maintain show coats

artificial vagina (və jī′nə) an apparatus used to collect semen from stallions for either laboratory examination and/or use in artificial insemination; usually consists of a rubber sheath surrounded by warm water inside a sealed metal cylinder

ascarid (as′ kə rid) a large nematode parasite found in the small intestine; also called *roundworm*

ascorbic acid (ə skor′ bik as′ id) vitamin C

aseptic (ā sep′ tik) refers to something being sterile; i.e., free from living germs and micro-organisms that cause disease, fermentation, or putrefaction

ash (as̲h̲) a mineral matter in feed from the residue remaining after complete burning of organic matter

Asiatic Wild Horse (ā′ z̲h̲ē at′ ik wīld hôrs) originating in Mongolia; still roams wild in Asia; has remained almost unchanged since the Ice Age; color: dun; mane and tail are black eel striped

asking the question (ask′ iŋ thə kwest′ s̲h̲ən) pushing a horse to make a supreme effort when he is near his physical limit in a competitive event

aspergillosis (as′ pər ji lō′ sis) a disease caused by the fungus *Aspergillus* and marked by inflammatory granular lesions in the skin, ear, orbit, nasal sinuses, and sometimes in the bones and meninges

aspermia (ə sper′ mē ə) failure of formation or emission of sperm

asphyxiation (as fik′ sē ā s̲h̲ən) suffocation

aspiration biopsy (as pə rā′ s̲h̲ən bī′ äp′ sē) a biopsy in which the tissue is obtained by the application of suction though a needle attached to a syringe

aspiration pneumonia (as′ pə rā′ s̲h̲ən nōō mōn′ yə) inflammation of the lungs due to food or other material entering the lungs through the trachea; can be associated with choke, esophageal strictures and bottle feeding of foals

ass   (as) a member of the horse family used for domestic work before horses were tamed

Assateague   a small pony believed to be the offspring from shipwrecked horses from colonial America; inbreeding caused a stunted appearance

Association of Parti-Colored Arabians (APA)   a registry of pinto-colored Arabians

association saddle   (ə sō sē ā′ ṣẖən sad′ əl) the standard saddle design approved in 1919 by the management of four large western rodeos

asterisk   (as′ tər isk) used in front of a horse's name on his registration papers; an asterisk (*) indicates "imported"; used in front of a jockey's name, it indicates that he is an apprentice rider

astride riding   (ə strīd′ rīd′ iŋ) riding with one leg on each side of the horse

astringent   (ə strin′ jənt) drugs that cause contraction of infected areas, such as tannic acid, alum, and zinc oxide or sulphate

ataractic   (at′ ə rak′ tik) a tranquilizer

ataxia   (ə tak′ sē ə)   failure or irregularity of muscular action producing a stumbling or staggering gait; see *Wobbler*

at grass   1. a horse that derives his complete feed needs from pasture 2. a horse resting from his usual routine

atlanto-occipital malformation   (at lan′ tō äk sip′ i təl mal′ fôr mā ṣẖən) disorder of Arabians; fusion of the first vertebra with the skull, causing weakness and inability to stand

atlas   (at′ ləs)   the first vertebra of the cervical region; see *skeletal system* (illus.)

atresia ani   (ə′ trē zẖə ā′ nē) congenital absence of a normal body opening at the anus; the foal shows signs of constipation, becomes colicky, and his abdomen swells; surgical correction is rarely beneficial

atresia coli   (ə trē′ zẖə cō′ lī) closure of the colon; severed large intestine; affected foals appear normal up to twenty-four hours, then become colicky and die within three to four days

atrial fibrillation   (ā′ trē əl fib′ rə lā′ ṣẖən) irregular heartbeats, rapid and ineffective contractions

atrial septal defect   (ā′ trē əl sep′ təl dē′ fekt) defect of the wall separating the two atria of the heart

atrium   (ā′ trē əm) smaller paired chambers of the heart receiving blood from the veins and transporting it to the ventricles via muscle contractions

atrophy   (a′ trə fē) a decrease in size or wasting away of a body part or tissue

atropine   (at′ rə pēn) a drug used to relax smooth muscles in various organs, to increase heart rate and to dilate the pupil when applied to the eye

attenuate   (ə ten′ yōō wāt) 1. to reduce or to make tissue thinner 2. to make a drug or compound less effective

---

a=fat; ā=ape; ä=car; â=bare e=ten; ē=even; i=is; ī=bite; ō=go; ô=horn; ōō=tool; ŏŏ=look; u=up; ʉ=fur; ŋ=ring; ə=sofa

at the girth   indicates the rider's legs are positioned properly, on or slightly behind the girth depending on saddle style, stirrup length and style of riding

attire   (ə tīr′) the rider's clothes

attitude   (at′ ə tōōd) a temporary behavior resulting from a specific situation and/or environmental conditions

auction   (ôk′ shən) a well-established method of selling horses whereby the auctioneer calls for bids or prices and the value of the animal keeps increasing until the people placing the bids, known as the bidders, decide to cease offering a bid; the person who made the highest bid is the purchaser of the animal

auscultation   (ôs′ kəl tā′ shən) the act of listening for sounds within the body; chiefly for determining the condition of the lungs, heart, pleura, intestines and other organs

Australian checker   (ô strāl′ yen chek′ ər) a flat, rubber device shaped like an inverted Y; the two bottom arms end in disks, which have holes in them so that they can be pulled over the bit rings; primarily used in racing

Australian Pony   (pō′ nē) a strong, attractive pony suitable for children; resembles the Welsh Mountain Pony

Australian simplex safety iron (sim′ pleks sāf′ tē ī′ ərn) a balloon loop forward on the outer side of the iron on the stirrup that ensures the foot cannot become trapped

autoimmune disease   (ôt ō i myōōn di zēz′) the production of antibodies against the body's own tissues resulting in disease

autoimmunity   (ôt′ ō i myōōn i tē) result of the production of autoantibodies; may cause damage to normal tissues

automatic timer   (ô′ tə mat′ ik tī′ mər) a device used for timed and speed-based events; the horse breaks an electronic ray as he goes through the start, triggering the mechanism, which starts the clock; as a horse goes through the finish, he breaks a similar device, which stops the clock

automatic water bowls   (wô′ tər bōlz) plumbed-in water bowls; the water flow is either controlled by a spatula that the horse pushes as he drinks or the bowls are calibrated to maintain a particular water level

autonomic nervous system   (ôt ə näm′ ik nʉr′ vəs sis′ təm) the part of the nervous system that regulates the internal environment of the body

autopsy   (ô′ täp sē) the examination of a body after death; generally to determine cause of death

Authorisation Speciale   (ô′ ther i zā′ shən spesh′ əl) a pink card issued to a rider by the National Equestrian Federation permitting him to compete in an international dressage, show-jumping, or combined training event

Autumn Double   (ô təm dub′ əl) an annual two-race event held in Newmarket, England; consists of the Cesarewitch Stakes and the Cambridge Stakes

Auxois   a French draft breed; a quiet, good-natured horse often branded with the letters TX on the left side of the neck; the breed dates back to the Middle Ages when it was used for drawing carriages and carts

Avelignese an Italian breed; height: 12–14 hands; easy-going nature; excellent for beginners

average (av' rij) when a rodeo has more than one go-round in an event, the contestants are paid off for the best ride or time in each go-round and for the best average of all go-rounds; the winner of the average is the event winner

average earnings index (ʉr niŋs in' deks) the yearly earnings of a horse or the average earnings of progeny as a proportion of the total amount of purses available in that year per horse

avermectin (āʹ vər mekʹ tin) a class of dewormer effective against many parasites including bots; includes ivermectin

avoidance (ə voidʹ əns) a type of negative reinforcement; the horse is first given a cue; with a correct response, no punishment is administered; with a latent or incorrect response, punishment is applied; see *negative reinforcement*

axilla (ak silʹ ə) area of the chest on the inside of the forearm

axis (akʹsis) **1.** the second cervical vertebra **2.** a line around which part of the body is arranged or is symmetrical; see *skeletal system* (illus.)

axle (aksʹ əl) the metal axis on which the wheels of the driving vehicle turn

azoturia (azʹ ō tōōrʹ ē ə) a disease of horses marked by a sudden onset of perspiration and paralysis of the hindquarters, and by the passing of light-red to dark-brown urine; occurs in horses that, after being engaged in continuous work, are rested for several days and well fed and then suddenly returned to work; also known as *Monday morning sickness* or *tying up*

Azteca (az tekʹ ə) a breed originating in Mexico by crossing Andalusian stallions with Quarter Horse mares or vice versa; an elegant horse; well suited to competition and leisure riding

---

a=f<u>a</u>t; ā=<u>a</u>pe; ä=c<u>a</u>r; â=b<u>a</u>re e=t<u>e</u>n; ē=<u>e</u>ven; i=<u>i</u>s; ī=b<u>i</u>te; ō=g<u>o</u>; ô=h<u>o</u>rn; ōō=t<u>oo</u>l; ŏŏ=l<u>oo</u>k; u=<u>u</u>p; ʉ=f<u>u</u>r; ŋ=ri<u>ng</u>; ə=sof<u>a</u>

B

babbler (bab' ə lər) a hound that bays and flings his tongue around when not on the line

babesiosis (bə' bē zē o' sis) an infection of red blood cells by *Babesia,* usually transmitted by ticks

back (bak) **1.** the flat backbone area of a horse between the withers and the loin; technically, the thoracic area from the eighth vertebra to and including the eighteenth dorsal vertebra; see *points of a horse* (illus.) **2.** a two-beat diagonal gait in reverse **3.** in racing, to place a bet on a horse

back aids when the rider alters his center of gravity as a cue; also called *weight aids, action of the loins, seat aids, pushing buttocks forward, braced back,* and *driving seat*

back at the knee a conformational fault visible in the front legs when viewing them from the side; the knees are bent too far back; also called *calf knee;* see *conformation comparisons* (illus.)

back band the strap on a single-harness driving apparatus that passes through the saddle and fastens to the shaft tugs; see *harness parts A* (illus.)

back bulge a saddle fork with a puffed-out shape on its backside; designed in an attempt to make a popular bronc-riding saddle

back combing a step in the process of mane thinning; to back comb, section out a strand of mane, comb back all but the longest hairs; to thin, wrap the longer hairs around the comb and quickly pull them out

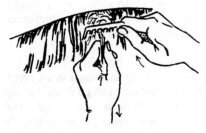

Back Combing

backer (bak' ər) a person who places a bet on a horse

back hander a polo stroke in which the player traveling forward hits the ball backward in the opposite direction

backing (bak' iŋ) **1.** a method of breaking and training when, by gradual stages, the handler eventually sits on the horse's back **2.** to move in reverse

back jockey the top skirt of a western saddle; leather flaps that cover and protect the tree bars from the back of the cantle to the end of the bars

back not round indicates that the horse is not using his back correctly and instead of arching upward toward the rider, he "holds" his back away, either flat or hollow

back of knee pisiform bones

backside (bak sīd) the stable and training area of a racetrack

back splice (bak splīs) a means of weaving the strands of a rope back into themselves to prevent the end of the rope from fraying; results in an increase in the diameter of the rope

20

back stay (bak′ stā) a support extending from the upper to the lower portions of the carriage platform; see *carriage parts* (illus.)

back strap (bak′ strap) on the driving apparatus, the strap that joins the crupper's dock (tail) piece to the saddle pad; some are buckled to allow easier tail entry, others are sewn solid; see *harness parts A* (illus.)

backstretch (bak strech) the side of the track furthest from the winning post

bacteremia (bak′ tə rē′ mē ə) presence of bacteria in the bloodstream

bacteria (bak tir′ ē ə) plural of *bacterium*; a group of single-celled microorganisms; widely distributed in nature; can have both beneficial and harmful effects on a horse

bacterial (bak tir′ ē əl) pertaining to any of a class of microscopic plants having single-celled or noncellular bodies often growing in clusters

bacterial population (bak tir′ ē əl pop′ yə lā shən) the count of bacteria found in the horse's cecum or colon for fiber digestion; enables him to digest roughage more effectively

bactericidal (bak tir ə sīd′ əl) having properties that destroy or kill bacteria

bacterins (bak tir′ ənz) suspensions of bacteria that have been killed by heat or chemical means; used as a vaccine to stimulate the production of antibodies

bacteriostatic (bak tir′ ē ō sta′ tik) an agent that inhibits the growth or action of bacteria

bacterium (bak tir′ ē əm) a single-celled organism that multiplies by simple division; can be either spherical, rod shaped, or spiral; some are beneficial; others cause disease

bad actor (bad ak′ tôr) a horse that is difficult, disagreeable, and uncomfortable to ride

bad doer a horse that does not eat well or does not digest much of what he does eat

Badge of Honor (baj uv än′ ər) an award presented to riders competing in Prix des Nations competitions with points given as follows: Bronze, 5; Silver, 25; Gold, 50; competing in an Olympic Game is counted as competing in five Prix des Nations

bad habit undesirable behavior usually related to handling or training; see *vice*

bad minded an uncooperative horse that resists training

Badminton (bad′ min tən) the Badminton Three-Day Horse Trials; one of the chief fixtures in the eventing calendar since its foundation in 1949; held at the Cotswold home of the Duke of Beaufort in Gloucestershire, England

bad traveler a horse that does not travel well; he will generally be nervous, hard to load into the trailer, and once loaded he will stomp his feet and possibly kick at the door; generally due to poor training or hauling practices

---

a=fat; ā=ape; ä=car; â=bare; e=ten; ē=even; i=is; ī=bite; ō=go; ô=horn; ōō=tool; ŏŏ=look; u=up; ʉ=fur; ŋ=ring; ə=sofa

bagman   (bag' man) a bagged fox; in countries where foxes are scarce, it is sometimes customary to bring a fox to the meet in a sack and turn him loose

balance   (bal' əns) **1.** in regard to movement, a state of equilibrium in keeping the center of gravity over the base **2.** in regard to conformation, desirable proportions

balance, central   equal weight on the front and back legs; a collected gait

balanced bit   a bit that naturally returns to the straight up-and-down position, releasing the curb strap

balanced ration   a ration that supplies proper amounts of all nutrients needed by the animal

balanced seat   the position of the mounted rider that requires a minimum of muscular effort to remain in the saddle and that interferes least with the horse's movements and equilibrium

balance, forward   more weight supported by the front legs than the rear legs; seen in gaits in which the horse moves forward energetically

balance not maintained   **1.** a horse that suffers momentary or overall lack of balance **2.** a change in the rider's seat, position, and/or leg placement that has caused or will cause the horse to perform less-desirable gaits

bald   (bôld) a horse with a wide blaze blanketing most of the face; the white can extend out and around the eyes and down to the upper lip and around the nostrils; see *markings, face* (illus.)

bale   (bāl) hay that is packed together and bound into a unit with wire or string; generally weighs 60 lb, but weight and size vary greatly depending on type of hay

Bali   (bä' lē) Indonesian breed with many primitive features; docile and cooperative; used for riding and pack

balk   (bôk) to be stubborn; to refuse to respond to aids; to refuse or cease forward motion

ball   (bôl) a medicinal compound enclosed in a gelatin capsule and administered with a balling gun; this can be a dangerous procedure and should only be done by a veterinarian; also called a *medicine pill*

ball and socket joint   ex: hip joint

balling gun   a syringelike device used to give large pills to horses

balling up   snow buildup in a horse's hooves; greasing the soles helps prevent this problem

ballatade   (bal' ə tād') the leap of a horse when four feet are in the air and only the shoes of the hind feet are showing; an air above the ground performed by a horse trained in the classical manner; the movement involves a half rear, then the horse jumps forward, drawing the hind legs up below the quarters, before landing on all four legs

balloted out horse   (bal' ə təd out hôrs) horses that have been nominated for a race or event but, because of entries greater than the designated safety limit, are not allowed to compete

band   (band) a group of horses, a herd

bandage   (ban' dij) used for protection against injury and for support, warmth, and general veterinary care

bandy legs (ban' dē legz) a horse that is pigeon-toed on his hind feet with the points of his hocks turned outward; also called *bow legs*

banged tail (baŋd' tāl) when the hair of a full-length tail is cut straight across; if cut just below the dock or bony part of the tail, it is known as *bang tailed*

bang tail (baŋ tāl) slang meaning "horse"

bank (baŋk) solid earthen ramp or wall that is used as a drop jump

banting (bant' iŋ) reducing a jockey's weight

bar (bär) 1. part of the saddle tree that runs along each side and parallel to the horse's spine 2. interdental space between the incisors and the molars where the bit lies; see *hoof* (illus.) and *bars*

barb (bärb) old breed similar to Arabians; originated in North Africa and widely used for cross-breed improvement; known as a docile riding horse

barbary pack (bär' bər ē pak) a rough, scratched-together pack of hounds not normally kenneled together but rounded up for the occasion with the hope that they will have sufficient nose and stamina to provide sport

barbed wire fence (bärbd' wīr fens) a special type of wire with small wire thorns evenly spaced along the wire; dangerous to horses; can cause a great deal of damage to a horse that becomes entangled in it

bar bit a bit consisting of a slightly curved bar with snaffle rings

barbiturate (bär bich' ər āt) a drug used as a sedative, hypnotic, or anesthetic

Bardi horse (bär' dē) see *Bardigiano*

Bardigiano breed originated in Italy; particularly well suited to hilly and mountainous regions; height: 13.1–14.2 hands

bareback riding (bâr' bak' rīd iŋ) 1. riding a horse without a saddle or blanket on his back 2. a rodeo event known as *bronc riding*; riders hold on to a leather strap and attempt to ride a bucking bronco

barefoot (bâr' fŏŏt) unshod

bareme the jumping competition table used in judging; table A covers jumping only and table C includes speed

barium (ber' ē əm) dye material given to horses by mouth to outline the intestines and stomach on radiographs

barker (bär' kər) a foal that is completely disoriented at birth or soon thereafter; the animal goes down, followed by violent convulsions; in the latter stage, he emits a sound like a yelping dog, hence the name

barn (bärn) a man-made structure used to shelter horses, tack, feed, etc.

barn crazy a horse that resents the

---

a=fat; ā=ape; ä=car; â=bare; e=ten; ē=even; i=is; ī=bite; ō=go; ô=horn; ōō=tool; ŏŏ=look; u=up; u=fur; ŋ=ring; ə=sofa

confinement of a barn and will kick and fight as a result; in some cases, this may be so severe the horse should be kept in a paddock with access to an open-faced shed

barn itch   see *ringworm*

barn sour   1. a horse that refuses to leave the stable area or a group of horses; the horse may attempt to bolt back to the barn or to his herdmates 2. any horse in which performance appears to be suffering due to excessive work, overtraining, inadequate rations, etc.

barnyard grass   *Echinochloa crusgalli*; poisonous plant that can accumulate nitrates and cause sudden death if eaten

bar plate   a wide metal plate connecting the branches of a horseshoe

bar pressure   pressure on the indenture gap in the lower jaw

barrage   (bə räzh′) the alternate name for a jump-off in which horses with equal scores at the end of a competition recompete against each other; the result can either be decided by the number of faults, time against the clock, or a combination of the two

barrel   (bar′ el) the part of a horse's body between the forelimbs and the loins; may also refer to the rib cage

barrel racing   barrel racing is a standard gymkhana event; the rules vary depending on the organization that sanctions the gymkhana, but the standard positioning of the barrels is a cloverleaf pattern; knocking over barrels results in a fault or time penalty; the fastest time wins the race

barren mare   (bar′ ən mâr) a mare that is not in foal; may also describe a mare incapable of breeding

barrier   (bar′ ē ər) the point at which a race starts; in timed rodeo events, the stock is given a predetermined headstart depending on arena conditions; a rope is stretched across the front of the box out of which the contestant's horse will come; the barrier rope is released by a measured length of twine that is pulled loose from the calf or steer as he reaches the designated distance

bar risers   strips of wood or leather placed on top of the bars behind the fork to shape the contour of the seat

bars   (bärz) 1. the lower portion of the jaw, devoid of teeth, where the bit rests; the open spaces on the jaw between the incisors and premolars 2. portions of the wall of the hoof that are turned inward at the heels and run more or less parallel to the sides of the frog 3. in a saddle, two long, horizontal tree bars rest on the back of the horse, one on each side of the spine, they support and anchor the fork and cantle of the saddle

bar shoe   a therapeutic shoe in which the heels are joined by a bar; helps relieve pressure from the heels and quarters; may also hold a leather pad over the sole in case of injury; horseshoe with no opening between the heels, forming a continuous circle

bars of the mouth   the portion of the horse's lower jaw that has no teeth; the space between the incisors and the molars where the bit lies

bascule   (bas′ kyōōl) the desirable arc a horse's body makes as it goes over a jump

base (bās) the rider's seat and weight

base narrow standing with front or rear feet closer together than the limbs are at their origin; see *conformation comparisons, front and rear limb* (illus.)

base wide a conformation fault in which there is greater distance between the horse's legs at the bottom than at the top; caused by an improper positioning at the elbow; see *conformation comparisons, front and rear limb* (illus.)

Bashkir (bäsh' kər) a Russian breed of riding pony; strong and hardy; color: bay, chestnut, or palomino

Bashkir Curly (bäsh' kər kʉr' lē) see *American Bashkir Curly*

basic halter (bā' sik hôl' tər) a web headpiece and nosepiece front; its rope shank forms the nosepiece rear; its disadvantage is that there is no throatlatch and therefore the halter comes off easily

Basque Pony (bask pō' nē) a breed that originated in Spain; very hardy, well adapted to survival in the wild; recently shown to be suited to riding, jumping, dressage, cross-country, etc.

bastard strangles (bas'tərd straŋ gəlz) a form of strangles that affects tissues in the whole body instead of only the lymph nodes of the head; can be fatal

Basuto (bə sōōt' ō) native to the Cape area of South Africa; a small, heavyset pony with short legs and hard hooves; tough and fearless, their endurance ability enables them to survive on poor rations

bat (bat) a short, flat, leather riding whip

Batak (bə' tak) a native breed of the island of Sumatra, the largest Indonesian island; this breed, a cross between specially imported Arab stallions and selected mares of other breeds, is a sought-after and valuable pony

bathing (bāth' iŋ) washing the horse with soapy water to remove dust and dirt from the coat

bay (bā) a body color in which the coat is dark red to yellowish brown in color and the mane, tail and lower limbs are black; black on the limbs is referred to as *black points*

bay brown (bā broun) primary coat color is brown, with black points, black mane and tail, and bay muzzle

Bayo Coyote (bā' ō kī ō' tē) a dun horse with a black dorsal stripe

bean (bēn) a puttylike mass of smegma that collects in the urethral diverticulum of the penis

beaning (bēn' iŋ) disguising an unsoundness in a horse

bean shooter (bēn shōō' tər) a horse that throws his front feet violently forward at the trot, with little flexion, "landing" about twelve inches above the ground; a very undesirable trait

bear grass (bâr gras) *Nolina texana*; poisoning causes liver damage and extreme sensitivity to sunlight

bearing rein a rein opposite the direction of desired movement; this rein is laid against the horse's neck in the

a=fat; ā=ape; ä=car; â=bare; e=ten; ē=even; i=is; ī=bite; ō=go; ô=horn; ōō=tool; ŏŏ=look; u=up; ʉ=fur; ŋ=ring; ə=sofa

direction of the turn; see *harness parts A, B and C* (illus.)

bearing rein hook   (hŏŏk) a hook found on the upper part of the harness to hold the bearing rein; see *harness parts A* (illus.)

bear trap saddle   a short-seated, wide-swelled saddle with a high cantle; a true bear trap saddle has the wide-swelled fork Vs located backward from the center; excellent for bronc busting, but dangerous if a horse falls, because it is almost impossible for the rider to get out of it

Beberbeck   (bē' bər bek) a breed, originating in West Germany, resulting from the cross between Arabs, Thoroughbreds, and local brood mares; a willing disposition is combined with a heavy Thoroughbred appearance

bedding   (bed' iŋ) material put down in a stall on which the horse may stand or lie; straw, sawdust, wood shavings, sand, peat moss, leaves, or sugarcane stalks are considered to be good bedding for horses

bed down   (bed doun) to put down a bed of straw, shavings, or other fibrous material for a horse in a stable or loose box

beef hide   (bēf hīd) a secondary grade of rawhide tree covering

beefy hocks   (bēf ē häks) thick, meaty hocks, lacking in quality

behavior   (bi hāv' yer) the way a person or horse behaves or acts

behind the bit   when a horse evades the bit by bending the head toward the chest; the horse becomes over-flexed and insensitive to the aids

behind the movement   when the body of the rider is behind the vertical; he may be putting too much weight on the loins of the horse and impeding the action of the hind legs and movement of the horse's back

Belgian   (bel' jən) a breed originating in Belgium; a heavy and closely coupled draft horse breed; common uses: draft work and shows

Belgian Brabant   (brə bant') a breed originating in Belgium; generally classed as a division of the French Ardennes; docile workers with exceptional endurance

Belgian Draft Horse Corporation of America   a registry for Belgians that requires lineage traceable to U.S. and Belgian studbooks

bell   (bel) an object rung in show competitions to signal competitors to start, restart, or stop, or to indicate elimination

bell boots   (bel bōōtz) rubber protective boots that are bell shaped, and fit over the coronet bands and bulbs of the heel

belly   (bel' ē) the large cavity that contains the stomach, liver, spleen, intestines, kidneys, and bladder; the soft underside of the horse's barrel behind the rib cage; also known as *abdomen*; see *points of a horse* (illus.)

bellyband   (bel' ē band') part of the driving apparatus on a two-wheeled cart; may be a separate band buckled onto the back band, or one continuous strap; serves to keep the shafts securely in position which is important for proper balance; see *harness parts A* (illus.)

Belmont (bel' mänt) third race of the Triple Crown series; horses race one and one-half miles; race is run by three-year-old Thoroughbreds

bench knee (bench' nē) a conformational flaw found in the front legs when the cannon bones are offset to the outside of the knee when viewed from the front; see *conformation comparisons, front limb* (illus.)

bend (bend) the curvature of the horse's body, most noticeable in the neck

bending (bend' iŋ) lateral arcing of the body characteristic of circular work; the uniform bending of the horse's entire body from poll to tail to follow the track on curves and circles; may be referred to as *lateral suppleness*

benign (bi nīn') a tumor, not malignant or recurrent, with a favorable outlook for recovery

bent-top iron (bent täp ī' ərn) an English stirrup that has a top that curves away from the rider's instep; this helps keep the heel down and is suitable for those riders who like to push their foot fully home in the iron

benzene hexachloride (ben' zēn hek sə klôr' īd) one of the products used to treat mange

benzimidazole (ben' zim ə da' zōl) generic name for a chemically and functionally similar family of dewormers that includes cambendazole and thiabendazole

Berlin (bər lin') **1.** a carriage for two persons that has four wheels and the body is suspended **2.** a formal, four-wheeled covered carriage with two facing seats and a seat outside for the

*Berlin Carriage for
Several Passengers*

Berlin Carriage

coachman; it is drawn by four or six horses

besnoitiosis (bes' noi tē ō' sis) an infectious disease caused by protozoa that involves the skin, subcutaneous tissue, blood vessels, and other tissue

bet (bet) a wager placed on a horse in a race or competition; to make a wager

betting (bet' iŋ) the quotation of the wager prices of horses in a certain race; to place a bet on a horse

betting shop (bet' iŋ shop) a licensed bookmaker's establishment, not on a racecourse, that takes bets on horse races

Bhutia (byŏŏ' shə) breed originating

---

a=fat; ā=ape; ä=car; â=bare; e=ten; ē=even;
i=is; ī=bite; ō=go; ô=horn; ōō=tool;
ŏŏ=look; u=up; ʉ=fur; ŋ=ring; ə=sofa

in India; strong with good endurance; suited for rough terrain; used for pack

biceps (bī′ seps) a muscle having two heads or parts

biceps femoris muscle (fem′ ôr es mus′ əl) the large muscle of the thigh area; see *muscular system* (illus.)

bifurcation (bī′ fər kā′ shən) the site where a single structure divides into two branches

big head the bony enlargements on both sides of the face below the eyes; caused by a deficiency in calcium or an excess of phosphorus

big hearted a horse with an exceptional desire to please his rider

bight (bīt) with closed reins, such as with an English bridle, the ends of the reins; even though western reins are often split, their ends are also referred to as the bight

big knees abnormal growth caused by epiphysitis resulting from concussion

big leg severe swelling of the hind legs or forelegs of working horses; usually occurs during a period of reduced activity

big race the principal race of the day at any race meeting

bilateral (bī lat′ ər əl) having two sides or pertaining to both sides

bilirubin (bil′ ə rōō′ bin) a bile pigment formed from the breakdown of red blood cells

billet (bil′ it) 1. a short, leather cinch strap that attaches to the rigging device or skirt slots on the off side of the saddle and to the cinch; used only with a buckle-type cinch, both front and rear; also called *half breed* used in lieu of a full latigo; see *English saddle, western saddle* (illus.) 2. droppings of a fox

binder (bīn′ dər) the top of a cut-and-laid fence; a sapling woven between upright stakes

binocular vision (bi näk′ yə lər vizh′ ən) focusing on the same object with both eyes; using both eyes at the same time

biochemical profile (bī′ ō kem′ ik əl prō′ fīl) a series of chemical tests run on blood or serum to evaluate organ function

bioelectric impulse (bī′ ō i lek′ trik im′ puls) an electrical impulse generated by living tissue such as muscle or nerve cells

biological (bī′ ə läj′ i kəl) of or relating to life or living processes; a medicinal preparation made from living organisms or their products, including vaccines, antitoxins, serums, etc.

biologically inert (bī′ ə läj′ i kəl lē in ʉrt′) not affecting body processes or eliciting a tissue reaction, as in a virus used to produce a vaccine

biopsy (bī′ äp′ sē) surgical removal and examination of living tissue as an aid to precise diagnosis

biotin (bī′ ə tin) a water-soluble vitamin of the B complex

biotransformation (bī′ ō trans′ fər mā′ shən) a change in the composition of a drug by the liver

bipartite (bī pär' tīt) having two parts or divisions

bishoping (bish' əp iŋ) the practice of artificially altering the teeth of an older horse in an attempt to make it sell as a younger horse

bit (bit) a device, normally made of metal or rubber, attached to the bridle and placed in the horse's mouth so as to regulate the position of the horse's head and to help control the pace and direction of the horse

bit bars outside portion of the bit where it attaches to the shanks and rests on the bars of the mouth

bite, angle of outer angle at which the upper and lower incisors meet

bit guard a rubber or leather ring that lies between the horse's cheek and the bit ring or shank to prevent skin pinching

biting (bīt' iŋ) a vice in horses, especially young horses, stallions, and spoiled horses; it can result from hand-fed treats, petting, or improper training

bitless bridle (bit' les brī dəl) **1.** any of a variety of bridles used without bits **2.** pressure being exerted on the nose and the curb groove instead of the mouth

bit pain when a horse is uncomfortable with a bit in his mouth; check for sharp teeth, sores, cuts on the tongue, and under the chin, as well as the fit of the bit

bit proportion the relationship of the distance of the shank above the mouthpiece to the distance below the mouthpiece

bitter rubberweed (bit' ər rub' ər wēd) a yellow-flowered weed that may be only a few inches tall or as much as two feet tall; an irritant to the digestive tract

bitting (bit' iŋ) **1.** a combination of bridle, harness pad, and cupper; a surcingle with rings through which driving lines may pass or to which reins may be attached **2.** teaching the horse to be supple and willing in the bit

black (blak) a body color where the skin, mane, tail, and body hair of the horse are black; no other color is present, except that white markings on the face and legs are permitted

Black Marks small areas of black hairs on any other color

black points when the mane, tail, and legs are black or darker than the rest of the horse

black saddler a saddler who specializes in making items of saddlery for riding horses

blacksmith (blak' smith) an artisan whose medium is iron and who, among other things, makes horseshoes

black type bold-face print on a horse's sales catalog that indicates a horse that has won or placed in a stakes race

black walnut in the form of shavings, black walnut trees can be toxic to horses; the tree may also be danger-

---

a=f<u>a</u>t; ā=<u>a</u>pe; ä=c<u>a</u>r; â=b<u>a</u>re; e=t<u>e</u>n; ē=<u>e</u>ven; i=<u>i</u>s; ī=b<u>i</u>te; ō=g<u>o</u>; ô=h<u>o</u>rn; ōō=t<u>oo</u>l; ŏŏ=l<u>oo</u>k; u=<u>u</u>p; ʉ=f<u>u</u>r; ŋ=ri<u>ng</u>; ə=sof<u>a</u>

ous to horses in the spring due to allergic respiratory reactions to the tree's pollen; if the horse chews on the bark, he may get colic or laminitis

bladder (blad' ər) a stretchable, membranous sac that temporarily stores urine secreted by the kidneys

blank day (blaŋk dā) when no fox is found within a covert; day in which hounds fail to start a fox

blanket (blaŋ' kit) 1. white or light-colored markings over the hindquarters of an Appaloosa 2. any padding placed between the horse and the saddle to ease the pressure of the saddletree bars on the horse and to absorb perspiration and prevent it from getting on the saddle; a blanket, as opposed to a pad, may be refolded in various ways on long rides to lessen pressure on sore spots on the horse's back 3. a body covering used to protect the horse from sun, wind, cold, rain or snow

blanket clip when only the areas covered by a blanket are clipped; the head, neck, and legs are left unclipped

blanketing covering a horse with a blanket to keep a horse clean, dry and warm and to help maintain a glossy coat; also used after a workout to cool a horse down gradually

blaze (blāz) a broad, white marking covering the forehead (but not the eyes or nostrils) and extending down the face covering the whole width of the nasal bones; see *markings, face* (illus.)

Blazer Horse Association a registry of 722 horses, no white skin above the knees or hocks, except on the face

bleeder (blēd' ər) a horse that bleeds after or during a workout or race; the result of a nasal hemorrhage caused from a ruptured throat vein or bleeding from the lung

blemish (blem' ish) any mark or deformity that diminishes the beauty of the horse, but does not affect his serviceability; there is no set classification to distinguish between an unsoundness or blemish; for example, a splint may be either depending on location, cause and lameness; see illustration

blind bucker a horse that bucks indiscriminately, heading into anything, when ridden

blind country (blīnd kun' trē) terrain so overgrown with weeds and underbrush that it is not possible to gauge the jumps and footing

blinders (blīn' dərz) see *blinkers*

blindfolding (blīnd fōld' iŋ) the practice of using a covering over the eyes, such as a towel, sack, or sweater; used to handle, load, and lead horses from burning buildings, etc.

blindness (blīnd' nis) partial or complete loss of vision; any evidence of defective vision constitutes grounds for rejecting a horse for unsoundness

blind spavin (blīnd spav' in) a spavin where the bone has degenerated, but there is no visible exostosis; a horse suffering from this condition will be lame without showing external signs of spavin

blind spot 1. the spot where the optic nerve enters the eyeball in the optic disk and spreads nerves out within the retina 2. zones in which a horse

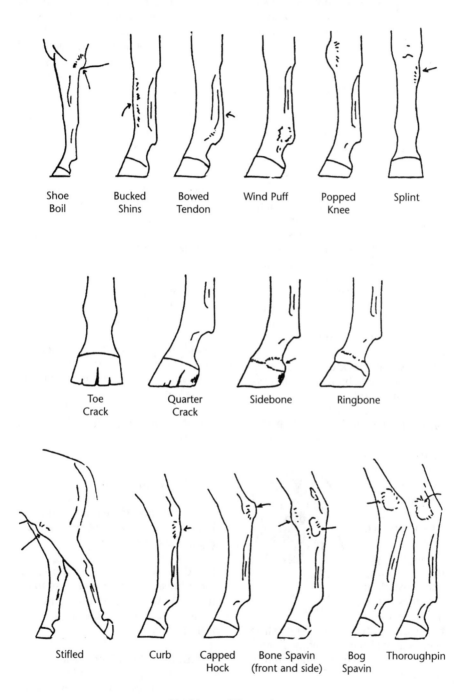

| Shoe Boil | Bucked Shins | Bowed Tendon | Wind Puff | Popped Knee | Splint |

| Toe Crack | Quarter Crack | Sidebone | Ringbone |

| Stifled | Curb | Capped Hock | Bone Spavin (front and side) | Bog Spavin | Thoroughpin |

Blemishes and Unsoundnesses

Blind Spot

cannot see; directly in front of and behind the horse; see illustration

blind switch an American term referring to a horse in a race that is behind a pocket of horses and is unable to get out and perform better

blinkers (bliŋk′ ərs) a pair of eye shields fixed to the bridle or on the head covering; used to prevent a horse from looking anywhere but directly in front of him; see *harness parts B and E* (illus.)

blinkers stay buckle a support attachment to hold blinkers in place; see *harness parts E* (illus.)

blister beetle (blis′ tər bēt′ əl) *Cantharis vesticatoria*; an insect with body fluids that contain the chemical cantharidin, which irritates the skin when applied externally, causing redness, burning, and blistering; inflames the intestine when taken internally; can be fatal; blister beetles may also be striped or spotted; blister beetles occur in alfalfa hay in certain areas

Blister Beetle

blistering (blis′ tər iŋ) application of an agent to the skin to produce blistering and inflammation of the skin; used to treat chronic or subacute inflammation of joints, tendons, and bones; increases the blood supply to the site of the blister and induces more rapid healing

blocks (bläks) anesthetic injections to numb certain parts of the body; used to diagnose location of lameness or to facilitate standing surgeries

blood (blud) makes up one-eighteenth of a horse's body weight; transports nutrients, oxygen and waste products, regulates temperature, equalizes water content, and produces immunities

blood blister a hematoma; a collection of clotted blood caused by a break in the wall of a blood vessel

blood brain barrier a barrier between the blood and brain tissues that only allows a limited number of substances to cross

blood culture growth of bacteria found in the blood of an infected horse

blood groups differences in antigens and antibodies found on red blood cells and in serum of different horses; can cause a problem when giving blood transfusions

blood horse a pedigreed horse; to most horsemen, the term is synonymous with Thoroughbred and, in some cases, more specifically the English Thoroughbred

bloodline the blood relationship among horses; it is generally accepted that all of a horse's progeny are said to belong to his bloodline

bloodlines   (blud līnz) the family lineage

blood poisoning   a general infection of the blood; also called *septicemia*

blood pressure   the pressure of the blood on the walls of the arteries; dependent on the energy of the heart action, the elasticity of the walls of the arteries, and the volume and viscosity of the blood

blood spavin   a varicose vein enlargement that appears on the inside of the hock, but immediately above the location of bog spavin; an enlargement of the saphenous vein on the inside of the hock

bloodstock   Thoroughbred horses, particularly race and stud animals

blood typing   used to help determine the parents of any particular horse; red blood cells can be divided into eight separate systems and these can be further subdivided into a number of factors

bloodworms   see *strongyle*

bloom   (blōōm) hair that is clean and glossy; denoting a healthy appearance; good body condition

blow   (blō) greatly increased force of respiration, as after hard exercise

blow a stirrup   to lose a stirrup iron; in some competitions, the rider would be disqualified

blowfly   (blō flī) several species of fly that breed in animal flesh

blow out   to walk or exercise a horse

either to loosen his muscles for further exercise or to prevent chilling and stiffening after a hard workout

blow up   a term used in the dressage arena or the show ring when a horse either breaks from the pace at which he is meant to be going, generally misbehaves, or bucks

blue dun   (blōō dun) coat color in which the skin is black with the body color a dilute black, the mane and tail are always black, and there may be a dark dorsal stripe running from the base of the tail to the mane; a dark stripe may also be present down the withers

blue eye   (blōō ī) an eye with a blue appearance; vision may or may not be affected, therefore it may or may not be categorized as an unsoundness; also known as *China eyed, glass eyed,* or *cotton eyed*

blue nose   (nōz) photosensitization occurring on the nostrils

blue roan   (rōn) coat color in which the coat has a blue tinge, which is the result of an equal mixture of white and black or black-brown hairs

bluetick   (blōō tik) a hound that is mostly white with small splashes of black mixed in, giving a bluish appearance

bluffter   (bluf′ tər) a thick, foam rubber noseband, covered in fleece; obscures the horse's vision below and behind him; reduces shying during a race; used mainly on trotters and pacers

---

a=f<u>a</u>t; ā=<u>a</u>pe; ä=c<u>a</u>r; â=b<u>a</u>re; e=t<u>e</u>n; ē=<u>e</u>ven;
i=<u>i</u>s; ī=b<u>i</u>te; ō=g<u>o</u>; ô=h<u>o</u>rn; ōō=t<u>oo</u>l;
ŏŏ=l<u>oo</u>k; u=<u>u</u>p; ʉ=f<u>u</u>r; ŋ=ri<u>ng</u>; ə=sof<u>a</u>

bobtailed	(bäb tāld') a horse with a short or docked tail

bodkin hitch	(bäd' kən hich) a farm hitch used in plowing heavy land

body	(bäd' ē) the sum of four main parts: neck and head, forequarters, body or trunk, and the rear quarters

body brush	a soft brush with fine bristles used to promote a healthy shine; a finishing brush

Body Brush

body clip	clipping the horse's entire coat including the legs

body colors	four basic coat colors exist in horses: black, brown, bay, and chestnut; these colors are further added to by the effects of greying, roaning, dilution, and spotting of the coat

body language	how a horse holds and moves his body to convey his feelings

boggy hock	(bäg' gē häk) similar to a bog spavin except that the entire joint swells

bog rider	(bäg rīd' ər) a cowboy whose job is to rescue cattle that have gotten trapped in mud or marshland

bog spavin	(bäg spav' ən) a filling of the natural depression on the inside and front of the hock; an inflammation of the synovial membrane; a bog spavin is much larger than a blood spavin and may be a blemish or an unsoundness; see *blemishes and unsoundnesses* (illus.)

boil	(boil) see *summer sores*

boil over	to start bucking

boil, shoe	see *shoe boil*

bolt	(bōlt) 1. to charge or run off; a serious bad habit 2. gulp food without chewing

bolt a fox	to make a fox leave his den or the drain in which he has taken refuge by putting a terrier behind him

bolus	(bō' ləs) a rounded mass of food or medicine given orally

bone	(bōn) 1. individual parts of hard tissue forming the skeleton 2. the measurement of the circumference around the cannon bone about halfway between the knee and fetlock joints

bone cutter	(cut' ər) a forcepslike instrument originally designed to cut bones; can be used successfully to remove the sharp points on a horse's teeth

bone marrow	(mar' ō) the soft material filling the cavities of bones; made up of a meshwork of connective tissue containing branching fibers; the mesh is filled with marrow cells; functions mainly in the production of red blood cells and some white blood cells

bones	(bōnz) any of the separate parts of the hard tissue forming the skeleton; there are four main classifications of bones: long, short, flat, and irregular

bone spavin	(spav' in) a serious unsoundness affecting the bones of the hock joint; a bony enlargement that appears on the inside and front of the hind legs below the hock at the point where the base of the hock tapers into the cannon bone; also called *jack spavin*; see *blemishes and unsoundnesses* (illus.)

bookie (bŏŏk′ ē) an abbreviated term for a bookmaker

bookmaker (bŏŏk mā′ kər) a professional betting man who is licensed to accept bets placed by others

booster (bōō′ stər) second or subsequent dose of a vaccine

boot hooks (bōōt hŏŏks) tools to help the rider pull on tall leather boots; they have a handle of bone, ivory, wood, or metal surmounting a metal hook; the hooks are used in pairs and are slotted into two cloth loops inside the boots

boot jack (jak) a wedging device to help in removing boots; one foot holds the jack to the ground while the other heel is placed in the jack wedge; the wedge grips the boot so that the rider can pull the foot out easily

boots (bōōts) 1. footwear used to protect the rider's legs or feet against injuries 2. protective legwear for the horse's cannon bone, fetlock, coronary band, etc. 3. markings; white area on leg extending from the hoof partway up the cannon 4. on a coach, the uncovered, box-shaped projections slung along the coach between the front and rear wheels

boot trees (trēz) wood, plastic, or metal formed of a number of shaped pieces and slotted together inside the boots to preserve the shape of tall leather boots; keeps boots from sagging at the ankles

borborygmus (bôr′ bə rig′ məs) sounds caused by the passage of food, fluid, and gas through the digestive system; these sounds are increased in spasmodic colic and diarrhea, and decreased in impaction

bordered (bôr′ dərd) a marking that is circumscribed by an area of mixed color

border-stamped saddle a saddle with the full edge trim stamped with a design; often, just the corner of the fenders and skirts are stamped

borium (bôr′ ē əm) common name for tungsten carbide, one of the hardest materials known; may be used to increase traction and durability in horseshoes

borna (bôrn′ ə) a meningoencephalitis caused by a virus found in food and water; the disease is highly fatal

bosal (bō′ səl) the braided rawhide or rope noseband of a bosal hackamore; the part of the hackamore that fits over the nose; it works on the principles of balance, weight, and pressure

Bosnian (bäs′ nē ən) breed originated in Yugoslavia, known for a calm temperament; widely used by farmers

bot block (bät bläk) a hard but porous synthetic black block used to remove botfly eggs from the horse's hair; the block can be sharpened by drawing it across a hard edge

bot egg knife (eg nīf) a small knife with a serrated edge used to remove

---

a=fat; ā=ape; ä=car; â=bare; e=ten; ē=even; i=is; ī=bite; ō=go; ô=horn; ōō=tool; ŏŏ=look; u=up; ʉ=fur; ŋ=ring; ə=sofa

Bot Egg Knife

botfly eggs from a horse's coat

botfly (flī) a parasite that deposits tiny eggs on horses' legs and bellies; if ingested, the eggs mature in the digestive system and the larvae attach themselves to the stomach wall

bots (bäts) the larvae of the botfly

botulism (bäch' ə liz əm) a type of food poisoning caused by a neuro-toxin produced by a bacterium; characterized by abdominal pain, nervous symptoms, secretion disturbances, and dilation of the pupils; can be caused by feeding poor-quality silage

Boulonnais breed originated in France; two distinct types: small and large; the small type is virtually extinct and the large type is used for draft work

boundary rider (boun' də rē rī' dər) a station (ranch) worker whose task is to ride the fencing on the property and repair any problems

bowed tendon (bōd' ten' dən) fairly severe front limb tendon strain in which the flexor tendons bulge instead of being straight and parallel to the cannon bone; the damage may be permanent; usually caused by poor conformation, poor shoeing, over-stretching, improper conditioning, overwork, or accident; see *blemishes and unsoundnesses* (illus.)

bow legged (bō legd') a conformation fault in which the hocks or knees are set too far apart and the feet are usually too close together; also known as *bandy legs*; see *conformation comparison, front and rear limb* (illus.)

bowler hats (bōl' ər hats) hats used for hunting dress for women other than farmers' wives and men other than farmers; made from a mixture of rabbit fur, gossamer, and shellac, and invariably black

bowline knot (bō' līn nät) a nonslip knot that will untie even if tightened very snugly; used for safety in re-straint procedures

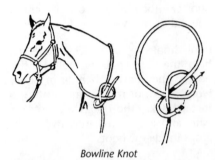

Bowline Knot

box (bäks) on a carriage, the seat from which the driving is done

boxstall (bäks stäl) a stall in the shape of a large box; standard dimensions are 10 x 10 ft to 12 x 12 ft

boxy feet (bäks' ē fēt) feet with a small frog and a high heel

brace (brās) an alcohol-based substance applied to horses' legs after exercise to prevent swelling

brace bandages (brās ban' dij es) resilient bandages on the legs of horses worn in some cases in an effort to support lame legs; worn in other cases to protect a horse from cutting and skinning his legs while racing

brachygnathia (brək' ig nā' thē ə) an abnormally short lower jaw; also known as *parrot mouth*

bracken fern (brak'ən fʉrn) plant known as *Pteridum aquilinum*; poisoning causes uncoordination, abnormal stance, and convulsions; can be fatal

bradycardia (brad' i kär' dē ə) an abnormally slow heart rate

bradykinin (brad' ə kin' in) factors formed by a group of enzymes produced by the body that maintain dilation of the blood vessels in the inflammatory process

braid aid (brād ād) a comb designed to separate the mane into three even segments for easier braiding

Braid Aid

braiding (brād' iŋ) weaving the horse's mane or tail into small, tidy braids either for show purposes or to protect and train the mane

Braiding

brain chain (brān chān) used by hunting horse trainers; a variation of the chambon; a gag runner is situated on both sides of the bridle just below brow band; a chain runs across the brow band and is attached to two straps that pass through the gag runner and to the girth; not to be used while the horse is being ridden

brain stem (brān' stem) part of the brain that controls basic body functions such as respiration, temperature, and heart rate

bran (bran) edible seed coats that are a by-product of grain milling, which, when freshly ground and dampened, acts as a mild laxative and aids digestion; a good source of thiamine and niacin

brand (brand) a registered mark of identification; may be on the cheek, neck, shoulder, or hip; may be a freeze brand or a hot brand

bran disease (bran di zēz') also called *big head*; nutritional imbalance resulting in bony deformities due to calcium reabsorbtion from bone

bray (brā) the vocal sound of a jack

break (brāk) to teach a young horse to obey commands, and to accept direction and control

breakage (brā' kij) in pari-mutuel betting, the odd cents left over, after paying the successful bettors to the nearest ten cents

break coach (kōch) an open, four-wheeled spring coach with two facing seats for the passengers, a front seat for the coachman,

Break Coach

and an auxiliary rear seat for the footman; has a team of four to six horses

break down (doun) to lacerate the

---

a=f<u>a</u>t; ā=<u>a</u>pe; ä=c<u>a</u>r; â=b<u>a</u>re; e=t<u>e</u>n; ē=<u>e</u>ven; i=<u>i</u>s; ī=b<u>i</u>te; ō=g<u>o</u>; ô=h<u>o</u>rn; ōō=t<u>oo</u>l; ŏŏ=l<u>oo</u>k; u=<u>u</u>p; ʉ=f<u>u</u>r; ŋ=ri<u>ng</u>; ə=sof<u>a</u>

suspensory ligament or fracture a sesamoid bone so the back of the fetlock drops to the ground

breaking (brāk' iη) when a horse leaves his gait and breaks into either a faster or slower gait

breaking cart a sturdy, two-wheeled, long-shafted vehicle pulled by one horse

breaking pen a round pen built with high, solid walls to help prevent injury to horse and rider during training sessions

breaking the barrier in rodeo and timed events, when the contestant rides through and breaks the barrier before it is released; the contestant receives a penalty or may be disqualified

breakover (brāk' ōv ər) the moment in a horse's stride between landing and takeoff

breast (brest) the muscular area between the front legs

breast collar western term for breastplate; the strap that passes around the front of the horse above the front legs and is attached to the cinch rings or breast collar D rings; its purpose is to hold the saddle forward on the withers

breast harness a breast piece elongated at each end to form long traces that pass through loops on the saddle and are coiled tightly around the length of the shafts of two-wheeled sulkies

breast-high scent a scent that is so strong that hounds run with their heads down, but with their noses off the ground

breastplate a short, wide strap that passes over the neck in front of the withers; two adjustable straps run from each end of the short strap back to the saddle; see *harness parts A* (illus.)

breech birth (brēch burth) delivery in which the fetus' rump or hind feet are presented first in the birth canal

breeches (brēch' əs) English riding pants

breeching the harness apparatus by which the horse holds back the vehicle when there is no brake; see *harness parts A* (illus.)

breeching dee a D-shaped metal fitting that connects the breeching strap to the shaft; see *harness parts A* (illus.)

breech strap a leather strap that passes around the buttocks of a horse to prevent the saddle from slipping forward; it is seldom used except in packing

breed (brēd) a group of horses having common origin and possessing certain distinguishable characteristics that are transmittable to their offspring

breed character (kar' ik tər) the quality of conforming to the description of a particular breed

breeder (brēd' ər) 1. owner of the dam at the time of service who was responsible for the selection of the sire to which the dam was mated 2. the owner of the mare that gives birth to a foal 3. the owner of a stud farm

breeding (brēd' iη) an attempt to regulate the offspring through intensive selection of parents

breeding hobbles a leg restraint used on mares being bred to keep them from kicking and injuring the stallion

breeding roll   a roll placed between the stallion and mare at the time of breeding to prevent the stallion from penetrating too far into the vagina and injuring the mare

breeding shed   designated enclosed area to mate horses; the breeding shed usually includes a teasing board as well as the necessary sterilizing and sanitizing equipment

breeding stock   horses used to produce offspring

breed registry   (rej' is trē) a group of breeders banded together for the purposes of recording the lineage of their animals, protecting the purity of the breed, encouraging further improvements of the breed, and promoting the breed

breedy   (brēd' ē) 1. smart and trim (refined) about the head and front part of body 2. of Thoroughbred type and build 3. showing strong breed characteristics

breeze   (brēz) an easy workout under stout restraint by the exercise rider to stabilize an already sharp horse's condition between engagements

breeze in   (brēz in) to win a race very easily

Breton   (bret' ən) a draft breed found in Europe and Japan; known for good endurance; used for heavy farm work

bridle   (brīd' əl) the part of a horse's saddlery or harness that is placed about the head; there are three components to a bridle: the reins, bit, and headstall

bridle cavesson   (kav' i sən) the standard noseband with many English bridles; used to encourage a horse to keep his mouth closed

bridle marks   an area of wear on the face; the absence of hair caused by an improperly fitted bridle

bridle noise   when a horse is held with his head pulled into his chest with the neck arched, he may produce a respiratory sound similar to roaring, but less pronounced; a whistling sound

bridle path   a section of the mane at the poll that is trimmed or clipped to allow for a space to rest the halter or bridle

bridling   (brīd' liŋ) the act of putting a bridle on the horse's head

bridoon   (bri dōōn') a small snaffle bit used in conjunction with the curb on the double bridle; sometimes *bradoon*

bright chestnut   (brīt ches' nut) coat color; primary color is bright golden red

brilliance   (bril' yəns) flash or dazzle, as related to performance

brisket   (bris' kit) the lower part of the horse's chest between the front legs; pectoral muscles

britches   (brich' iz) 1. the musculature of the rear quarters, especially of the gaskins, stifle, and thigh   2. pants

brittle hooves   (brit' əl   hōōvs) hooves that are abnormally dry and fragile

---

a=f<u>a</u>t; ā=<u>a</u>pe; ä=c<u>a</u>r; â=b<u>a</u>re; e=t<u>e</u>n; ē=<u>e</u>ven; i=<u>i</u>s; ī=b<u>i</u>te; ō=g<u>o</u>; ô=h<u>o</u>rn; ōō=t<u>oo</u>l; ŏŏ=l<u>oo</u>k; u=<u>u</u>p; ʉ=f<u>u</u>r; ŋ=ri<u>n</u>g; ə=sof<u>a</u>

britzka (brits' kə) a Polish carriage used for hire; the front wheels are much smaller than the rear pair

Britzka

broad spectrum (brôd spek' trəm) a wide range of activity, as in a wide range of bacteria affected by a broad-spectrum antibiotic

broke (brōk) **1.** a horse that has been ridden enough to be fairly manageable; tamed and trained to a particular function **2.** when the horse changed gaits of his own will; i.e., if the horse was in the canter and fell for a moment to trot and then went back to canter

broken bit a bit with a break or hinge in the center of the mouthpiece

broken crest a heavy neck that breaks over and falls to one side

broken knees knees showing scars or broken skin due to an open injury caused by a fall; these scars may be an indication that the horse is awkward and inclined to stumble

broken wind an inability to empty the lungs of air; caused by the rupture of some alveoli and characterized by difficult breathing; a chronic cough and generally poor condition

bronc (bränk) from Spanish meaning *wild*, now used to denote meanness or wildness in a derogatory sense

bronc-busting saddle a loose designation for any wide-swelled, high-backed, short-seated saddle designed to keep the rider in the saddle on a bucking horse

bronchi (brän' kī) tubes extending from the trachea into both lungs; either or both of the two main branches of the trachea, one going into each lung

bronchial dilator (brän' kē əl dī' lāt ər) a drug that will dilate (enlarge) the bronchi and other air passages of the respiratory system

bronchial pneumonia (brän' kē əl nōō mōn' yə) inflammation of the bronchi and the lung, characterized by fever, difficulty breathing, nasal discharge, depression, dull eyes, coughing, and a rasping, cracking sound in the horse's rib cage

bronchial tree (trē) the many divisions of the bronchi before they reach the lung tissue

bronchitis (brän kī' tis) inflammation of the bronchial tubes; often marked by fever, coughing, and difficulty breathing

bronchopneumonia (brän' kō nōō mōn' yə) an inflammation of the lungs that begins in the terminal bronchioles, which become clogged with mucus and pus; also see *bronchial pneumonia*

bronco (bräŋk' ō) an unbroken or imperfectly broken wild horse

broncobuster (bus' tər) a person who breaks and trains broncos

bronc riding one of the standard rodeo events; contestants attempt to ride a bucking horse for a specified period of time

bronc saddle a saddle used in breaking broncos

brood mare (brōōd mâr) a mare kept for breeding or reproductive purposes

broom tail (brōōm tāl) a western range horse; a poor, ill-kept horse of uncertain breed and inferior quality

brougham (brōō′ əm) an elegant, closed carriage with two or four wheels designed for city use and drawn by one horse; named after an English lord

Brougham

brow band (brou band) the part of the bridle that lies across the horse's forehead below the ears; see *English bridle; harness parts B and E* (illus.)

brown (broun) coat color; dark skin with black and dark-brown hair mixed; mane and tail are black; hairs on the muzzle are the best indicator of the true color of the horse

brucellosis (brōō′ sə lō′ sis) bacterial infection found in poll evil and fistulous withers; causes variable fever, stiffness, and bursa enlargement at the poll or the withers

bruise (brōōz) a contusion caused by blunt impact without laceration

bruised sole (brōōzd′ sōl) a bruise or blood clot that has developed on the laminae of the hoof and can be seen on the sole of the hoof; the horse may be lame and show pain when pressure is applied to this area

Brumby (brum′ bē) an Australian wild horse; cunning, resistant, and at times unmanageable; extinction is possible due to heavy culling of wild herds since the 1960s

Brumby runner an Australian bush horseman who captures wild horses

brush (brush) 1. to force a horse to top speed over a short distance 2. a jump made of shrubs and brush with a clearly visible bar 3. the tail of a fox 4. a grooming tool

brushing (brush′ iŋ) 1. limb contact during movement in which a foot strikes another foot or part of the leg 2. grooming

brushing boot (brush′ iŋ bōōt) legwear designed to protect the legs from the sores and lameness caused by one foot striking the other foot or leg

bruxism (bruk′ sizm) grinding of teeth; usually a reflection of severe pain

buccal (buk′ əl) pertaining to the cheek

buck (buk) 1. when a horse leaps into the air, keeping his back arched, and comes down with his forelegs stiff and his head held low 2. a kick into the air either during a ride or when, for example, a change of pace is mandated

buckaroo (buk′ a rōō) a cowboy from the far western U.S. who follows the horsemanship and bridling traditions of the old-time California vaqueros

---

a=f<u>a</u>t; ā=<u>a</u>pe; ä=c<u>a</u>r; â=b<u>a</u>re; e=t<u>e</u>n; ē=<u>e</u>ven; i=<u>i</u>s; ī=b<u>i</u>te; ō=g<u>o</u>; ô=h<u>o</u>rn; ōō=t<u>oo</u>l; ŏŏ=l<u>oo</u>k; u=<u>u</u>p; ʉ=f<u>u</u>r; ŋ=ri<u>ng</u>; ə=sof<u>a</u>

buckboard   a springless, four-wheel carriage

bucked shin   an inflammation of the periosteum (bone skin) on the front side of the cannon bone, usually occurring on the forelegs of young horses that are strenuously exercised; typically a temporary racing unsoundness; see *blemishes and unsoundnesses* (illus.)

buckeye   Aesculus plant species; poisonous plant that causes a neurological disturbance if eaten

bucking roll   an "extra set of swells" fastened onto the saddle horn to protect a rider when riding bucking horses; allows the rider to wedge himself in, making it harder for the horse to buck him off

buck-kneed   conformational fault; horse stands with knees slightly bent forward; also known as *knee sprung* or *over at the knees*; see *conformation comparisons* (illus.)

buckle guard   a protective leather covering over a buckle on one or both sides; see *English saddle* (illus.)

buckling over   when the knee appears bent over; often seen in old horses due to hard work and strain in younger years

buckskin   1. a diluted bay coat color; a form of dun with a yellowish or gold body color, black mane and tail, and black on the lower legs; the hair shaft appears to have pigment on only one side 2. a color registry (Buckskin) originating in the U.S.; includes buckskin, dun, red dun, and grullo coat colors; common uses: cow horse, pleasure, and show

buckstitch   a contrasting thong of leather or vinyl, usually white, woven in and out of a piece of leather for decoration or to bind the leather together

buck strap   a leather loop attached to the saddle horn or around the fork to provide a handhold when riding a bucking horse; usually used by a novice and, hence, also known as a *fraidy strap*

buckwheat   *Fagopyrum* plant species; poisonous plant that causes liver damage and sensitivity to light

Budyonny   a Russian breed resulting from the cross between the Don and the English Thoroughbred; officially recognized in 1948, a sturdy horse with a balanced appearance and great freedom of movement at all paces

bug boy   (bug boi) an apprentice jockey, so-called because of the "bug" or asterisk denoting the 5-lb weight allowance in the official program

buggy   (bug' ē) a small, light, one-horse carriage with or without a hood; four wheeled in the U.S., two wheeled in the U.K.

bulb of the heel   (bulb) structure of the foot; located at the back of the hoof

bulbo-urethra   (bul' bō yōō rē' thrä) two small glands, present in the male, that produce a secretion that helps provide a medium for the conveyance of spermatozoa during ejaculation; also called *Cowper's gland*

bulge   (bulj) the swell on the saddle formed when the outer edges of the fork curve back to the bar

bulldogging   see *steer wrestling*

bulldogging horse   a horse used for steer wrestling

bullfinch   (bŏŏl′ finch) a type of jump found in England; a thick hedge too high to be jumped and through which the rider must bore

bull hide   (bŏŏl hīd) the best grade of rawhide tree covering

bull pen   auction ring

bull riding   one of the standard events in a rodeo; the contestant has to ride a bull, which is equipped only with a rope around his middle that the rider holds with one hand, and a flank strap

bumper   (bum′ pər) an amateur race rider; an amateur race

bumping the bit   (bum′ piŋ thə bit) lightly applying and then releasing pressure on the bit through the reins

bur   (bʉr) the part of the bar that extends forward in front of the fork

Burghley   (bʉr′ lē) the seat, near Stamford in Lincolnshire, of the Marquis of Exeter; the home of Britain's principal autumn three-day event, the Burghley Horse Trials

Burmese   (bʉr mēz′) breed found in Burma; may be unreliable; has good endurance

burning bush   (bʉr′ niŋ) see *fireweed*

burning scent   (bʉr′ niŋ sənt) a scent so hot and strong that hounds tear along the line without hesitation; also called *screaming scent*

bursa   (bʉr′ sə) a sac or saclike cavity filled with fluid and situated at places in the tissues where friction would otherwise develop

bursatti   see *summer sores*

bursitis   (bər sī′ tis) an inflammation of the bursa, occasionally accompanied by the formation of a calcified deposit in the underlying tendon

burst   (bʉrst) when hounds get away quickly on their fox or when there is a fast run during a hunt

bush track   (bŏŏsh′ trak) an unofficial race meeting in the U.S.

butcher boots   (bŏŏch′ ər bōōts) the most common of the tall English boots; plain, full-length hunting boots fitted with garters

bute   (byōōt) a slang term for phenylbutazone; an anti-inflammatory agent

butorphanol   (byŏŏ tôr′ fə nōl) narcotic tranquilizer used in horses

buttress   (but′ ris) thickened angle at the heel of a horse's hoof wall; see *hoof* (illus.)

buttress foot   (fŏŏt) when the horse's hoof becomes pyramidal in shape, which can be caused by a form of low ringbone

buy a lot   (bī ə lät) an expression used in racing circles for falling off the horse

---

a=f<u>a</u>t; ā=<u>a</u>pe; ä=c<u>a</u>r; â=b<u>a</u>re; e=t<u>e</u>n; ē=<u>e</u>ven; i=<u>i</u>s; ī=b<u>i</u>te; ō=g<u>o</u>; ô=h<u>o</u>rn; ōō=t<u>oo</u>l; ŏŏ=l<u>oo</u>k; u=<u>u</u>p; ʉ=f<u>u</u>r; ŋ=ri<u>ng</u>; ə=sof<u>a</u>

by-day (bī dā) a day not regularly scheduled on the fixture card, but the master of huntsman takes hounds out anyway

Byerley Turk an Arab stallion that was one of the three founders of the English Thoroughbred; Byerley Turk was captured from the Turks at the siege of Budapest and brought back to England by Captain Byerley, hence the name; never raced, the horse proved to be a top-class sire

by or sired by (bī or sī ərd bī) a term used to indicate the male parent of the horse; i.e., Alysheba (the offspring) is by Alydar (the stallion)

C

cachexia   (kə kek′ sē ə) wasting and malnutrition

Cactus   (kak′ təs) famous dwarf horse born from full-size parents

cade   (kād) an English term for a foal raised by hand

cadence   (kād′ əns) the rhythm, tempo, and the horse's paces; when the horse covers equal distances on the ground in equal spaces of time; the gait is rhythmical, steady, elevated, and regular

Calabrese   a breed found in Italy derived from the Arab, Andalusian, and English Thoroughbred bloodlines; an attractive horse with good endurance

calash   (kə lash′) a carriage that may or may not have a fold-down top and is drawn by one horse

calcification   (kal′ sə fi kā′ shən) the process of tissue becoming hardened by a deposit of calcium

calcium   (kal′ sē əm) a mineral that aids in muscular activity, blood clotting, enzyme activation, and bone formation

calcium lactate   (kal′ sē əm lac′ tāt) a calcium salt of lactic acid; used to induce thickening and more rapid clotting of the blood

calf horse   (căf hôrs) a specially trained horse used for calf roping

calf knee   a conformational flaw in which the knee bends backward; opposite of over at the knee or knee sprung; considered a serious flaw because of the strain it puts on the knee; also called *back at the knee*; see *conformation comparisons* (illus.)

calf roping   one of two events that originated on the early ranches; one of the standard events in a rodeo in which the rider ropes a calf and then swiftly dismounts to tie the calf by three legs

calico   (kal′ ə kō) a paint horse that has irregular, splashy, scattered markings

calico pinto   (pin′ tō) a multicolored or spotted pony

California saddle   (kal′ ə fôr′ nye sad′ əl) a saddle, developed in the 1800s, characterized by rounded skirts, long tapaderas, and a small horn

California skirt   (skʉrt) round saddle skirts, so called because of their popularity in California

calk   (kôk) grips on the ground surface of the shoe, usually at the heels and toes of the shoes of horses; designed to give the horse better footing and prevent slipping

calking   (kôk iŋ) injury to the coronary band by the shoe of the horse; usually incurred by horses with shoes that have calks or by horses that are roughshod

call over   (kôl ō vər) 1. the naming of the horses in a race 2. when the latest betting odds on each horse are given

---

a=fat; ā=ape; ä=car; â=bare; e=ten; ē=even; i=is; ī=bite; ō=go; ô=horn; ōō=tool; ŏŏ=look; u=up; ʉ=fur; ŋ=ring; ə=sofa

callus (kal' əs) **1.** a localized thickening of the outer layer of the skin due to friction or pressure **2.** an unorganized woven meshwork of bone that forms at the site of a fracture and is eventually replaced by hard adult bone

Camargue a French breed, height: 13–15 hands; usually white or light gray; hardy with good endurance

camera patrol (kam' ər ə pə trōl') equipment for filming a race while it is in progress

camp (kamp) extending the forelegs out in front and the hind legs out behind; an indication of a kidney disorder if done naturally; in some breeds, it is the accepted show stance

camp drafting (dräft iŋ) a uniquely Australian rodeo contest in which a rider separates a large bull from a group of cattle and drives it at the gallop around a course marked with upright poles

camped out a conformational defect of the hind legs in which the horse, taking its natural stance, has too little angulation in the hock, causing hoof placement to fall too far behind the horse; see *conformation comparisons* (illus.)

camuse (kam' ōōs) another term for a dished face

Canadian Cutting Horse a breed skilled at working large herds of free-roaming cattle; bred from the American Quarter Horse, which it resembles in temperament and appearance

Canadian Horse Breed Association a registry of 1,500 Canadian horses

Canadian Mountain and Moorland Society a registry in which all breeding stallions must be licensed and blood typing is required

Canadian Pacer see *Standardbred*

cancellous (kan' sə ləs) spongy bone tissue

cancer (kan' sər) an anaplastic cellular mass that has a tendency to spread to other tissues or organs and that has a naturally fatal course; also called *neoplasia*

canine teeth (kā' nīn tēth) teeth appearing in the interdental space of male horses at five years of age; also known as *tushes* or *bridle teeth*

canker (kaŋ' kər) an ulceration; a chronic softening of the horn of the horse's foot; generally caused by horses continually standing in damp, moist, unclean areas

cannon bone (kan' ən bōn) the long bone between the knee or hock and the fetlock; also called the *third metacarpal bone* in the front and the *third metatarsal bone* in the rear legs; see *points of the horse; hoof* (illus.)

cannula (kan' yŏŏ lə) a tube inserted into a body cavity to transfuse or draw off fluid

canter (kan' tər) a slow, restrained gallop or run; a three-beat gait in which the two diagonal legs are paired, thereby producing a single beat that falls between the successive beats of the other unpaired legs

canter broken (kan' tər brō' kən) when the three-beat gait of the canter is not entirely accurate; may refer to a horse with a high croup, which gives the impression of the horse cantering

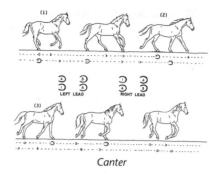

Canter

in two parts—first the forehand and then the hindquarters

cantharidin (kan t͟har′ i din) an agent occurring in crystal form that has a bitter taste; may be given as a diuretic and applied externally to produce blistering; the poison found in a blister beetle

cantle (kan′ təl) the back portion or the rear of the saddle seat; see *English saddle; western saddle* (illus.)

cantle binding rolled leather bead stitched over the perimeter of the cantle

cantle drop the outside of the back of the cantle

cantle rider one who rides pressing against the cantle because of a badly slanted seat or stirrups that are too far forward

cantle roll a long welt protruding a third of an inch or more from the front face of the cantle just under its top rim; designed to prevent the rider from sliding backward out of the saddle or from moving skyward when riding a bucking horse

cap (kap) **1.** the fee payable by a visitor for a day's hunting **2.** to encourage

the hounds by waving them onto the line, cap in hand

capillary (kap′ ə ler′ ē) the smallest vessel of the circulatory system; minute vessels that connect the arterioles and venules, forming a network in the body; semipermeable membranes for the interchange of various substances between blood and tissue fluids

capillary action (ak′ s͟hən) the action by which a liquid is elevated in a tube through the attraction of its surface molecules to those of the tube

capillary refill time (rē′ fil tīm) the time required for normal blood flow and color to return to an area of the gums after the application of pressure; slow refill time may indicate anemia, low blood pressure, blood loss, shock, or dehydration

capped elbow a soft, flabby swelling over the point of the elbow due to trauma

capped hock a swelling at the point of the hock; comparable to capped elbow of the forelimb; usually caused by repeated injury from kicking in stalls, lying on hard or concrete floors, or trauma from other sources; see *blemishes and unsoundnesses* (illus.)

capped knees an inflammation of the joint capsules and associated structures of the knee; sometimes the result of a bruise often repeated or self-inflicted by a horse that has a habit of pawing while in the stable

---

a=f_at; ā=_ape; ä=c_ar; â=b_are; e=t_en; ē=_even;
i=_is; ī=b_ite; ō=g_o; ô=h_orn; ōō=t_ool;
ŏŏ=l_ook; u=_up; ʉ=f_ur; ŋ=ri_ng; ə=sof_a

capriole (kap' rē ōl') an intricate movement performed by Lipizzan horses in which the horse leaps high into the air and kicks out with his hind legs

caps (kaps) temporary teeth that sometimes fail to fall out when they are being replaced by permanent teeth

carbohydrates (kär' bə hī' drāts) the main energy nutrient; compounds made up of carbon, hydrogen, and oxygen

carcass (kär' kəs) a dead animal body

carcinoma (kär' sə nō' mə) a malignant new growth of epithelial cells that tends to spread quickly; cancer that originates from epithelium

cardia (kär' dē ə) the opening of the esophagus into the stomach

cardiac (kär' dē ak') pertaining to the heart

cardiac cycle (sī' kəl) the actions of the heart during one complete heartbeat

cardiac murmur (mʉr' mʉr) abnormal heart sound that can be heard by listening to the heart with a stethoscope; usually due to increased turbulence of the blood leaking through the heart valves or through other defects in the heart

cardiac output (out' pŏŏt) the amount of blood pumped from the heart during each beat

cardiovascular (kär' dē ō vas' kyŏŏ lər) pertaining to the heart and blood vessels

cardiovascular system (kär' dē ō vas' kyŏŏ lər sis' təm) consists of the heart and blood vessels; responsible for transporting blood to all tissues in the body and then returning it to the heart

carleitas a solid-color wool Mexican blanket used as a saddle blanket; similar to a Navajo blanket

carotid artery (kə rät' id är' tər ē) the artery that supplies blood to the brain, head, and face

carpal (kär' pəl) pertaining to the knee

carpitis (kär pī' tis) inflammation of the knee joint accompanied by swelling and pain

carpus (kär' pus) another name for the knee (front legs); see *skeletal system* (illus.)

carpus valgus (val' gəs) deformity of the knee when the cannon bone points away from the midline when viewed from the front; bowlegged

carpus varus (vär' əs) deformity of the knee when the cannon bone deviates toward the midline when viewed from the front; knock kneed

carriage (kar' ij) **1.** a horse-drawn vehicle; any of the more elegant, four-wheeled family driving vehicles **2.** the bearing of a horse; how he holds his head, neck, and tail

carriage, berlin   see *berlin*

carriage, break   see *break coach*

carriage, britzka   see *britzka*

carriage, brougham   see *brougham*

carriage, calash see *calash*

carriage, cart see *cart*

carriage, charabanc see *charabanc*

carriage, clarence see *clarence*

carriage, coupe see *coupe*

carriage, derby see *derby*

carriage, dogcart see *dogcart*

carriage, dorsay see *dorsay*

carriage, drag see *drag*

carriage, duc see *duc*

carriage, fiacre see *fiacre*

carriage, gig see *gig*

carriage, hansom cab see *hansom cab*

carriage, landau see *landau*

carriage, mail coach see *mail coach*

carriage, mylord see *mylord*

carriage, omnibus see *omnibus*

carriage, parts of see *carriage parts* (illus.)

carriage, phaeton see *phaeton*

carriage, stage coach see *stage coach*

carriage, stanhope see *stanhope*

carriage, sulky see *sulky*

carriage, tandem see *tandem*

carriage, tilbury see *tilbury*

carriage, tilbury phaeton see *tilbury phaeton*

carriage, tonneau see *tonneau*

carriage, victoria see *victoria*

carriage, vis-a-vis see *vis-a-vis*

carriage, wagonette see *wagonette*

carriage, whiskey see *whiskey*

carrier (kar' ē ər) infected animal that harbors a specific infectious agent in the absence of discernible clinical disease and serves as a potential source of infection for other animals; an animal that carries a recessive gene or the organisms of a disease without showing signs of the condition

cart (kärt) an open, long-shafted vehicle with two large wheels; drawn by one horse and carries four people on seats running lengthwise

Carthusian (kär thōō' zhən) a Spanish breed used by monks; quiet, docile, and intelligent with a strong athletic build

cartilage (kärt' əl ij) a specialized type of fibrous connective tissue; may form the shape of a part, such as the nose or ear, or may serve as a soft, somewhat flexible end of a long bone, such as on the distal end of the ribs

caruncle (kär' əŋ kəl) a small, fleshy outgrowth

caseous (kā' sē əs) resembling cheese or curd

---

a=fat; ā=ape; ä=car; â=bare; e=ten; ē=even; i=is; ī=bite; ō=go; ô=horn; ōō=tool; ŏŏ=look; u=up; ʉ=fur; ŋ=ring; ə=sofa

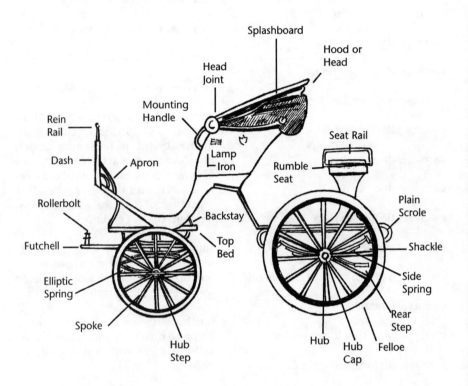

Splashboard

Hood or
Head

Head
Joint

Mounting
Handle

Rein
Rail

Seat Rail

Dash

Apron

Lamp
Iron

Rumble
Seat

Plain
Scrole

Rollerbolt

Backstay

Shackle

Futchell

Top
Bed

Side
Spring

Elliptic
Spring

Rear
Step

Spoke

Hub

Hub
Cap

Felloe

Hub
Step

Carriage Parts

Caslick's operation   an operation to correct pneumovagina that involves suturing the upper vulvar lips together to help reduce infection and improve reproductive rates

Caspian Pony   (kas' pe ən pō' nē) Iranian breed thought to be extinct until 1965; quiet and docile; used for riding and jumping

cast   (kast) **1.** falling down or lying close to a wall or fence so the horse's legs are trapped and he cannot get up without assistance **2.** a stiff casing made up of bandages and solidified with plaster of paris or other hardening material that is used to immobilize a part of the body in cases of fractures, dislocations, or infected wounds **3.** to throw a horse onto the ground, by use of casting ropes and/ or hobbles, as part of the breaking process or to perform some type of operation on the horse

castile soap   (kas tēl' sōp) fine, hard soap made from olive oil and caustic soda

castor bean   (kas' tər bēn) a poisonous plant also known as *Ricinus communis*; ingestion causes diarrhea, uncoordination, and can result in death

castrate   (kas' trāt) to remove the testicles from a male animal; to geld; the horse is then known as a *gelding*

catalyst   (kat' əl ist) a substance that brings about a reaction without being consumed by that reaction

cataplasm   (kat' ə plaz' əm) see *poultice*

cataract   (kat' ə rakt) loss of transparency of the lens of the eye or its capsule

catch hold   (kach hōld) the collection of hounds by the huntsman who takes them forward at a check or in answer to a halloo indicating that the fox has been seen

catch pigeon   (pig' ən) racehorse capable of sprinting faster than most

catch rope   (rōp) working rope or lariat

catch weight   (wāt) the random or optional weight carried by a horse when the conditions of a race do not specify a weight

cat foot   (cat fŏŏt) a hound's foot; so called because the foot is rounder than the more elongated pad of the fox and hare

cathartic   (kə thär' tik) an agent that causes evacuation of the bowels

catheter   (kath' ə tər) a flexible, tubular instrument for withdrawing fluids from or introducing fluids into a body cavity or into a blood vessel

caudad   (kô' dad) toward the tail, opposite of *craniad*

cauda equina   (kou' də ē kwe' nə) the end of the spinal cord where it divides into a number of nerves; situated in the tail

caudal   (kôd' əl) referring to a position near the tail; opposite of *cranial*

caudal epidural anesthesia   (ep' i dōō' rəl an' is thē' zhə) type of nerve block when the local anesthetic is infiltrated into the space around the

---

a=fat; ā=ape; ä=car; â=bare; e=ten; ē=even; i=is; ī=bite; ō=go; ô=horn; ōō=tool; ŏŏ=look; u=up; ʉ=fur; ŋ=ring; ə=sofa

spinal cord thus numbing large areas of the hind legs

caul (kôl) the inner membrane enclosing a foal before birth

caustic (kôs' tik) burning, corrosive, and destructive to living tissue

cauterize (kôt' ər īz') to burn away unhealthy tissue with a hot iron, electric current, or chemical substance

cavalletti (kav' əl et ē) a series of small wooden rails used in the basic training of a riding horse in order to encourage him to lengthen his stride, improve his balance, and loosen up and strengthen his muscles; a ground rail suspended between two X-shaped supports

caveat emptor (kä' vē ät' emp' tôr) Latin for "let the buyer beware"

caverna (kav' ərn ə) a general term used to designate a hollow place within the body or organ

cavesson (kav' i sən) another name for a noseband; a stiff noseband on a halter used with a longe strap in training; also used in conjunction with a bridle to keep the horse's mouth closed; see *English bridle* (illus.)

cavity (kav' ə tē) a real or potential hollow space within the body or organ

cavy (kā' vē) a collection of horses

cayuse (kī' ŏŏs') a general term used to describe a horse of nondescript breeding; may also refer to an Indian horse or pony

cecum (sē' kəm) a large, sock-shaped pouch between the small and large intestines of the horse; important in digestion and water absorption

cell (sel) the microscopic unit of body construction; the building blocks of the body

cellulitis (sel' yŏŏ līt' is) inflammation of connective tissues below the skin

cellulose (sel' yŏŏ lōs) a carbohydrate that appears only in plants and cannot be digested by horses; also referred to as *fiber*

Celsius (sel' sē əs) the name of a Swedish astronomer who calibrated a thermometer to indicate the freezing point at 0 degrees and the boiling point at 100 degrees

CEM see *contagious equine metritis*

centaur (sen' tôr) a mythological creature that had a head, torso, and arms of a man, and the body and legs of a horse

center bar cinch ring (sen' tər bär sinch riŋ) a cinch ring with the bar across the center to which the buckle tongue is attached

center fire (sen' tər fīr) a western saddle with a single rigging ring suspended halfway between the fork and the cantle on each side

center marker (mär' kər) used to denote the top and bottom of a dressage ring; generally A and C are used; see *dressage ring*

center of gravity (grav' i tē) a horse's center of gravity at a standstill is about six inches behind the elbow

center of motion   (mō' shən) in a horse, the center of motion will vary according to the balance of the horse but generally is over the fifteenth vertebra or ten inches behind the center of gravity

central nervous system   (sen' trəl nʉr' vəs sis' təm) the part of the nervous system that supervises and coordinates all the activities of the body; consists of brain and spinal cord; transmits nerve impulses from the brain to the peripheral nerves and returns external stimuli back to the brain

centrals   (sen' trälz) middle incisors of the lower and upper jaws; first teeth to appear in foals

cephalosporin   (sef' ə lō spôr' in) type of broad-spectrum antibiotic commonly used in foals

cerebellar abiotrophy   (ser' ə bel' ər ab' ē ät' rō fē) lack of formation of the cerebellum before birth of the foal

cerebellum   (ser' ə bel' əm) the part of the brain that controls the coordination of movements

cerebrospinal fluid   (ser' ə brō spīn' əl flōō' id) fluid containing salts, proteins, and sugar that bathes the spinal cord and brain

cerebrum   (ser' ə brəm) main part of the brain

certainty   (sʉr' tən tē) a horse regarded as certain to win a particular race; may or may not be the official favorite

cervical   (sʉr' vi kəl) pertaining to the neck, or to the neck of any organ or structure; there are seven cervical vertebrae in the horse

cervicitis   (sʉr' və sīt' əs) an inflammation of the cervix

cesarean section   (si zer' ē ən sek' shən) an incision made through the abdominal and uterine walls to deliver a fetus

cestode   (ses' tōd) tapeworm

Chadwick spring   (chad' wik spriŋ) a V-shaped steel spring fitted to the bottom of the foot; keeps constant pressure on the bars of the foot

chaff   (chaf) meadow hay or green oat straw cut into short lengths for use as feed

chain twitch   (chān twich) a means of restraint; a wooden stick with a loop of chain; the upper lip is pulled out and the chain is tightened around it; the application causes the release of endorphins, natural opiates that relax the horse

chalk   (chälk) the favorite or most heavily played horse in a race; the term originated in the days of bookmakers when the odds were written on slates with chalk

Chain Twitch

champing   (champ' iŋ) a term that describes the horse playing with the bit; a young horse's development is encouraged by using a bit with keys attached to the mouthpiece, which tends to make the saliva flow and keep the mouth moist; it is considered by some to be an aid in producing a 'soft' mouth

a=fat; ā=ape; ä=car; â=bare; e=ten; ē=even; i=is; ī=bite; ō=go; ô=horn; ōō=tool; ŏŏ=look; u=up; ʉ=fur; ŋ=ring; ə=sofa

champion (cham′ pē ən) the highest award in a particular division

change of diagonal (chānj uv dī ag′ ə nəl) when the rider changes the diagonal to which he is posting

change of hand to change direction by crossing the long diagonal of the riding arena; also known as *change of rein*

change of lead to change the leading leg at the canter or lope

change of rein see *change of hand*

changing rhythm (chānj′ iŋ rith′ əm) the alteration of steps within a pace; instead of moving with regular, steady strides, the horse, for one reason or another, breaks the length of the stride for one or more steps, altering the rhythm

channel (chan′ əl) the long narrow area between the bars of the tree; uncovered on the McClellan saddle, but in the stock saddle it is usually covered with the seat leather and a metal plate; it allows some air to circulate above the horse's spine

channel keeper (chan′ əl kē′ pər) a stationary keeper, three or more inches long; used on a flank cinch to keep the flank billets from flapping and the ropes from catching on the loose billet

chaps (shaps) outer garment, usually made of leather; worn to protect the rider's legs from brush, cacti, and cold; two kinds: batwings (flared) and shotguns (fit close to the leg)

charabanc (shar′ ə bäŋ′) a long, light, four-wheeled vehicle, completely open with seats arranged in parallel rows; drawn by pairs of horses; originally used for hunting

Charabanc

character (kar′ ik tər) the nature or type of behavior of the horse

characteristics (kar′ ik tə ris′ tiks) traits, features, or qualities different from others

charbon see *anthrax*

charging (chärj′ iŋ) 1. when a horse suddenly attacks or savages a person, horse, or other animal 2. to rush into a fence in jumping

charro horse (chä′ rō hôrs) a type of Spanish ranch horse; trained in roping and other ranch work

charro saddle (sad′ əl) a "gentleman rider's" ornate Mexican saddle; many such saddles are used in parades and shows

check (chek) 1. short for checkrein 2. when the hounds lose the scent and stop 3. the western version of the half halt

check guards simple, flat rubber circles with hoses in the center to accommodate the bit mouthpiece; designed to stop the bit cheeks from chafing the lips

checkrein a rein designed to keep a horse's head in a certain position by attaching to the bridle and then to the saddle or harness

cheek (chēk) the skin that covers the sides of the face

cheek piece   the part of the bridle that attaches the bit to the headpiece; so called because it lies across the cheek; see *English bridle; western bridle; harness parts B and E* (illus.)

cheek strap   part of the bridle that runs down the cheek connecting the top of the bridle with the bit

cheer   (chēr) when the huntsman in a foxhunt calls to his hounds; an encouraging cry

chef d'equipe   the manager of an equestrian team responsible for making all the arrangements, both on and off the field, for a national team competing abroad

chemotherapy   (kēm' ō ther' ə pē) the treatment of a disease by chemical agents

chest   (chest) the front third of the trunk; that portion of the body from which the front legs extend; see *points of the horse* (illus.)

chestnut   (ches' nut) coat color; brown hair and points with wide variation from dark reddish brown to light golden brown; mane and tail should be close to coat color

chestnut roan   (ches' nut rōn) coat color; chestnut with equal parts of white hair mixed in; lower legs may be solid color; also called *strawberry roan*

chestnuts   (ches' nuts)   horny growths on the inside of a horse's leg above the knees and below the hocks; also called *night eyes*; see *points of the horse* (illus.)

Cheyenne roll   (shī en' rōl) a wide, flat backward extension of the cantle binding

Cheyenne saddle   see *Texas trail saddle*

Chickasaw   (chik' ə sô) the name for east coast Indian horses

Chilean Corralero Registry International   a registry for Chilean Corraleros descended from sires and dams registered in the studbook of Chile, South America

chin   (chin) the part of the face between the lower lip and the front of the lower jaw; see *points of the horse* (illus.)

Chincoteague Ponies   ponies found in the eastern U.S. that are the descendants of the survivors of a shipwreck off the coast of Virginia

Chinese horse   (chī' nēz hôrs) breed found in China; usually dun colored with a primitive zebra or eel stripe; good endurance, but may be rebellious

chin groove   (chin grōōv) the small indentation between the chin and the branches of the jaw; see *points of the horse* (illus.)

chinks   (chinks) chaps that extend slightly beyond the knee; they do not cover the rider's shins

chlorhexide   (klôr heks' īd) a soap or solution used for disinfection of skin and surfaces

---

a=fat; ā=ape; ä=car; â=bare; e=ten; ē=even; i=is; ī=bite; ō=go; ô=horn; ōō=tool; ŏŏ=look; u=up; ʉ=fur; ŋ=ring; ə=sofa

chlorophyll (klôr′ ə fil′) the green coloring of plants

choke (chōk) a partial or complete esophageal obstruction that may cause death through perforation of the esophagus or degeneration and death of the tissue due to pressure

choke cherry (chōk cher′ ē) a shrub or bush with leaves and bark that contain cyanide; poisoning causes difficulty in breathing and can result in death; see *cyanide*

cholagogue (kō′ lə gog) a drug or compound that stimulates the flow of bile from the liver

chondritis (kän′ drīt′ əs) inflammation of cartilage

chondromalacia (kon′ drō mə lā′ shē ə) softening of cartilage, especially in the patella

chop (chäp) the capture and killing of the fox before he has escaped and there has been no run; also called *mobbed*

chorioallantoic sac (kôr′ ē ō ə lan′ tō ik sak) the placenta

chorioptic mange (kor′ ē op tik mānj) a skin disease caused by mite infection on the legs of the horse; frequently results in secondary infection and grease heel

chorioretinitis (kō′ rē ō ret′ i nī′ tis) an inflammation of the choroid and the retina of the eye

choroid (kôr′ oid) the layer in back of the eyeball containing blood vessels

chromosome (krō′ mə sōm) the structure in the cell that carries genes; each species has a constant number of chromosomes set in pairs; the horse has 32 pairs

chronic (krän′ ik) persisting or continuing over a long period of time; the opposite of *acute*

chronic obstructive pulmonary disease heaves; a respiratory disease caused by allergies, usually due to dust or pollen

chukka (chuk′ ə) a period of play in polo lasting seven and one-half or eight minutes

chukker (chuk′ ər) see *chukka*

chute (shōōt) 1. the straightaway entering into the main oval track for races at six furlongs (1.2 km) 2. the straight part of the track behind the barrier 3. the box from which livestock is released into the arena in rodeo events

chyme (kīm) the semifluid, creamy material produced by gastric digestion of fatty foods

CID see *combined immunodeficiency*

ciliary muscle (sil′ ē er′ ē mus′ əl) muscle that changes the shape of the lens to adjust focus

cinch (sinch) a part of the western saddle, that is a band that runs underneath the barrel of the horse just behind the front legs and fastens the saddle in place; see *western saddle; girth* (illus.)

cinch connector strap the strap connecting the center of the front cinch to the center of the flank cinch on the horse's belly; gives stability of position to the flank cinch and keeps it from sliding back and causing the horse discomfort, which could induce bucking

cinch crossbar the band that crosses the center of the cinch; holds the strands together and keeps the cinch straight

cinched up when the cinch is properly tightened so that the saddle is secured to the horse, one should be able to get three or four fingers between the cinch and the horse's belly

cinch knot a latigo knot used on the rigging ring on the near side of the saddle; serves as a hitch when a buckle is not in use; made the same as the windsor knot in a man's tie; a four-in-hand knot; also called a *cinch*

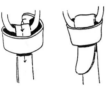

Cinch Knot

cinch ring buckle a type of cinch that has buckle-style rings for attaching the half-breed straps

cinch strap holder a small, bell-shaped leather flap slotted at the bottom, usually near the base of the fork or cantle; used only to hold the long free end of the latigo strap when the saddle is cinched up with a cinch ring buckle

cinchy (sinch′ ē) a horse that is touchy and bites or kicks when being cinched up

circle and strap two circular pieces of leather placed around the ends of a mullen mouthpiece and connected by an adjustable strap that is attached to the noseband by a small strap in the middle; puts pressure on the horse's

nose and raises the bit in his mouth, making it hard for him to get his tongue over the bit

circle cheek snaffle a bit with large ring cheeks similar to those of the Liverpool bit used for driving; rein attachment is in the center of the cheek; produces a squeezing action that, combined with the extra large cheeks, helps to keep the horse straight

circle too large/small/square in riding classes that include patterns, judges often deduct points for these incorrectly executed circles

circulatory system (sʉr′ kyə la tôr′ ē sis′ təm) the body system that consists of the heart, blood, veins, and arteries

circumduction (sʉr′ kəm duk′ shən) the circular movement of an eye or leg

Circus Maximus (sʉr′ kəs mak′ si məs) the famous location of Roman chariot races

cirrhosis (sə rō′ sis) a liver disease characterized by loss of the normal structure and fibrous regeneration; hardening and enlargement of the liver caused by chronic poisoning or liver disease; impairs metabolic and digestive functioning of the liver

CITE foal test used to test foal blood for antibodies; indicates amount of colostrum received from the dam

claim full allowance (klām fŏŏl ə lou′ əns) the weight allowance allowed

a=fat; ā=ape; ä=car; â=bare; e=ten; ē=even; i=is; ī=bite; ō=go; ô=horn; ōō=tool; ŏŏ=look; u=up; ʉ=fur; ŋ=ring; ə=sofa

to apprentice jockeys due to their inexperience; these riders are allowed to ride at a lesser weight than their more-experienced counterparts; it is possible for a highly successful apprentice to exhaust his weight allowance before his apprenticeship is completed

claiming price   the predetermined price at which a horse in a claiming race must be sold if it is claimed

claiming race   a race in which all the horses are entered at stated prices and may be claimed (purchased) by any other owner or starter in the race; in effect, all horses in a claiming race are offered for sale

Clarence   (klar′ əns) a carriage named after the English Duke of Clarence; a closed, four-wheeled vehicle with one seat inside and one outside for the coachman

Clarence Carriage

classic   (klas′ ik) any one of the five chiefly English flat races for three-year-old horses; the Derby, the Oaks, the St. Leger, the 1,000 Guineas, and the 2,000 Guineas

classical art of riding   (klas′ i kəl ärt uv rīd′ iŋ) the method of riding promoted by schools such as the Spanish Riding School in which the natural movements of the horse are controlled and perfected

classification   (klas′ ə fi kā′ shən) arrangement according to some orderly plan; division into groups or classes

claybank   (klā baŋk′) coat color; vari-

ation of the dun color; coat is light copper, with mane and tail a darker shade; the very light red dun color

clean bred   (klēn bred) a horse of any breeding with an ancestry that can be traced back and shown to contain nothing other than pureblood; all ancestors are registered to the same breed registry

clean gaits   the ability of an American Saddlebred to maintain, without pause or missing, all five artificial gaits

clean legs   no blemishes or unsoundnesses on the legs; when the horse's legs, especially from the knee or the hock down, are smooth

clearance (klēr′ əns) a document from any organization controlling any aspect of horse activities that permits any horse and/or rider to be able to participate in events outside their area

clear round   a show-jumping or cross-country round that is completed without jumping or time faults

cleft of the frog   (kleft uv thē frog) the division in the middle part of the frog; see *hoof* (illus.)

cleft palate   (kleft pal′ it) congenital defect; the roof of the mouth is split and allows food to regurgitate into the nose

Cleveland Bay   (klēv′ lənd bā) a breed found in Great Britain; always solid bay with black legs; used as a saddle horse; frequently used to increase quality of other breeds; larger than most light horse breeds; height: 16–16.2 hands

Cleveland Bay Horse Society of

North America a registry in which partbred registration requires one parent to be a purebred Cleveland Bay

clicking (klik′ iŋ) striking the forefoot with the toe of the hind foot on the same side; also known as *forging*

climbing (klīm′ iŋ) Thoroughbred's striding in an unnatural, upward fashion, not reaching out forward as in a coordinated gait

clinical (klin′ ik əl) based on actual observation of signs or symptoms

clinical diagnosis (klin′ i kəl dī′ əg nō′ sis) diagnosis based on signs or symptoms

clinker (kliŋk′ ər) a first-rate or top-class horse

clip (klip) **1.** a thin, metal projection on the outside of a horseshoe that lies against the hoof to help stabilize the shoe **2.** to cut or shave a horse's hair **3.** a sharp blow, such as when one hoof strikes another

clippers (klip′ ərs) either electric or hand-operated units used to cut the horse's hair

clipping (klip′ iŋ) cutting the horse's long winter coat with clippers; trimming ears, chin, and fetlocks for show

clitoris (klit′ ər əs) the female version of the penis situated on the floor of the vagina just inside the vulva

clocker (kläk′ ər) the person who times a horse's workouts; the times are published for the benefit of the public; almost all workouts are done early in the morning during training hours

close breeding the mating of closely

related animals such as sire to daughter, son to dam, brother to sister, etc.; see *inbreeding*

close coupled short and strong; often considered an advantage in a back

close nail a shoeing nail that puts pressure on but does not penetrate sensitive tissue

Clostridium tetani (klos trid′ ē əm tə tan′ ē) the bacterium causing tetanus (lockjaw); often introduced into the body via a puncture wound

closure time (klō′ zhər tīm) the date and time at which nominations are finally accepted for a race or event

clot (klät) a semisolidified mass of blood

club foot (klub fŏŏt) an abnormally upright foot with a high heel and short toe, resulting from the inability to straighten the coffin joint

cluck (kluk) to move the tongue in such a way as to produce sounds; the command to go, proceed; the signal to increase speed

clucking and chirping sounds made to encourage more speed; they should not be used when riding with others

Clydesdale (klīdz′ dāl) originating in Scotland and Great Britain; a popular draft, carriage horse; one of the feathered breeds (those with long hair on the fetlocks); the shape of the foot is considered important to breed character

---

a=fat; ā=ape; ä=car; â=bare; e=ten; ē=even; i=is; ī=bite; ō=go; ô=horn; ōō=tool; ŏŏ=look; u=up; ʉ=fur; ŋ=ring; ə=sofa

Clydesdale Breeders of the U.S.A.   a registry for Clydesdale stallions, mares, or geldings; horses will be admitted to the registry if both sire and dam are recorded in the Clydesdale studbook

coagulate   (kō ag′ yōō lāt) to cause to clot, forming an insoluble fibrin clot

coarse   (kôrs) lacking in quality; thickness or roughness in texture of hair; hairy fetlocks; lack of refinement

coat colors   there are five basic coat colors in horses: bay, black, brown, chestnut, and white

cob   (käb) a type rather than a breed; a short-legged animal with a maximum height of 15.1 hands with the bone and substance of a heavyweight hunter; capable of carrying a substantial weight

cobalt   (kō′ bôlt) mineral required for the synthesis of vitamin B12 in the intestinal tract

cobby   (käb′ ē) close coupled and stoutly built

coccidioidomycosis   (käk sid′ ē oi′ dō mī kō′ sis) a fungal disease that has two forms: primary and secondary; the primary form is an acute respiratory infection from inhalation of spores; the secondary type is a virulent granulomatous disease that involves the viscera, central nervous system, lungs, etc.

coccidiosis   (käk sid ē′ ō′ sis) intestinal infection usually causing diarrhea

coccidiostat   (käk sid′ ē ō stat) any of a group of chemical agents mixed in feed or drinking water to control coccidiosis

coccygeal vertebra   (kok′ sij′ ē əl vʉr′ tə brə) also called *caudal vertebra*; the bones in the tail; the number of bones ranges from fifteen to twenty-one, depending on the horse and the breed; see *skeletal system* (illus.)

cocked ankles   (kokd ank′ əlz) a condition usually limited to the hind feet; partial dislocation of the ankle or fetlock joint brought on by a shortening of the tendons on the back side of the leg; horses having this condition stand bent forward on the fetlocks in a cocked position

cockhorse   an extra horse used with English stagecoaches; ridden behind the coach in ordinary going, but hitched before the team for added draft when approaching steep hills or heavy going

cocktail   an English expression meaning a coldblooded hunter; one that is not a Thoroughbred; the tails of such horses were frequently docked in England

cofavorite   (cō fā′ vər it) one of two or more horses given equal odds to win a race

coffin bone   (kôf′ in bōn) the lowest bone in the horse's hoof; also known as the *distal phalanx* or *third phalanx*; see *hoof* (illus.)

Coggin's test   a test used to determine the presence of equine infectious anemia antibodies in a blood sample

coital exanthema   (kō′ i tal eks an thē′ mə) a contagious disease carried by a Herpes virus that results in temporary sterility in mares and is characterized by the development of many small blisters on the mucous membranes of the vulva and vagina

coitus (kō′ it əs) sexual intercourse

colas the Spanish term used to describe the roping classes

cold back (kōld bak) a horse that objects to the saddle being fitted and the girth being tightened

cold backed a horse that humps his back and does not settle down until the saddle has been on a few minutes

coldblood having ancestors that trace to heavy war horses and draft breeds; characteristics might include more substance of bone, thick skin, heavy hair coat, shaggy fetlocks, and lower red blood cell and hemoglobin values; may be used in some cases to refer to a grade horse with unknown breeding

cold jawed a horse that has a hard (insensitive) mouth; often due to the rider's misuse of the bit

cold lameness incapable of normal movement on the first starting exercise

cold line the faint scent of a quarry that may have lain for some time; in certain scenting conditions, a scent may be quite "fresh," but still so faint as to be termed *cold*

cold-water therapy walking a horse in a cold stream or putting on ice boots after a horse has been cooled down after a hard workout; the cold will make the blood vessels in the legs dilate, prevent excessive swelling, and ease muscle soreness

colic (käl′ ik) abdominal discomfort; the pain ranges from mild to excruciating; may be caused by gas, impaction, intestinal damage from parasites, etc.

colitis (kō līt′ is) inflammation of the colon

colitis X a complex, severe, often fatal disorder characterized by fever and diarrhea; related to stress

collagen (käl′ ə jən′) a main fibrous protein of skin, bone, tendon, cartilage, and connective tissue

collar (käl′ ər) the padded part of the harness that goes around the horse's neck; see *harness parts A* (illus.)

collar work (käl′ ər wʉrk) any type of work that requires a harness or draft horse to push against a collar to move his load

collect (kə lekt′) to bring a horse into complete balance between the hands and legs by the use of rein aids and leg cues by creating impulsion with the legs and containing it with the hands; the horse brings his hind legs further under his body

collected (kə lekt′ əd) when a horse is ridden well up to his bit with his neck flexed, jaw relaxed, and hocks well under him; a collected horse has full control over his limbs at all gaits and is ready and able to respond to the signals or aids of the rider; a controlled gait; correct, coordinated actions

collection (kə lek′ shən) the shortening of the horse's body length

---

a=fat; ā=ape; ä=car; â=bare; e=ten; ē=even; i=is; ī=bite; ō=go; ô=horn; ōō=tool; ŏŏ=look; u=up; ʉ=fur; ŋ=ring; ə=sofa

caused by the rider driving him forward into the bit, thus flexing at the poll, raising the action, lowering the croup, and bringing the hindquarters under him; the horse remains on the bit, is light and mobile, and is ready to respond to the requests of the trainer

collodion (kə lō′ dē ən) a clear, viscous liquid that dries to a transparent film when applied to wounds; a protective covering

colon (kō′ lən) the part of the large intestine extending from the cecum to the rectum

Colorado Ranger Horse Association a registry in which most horses are Appaloosa-colored, but this is not a requirement

Color Class (kul′ ər klas) the class in which coat color and pattern, not conformation, is a deciding factor

color registry (rej′ is trē) the registry that has certain color requirements for registration, such as palomino or pinto; a horse may be double registered, e.g., a palomino Quarter Horse

colors (kul′ ərs) the jockey's silk or nylon jacket and cap provided by the owner

colostrum (kə läs′ trəm) mare's milk produced in the first few days after a foal's birth; contains globulin, a protein that provides the foal with temporary immunity against infectious disease

colt (kōlt) a young male horse under three years of age; some extend the age to four years

coma (kō′ mə) a state of uncon-sciousness from which the animal cannot be aroused

combination bit (käm′ bə nā′ shen bit) a set of two bits using one mouthpiece and four reins

combination horse (hôrs) a horse that can be ridden or driven in harness

combination obstacle (ob′ stə kəl) in show jumping, an obstacle consisting of two or more separate jumps that are numbered and judged as one obstacle

combination rein (rān) using neck and direct reining at the same time; a training technique in which direct reining dominates initial training and leads into full neck reining

combined immunodeficiency disease (kem bīnd′ im′ yə nō di fish′ ən sē di zēz′) a heritable deficiency in the immune system of Arabian foals that is usually fatal; affected foals are unable to produce their own antibodies, making them defenseless to infection; also called *CID*

combined training a comprehensive test of both horse and rider, consisting of the following three phases: dressage, cross-country, and show jumping; held over a period of one, two, or three days, depending on the type of competition

come a cropper an English term for falling off the horse

commissure (käm′ i shŏŏr′) deep groves located on each side of the frog, giving elasticity to the foot

Committee saddle see *association saddle*

common botfly see *botfly*

communicable disease (kə myōō′ ni kə bəl di zēz′) illness due to a specific infectious agent or its toxic products arising through transmission of that agent or its products from a reservoir to a susceptible host

compost (käm′ pōst) a mixture of manure, grass, and/or vegetable leftovers, aged and used for fertilizing the soil

compound fracture (käm′ pound frak′ chər) a fracture that has broken the skin

compression bandage (kəm presh′ ən ban′ dij) a bandage that is applied tightly over inflammation to provide pressure to the area and reduce swelling

compression screw (kəm presh′ ən skrōō) a special kind of screw used to fix bone fragments together

Comtois a very old French breed; used as a war-horse; noted for being active and surefooted; well suited to mountainous regions

concave (kän kāv′) hollowed or rounded inward like the inside of a bowl; opposite of *convex*

concave shoe (shōō) a horseshoe the ground surface of which is concave, forming inner and outer rims; rimshoe

concentrates (kän′ sən trāts) feeds that are low in fiber and high in total digestible nutrients; examples of this class of feeds are the various grains and high-grade by-products

conception (kən sep′ shən) the fertilization of the egg and the beginning of growth of the embryo inside the mare's body

concho (käŋ′ chō) a silver or other metal coin-size decorative piece with two slots or a screw base placed on top of the rosette or rosettes through which the saddle strings are passed and tied holding the skirts and jockeys to the saddletree; see *western saddle* (illus.)

concussion (kən kush′ ən) a shock from impact

condition (kən dish′ ən) the state of health as evidenced by the coat, state of flesh, and general appearance

conditioned response an acquired or learned reaction

conditioning the process of developing tolerance to exercise and new capacities of performance; preparing a horse mentally and physically for the demands of an event

condition race a race in which certain conditions are specified (usually number of wins up to a certain date, weights carried, distance, and so on); a calendar of races that includes the stipulations and provisions under which each race is to be run is published in the condition book

conformation (kän′ fôr mā′ shən) the shape or contour of the body or body structures; overall picture of the horse; symmetry and correctness of all parts of the body; the physical structure as compared to an ideal

conformation hunter (hunt′ ər) class judged 40 percent on conformation and 60 percent on performance

a=fat; ā=ape; ä=car; â=bare; e=ten; ē=even; i=is; ī=bite; ō=go; ô=horn; ōō=tool; ŏŏ=look; u=up; ʉ=fur; ŋ=ring; ə=sofa

Front Limb Comparisons
(Side View)

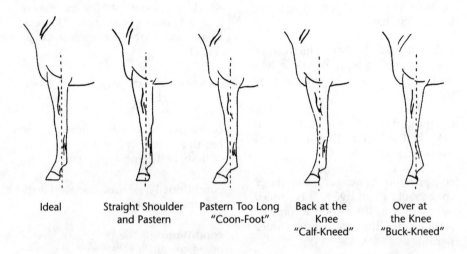

| Ideal | Straight Shoulder and Pastern | Pastern Too Long "Coon-Foot" | Back at the Knee "Calf-Kneed" | Over at the Knee "Buck-Kneed" |

Rear Limb Comparisons
(Side View)

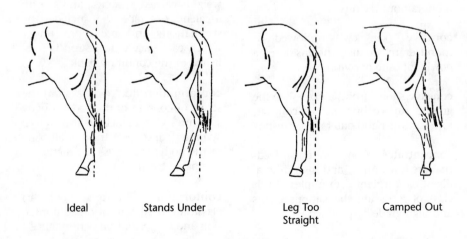

| Ideal | Stands Under | Leg Too Straight | Camped Out |

Conformation Comparisons

Front Limb Conformation Comparisons
(Front View)

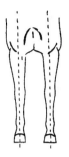

Ideal

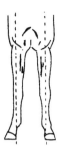

Base Wide
Narrow Chest
Toes Out

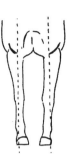

Base Narrow
Toes In
"Pigeon-Toed"

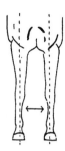

Offset Knees
"Bench Knees"

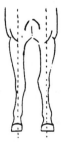

Knock Kneed

Bow Legged

Base Wide

Base Narrow

Conformation Comparisons

Rear Limb Conformation Comparisons
(Rear View)

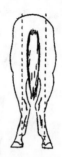

Ideal

Cow Hock
(Toed-Out)

Bow Legged
(Toed-In)

Base Narrow

Base Wide

Narrow

Conformation Comparisons

congenital   (kən jen' ə təl) existing at and usually before birth; these conditions may or may not be inherited

congestion   (kən jest' shən) presence of abnormally increased amounts of blood in an organ or tissue

conjunctiva   (kän' jəŋk tī' və) membrane lining the inside of the eyelid and covering the exposed surface of the eyeball around the cornea

conjunctivitis   (kən juŋk' tə vīt' is) inflammation of the membrane that lines the eyelid and covers part of the eyeball

connecting bar   (kə nekt' iŋ bär) the bar connecting the shanks where the rein loops are attached; also called the *stabilizer bar, bit bar,* and *roper's bar*

connection   (kə nek' shen) the relationship between the handler's aids and the performance of the horse

connective tissue   (kə nek' tiv tish' ōō) tough, fibrous tissue that supports and connects other tissues in the body

connector strap   (kə nek' tər strap) the strap that connects the front and rear rigging rings just under the skirts; adds stability and strength to the rigging assembly when the horse is in action

Connemara   (kän' ə mär' ə) an Irish breed; docile riding and light-work pony; particularly well suited as a riding mount for young riders; height: 13–14.2 hands; famed for their jumping ability

consolidation   (kən säl' ə dā' shən) the process of becoming solid, as when, in pneumonia, the lung becomes firm as the air spaces fill with pus

constipation   (kän' stə pā' shən) infrequent or difficult evacuation of the feces

constriction   (kən strikt' shən) an area of compression and of drawing together

contact   (kän' takt) the "feel" between the rider's hands and the bit (through the reins);   light contact is desirable, because its sensitivity makes for a responsive horse

contactual behavior   (kän' takt yōō' əl bē hāv' yər) the grouping or touching of horses when they are seeking protection or affection

contagious   (kən tā' jəs) capable of spreading from one animal to another

contagious acne   (ak' nē) an infection caused by a small intracellular parasite; usually limited to areas in contact with the harness or tack;   lesions are small, painful, and take a week to heal

contagious equine metritis   (ē' kwīn mi trī' tis) a bacterial infection of the uterus passed from infected stallions to mares during breeding; causes infertility; sometimes referred to as *CEM*

contaminant   (kən tam' ə nənt) something that causes the introduction of foreign material by contact, as with the introduction of microorganisms into a wound through a dirty bandage

contracted heel   (kən trak' təd hēl) a

---

a=fat; ā=ape; ä=car; â=bare; e=ten; ē=even; i=is; ī=bite; ō=go; ô=horn; ōō=tool; ŏŏ=look; u=up; ʉ=fur; ŋ=ring; ə=sofa

condition in which the foot is contracted and narrowed at the heel; could be due to incorrect trimming or shoeing, lack of weight bearing or lack of moisture

contracted tendons   (ten′ dənz) abnormal condition of the flexor tendons at the back of the leg preventing normal extension of the fetlock and/or coffin joint

contraindicate   (kän′ trə in′ də kāt′) to render a method of treatment as undesirable or improper

contralateral   (kän′ trə lat′ ər əl) on the opposite side of midline

control   (kən trōl′) to maintain command of a horse without domination

contusion   (kän tōōz′ zhən) a bruise or injury incurred without breaking the skin

convalescence   (kän′ və les′ əns) period of recovery from surgery or injury

convex   (kän veks′) curved or rounded like the outside of a ball; opposite of *concave*

cooler   (kōō′ lər) a light, woolen blanket that can be thrown over the horse after strenuous exercise to keep him from cooling off too quickly and getting chilled

cool out   (kōōl out) to cause a horse to move about quietly after heavy exercise until the horse is neither hot to the touch nor breathing hard

coon foot   (kōōn fŏŏt) a conformational defect in which there is too great an angulation of the pastern; so called because the pastern looks similar to a raccoon foot; see *conformation comparisons* (illus.)

Cooler

coordination   (kō ôr′ də nā′ shən) harmonious working of various muscles in a smooth, correct way with precise timing; a flowing movement as opposed to jerky, awkward motion

COPD   see *chronic obstructive pulmonary disease*

copper   (käp′ ər) a mineral required by the horse, the lack of which can cause anemia

coprophagy   (kä präf′ ə jē) eating feces

copulation   (kop′ yə lā′ shən) sexual intercourse

cording up   see *tying up*

corium   (kôr′ ē əm) the covering of the bony and elastic structures of the foot; the layer of skin below the epidermis (hoof or skin) consisting of a dense bed of vascular connective tissue

corn   (kôrn) **1.** the seeds of plants that grow in ears; the grain lowest in protein, fiber, calcium, and phosphorus **2.** a bruise to the soft tissue underlying the horny sole of the foot that manifests itself in a reddish discoloration of the sole immediately below the affected area; can cause severe lameness

cornea (kôr′ nē ə) the convex structure covering the lens of the eye; the transparent membrane forming the front part of the eyeball; light passes through the cornea and lens to the retina; see *eye, horse's* (illus.)

corneal (kôr′ nē əl) pertaining to the cornea

corneal injuries (in′ jə rēz) injuries that occur to the cornea or surface of the eye

corneal opacity (ō pas′ i tē) clouding of the surface of the eye

corneal ulcer (ul′ sər) abrasion or erosion of the outermost covering of the eye; usually due to trauma or infection

corners (kôr′ nərz) teeth located in back of and next to the forward edge of the interdental space; the third set of incisors

corona blanket (kə rō′ nə blāŋ′ kit) a saddle pad cut to fit the shape of the saddle skirt with a large roll around the edge; usually two colored

coronary (kôr′ ə ner′ ē) 1. pertaining to the heart 2. encircling in the manner of a crown, as applied to blood vessels, ligaments, or nerves (a coronary band encircles the hoof)

coronet (kôr′ ə net′) 1. a band around the top of the hoof from which the hoof wall grows; coronary band; see *hoof; points of horse* (illus.) 2. a leg marking in which white is found on the coronet; see *markings, leg* (illus.)

coronet boot (bōōt) a double-strapped felt boot, usually lined with leather for strength; protects the back of the heel and coronary band

corpora nigrans (côr′ pôr ə nī grans) small, brown, irregularly shaped masses normally found along the edge of the pupil of horses

corpus luteum (kôr′ pəs lōō′ tē əm) a solid mass that forms in the ovary after ovulation; produces the hormone progesterone that helps maintain pregnancy

corrective shoeing (kə rek′ tiv shōō′ iŋ) the practice of trimming and shoeing a horse's hoofs in such a way as to correct a defect in the way of traveling or to reduce pain

corticosteroid (kôr′ tə kō ster′ oid) hormones of the adrenal cortex or any other natural or synthetic compounds having a similar activity; they have a systemic and metabolic effect and inhibit inflammatory processes

cortisol (kôr′ tə säl) adrenal hormone affecting fat and water metabolism, muscle tone, nerve stimulation and inflammation

cortisone (kôrt′ ə sōn′) an anti-inflammatory hormone related to similar natural hormones produced by the adrenal glands; a type of corticosteroid

corus rig (kôr′ əs rig) a rig with leather completely covering the rawhide of the tree; a mochila covering; originally made in two pieces laced together with a slot for the

---

a=f<u>a</u>t; ā=<u>a</u>pe; ä=c<u>a</u>r; â=b<u>a</u>re; e=t<u>e</u>n; ē=<u>e</u>ven;
i=<u>i</u>s; ī=b<u>i</u>te; ō=g<u>o</u>; ô=h<u>o</u>rn; ōō=t<u>oo</u>l;
ŏŏ=l<u>oo</u>k; u=<u>u</u>p; ʉ=f<u>u</u>r; ŋ=ri<u>ng</u>; ə=sof<u>a</u>

cantle and buckled or laced in front of the horse

costal arch (käs' təl ärch) where the last ten ribs join each other along a row of cartilage on each side of the rib cage

coster harness (käs' tər här'nis) similar to a trade harness, but more flamboyant; colored kidney beaters are attached to the crupper back strap and these match the leather on the face drop and under the saddle; at shows, coster horses and ponies are hitched to gaily painted vehicles

cotton mules (kät' ən mūlz) used primarily by cotton growers in the South to plant, cultivate, and harvest the cotton crop; somewhat lighter and more angular than sugar mules, they also possess less quality

coughing (kôf' iŋ) a protective mechanism to keep the breathing passages clear of obstruction so that air can move in and out freely; excessive coughing irritates and inflames the mucous membrane lining the respiratory tract; horses in stables or barns are more susceptible to coughs than those in yards or paddocks, mainly because of poor ventilation

counter (koun' tər) when a hound runs a line in reverse

countercanter (koun' tər kan' tər) horse canters on the opposite lead to the direction of travel yet retains bend to the counter lead; a suppling exercise; the horse leads with the outside leg while remaining bent to the leading leg; should not be confused with cantering on the wrong lead

counterirritant (koun' tər ir' i tənt) an agent that produces a superficial irritation to relieve another irritation

country (kun' trē) the area over which a certain pack of hounds may hunt

coupe (kōōp) a closed, four-wheeled carriage for two or three persons, with a front seat outside for the coachman

Coupe

coupled (kup' əld) when two or more horses are grouped in the betting and bets on them are decided by the position of the foremost horse

coupled entry (kup' əld en' trē) two or more horses belonging to the same owner or trained by the same person; they run as an entry, comprising a single betting unit

couples (kup' əls) a manner in which to count; thirteen hounds are known as six and one-half couple

coupling (kup' əl iŋ) region of the lumbar vertebrae, loin, or space between the last rib and hip; the width of four fingers is considered to constitute a short coupling; see *points of the horse* (illus.)

coupling rein the inside rein connecting harness horses; see *harness parts D* (illus.)

courbette (kōōr' bət) dressage term for an air above the ground wherein the horse executes little leaps from the levade position (reared into an almost upright position) without allowing the forefeet to touch the ground; also called *curvet*

course (kôrs) **1.** a racecourse **2.** prescribed route that the horse and exhibitor must take **3.** for hounds to hunt by sight rather than by scent

course builder the person responsible for designing and building a show-jumping or cross-country course

course designer a person who designs a show-jumping or cross-country course; they may or may not actually build the course

course pattern a diagram showing the arrangement of obstacles in a course and the sequence and gaits the rider should follow

covering (kuv′ ər iŋ) the mating of a stallion with a mare; the stallion is said to cover the mare

covert (kō′ vərt) a hunting term denoting a wood or thicket that might hold a fox or other quarry; any wooded area in which a fox might hide

covert hack (kō′ vərt hak) a horse that is ridden to the covert site, but is not used in the hunt

cow (kou) **1.** bovine **2.** the mental abilities of a horse used to work cattle

cowboy a man who herds and tends cattle on ranches; work is done mainly on horseback

cowboy polo can be played both indoors and outdoors; a more aggressive

game and involves considerably more contact than polo

cowboy shoe shoe used for most pleasure horses

cowgirl the female equivalent of a cowboy

cow hocked a conformational flaw in which the hocks, when viewed from the rear, are too close together; see *conformation comparisons, rear limb* (illus.)

cow horse the horse that a cowboy rides while working cattle

cow kick a quick forward kick with a hind leg that can catch a handler at the horse's side

cow milking a sport held at some rodeos; a timed event; the winner gets the most milk from a herd of wild cows in the least amount of time

coxitis (käk sī′ tis) inflammation of the hip joint

coxofemoral (käk′ sō fem′ ō ral) pertaining to the hip and thigh

coyote dun (kī′ ōt dun) a dun with black points and a black dorsal stripe

crab bit (krab bit) a bit with prongs extending at the horse's nose; its purpose is to tip the horse's head up and help prevent him from ducking his head, bowing his neck, and pulling hard on the reins

cracked hooves (krakt ho͝ovz) cracks

---

a=fa̱t; ā=āpe; ä=ca̱r; â=ba̱re; e=te̱n; ē=e̱ven;
i=i̱s; ī=bi̱te; ō=go̱; ô=ho̱rn; ōō=too̱l;
o͝o=lo͝ok; u=u̱p; ᵫ=fu̱r; ŋ=ri̱ng; ə=sofa̱

in the hoof wall due to dryness, brittleness, or injury

cracks (krakz) **1.** separations or breaks in the hoof wall; can vary markedly from short and shallow to long and deep **2.** the outstanding horses in a stable at any given time

cradle (krā′ dəl) a device made of wood or aluminum, worn around the neck of the horse, that prevents him from chewing at sores, blankets, bandages, etc.

craniad (krā′ nē ad) toward the head; opposite of *caudad*

cranial (krā′ nē əl) pertaining to the cranium (skull) or the end of the body toward the head

cranial cavity (kāv′ i tē) part of the skull that protects the brain

cranial nerve (nʉrv) paired nerves that emanate from the lower surface of the brain and pass through openings in the skull to nearby parts of the body, mostly the head

cranium (krā′ nē əm) may refer to all the bones of the head, except the mandible; the eight bones that form the vault that contains the brain

crash (krash) when hounds all give tongue at once on finding a fox

cream (krēm) coat color; very light-yellow coat on unpigmented skin, eyes may be blue or pink; also called *cremello*

creep feeder (krēp fēd′ ər) the enclosure or feeder that is accessible to the foal, but not the dam

cremello (krəm′ əl ō) a coat color resulting from the action of dilutant genes on the chestnut coat color; see *cream*

crepitation (krep′ ə tā′ s͟hən) the noise made by the ends of a fractured bone rubbing together; a sound like that made by rubbing the hair between the fingers

crest (krest) upper part of the neck, from the withers to the ears; see *points of the horse* (illus.)

crest of the neck the topline of the neck and the area where the mane grows; stallions tend to have a more pronounced crest than mares

cretinism (krēt′ ən iz′ əm) a form of idiocy present at birth; caused by thyroid deficiency and characterized by stunted mental and physical growth

cribbing (krib′ iŋ) biting or setting teeth against the manger or some other object while sucking air; a condition that may be a habit of boredom or endorphin addiction but is dangerous in that these horses are subject to colic

cribbing strap a strap that is fastened tightly around the throatlatch; as the neck is arched and muscles flexed, the neck expands and the strap inflicts pain or inhibits breathing to deter cribbing

cricket (krik′ it) the attachment on a bit's port that will spin in the horse's mouth as he moves his tongue

Criollo (krē ô′ yô) a breed originated in South America; known for their good resistance to disease, endurance, speed, and ability to carry weight

crock (kräk) a worthless horse

crooked halt (kr͝ook′ id hôlt) when the horse stops with his hindquarters to one side of his forehand; he is not straight

crop (kräp) a riding whip with a short, straight stock and a loop

crop-eared an animal that has had the tips of his ears either cut off or frozen off

cropout a horse out of two registered parents that is not eligible for registration because of his coloring

cross (krôs) 1. the point where a jockey joins the reins; American riders generally ride with a shorter cross than elsewhere in the world 2. a dark stripe across the shoulders

cross-bar shoe the cross-bar shoe is similar to the regular bar shoe, but the bar joins the two branches of the shoe or a branch to a heel; it protects the bottom of the hoof

crossbred the offspring of a sire and dam of different breeds

Crossbred Pony Registry a registry in which offspring must be by a registered purebred stallion and one of the parents must be a pony

cross country includes such universal events as hunter trials and the newer team chasing events; both of these are timed and ridden at speed over natural fixed fences

cross-fire 1. a defect in the way of going, generally confined to pacers; consists of a scuffing on the inside of the diagonal forefeet and hind feet; a condition in which the inside toe or wall of a hindfoot strikes the inner quarter or undersurface of the oppo-

site forefoot 2. when a horse is cantering in different leads on the front quarters than on the hindquarters; disunited

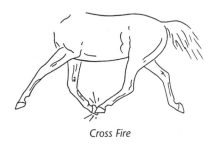

Cross Fire

cross matching the process of testing the blood of one individual against that of another prior to transfusion or a foal nursing his first colostrum

cross reins method of holding single reins where reins overlap in hands across the horse's neck

cross saddle any saddle ridden astride, with the legs across the horse; distinguished from sidesaddle

cross ties a form of restraint in which short lead ropes are attached to each cheek ring of the horse's halter and then to eyes set into posts or the walls of a barn aisle; this restraint is used when grooming or saddling

croup (kr͞oop) sloping portion of the back between the tail and the loin; it is most easily visualized as the area that slopes off from the hip to the tail; see *points of the horse* (illus.)

croupade (kr͞oop′ ād) an air above the ground in which the horse rears

---

a=fat; ā=ape; ä=car; â=bare; e=ten; ē=even;
i=is; ī=bite; ō=go; ô=horn; ōō=tool;
o͝o=look; u=up; u=fur; ŋ=ring; ə=sofa

and then jumps vertically with the hind legs drawn up toward the belly

croup high (krōōp hī) when the croup of the horse is going up at each stride, but the quarters should lower and come under the horse more

crow hop (krō hop) mild, bucking motion

crown knot (kroun nät) a knot used on the end of a rope to keep it from unraveling

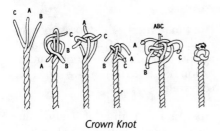

Crown Knot

crown of tooth the portion of the tooth that protrudes from the gum

crown piece the part of the bridle that goes over the horse's head behind the ears

crude protein (krōōd prō' tēn) the total protein content; the digestible protein is the protein in feed used by the horse

crupper (krup' ər) a leather strap attached to the rear of the saddle, extending to the horse's tail; a round leather at the posterior end circles underneath the horse's dock (bony part of the tail) to prevent the saddle from sliding forward; see *harness parts A* (illus.)

crura (krōō' rə) pertaining to the legs, from knee to foot

cry (krī) the bay of a hound; varies according to whether he is running a hot or cold scent

crying room (krī' ing rōōm) the main office or headquarters of a rodeo where excuses and grievances are aired

cryosurgery (krī' ə sʉr' jə rē) the destruction of tissue by the application of extreme cold; used in the treatment of sarcoids, etc.

cryptococcosis (krip' tō kä kō' sis) an infection caused by a yeastlike fungus that results in lesions in the nasal cavity and lips, in the lungs, and in the meninges; usually fatal

cryptorchid (krip' tôr' kid) a male horse with one or both testicles retained in the abdomen that have not dropped into the scrotum; also called *ridgling*

cub (kub) a young fox

cue (kyōō) a signal or composite of trainer aids designed to elicit certain behavior in a horse

culture (kul' c͟hər) a growth of microorganisms or living tissue cells

cups (kups) the hollow space on the wearing surface of incisors

curb (kʉrb) a thickening of the plantar ligament at the back of the hock, resulting in an enlargement below the point of the hock; see *blemishes and unsoundnesses* (illus.)

curb bit a bit with various mouthpieces and shanks; solid mouthpieces usually have a rise that will relieve pressure on the tongue and put pressure on the roof of the mouth; see *English bridle; western bridle* (illus.)

curb chain   a metal chain that is fitted to the eyes of a curb or pelham bit and lies in the curb groove of the horse's jaw; see *English bridle* (illus.)

curb groove   the groove of the lower jaw just behind the lower lip

curb strap   the leather strap on the bit that passes under the horse's chin; see *western bridle* (illus.)

curette   (kyŏŏ ret') **1.** to scrape or clean with a small surgical scoop, loop, or ring **2.** a spoon-shaped instrument used to remove material from the uterus, bony surface, etc.

curly coat   (kʉr' lē kōt) a genetic defect that causes the hair to be curly

currant jelly   (kʉr' ənt jel' ē) an English expression meaning hunting hare; harriers are sometimes called "jelly dogs"

curry   (kʉr' ē) the act of cleaning (grooming) with a curry tool, using circular motions to loosen hair and dirt

curry comb   (kōm) a grooming tool made of rubber used to remove dirt; should be used in a circular motion; the metal curry comb is too harsh for use on the horse, but it may be used to remove dirt and hair from body brushes

curvet   (kʉr' vit) a leap in which a horse simultaneously raises both forelegs and, as they are falling, raises the hind legs; all legs are in the air for an instant

Cushing's disease   (kŏŏsh iŋz di zēz') a hormonal disorder causing an abnormally long hair coat and abnormal shedding

cushion   (kŏŏsh' ən) the loose top surface of the racetrack

cut   (kut) **1.** to geld or castrate a colt or stallion **2.** to separate a cow from a herd

cut-and-laid fence   a type of thorn fence that has been partly cut through and then turned back and bound to form a firm barrier

cutaneous papillomatosis   (kyŏŏ tā' nē əs pap' ə lō' mə tō' sis) equine warts, most commonly found on the nose and lips

cutback saddle tree   a long, flat English saddle tree that rests low on the horse's back and is designed to place the rider's weight toward the rear;   the name is derived from the U-shaped cutaway slot for the withers; primarily used for showing

Cutback Saddle Tree

cut out   to separate certain animals in a herd

cut out under the knee   a conformation fault in which there is an indentation just below the knee on the front of the cannon bone

cutting class   a class designed to show "cow sense" by asking a horse

a=fat; ā=ape; ä=car; â=bare; e=ten; ē=even; i=is; ī=bite; ō=go; ô=horn; ŏŏ=tool; ŏŏ=look; u=up; ʉ=fur; ŋ=ring; ə=sofa

and rider to separate one cow from the others and block his efforts to return to the herd; in the cutting class, a rider is penalized for cueing the horse with the reins

cutting corners   a rider who stays far away from the corners of an arena and does not make good use of the full arena

cutting horse   a horse trained to separate one animal from a herd; a horse used to compete in the Cutting Class

cutting saddle   a western saddle with a flat seat, which allows the rider freedom of movement; may have flat bottom or oxbow stirrups

Cutting Saddle

cyanide   (sī′ ə nīd′) a type of poison that can be found in arrow grass, johnson grass, sudan grass, pincherry, common sorghum, wild black cherry, choke cherry, or flax

cyanosis   (sī′ ə nō′ sis) a bluish discoloration of skin and mucous membranes due to deficient oxygenation of the blood

cyst   (sist) any normal or abnormal closed cavity or sac lined by epithelium, particularly one that contains a liquid or semisolid substance

cystitis   (sis′ tī tis) inflammation of the bladder; not a common problem in horses; mares are affected more frequently than males

cytology   (sī täl′ ə jē) the microscopic study of cells suspended in fluid and obtained from the body by aspiration through a fine needle

cytoplasm   (sīt′ ə plaz′ əm) the contents of a cell outside its nucleus; the portion essential to all functions

D

daisy cutter (dā′ zē kut′ ər) a horse that seems to skim the surface of the ground at the trot; such horses are often predisposed to stumbling

Dale (dāl) a breed from the valleys or "dales" of Great Britain; known as a solidly built pony with good endurance and a calm, agreeable nature; height: not more than 14.2 hands

dally (dal′ ē) to take a wrap with a rope around the saddle horn of a western saddle

dally horn (hôrn) a type of horn used by the dally ropers; there must be enough room on the horn's neck for the lariat to be wrapped around it counterclockwise one or two times so that the dally roper can play out his lariat to absorb the shock when the roped animal reaches the end of the rope

dam (dam) a name for a mare that has a foal; the female parent of a horse

Damalinia equi (dam′ ə lin′ ē ə ē′ kwī) horse louse

dandy brush (dan′ dē brush) a hard bristled brush used to remove excess hair and loose dirt

Dandy Brush

danger zone (dān′ jər zōn) directly in front of or directly behind a horse; in a horse's blind spot

Danubian (dan′ yōō bē ən) a breed developed in Bulgaria; a powerful, light draft horse, sometimes used under saddle; a strong and enduring breed; color: dark chestnut and black

dapple (dap′ əl) small spots, patches, or dots on the coat that contrast in color or shade with the base color such as dapple gray

dappling (dap′ əl iŋ) mottled pattern on the coat resulting from a mosaic of two shades of hair; the pattern can vary with age and season

dark bay (därk bā) coat color; same as bay with the primary coat color a reddish brown

dark gray when the skin is dark and the coat is an uneven mixture of white and black or black-brown hairs; the percentage of white hairs increases with age and white tends to predominate on the face

dark horse in racing, a horse with a form that is little known outside his own stable

Dartmoor (därt′ mŏŏr) a breed of pony that has been living wild on Dartmoor, a rugged moorland area in the southwest part of the county of Devon in Great Britain; known for a kind nature and well-balanced appearance; white markings not encouraged

dash (dash) **1.** a race decided in a single trial **3.** a screen at the front of the carriage to protect against splashing; see *carriage parts* (illus.)

---

a=fat; ā=ape; ä=car; â=bare; e=ten; ē=even; i=is; ī=bite; ō=go; ô=horn; ōō=tool; ŏŏ=look; u=up; ʉ=fur; ŋ=ring; ə=sofa

daylight, length of   the gauge of victory in a race; if there is room for one horse's body between the first and second horse in the race, he may be called a winner by one length of daylight

day money   the amount of prize money paid to the winners of each go-round

day rug   a light horse blanket that has a braided string looped round the quarters;   may have a hood for warmth during traveling;   it is customary for the owner's initials to be shown on a rug's rear corners

DDS   see *diaminodiphenylsulfone*

dead heat   (ded hēt) a racing term referring to two or more contestants that arrive simultaneously at the finish line

debilitate   (di bil' ə tāt') to weaken

debride   (di brīd) to remove foreign material and contaminated or dead tissue; often a part of wound treatment

deciduous teeth   (di sij' ōō əs tēth) the teeth that are shed at maturity; by the age five years, all of the deciduous teeth should be shed; milk teeth

declaration   (dek' lə rā' shen) a written statement from an owner, trainer or his representative, submitted before a race, confirming that a particular horse will take part

decubitus   (dē ku' bi tus) ulcers or sores formed from prolonged lying down; especially on the stifle, elbow, and bony prominences of the head

dee   (dē) a D-shaped metal fitting through which various parts of the harness pass

deep flexor tendon   (dēp flek' sər ten' dən) tendons connecting the deep muscles of the back of the leg to the coffin bone in the foot; see *hoof* (illus.)

deerfly   (dēr flī) a flying insect that inflicts a painful bite

defecation   (def' ə kā' shən) the elimination of solid waste products from the body

deficiency   (di fish' ən sē) lack of one or more basic nutrients, such as a vitamin, mineral, or amino acid

degenerative   (di jen' ə ra' tiv) pertaining to deterioration and change of a tissue to a less functional form

degenerative joint disease   (di jen' ə ra' tiv joint di zēz') progressive deterioration of joint cartilage causing lameness

deglutition   (dē' glōō tish' ən) the act of swallowing

dehiscence   (di his' əns) separation of the layers of a surgical wound

dehydration   (dē hī' drā shən) condition resulting from excessive loss of body water or inadequate intake of water

demineralization   (dē min' ər al i zā shən) to eliminate excessively mineral or organic salts; as in tuberculosis, cancer, and osteomalacia

demodectic mange   (dem' ō dek' tik mānj) a skin disease caused by mites living in hair follicles and sebaceous glands, causing tissue damage through the production of toxins

den (den) **1.** the home of a fox **2.** when hounds pursue a fox into his hole, they are said to den him

den bark (bärk) the peculiar cry the hounds give when they have run their prey to the ground

dental float (den' təl flōt) file used to remove sharp edges on molar teeth

dental pulp soft core within the tooth where nerves and blood vessels are located

dental star a star-shaped or circle-like structure near the center of the wearing surface of the permanent incisors; used in judging age

dentigerous cyst (den tij' ər əs sist) a tumor containing different types of material such as hair or tooth tissue; also known as *ear fistula* or *conchal sinus*

dentition (den tish' ən) the number and type of teeth and their arrangement in the horse's mouth

deoxyribonucleic acid (dē ok' se rī' bō nōō klē' ik as' id) DNA; protein chains present in cell nuclei that determine individual hereditary characteristics; the material that makes up genes; a large molecule consisting of two chains of nucleotides wound helically around one another

depression (di presh' ən) a lowering of functional activity

derby (dur' bē) **1.** a stakes race exclusively for three year olds **2.** a carriage originally built for Lord Derby; an open, four-wheeled carriage; designed for

Derby

carrying four passengers **3.** an elegant, traditional show hat

Derby Carriage

dermatitis (dur' mə tī' tis) inflammation of the skin

dermatitis granulosa see *summer sores*

dermatomycosis (dur' mə tō mī kō' sis) referring to a superficial fungal infection of the skin

dermatophilosis (dur' mə tō fi lō' sis) a skin bacterial condition caused by an infection by *Dermatophilus*; usually found in humid areas of the country; also called *swamp fever*

dermatophyte (dur' mə tō fīt') a fungus that affects the hairs; the cause of ringworm

dermis (dur' mis) the sensitive, vascular inner layer of the skin

Desert Bred (dez' ərt bred) an Arabian horse directly descended from horses that have been proven to have Bedouin heritage

desmitis (des mī' tis) inflammation of a ligament

desmotomy (des mot' ō mē) the cutting or division of ligaments

Devonshire boot see *Devonshire slipper iron*

Devonshire slipper iron (dev' ən

---

a=fat; ā=ape; ä=car; â=bare; e=ten; ē=even; i=is; ī=bite; ō=go; ô=horn; ōō=tool; o͝o=look; u=up; u=fur; ŋ=ring; ə=sofa

s͟hē͞r slip' pər ī'
ərn) shaped
like a heelless
slipper   and
hung on a re-
volving   bar
from the stir-
rup   leather;
the slipper itself is leather and covers
the front of the rider's foot

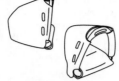

Devonshire Slipper Iron

dew poisoning   (dōō poi' zən iŋ) irritated weepy patches on the face and
legs caused by contact with certain
plant juices; examples are small-
headed sneezewood, stinging nettles,
and spurge

dewormer   (dē wʉrm' ər) any number of commercial products administered by stomach tube, syringe or
through feed to control internal parasites

diabetes   (dī' ə bēt' is) any of several
metabolic disorders characterized by
excessive urination and persistent
thirst

diabetes insipidus   disease of the
brain or kidney that results in the
horse excreting abnormally large
amounts of urine

diabetes mellitus   inability of the
body to utilize sugars; results in an increase of blood sugar and an increase
in urine production

diagnosis   (dī' əg nō' sis) distinguish-
ing one disease from another or iden-
tifying a disease from its characteristics and/or causative agents

diagonal   (dī ag' ə nəl) 1. when the
forefoot moves in unison with the opposite hind foot 2. a maneuver from
one corner of an arena to another
through the center

diagonal aids   (dī ag' ə nəl ādz)
refers to the rider's aids; opposite hand
and leg, e.g., right hand and left leg

dialysis   (dī al' ə sis) removal of
waste products from the blood

diaminodiphenylsulfone (di am' i no
di fen' əl sul' fōn) DDS; administered by
mouth, by stomach tube or enema to
soften the stool

diaphragm   (dī' ə fram') the muscle
that separates the abdominal and the
thoracic cavities

diaphragmatic   (dī' ə frag mat' ik)
relating to the muscular partition separating the cavities of the chest and
the abdomen

diaphragmatic flutter   (flut' ər) also
called *thumps*; contractions of the diaphragm with each heartbeat due to
electrolyte imbalances

diaphragmatic hernia   (hʉr' nē ə)
defect in the diaphragm that allows
organs of the abdominal cavity to
enter the chest cavity

diaphysis   (dī af' ə sis) the shaft of a
long bone between the ends

diarrhea   (dī' ə rē' ə) stool of abnormal liquidity and frequency

diazepam   (dī az' e pam) a tranquilizer and anticonvulsant used in
horses; also known as *Valium*

dichlorvos   (dī klôr' vəs) organophosphate wormer; an overdose can
cause neurological and intestinal malfunction

dicoumarin   (dī kōō' mər in) a toxin
that might be found in spoiled or
moldy sweet clover

did not change diagonal   a posting error on the part of the rider in which the rider does not change diagonals correctly

diestrus   (dī es′ trəs) a short period of sexual quiescence between metestrus and proestrus; 14–15 day average

digestion   (di jes′ chən) the process of converting feed nutrients into substances the body is able to use

digestive organs   (di jes′ tiv ôr′ ganz) includes the mouth, pharynx, esophagus, stomach, small intestine, cecum, large intestine, rectum and anus

digestive system   (sis′ təm) the body system that digests nutrients and consists of the digestive tract

digestive tract   (trakt) the body parts that aid in digestion

digital cushion   (dij′ it əl kŏŏsh′ ən) tissue located below the heel of the foot; functions as a shock absorber

digital extensor tendons   (ek sten′ sôr) cords of tough, fibrous connective tissue in which muscle fibers end and muscles are attached to bones; tendons of the fore and hind limbs that act to help move the hoof forward and lift the toe; see *muscular system* (illus.)

digitalis   (dij′ ə tal′ is) medication derived from the foxglove plant; used to increase the strength of the heart contraction during heart failure

dilution   (di lŏŏ′ shən) the lessening of the intensity of the basic color hair; e.g., palomino to cremello

dimethyl sulfoxide   (dī meth′ il sul fok′ sīd) DMSO; an organic chemical that has a number of medical proper-

ties, including anti-inflammatory, antibacterial, and anagelsic; able to pass readily through the skin; can be used topically and internally

dinner plate   large, round, flat horn cap on a Mexican saddle; often several inches in diameter

dipping   (dip′ iŋ) the soaking of an animal's entire body in a solution; a dip of lindane, for example, would be used on a horse with ringworm

dipstick   (dip′ stik) a plastic strip with a small pad that is sensitive to certain substances in the blood or urine; used to quickly evaluate certain chemicals found in blood or urine

directness   (di rekt′ nəs) straight forward, a straight course, the quality of being direct

direct rein   (di rekt′ rān) pressure on the bit resulting from a pull straight back on the rein; a gentle tug on the right rein to cue the horse to turn right

dirt track   (trak) a racetrack with a surface of sand and soil

discipline   (dis′ ə plin) to correct or punish in order to produce desired results

disease   (di zēz′) an illness, ailment, or general state of sickness

dish   (dish) 1. the degree of horizontal rounding of the cantle to conform to the rider's outline; a deep-dished cantle is a well-rounded, scooped

---

a=fat; ā=ape; ä=car; â=bare; e=ten; ē=even;
i=is; ī=bite; ō=go; ô=horn; ōō=tool;
ŏŏ=look; u=up; ʉ=fur; ŋ=ring; ə=sofa

cantle **2.** the indentation below the forehead of an Arabian horse

dish-faced   (dish fāst) when a face is concave below the eyes; used especially to refer to Arabians if the profile shows a definite depression below the level of the eyes

dishing   (dish' iŋ) throwing the feet sideways in an outward arc; also called *paddling*

dishonest   (dis än' ist) a negative attribute,   generally illustrated by a horse that tries to evade his rider's commands and thus threatens the safety of the rider

disinfect   (dis' in fekt') to destroy disease-producing bacteria in and about the premises and make conditions unfavorable for their development

disinfectant   (dis' in fekt' ənt) used to clean infected areas; most disinfectants are considered too toxic for use on animals

dislocation   (dis' lō kā' shən) the displacement of any part; usually refers to a bone

dismounting   (dis mount' iŋ) getting off a riding horse; this is customarily done on the "near" or left side of the horse

disobedient   (dis' ə bē' dē ənt) the horse's evasion of the rider's aids; not performing the movement required; misbehavior

displacement of the soft palate   (dis plās' mənt əv the sôft pal' it) abnormal location of the soft palate on the roof of the horse's mouth; causes abnormal noises when the horse is breathing hard, such as during exercise

disposition   (dis' pə zish' ən) the nature and temperament the horse possesses; a horse's general attitude toward his handlers and other horses

disqualification   (dis kwäl' ə fi kā' shən) a fault so serious that it eliminates a horse from registry or show

disseminated intravascular coagulation   (di sem' ə nā ted in' trə vas' kyə lər kō ag' yə lā' shen) clotting of blood inside the blood vessels throughout the body; can be the result of overwhelming infection, snakebite, or toxemia

distaff side   (dis' taf sīd) the female side of a pedigree

distal   (dis' təl) remote; farther from the point of attachment or any other point of reference

distal sesamoid   (dis' təl ses' ə moid) also known as the *navicular bone*; located in the hoof capsule between the second and third phalanx; see *skeletal system* (illus.)

distemper   (dis tem' pər) a widespread contagious disease of horses, especially among young animals, caused by the bacterium *Streptococcus*; characterized by a mucopurulent inflammation of the respiratory mucous membrane; see *strangles*

distension   (dis ten' shən) the state of being swollen or enlarged from internal pressure

disunited   (dis' yŏŏ nīt' əd) cantering or loping on different leads front and hind; also known as *cross firing, cross canter*

diuretic   (dī' yŏŏ ret' ik) an agent

that increases the secretion of water in the urine

diverticulum   (dī' vər tik' yŏŏ ləm) a pouch or sac of variable size confined to a limited space occurring normally or created by herniation

dividend   (div' ə dənd) the amount paid to a person who has backed a winner or a placed horse;   in the U.S., called the *payoff*

diving   (dī' viŋ) in jumping, a horse that leaves the ground too early and struggles to clear the jump may stretch his front legs forward in such a manner that he appears to be diving

DMSO   see *dimethyl sulfoxide*

DNA   see *deoxyribonucleic acid*

dock   (däk) the fleshy part of the tail; see *points of the horse* (illus.)

docked   (däkt) a tail in which part of the dock has been removed;   occasionally done in driving horses to prevent the tail from interfering with the reins

docking and setting   (däk' iŋ and set' iŋ) removing part of the dock of the tail, cutting the tendons, and setting the tail to make the horse carry it high

dog   (dôg) horse of little value; usually one that is stubborn and of poor conformation

dogbane   *Apocynum* species of poisonous plant;   can cause sudden death due to heart failure if eaten

dogcart   a two-wheeled vehicle with a low, closed body;   drawn by a single horse, often a pony

Dogcart

dog hound   the male hound, as distinguished from the bitch hound; males used for breeding are sometimes called *stallion hounds*

doghouse   the old, wide, bent wooden stirrup;   so called because "it had enough wood in it to build a doghouse"

dogie   (dō' gē) a calf without a mother

dog soldier   a stallion cast out from a wild herd

Dole Gudbrandsdal   a breed originating in Norway from the cross of Thoroughbred, trotting horses, and draft horses;   displays a natural aptitude for trotting

domestication   (də mes' tə kā' shən) to adapt wild animals to human use

dominance   (däm' ə nəns) showing authority or influence;   controlling others in the group

dominance hierarchy   (däm' ə nens hī' ə rär' kē) a method of deciding who is the boss through fighting; the winner is then in control; pecking order

dominant   (däm' ə nənt) **1.** pertaining to a gene that guarantees the appearance of its trait in the offspring, regardless of the nature of the gene

---

with which it is paired **2.** top horse in a herd

don   (dän) a breed small of stature, energetic, and sturdy; improved with eighteenth century crossing with Karabakh, Turkmene, and Karabair stallions

donut   (dō′ nut) a round, rubber lip guard that goes over the bit; used mainly on swivel-shanked or joint-shanked bits

dope   (dōp) to administer drugs to a horse, either to improve or hinder his performance in a race or competition; an illegal practice with heavy penalties in all forms of equestrian sport

doping   (dōp′ iŋ) the administration of a drug to a horse to increase or decrease his speed in a race; racecourse officials run saliva tests and urine tests to detect any horses that have been doped; if doping is proved, the horse may be banned from the track

dorsal (dôr′ səl) pertaining to the back or denoting a position more toward the back surface than some other point of reference

dorsal stripe   a body marking that is a continuous black, brown or dun-colored stripe that runs down the back of the horse from mane to tail; also called *eel stripe*

dorsay   (dôr′ sē) a covered carriage for two persons; has four wheels and is very softly sprung on long springs; the coachman's seat is outside and open

Dorsay

double   (dub′ əl) **1.** two fences with only a short distance between them that the rider has to jump as a combination **2.** the backing of two horses to win in separate races

double bridle   a bridle consisting of two bits, a curb, and a snaffle that are attached by means of two sets of cheek pieces; are operated independently

double-gaited   refers to a horse that can both trot and pace with good speed

double-rigged   a saddle with two cinches; full-rigged with one rigging ring directly below the fork and one directly below the cantle

doughnut   (dō′ nut) a roll placed around a horse's pastern to prevent capped elbows or shoe boils

dourine   (dŏŏ rēn′) a contagious disease marked by lymph gland swelling, genital inflammation, and paralysis of the hind limbs

down in front   a horse that carries his head too low, putting too much weight on the forehand

down on the front end   refers to a horse that shifts his weight to his front end while working a cow

Draft Breton   (dräft bre tōn) a draft breed originating in France; the largest of its morphological type; used during the Middle Ages when it was sought after as a popular, long-journey war-horse; height: 16 hands

draft horse   horse used for power or work; height: as tall as 17.3 hands; weight: 1,400 pounds or more; the major draft breeds are the Percheron, Clydesdale, Shire, Belgian, and Suffolk

Draft Horse and Mule Association of America an association that promotes the breeding and use of draft horses

draft mules regarded by some as the finest mules in type and quality; weight: 1,200 to 1,600 lbs, height: 16–17.2 hands; limited numbers are still exhibited in livestock shows

draft rein outside rein of the harness; see *harness parts D* (illus.)

drafty (draft′ ē) having the characteristics of a draft horse; heavy and lacking in refinement

drag (drag) the classic covered Berlin, drawn by at least four horses; designed to carry passengers and their luggage

drawing (drô′ iŋ) a horse's intuitive ability to compel the curious cow to move closer to him by maintaining an appropriate distance

drawn down (drôn doun) the state of a horse that is thin and tucked up in the waist; often used in reference to racehorses

drench (drench) a method used for giving liquid medication to a horse by pouring it down his throat from a bottle

dressage (drə säzh′) a French word for training; the continued training of the horse to increasing levels of performance in the execution of various gaits and movement

dressage ring the riding area for schooling or showing dressage horses. The standard ring is 20 m x 40 m (66 ft x 132 ft) and the Olympic size is 20 m x 60 m (66 ft x 198 ft); A and C mark the midpoints of the far and

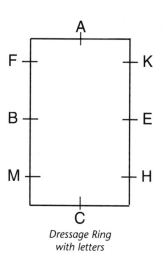

Dressage Ring with letters

near ends of the ring, respectively; other letters mark various locations in the ring

dressage saddle a type of saddle that has a deep spring tree that places the rider securely in the center of the saddle

Dressage saddle

D-ring snaffle (dē riŋ snaf′ əl) a bit with large D-shaped rings that prevent pinching and will not allow the bit to be pulled through the mouth; usually has a jointed mouthpiece with thin arms that provide greater control on racehorses and other mounts that are difficult to manage

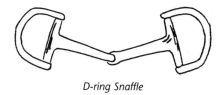

D-ring Snaffle

a=fat; ā=ape; ä=car; â=bare; e=ten; ē=even; i=is; ī=bite; ō=go; ô=horn; ōō=tool; ŏŏ=look; u=up; ʉ=fur; ŋ=ring; ə=sofa

driving (drīv' iŋ) **1.** handling one or more horses to pull some form of cart or carriage **2.** a training method used prior to riding a horse; the handler follows the horse from behind, guiding the horse by long lines attached to the bridle or halter **3.** moving cattle

driving reins (drīv' iŋ rānz) the reins by which the handler directs the horse or team

dropped   noseband (dropt nōz' band) a noseband that goes around the horse's muzzle; generally lower than a regular noseband; used to prevent the horse from opening his mouth

Dropped Noseband

drug eruption (drug i rup' shən) allergic skin reaction to drugs, usually in the form of hives

drug excretion (ek skrē' shən) elimination of drugs from the body; usually by the kidneys or the liver

dry work (drī wʉrk) conducting training exercises on a cutting horse while the cow is standing still

duc (duk) an open, four-wheeled carriage with facing seats for four passengers; came into use in the midnineteenth century

Duc Carriage

duct (dukt) tubular structure that releases substances formed in a gland

ductus arteriosus (duk' tus ar tēr' ē ō sis) a fetal blood vessel that connects the pulmonary artery directly with the aorta to prevent circulation of blood through the nonfunctional lungs, closes at or shortly after birth

dummy foal syndrome (dum' ē fōl sin' drōm) a condition of newborn foals believed to be caused by the cutoff of oxygen during birth, rendering the foal unable to nurse; may be characterized by more than one stage, including barking foal

dun body color yellowish or gold; mane and tail are black or brown; has dorsal stripe and usually zebra stripes on legs and transverse stripe over withers; see *buckskin* and *red dun*

duodenitis (dōō ō de nī' tis) inflammation of the duodenum

duodenum (dōō' ə dē' nəm) part of the small intestine

Dutch Draft (duch draft) a breed originating in Holland in 1918 when Zeeland-type mares were crossed with Belgian Heavy Draft, then Belgian Ardennes stallions; agile for its massive size

Dutch Warmblood (wôrm' blud) this breed traces back to the two much older Dutch breeds, the Groningen and the Gelderland; used for light draft work; gives outstanding performances in sporting events; distinguished both in jumping and dressage; height: 16.2 hands on average

dwarfism (dwôrf' izm) hormone imbalance that results in a decreased body size

dwell time (dwel tīm) the time taken between each maneuver in the training process to help keep the horse calm and help him learn faster

dying in the herd (dī' iŋ in thə hʉrd) in a cutting competition, the rider "dies in the herd" if the buzzer goes off before the rider has a chance to select another cow to cut from the herd

dyspnea (disp' nē ə) difficulty breathing

dystocia (dis tō' sē ə) difficulty in giving birth

---

a=fat; ā=ape; ä=car; â=bare; e=ten; ē=even; i=is; ī=bite; ō=go; ô=horn; ōō=tool; ŏŏ=look; u=up; ʉ=fur; ŋ=ring; ə=sofa

E

each way (ē<u>ch</u> wā) in racing, to back a horse to win and to place in the first three

ear (ēr) the hearing organ of the body; see *points of the horse* (illus.)

ear cones small hoods made of cloth; they are slipped over the ears to deaden the sound of horses coming from behind

ear down to restrain a horse by biting or twisting his ear

eardrum (ēr drum) the membrane that stretches across the entrance of the inner ear and transmits sound; tympanum

ear fistula see *dentigerous cyst*

early to walk/trot (ʉr' lē tōō wôk trät) a horse that performs gait transitions too soon rather than waiting for his cue at various markers

ears (ērz) the circular pieces at the corners of the seat and the jockeys, through which the saddle strings are passed; their purpose is for anchorage

earth (ʉrth) any hole in which the fox takes refuge

earth stopper (ʉrth stop' pər) a person employed to stop up fox holes prior to a hunt

ear twitch restraint by twisting the ear at its base

East Bulgarian (ēst bul' gär ē ən) a breed developed at the end of the nineteenth century in Bulgaria by crossing Thoroughbreds, Arabs, and Anglo-Arabs; an excellent saddle horse and a good jumper; lively, but mild mannered with good endurance

eastern (ēs' tərn) applied to horses of Arab, Barb, or similar breeding

eastern equine encephalitis (ēs' tərn ē' kwīn en' sef ə lī' təs) a viral disease similar to western equine encephalitis; occurring in the U.S. in a region extending from New Hampshire to Texas and as far west as Wisconsin; also found in Canada, Mexico, the Carribean, and parts of Central and South America

easy gaited (ē' zē gāt' əd) a horse that has reactions to the rider's cues that are pleasant and enjoyable

ecchymosis (ek' i mō' sis) small patches of skin discoloration or mucous membranes caused by the escape of blood from vessels into the tissue

eccrine (ek' rin) referring to outward secretion from the sweat gland

ECG see *electrocardiogram*

Echinochloa see *barnyard grass*

eclampsia (e klamp' sē ə) convulsions and coma in heavily milking mares due to loss of calcium through the milk

Eclipse (i klips') the racehorse that was unbeaten in twenty-four races in 1764; nearly 90 percent of all Thoroughbreds trace back to this sire

ectoparasite (ek' tō par' ə sīt') a parasite that lives on the skin surface, such as lice, fleas, and mites

88

ectopic (ek täp′ ik) tissue or organ found in an abnormal location

ectropion (ek′ trō pē än) the outward turning of the edge of the eyelid

eczema (ek′ sə mə) **1.** a condition involving the skin; inflammation of the skin with lesions of either a dry or weeping nature; allergies are probably the most common cause **2.** any nonspecific inflammation of the outermost layer of skin

edema (i dē′ mə) an accumulation of abnormally large amounts of fluid in the tissues

EEE *see eastern equine encephalitis*

eel stripe a dorsal stripe; a continuous stripe that runs down the back of a horse from mane to tail

efferent (ef′ ər ənt) carrying away from a center

efficacy (ef′ i kə sē) effectiveness or the ability to produce a desired effect

effusion (e fyōō′ zhən) the leaking of the blood fluid; exuding the blood fluids through the walls of the blood vessels

egg bar shoe (eg bär shōō) horseshoe with a curved bar connecting the heels, giving the shoe an "egg shape"; provides support to the heel of the foot and the fetlock

egg butt snaffle (eg but snaf′ əl) a snaffle bit with oval (egg-shaped) rings that join to the mouthpiece with a protective sheath that prevents lip pinching

Ehrlichia (är lik′ ē ə) an organism causing Potomac horse fever

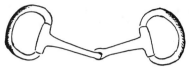

Egg Butt Snaffle

eight-string seat (āt striŋ sēt) a saddle with a front jockey separate from the side jockey requiring four saddle strings on each side to anchor all the leather parts

Einsiedler a breed named after a town called Einsiedeln in the Swiss Canton of Schwyz in Switzerland; generally these horses are docile and make good jumpers and saddle horses

EIPH see *exercise induced pulmonary hemorrhage*

ejaculate (i jak′ yə lāt′) the liquid, consisting of sperm and associated fluids, produced by the stallion at the time of service of a mare

elasticity (ē′ la stis′ ə tē) springiness in the step, making the horse barely seem to touch the ground

elbow (el′ bō) bony projection at the upper back of the foreleg; joint that permits forward bending of the leg; see *points of the horse* (illus.)

elbow boots (el′ bō bōōts) sheepskin-lined pads worn high on the front legs to protect the elbows from the front feet as they are folded back in top stride; needed on high-gaited trotters

elderberry (el′ dər ber′ ē) *Sambucus*

---

a=f<u>a</u>t; ā=<u>a</u>pe; ä=c<u>a</u>r; â=b<u>a</u>re; e=t<u>e</u>n; ē=<u>e</u>ven;
i=<u>i</u>s; ī=b<u>i</u>te; ō=g<u>o</u>; ô=h<u>o</u>rn; ōō=t<u>oo</u>l;
ŏŏ=l<u>oo</u>k; u=<u>u</u>p; ʉ=f<u>u</u>r; ŋ=ri<u>ng</u>; ə=sof<u>a</u>

species of poisonous plant that contains cyanide and can cause sudden death if eaten

electric fence   (i lek' trik fens) a type of fence in which an electric current is run through smooth wire or woven-plastic wire strands or ribbons;   also called *hot wire*

electrocardiogram   (i lek' trō kär' dē ə gram') a graphic tracing of the electric current produced by the heart muscle; ECG

electrocautery   (ē lek' trō kô ter' ē) to use an electrical device that, when heated, is used to cut and/or sear tissue and stop bleeding; the apparatus consists of a heating element (usually platinum wire or iron), a holder, and an electric rod

electrocution   (i lek' trə kyōō' shan) the passing of electric current through the body; may result in death

electrolytes   (i lek' trə līts) simple inorganic compounds that dissolve in water; in body fluids, they are capable of conducting electricity in various body functions such as nerve impulses, oxygen and carbon dioxide transport, and muscle contraction; the important electrolytes in horses are sodium, potassium, chloride, and calcium

electron microscopy   (i lek' trän mī kräs' kə pē) technique of ultrafine visual examination utilizing a microscope that produces magnified images on a screen or photographic plate with a beam of electrons rather than visible light

electroretinograph   (ē lek' trō ret' ə nō grəf) an instrument for measuring the electrical response of the retina of the eye to light stimulation

electuary   (i lek' chŏŏ er' ē) a medicinal preparation consisting of a powdered drug made into a paste with honey or syrup; a confection

elements   (el' ə ments)   a show-jumping word meaning one jump in a combination; a double has two jumps and a treble has three obstacles

elephant-eared Cheyenne roll   (el' ə fənt ērd shī an rōl) Cheyenne roll with enlarged ends where the cantle attaches to the bar; see *Cheyenne roll*

eleuin   (el' yōō' ən) one of the many cries used by the huntsman to encourage his hounds; this particular one tells them to draw a covert

elimination   (i lim' ə nā' shən) dropping a contestant from further rounds in a competition

eliminative behavior   (i lim' ə na tiv bē' hāv' yər) the behavior of selecting a place to urinate or defecate; if given enough room, a horse will usually walk some distance to an elimination spot

elk lip   (elk lip) an overhanging top lip; normally considered a conformational flaw

Ellensburg tree   (el' ənz bʉrg) the basic saddletree modified to become the official bucking contest tree

elliptic spring   (i lip' tik sprin) a spring used under the seats of carts and carriages to absorb shock; see *carriage parts* (illus.)

elongate   (i lôn' gāt) to increase in length

emaciated   (i mā' shē āt' əd) the condition of being excessively thin; in a wasted condition

emaciation   (i mā' shē ā shən) wasted condition of a body characterized by degeneration of fatty tissues and muscles

embolism   (em' bə liz' əm) the sudden blocking of an artery by a clot or foreign material carried by the blood

embryo   (em' brē ō') unborn animal in the earliest stages of growth and development within the womb

embryonated   (em' brē än ā' təd) fertilized and developing egg

embryonic   (em' brē än' ik) pertaining to offspring during the period of most rapid development before birth; generally forty days after conception

embryotomy   (em' brē ät' ə mē) the dismemberment of a fetus in the uterus to facilitate delivery

embryo transfer   (em' brē ō' trans fur') the process of recovering a fertilized egg from the uterus of one mare and transferring it to the uterus of another for gestation

emollient   (i mäl' yənt) a softening or soothing agent

emphysema   (em' fə sē' mə) an abnormal accumulation of air in tissues or organs

empirical   (em pir' ik əl) based on experience

empyema   (em' pī ē' mə) a collection of pus in a structure

emulsifier   (i mul' sə fī' ər) an agent used to protect an emulsion

emulsion   (i mul' shən) a preparation of one liquid distributed in small globules throughout another liquid

enamel   (i nam' əl) the white, compact, and very hard substance that covers and protects the dentine of the crown of a tooth

enarthrodial   (en' är thrō' dē əl) pertaining to a ball and socket type of joint

encephalitis   (en sef' ə līt' is) inflammation of the brain

encephalomalacia   (en sef' ə lō mə lā' shē ə) softening of the brain

encephalomyelitis   (en sef' ə lō mī' ə līt' əs) inflammation of the white matter in the brain and spinal cord; often caused by a virus; three primary strains of the virus are eastern, western and Venezuelan;   also called *sleeping sickness*

encystation   (en sist' ā shən) the process or condition of being or becoming enclosed in a sac, bladder, or cyst

endemic   (en dem' ik) constant presence of a disease or infectious agent within a given geographic area; may also refer to usual prevalence of a given disease within such an area

endocarditis   (en' dō kär dīt' is) inflammation of the membrane lining the heart muscle

endocardium   (en' dō kär' dē əm) the tough membrane that lines the four chambers of the heart

endocrine   (en' də krin) secreting internally; applies to various organs and structures that secrete hormones into the blood or lymph systems and have an effect on other parts of the body

endocrine glands a group of ductless glands that secrete hormones directly into the bloodstream

endocrine system the system in which a number of ductless glands of the body produce hormones to regulate growth, reproduction, metabolism, and digestion

endocrine tissues the structures in the horse's body that produce hormones; there are nine endocrine tissues found in a horse's body: hypothalamus, pituitary, pancreas, thyroid, parathyroid, adrenal glands, ovaries, testes, and uterus

endocrinology (en' dō kri näl' ə jē) the study of endocrine glands and their hormones

endogenous (en däj' ə nəs) originating within the body

endometritis (en' dō me trī' tis) inflammation of the endometrium of the uterus

endometrium (en' dō mē' trē əm) the lining of the uterus

endoparasites (en dō par' ə sīts) parasites that live in the internal organs and tissues; also called *internal parasites*

endopyrogen (en' dō pī' rō jen) a substance released from the infection-fighting cells of the body that stimulates the hypothalamus to cause a fever

endorphin (en dôr' fin) a morphine-like protein produced by nerve tissue to suppress pain and regulate emotional state

endoscope (en' də skōp) an instrument for the examination of the interior of a hollow organ such as the bladder or the stomach

endoscopic (en' dō skop' ik) an examination performed by means of an endoscope

endothelium (en' dō t̲h̲ē' lē əm) the layer of cells lining the cavities of the heart, the blood and lymph vessels, and the serous cavities of the body

endotoxemia (en' dō täk sē mē ə) the presence of specific bacterial poisons in the blood; may cause shock

endotoxic founder (en' dō täk' sik foun' dər) internal deformity of the foot induced by endotoxins

endotoxin (en' dō täk' sin) a heat-stable toxin present in the bacterial cell; a poisonous substance produced within bacterial cells and released when the cells are destroyed

ends (endz) the place in a pen where the horse stops to turn around

Endurance Horse Registry of America a registry of endurance horses

endurance ride (en dŏŏr' əns rīd) trials of speed and endurance; there are several well-known 50- to 100-mile competitive endurance rides in the U.S.

enema (en' ə mə) a liquid injection into the rectum

energy nutrients (en' ər jē nōō' trē ənts) the nutrients that usually make up the greatest bulk of feed; supply energy to the horse

engage (en gāj') to use the horse's back and hindquarters to create energy and impulsion to forward movement; an engaged horse has a rounded top line, dropped croup, flexed abdominals, and elevated head and neck

engaged (en gājd') 1. a term applied to a horse entered in a particular race 2. a horse's use of his hindquarters for impulsion

English bit (iŋ' glis̲h̲ bit) a variety of bits that can be placed into three categories: the curb, the snaffle, or a combination of both

English bridle a bridle that consists of the headstall, cavesson, reins, and bit; the reins are usually single, closed reins; may also be a double bridle using the English curb bit and snaffle bit; see illustration

English curb bit a bit that presses on the bars of the mouth and the tongue; the curb chain acts on the chin groove and the crown piece

English saddle a saddle distinguished from a western saddle by its small, flat shape, large, rounded fenders or flaps, and absence of skirt and horn; features a single, wide girth usually made of leather or canvas and light, open, steel stirrups; see illustration

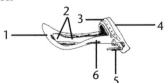

English Saddle Tree
Spring Tee

1. Cantle
2. Springs
3. Gullet Plate

4. Head
5. Bar
6. Waist or
    Twist

engorge (in gôrj) hyperemia; local congestion; excessive fullness of any organ or vessel

encephalin (en sef' ə lin) a chemical produced in the brain and spinal cord that prevents pain perception by shielding specific nerve endings

enophthalmos (en' of t̲h̲al' mus) protrusion of the eye

enter (en' tər) 1. hounds are entered when they are first put into the pack during the cubbing season; young riders are entered by being brought by their parents; both are known as the young entry 2. to pay fees to participate in a competition

enterectomy (en' ter ek' tō mē) resection of the intestines

enteric (en ter' ik) pertaining to the intestines

enteritis (en' tə rīt' is) inflammation of the intestines, especially the small intestine

enterolith (en' ter ō lit̲h̲') a stonelike mass that forms around a foreign object in the intestines of horses

enterostomy (en' tə räs' tə mē) a surgical incision into the intestines; used in such conditions as colic

enterotoxemia (en' tə rō täk sē' me ə) a condition characterized by the presence of toxins in the blood produced in the intestines

enterotoxin (en' ter ō täk sin) toxin that affects the intestinal mucus membranes, causing diarrhea

---

a=f<u>a</u>t; ā=<u>a</u>pe; ä=c<u>a</u>r; â=b<u>a</u>re; e=t<u>e</u>n; ē=<u>e</u>ven; i=<u>i</u>s; ī=b<u>i</u>te; ō=g<u>o</u>; ô=h<u>o</u>rn; ōō=t<u>oo</u>l; ŏŏ=l<u>oo</u>k; u=<u>u</u>p; ʉ=f<u>u</u>r; ŋ=ri<u>ng</u>; ə=sof<u>a</u>

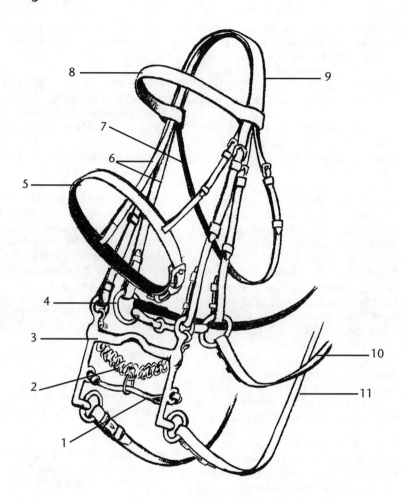

1. Lip Strap
2. Curb Chain
3. Curb Bit (Weymouth)
4. Snaffle Bit (Bridoon)
5. Cavesson
6. Cheek Piece

7. Throatlatch
8. Browband
9. Crown Piece
10. Snaffle Rein
11. Curb Rein

English Double Bridle

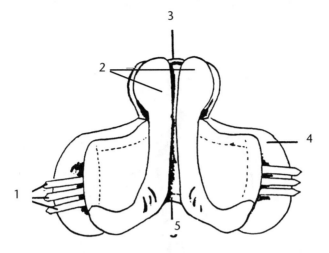

1. Billets
2. Panels
3. Cantle
4. Flap
5. Gullet

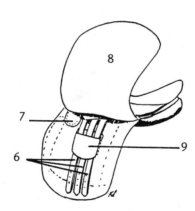

6. Billets
7. Point Pocket
8. Flap
9. Buckle Guard

English saddle

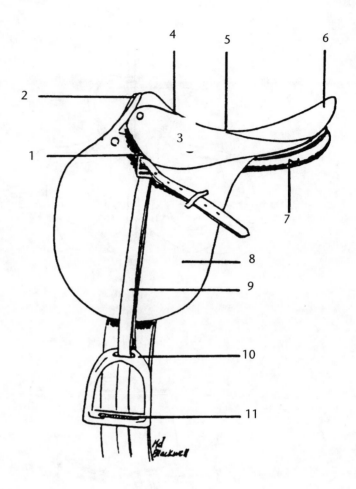

1. Stirrup Bar Under Skirt
2. Pommel
3. Skirt
4. Twist or Waist
5. Seat
6. Cantle

7. Panel
8. Flap
9. Stirrup Leather
10. Stirrup Iron
11. Tread of Stirrup Iron

English saddle

entire   (in tīr′) an ungelded male; a stallion

entropion   (en′ trō pē ən) the inward turning of the eyelid; causes the eyelashes to rub on the surface of the eyeball

entry   (en′ trē) **1.** two or more horses belonging to same owner or trainer that compete in the same race; a bet on one is a bet on the other **2.** a participant in a horse show or competition

entry fee   (en′ trē fē) the money paid by the contestant before he can compete at an event

enzootic   (en′ zō ät′ ik) a disease present in an animal community at all times, but occurring only in small numbers of cases

enzyme   (en′ zīm) any of a series of complex organic substances produced by living cells that initiate, sustain, or accelerate biological chemical reactions; especially the chemical reactions of digestion

eohippus   (ē′ ō hip′ əs) the oldest known ancestor of the modern horse; tiny, rodentlike, four-toed creature that inhabited the swamps and river beds of North America during the Eocene

eosinophil   (ē′ ō sin′ ə fil′) type of white blood cell that increases in number during certain chronic infections, allergies, and parasitic infestations

eosinophilic   (ē′ ō sin ə fil′ ik) relating to a structure, cell, or histological element readily stained by eosin dye

ephippium   (i fip′ ē əm) a Greek pad-type saddle

epicondyle   (ep′ ə kän′ dīl) a projection on a bone

epidemic   (ep′ ə dem′ ik) occurrence in a community or region of cases of an illness; a disease that is not normally present that attacks many animals in a community simultaneously

epidemiology   (ep′ ə dē′ mē äl′ ə jē) the science or the study of the causes and control of epidemics

epidermis   (ep′ ə dʉr′ mis) the outermost layer of skin that is not supplied with blood vessels; the layer of the skin from which the hair and hooves grow

epididymis   (ep′ ə did′ i məs) the mass of tubes connected to the testicle; sperm are stored there while they mature

epidural   (ep′ i dʉr′ əl) on or outside of the fibrous covering of the brain and spinal cord

epiglottis   (ep′ ə glät′ is) the thin plate of cartilage in front of the entrance to the larynx that prevents food from entering the larynx and trachea while swallowing

epilation   (ep′ i lā′ sḥən) the removal of hair by the roots

epilepsy   (ep′ ə lep′ sē) transient disturbances of brain function that may show as a loss of consciousness, seizures, etc.

epimeletic behavior   (ep′ ə mel ət ik bi hāv′ yər) the showing and giving of

a=f<u>a</u>t; ā=<u>a</u>pe; ä=c<u>a</u>r; â=b<u>a</u>re; e=t<u>e</u>n; ē=<u>e</u>ven; i=<u>i</u>s; ī=b<u>i</u>te; ō=g<u>o</u>; ô=h<u>o</u>rn; ōō=t<u>oo</u>l; ŏŏ=l<u>oo</u>k; u=<u>u</u>p; ʉ=f<u>u</u>r; ŋ=ri<u>ng</u>; ə=sof<u>a</u>

affection between two horses; commonly seen between a mare and foal

epinephrine (ep′ ə nef′ rin) a hormone secreted by the adrenal gland that stimulates the sympathetic nervous system, causing contraction of the capillaries and arteries, an increase in blood pressure and heart rate, and stimulation of the heart muscle; also called *adrenaline*

epiphora (e pif′ ō rä) tearing

epiphyseal plates (ep′ i fiz′ ē əl plāts) plates of cartilage near the ends of the long leg bones where lengthening of the bone occurs; the lengthening process, during which new cartilage cells are changed into bone, may be accelerated, causing swelling, leg pain, and/or plate collapse

epiphysis (i pif′ ə sis) the growth plates at the ends of long bones that develop separately from the shaft of the bone during the growth period; during this time, the plate is separated from the main portion of the bone by cartilage

epiphysitis (i pif i sī′ tis) inflammation and swelling of the epiphyseal plates (cartilage growth plates) above and below the joints; associated with excessively rapid growth in young horses

episiotomy (i pē′ zē ät′ ə mē) a surgical incision of the vulva

epistasis (i pis′ tə sis) a type of phenotypic expression in which one pair of genes on one pair of chromosomes affects the phenotypic expression of another pair of genes carried on a different pair of chromosomes

epistaxis (ep′ ə stak′ sis) nosebleed

epithelial (ep′ ə thē′ lē əl) pertaining to the epithelium

epithelium (ep′ ə thē′ lē əm) the covering of internal and external surfaces of the body; includes the lining of vessels and other small cavities; consists of cells joined together by small amounts of cementing substances

epizootic (ep′ i zō ät′ ik) any widely diffused and rapidly spreading disease of animals; attacks many animals in any region at the same time

epsom salt (ep′ səm sôlt) magnesium sulfate; used either as a laxative or to treat foot abscesses

epsom salt packs (ep′ səm sôlt paks) used to treat bruises

equal favorite (ē kwəl fā′ vər it) one of two horses that are bet at the shortest and similar odds in a race

equestrian (i kwes′ trē ən) pertaining to horsemen or horsemanship; a rider or performer on horseback

equestrienne (i kwes′ trē en′) a female rider or performer on horseback; a female equestrian

equine (ē′ kwīn or ek′ wīn) pertaining to a horse; belonging to the family Equidae; includes horses, asses, and zebras

equine distemper (dis tem′ pər) acute contagious bacterial infection of the salivary glands; may cause fever of 104–106 degrees and intense swelling of the submaxillary and parotid glands; see *strangles*

equine infectious anemia (in fek′ shəs ə nē′ mē ə) the infectious disease of horses characterized by intermittent fever, depression, progressive weakness, weight loss, edema, and anemia; also known as *swamp fever*

equine influenza (in′ floo en′ zə) an infectious disease caused by a virus that has properties of the type A influenza virus

equine piroplasmosis (pī′ rō plas mō′ sis) caused by *Babesia caballi* or *B. equi;* protozoan parasites that invade the red blood cells

equine viral rhinopneumonitis (vī′ rəl rī′ nō nŏŏ′ mō nī′ tis) equine viral abortion syndrome; EVR can cause abortion or respiratory disease

equitation (ek′ wə tā′ shən) the art of riding horseback correctly; there are three main styles of equitation: hunter seat, saddle seat, and stock seat

Equus (ek′ wus) the genus of the horse; the species of the modern horse is *Equus caballus*

Equus caballus (ek′ wus kā′ bə ləs) the scientific name of the horse

ergot (ʉr′ gət) a horny growth behind the fetlock joint; see *points of the horse* (illus.)

ergotism (ʉr′ gə tiz′ əm) due to clavicep fungus on seed heads; causes dry gangrene of the feet, ears, and tail

erosion (i rō′ zhən) an eating away; a kind of ulceration

errectores pilorum the muscles that cause hair to stand on end and increase the insulating effect

erupt (i rupt′) the act of breaking out or appearing; becoming visible

erythrocytes (i rith′ rə sīts) red blood cells; transport oxygen from the lungs to body tissues

erythrocyte sedimentation rate (i rith′ rə sīt sed′ ə men tā′ shən rāt) the rate of settling and separation of red blood cells in a volume of drawn blood

Escharotic (es′ kə rät′ ik) a corrosive or causative agent, such as butter of antimony, used to remove granulation tissue

Escherichia coli (esh′ er ēk ē ə kō′ lī) a species of rod-shaped bacteria normally present in the intestinal tract of humans, horses, and other animals; occasionally causes severe infection

escutcheon (i skuch′ ən) a slotted brass plate covering the mortise (slot) on a McClellan saddle

esophageal (i säf′ ə jē əl) pertaining to the esophagus

esophageal stricture (i säf′ ə jē′ əl strik′ chər) narrowed section in the esophagus, usually due to scarring after a choke, esophagitis or esophageal surgery

esophagitis (i säf′ ə jī′ tis) inflammation of the esophagus; can be the result of a previous choke

esophagus (i säf′ ə gəs) muscular tube for passage of food from the pharynx to the stomach; about fifty to sixty inches in length

ESR see *erythrocyte sedimentation rate*

---

a=fat; ā=ape; ä=car; â=bare; e=ten; ē=even; i=is; ī=bite; ō=go; ô=horn; ōō=tool; ŏŏ=look; u=up; ʉ=fur; ŋ=ring; ə=sofa

estradiol   (es' trə di' ōl) feminine hormone

estriol   (es' tri ōl) feminine hormone

estrogen   (es' trə jən) feminine hormone produced by developing follicles in the ovaries

estrogenic hormone   (es' trə jən' ik' hôr' mōn) hormones that stimulate the development and maintenance of female sexual characteristics; there are three principal estrogenic hormones: estradiol, estrone, estriol

estrone   (es' trōn) feminine hormone

estrous cycle   (es' trəs sīk' əl) the entire reproductive cycle of the mare; twenty-one days is average

estrus   (es' trəs) the period of sexual excitement (heat) during which the female will accept the male in the act of mating; average is 5–7 days

ET   see *embryo transfer*

ethmoid hematoma   (eth' moid hē' mə tō' ma) a collection of blood below the mucous membranes at the back of the nasal cavity

etiologic   (ēt' ē äl' ə jik) pertaining to the causes of disease

eustachian tube   (yōō stā' shən tōōb) a channel between the middle ear and the nasopharynx that allows adjustment of the pressure of air in the cavity to equal the outside air pressure

euthanasia   (yōō' thə nā' zhə) an easy or painless death; mercy killing

evacuation   (i vak' yōō wā' shən) an emptying, as of the bowels

evasion   (i vā' zhən) avoidance of an aid; for example, the behavior of a horse that overflexes or gets behind the bit to keep from accepting contact with the bit

evens   (ē' vəns) in racing, the betting odds given a horse when the person who places the bet stands to win the same amount as his stake

event horse   (i vent' hôrs) a horse that competes or is capable of competing in a combined training event

eventing   (i ven' tiŋ) combined training including dressage, cross-country, and stadium jumping

ewe-necked   (yōō' nekt') when the top profile of the neck is concave like a female sheep's neck; instead of a crest, the horse has a dip in the neck; also known as *turkey neck* or *upside-down neck*

exacta   (ig zak' tə) a type of wagering in which the bettor must select the first and second place finishers in exact order

excision   (ek sizh' un) removal of an organ or structure by cutting

excretion   (eks' krē shən) the act of eliminating the body's waste materials

exercise bandage   (ek' sər sīz' ban' dij) a bandage applied to a horse's legs before exercising to provide support to the tendons and ligaments

exercise boy   (boi) a jockey or other rider who gallops horses in workouts

exercise-induced pulmonary hemorrhage   (in' dōōsd' pul' mə ner' ē hem' ər ij) bleeding from the lungs during strenuous exercise; EIPH; also called *bleeder*

exertional myopathy (ig zᵤr′ shən′ əl mī äp′ ə thē) stiffness and muscle pain after strenuous exercise; in severe cases, the urine has a brownish color due to muscle cell breakdown; also called *azoturia, tying up,* or *exertional rhabdomyolysis*

exertional rhabdomyolysis (ig zᵤr′ shən′ əl rab′ dō mī ōl′ i sis) see *exertional myopathy*

Exmoor (eks′ mŏŏr) an old breed of British pony; a native of the wild moorland of southwest England from which the breed takes its name; a solidly built, well-proportioned pony well suited to drawing large, elegant carriages

exocrine (ek′ sə krin) a glandular secretion that is delivered to a body surface; e.g., sweat glands or digestive juices secreted by the pancreas into the intestines

exogenous (ek säj′ ə nəs) originating from outside the body

exophthalmos (ek′ säf thal′ məs) protruding eyeball

exostosis (eks′ ō stō sis) abnormal growth in the periosteum; a benign bony growth projecting outward from the surface of a bone

exotoxin (ek′ sō täk′ sən) a toxin produced by certain species of bacteria; found outside of the bacterial cell

expectorant (ik spek′ tər ənt) a substance that promotes ejection by coughing up of mucus or other fluids from the lungs and trachea

expiration (ek′ spə rā′ shən) the act of exhaling or expelling air from the lungs

extended trot (ik sten′ did trät) moving the horse at a very energetic, reaching trot; lengthening of the trot stride without an increase in tempo

extension (ik sten′ shən) the lengthening of the horse's body by causing the horse to reach forward with his head and neck while its forelegs and hind legs also extend forward; lengthening of a particular frame and stride while maintaining the original rhythm

extensor (ik sten′ sər) any muscle that extends or straightens a joint

external abdominal oblique (ik′ stᵤr′ nəl ab däm′ ə nəl ə blēk′) muscles of the abdomen that are placed neither perpendicular nor horizontal, but are inclined; see *muscular system* (illus.)

external coaptation (ik stᵤr′ nəl cō′ ap tā shən) alignment of a fractured bone using externally applied pins and rods

extinction (ik stiŋk′ shən) removal of a pleasant stimulus to discourage the behavior that follows

extravasation (ik strav′ ə sā′ shən) a discharge or escape of blood or other substance from a vessel into the tissues

exudate (eks′ yə dāt) discharge of fluid and tissue material from a sore or

a=fat; ā=ape; ä=car; â=bare; e=ten; ē=even; i=is; ī=bite; ō=go; ô=horn; ōō=tool; ŏŏ=look; u=up; ᵤ=fur; ŋ=ring; ə=sofa

wound; matter discharged from an incision or wound (drainage)

eye (ī) the organ of sight; see illustration; *points of the horse* (illus.)

eyelid (ī' lid) moveable folds of skin that open and close over the eyeball; see *eye, horse's* (illus.)

eye splice a loop that is back spliced into the end of a rope

eye to hounds a person is said to have a good eye to hounds when, by watching their actions and listening to them, he can tell what the fox has done and what the hounds are going to do

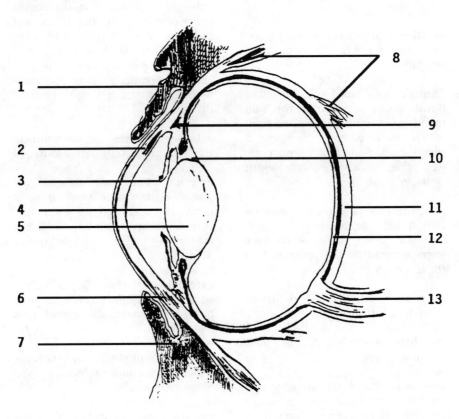

1. Upper Eyelid
2. Cornea
3. Iris
4. Pupil (opening in iris)
5. Lens
6. Sclera
7. Lower Eyelid
8. Muscles that move the eyeball
9. Ciliary Muscle (changes lens shape for distance vision)
10. Suspensory ligament of lens
11. Sclera
12. Retina
13. Optic Nerve

The Horse's Eye

F

face flies (fās flīz) flies that gather in large numbers on the face of horses, especially around the eyes and nose

face masking shading of black, brown, or red on the bridge of the nose, usually with the same color around the eyes; masking may spread to the jaw and muzzle or may outline the lips and nostrils

face piece the leather strap extending below the brow band of the harness bridle; see *harness parts B and E* (illus.)

facet (fas' it) a small plane or surface on a hard body; as on a bone

face the bit when the horse takes hold of the bit, reducing the effectiveness of the bit

facing up to a cow when a cutting horse turns his body to form a 90-degree angle with the cow after the cow has stopped, as opposed to the horse remaining parallel to the cow

fadge (faj) an old term for a pace between a walk and a trot; to ride at a very slow pace

Fagopyrum (fəg op' i rəm) see *buckwheat*

failure of passive transfer (fāl' yər uv pas' iv trans fur') failure of the newborn foal to receive adequate protective antibodies from the dam's colostrum during the first few hours of life

fainting foal syndrome (fān' tiŋ fōl sin' drōm) see *neonatal maladjustment syndrome*

Falabella the miniature horse of Argentina; developed from the Shetland and other breeds and now a much more refined animal than the Shetland

Falabella Miniature Horse Association a registry in which both sire and dam must be Falabella in order to register an offspring

fall (fôl) **1.** when the horse's shoulders and quarters on the same side touch the ground **2.** when there is separation between the rider and the horse that necessitates remounting

fallen neck see *broken crest*

falling in a horse that, at any pace, goes around a corner or circle leaning over to the inside; putting too much weight on the inside shoulder

falling off a cow the gradual or immediate increase in the space between a cutting horse and the cow as the two go across the pen; losing ground

falling on his head a clumsy unbalanced turn; when a horse puts too much weight on the front end during a turn

falling out when the horse's outside shoulder escapes on a corner or circle

false distemper (fôls dis tem' pər) abscesses resulting from contagious acne and related disorders

false moves (mōōvs) incorrect movements that a cutting horse

---

a=f<u>a</u>t; ā=<u>a</u>pe; ä=c<u>a</u>r; â=b<u>a</u>re; e=t<u>e</u>n; ē=<u>e</u>ven;
i=<u>i</u>s; ī=b<u>i</u>te; ō=g<u>o</u>; ô=h<u>o</u>rn; ōō=t<u>oo</u>l;
ŏŏ=l<u>oo</u>k; u=<u>u</u>p; u=f<u>u</u>r; ŋ=ri<u>ng</u>; ə=sof<u>a</u>

makes when he anticipates actions of the cow

false nostril   (nos' trəl) also called *alar fold*; an extra flap of skin between the outer nostril and the passageway through which the horse breathes

false quarter   (kwôr' tər) when the horn in the wall of the hoof in the region of the quarter is indented because of a defect in the coronary band

false ribs   (ribz) the last ten pairs of ribs that are not connected to the sternum

false start   (stärt) a start of a race that is recalled to commence again because of some infringement of the rules; generally, a horse breaking the start early

false tail   (tāl) taking hair from other horses' tails and attaching or weaving it into a tail to produce a longer thicker tail

family   (fam' ə lē) the lineage of an animal as traced through either the males or females depending on the breed

fan   (fan) the part of the sidebar of the saddle that extends backward behind the cantle

fancied   (fan' sēd) a horse likely to win a particular race; also called *favorite*

farcy   (fär' sē) a dangerous, highly contagious disease of the lymphatics caused by bacteria; prevention and treatment are ineffective

farm chunks   (färm chunks) the term *chunk* is descriptive of the farm chunk type of animal; a horse standing 15–16

hands in height and weighing from 1,300 –1,400 lb

farm mules   (mūlz) mules that are often plainer looking, thinner in flesh, and show less evidence of quality than draft mules

farrier   (far' ē ər) a person who shoes horses and trims horses' hooves

far side   (fär sīd) the right side of the horse; off side

fascia   (fash' ē ə) a sheet or band of fibrous tissue lying below the skin or surrounding muscles and various organs of the body

fasciculation   (fə sik' yə lā' shən) 1. a small local contraction of muscles visible through the skin   2. a spontaneous discharge of a number of fibers innervated by a single motor nerve filament

fast-twitch muscles   (fäst twich) thick, glycogen-storing muscle fibers that are used to accomplish vigorous exercise

fatigue fracture   see *stress fracture*

fats   (fats) organic compounds that provide a source of heat and energy; small amounts of fat are necessary in the horse's diet because fat is a carrier of vitamins A, D, E, and K; also known as *lipids*

fault   (fôlt) scoring unit to keep track of knockdowns, refusals, or other offenses committed by a competitor during his round

favor   (fā' vər) to show pain by limping or shortening stride in the affected leg; to limp slightly

favorite   (fā′ vər it) the horse in a race having the shortest odds offered against it

feather   (feth′ ər) long hair around the fetlock; usually associated with draft or coldblood horses

feathered   where hairs from two directions meet along a line, but at an angle so that a feathered pattern is formed

featheredged shoe   a shoe that helps to prevent horses from damaging themselves when they brush; the inside branch of the shoe is beveled to a feather edge

feather in eye   a mark across the eyeball, not touching the pupil; often caused by an injury; it may be a blemish or some other defect

feathering   a hound following a line moving his stern from side to side, but giving little if any tongue; indicating that he is not yet sure of the scent

fecal   (fē′ kəl) relating to the bodily waste discharged from the intestines, consisting of bacteria, cells from the intestines, secretions (mainly of the liver), and food residue

fecal flotation   (flō tā′ shən) laboratory procedure to test stools for worm eggs

fecaliths   (fē′ kə liths) small objects, such as wood, that become balls of ingesta in the intestines and sometimes cause chronic colic

feces   (fē′ sēz) bowel movements; excrement from the intestinal tract

Federation Equestre Internationale
FEI; the international governing body

of horse shows that makes the rules and regulations for the conduct of the three equestrian sports that comprise the Olympic Equestrian Games: show jumping, three-day event, and dressage, as well as international driving competitions; also known as the *International Equestrian Federation*

feeds   (fēds) standard feeds for a horse are hay, grass, oats, barley, corn, sweet feed, and bran; three main types of feed are roughages, concentrates, and supplements

feel   (fēl) the ability of the rider to sense the motion and anticipate the horse's movements by sensations reaching him through his legs, seat, and hands; the communication between horse and rider

feet of daylight   (fēt uv dā′ līt) the measurement of the number of feet between the first two horses in a race

FEI   see *Federation Equestre Internationale*

Fell   (fel) a breed of pony that takes its name from its place of origin, the fells or hilly moorland on the northwestern edge of the Pennines in Great Britain; the outward appearance of this pony combines strength and sturdiness with a certain elegance of form; heavy feathering on the limbs

fell into trot   (fel in′ tōō trät) horse's lack of balance at the canter; as the aid to slow is given, the weight rushes forward so the whole forehand is overloaded at the point when the transition to a trot is made

---

a=fat; ā=ape; ä=car; â=bare; e=ten; ē=even;
i=is; ī=bite; ō=go; ô=horn; ōō=tool;
ŏŏ=look; u=up; u=fur; ŋ=ring; ə=sofa

felloe (fel' ō) the rim of a spoked wheel, see *carriage parts* (illus.)

femur (fē' mər) the thighbone; the largest bone in a horse's body

fenbendazole (fen' ben' də zōl) a dewormer commonly used in horses

fence (fens) 1. any obstacle to be jumped in steeplechasing, cross-country, show jumping, or hunting 2. when a horse is turned into a fence to teach rollbacks and stops

fender (fen' dər) the leather piece between the saddle seat and stirrup on which the rider's legs rest; see *western saddle* (illus.)

fenestration (fen' ə strā' shən) to pierce with one or more openings

feral (fer' əl) a wild horse; one that has escaped from domestication and become wild, as opposed to one originating in the wild

fermentation (fur' mən tā' shən) enzymatic decomposition

fertilization (fur' tə li zā' shən) the process of uniting sperm and ova

fescue (fes' kyōō) a tufted perennial grass often grazed by horses

fetid (fet' id) having a rank or disagreeable smell

fetlock (fet' läk') 1. the area or joint of the lower leg above the pastern and below the cannon; the ankle; see *points of the horse* (illus.) 2. a coat marking in which a white area extends from the hoof up to the fetlock; see *markings* (illus.)

fetlock joint the junction where the

cannon bone meets with the pastern; see *points of the horse* (illus.)

fetlock ring boot a hollow rubber ring that fits over the fetlock; this simple device is effective as a buffer against brushing; gives no added support

fetus (fēt' əs) later stage of individual development within the uterus; generally, the new individual is regarded as an embryo during the first half of pregnancy and as a fetus during the last half

fever (fē' vər) elevation of body temperature above the normal

fiacre (fē ä' kər) a carriage built in 1640; named for the Hotel St. Fiacre outside of which many of these carriages were parked; the first carriage used for public service

Fiacre Carriage

fiador (fī' ə dôr) a throatlatch made of cord that fastens the bottom of the bosal to the headstall; used with a bosal, the old Spanish type of hackamore; a series of special knots on the fiador are the hackamore knot

fiber-optics (fī' bər op' tiks) flexible fibers used to deliver light to internal organs for an accurate visual image

fibrils (fī' brəl) fine, elongated threads of protein that make up the muscle fiber in voluntary muscles

fibrin (fī' brən) protein created during normal blood clotting that forms the structural basis of the clot; the essential fibrous protein portion of the blood

fibrinogen   (fī brin′ ə jən) a protein in the blood essential to the clotting process

fibrinous inflammation   (fī′ brə nəs in′ flə mā′ s̲h̲ən) inflammation characterized by a fibrin discharge

fibrocartilaginous   (fī′ brō kär′ ti laj′ i nəs) related to cartilage that contains a large amount of fibrous connective tissue

fibroma   (fī′ brō′ mə) a benign tumor of fibrous tissue

fibrosis   (fī brō sis) the formation of fibrous tissue

fibrous   (fī′ brəs) related to tissue consisting of elongated cells, fibroblasts, and collagen

fibrous adhesion   (fī′ brəs ad′ hē′ z̲h̲ən) a fibrous band or structure by which parts abnormally adhere

fibula   (fib′ yŏŏ lə) a small bone fused to the tibia; see *skeletal system* (illus.)

field   (fēld) 1. the entire group of starters in a race 2. all horses not individually favored in the betting 3. paddock 4. the mounted followers of a hunt

field horses   (fēld hôrs ez) two or more horses coupled as one betting interest; a field appears when there are more than ten entries in a race

fifth leg   (fift̲h̲ leg) the ability of a horse to be able to save himself or recover after having made a mistake, as if the horse had another leg to help him out of an unfortunate situation

figure eight   (fig′ yer āt) a riding pattern that looks like an eight laid on its side; when performed correctly, the rider should hold the horse on a straightaway for a few steps before beginning the next circle

figure eight bandage   a style of bandaging; a bandage applied in a figure eight fashion, which allows for expansion at the flexing of hocks and knees

figure eight nose-band   a noseband popular with event horses; straps cross in an X on the bridge of the horse's nose

Figure Eight Noseband

filing   (fīl′ iŋ) the act of filing down the teeth to remove sharp edges; also referred to as *floating*

filly   (fil′ ē) a female horse up to three years of age; in Thoroughbreds, the term may include four-year-olds

fimbria   (fim′ brē ə) the small, finger-like projections at the end of the uterine tube

find   (fīnd) a hound's first smell of the scent of a fox

finish   (fin′ is̲h̲) a horse passing the winning post mounted, providing, in the case of a steeplechase or hurdle race, he has jumped all the obstacles with his rider

finish a horse   to complete the schooling of a horse; a finished horse is one that has been completely schooled

a=f<u>a</u>t; ā=<u>a</u>pe; ä=c<u>a</u>r; â=b<u>a</u>re; e=t<u>e</u>n; ē=<u>e</u>ven; i=<u>i</u>s; ī=b<u>i</u>te; ō=g<u>o</u>; ô=h<u>o</u>rn; ōō=t<u>oo</u>l; ŏŏ=l<u>oo</u>k; u=<u>u</u>p; ᵾ=f<u>u</u>r; ŋ=ri<u>ng</u>; ə=sof<u>a</u>

Finnish horse a breed originating in Finland; the country's only native breed; a good, general-purpose breed

fireweed (fīr wēd) a species of poisonous plant; causes nitrate poisoning, results in difficulty breathing, brown coloration to the blood, and possible death

firing (fī ər' iŋ) applying a hot iron or needle to a blemish or unsoundness as a treatment

firing scar (fi ər' iŋ skär) any permanent mark produced on a horse as a result of firing

first-intention healing (fɨrst in ten' shən hēl' iŋ) the preferred method of healing in which the opposing edges of a wound are perfectly aligned and no granulation tissue fills the defect

first jockey the principal person engaged by an owner or trainer to ride for him

first lock the first lock of the mane on or in back of the poll; the first lock is sometimes braided with a ribbon, as is the foretop

fissure (fish' ər) any normal or abnormal cleft or groove

fistula (fis' chŏŏ lə) 1. an inflamed condition in the region of the withers, commonly thought to be caused by bruising 2. abnormal passageway or tube extending between two organs or draining an internal organ to the outside surface of the body

fistulous withers (fis' chŏŏ ləs with' ərz) a condition in which an infection of the withers leads to an abscess; often caused by the bacteria *Brucella*

five-eighths rigged (fīv ātths rigd') a saddle with the rigging ring halfway between the three-quarters and the center fire position

five gaited (fīv gā' tid) a saddle horse trained to perform in five gaits: the walk, trot, canter, slow gait, and rack

fixed hand (fikst hand) a rider who does not give to the motion of the horse, rather the hands are set and hold the reins rigidly in one place

fixed reins (fikst rānz) reins crossed and rested on top of the horse's withers so that the horse pulls against himself

fixture card (fiks' chər kärd) sent to all members of a hunt; tells the coverts to be drawn on specific days

Fjord (fyôrd) a breed that bears a resemblance to the wild horses of the Ice Age; it is an undemanding pony with good endurance, and is widespread throughout northern Europe; sometimes used as a pack animal; color: light dun, with black and silver mane and tail with extensive eel stripe; legs sometimes have zebra markings

flaccid (flas' id) flabby, limp, relaxed, without firm shape or consistency

flag race (flag rās) a gymkhana event in which competitors have to remove separately the small flags placed on the top of individual poles; the winner removes all the flags in the least amount of time

flag red a marker used in horse events to define the right-hand extremity of any jump or obstacle

flag white a marker used in horse

events to denote the left-hand extremity of any jump or obstacle

flame   (flām) a few white hairs in the center of the forehead

flank   (flaŋk) the area on the horse's body just in front of the upper part of the rear leg; usually very sensitive; see *points of the horse* (illus.)

flank cinch   (sinch) the back cinch on a double-rigged saddle; used to prevent the saddle from tipping up and flipping forward during roping

flank strap   (strap) a leather strap or rope that is tightened around the flank area of a rodeo horse or bull to induce him to buck

flap   (flap) a part of the English saddle on which the lower leg rests; see *English saddle* (illus.)

flapper   (flap' ər) a horse that runs at an unauthorized race meeting

flapping   (flap' iŋ) an unofficial race meeting that is not held under the rules of racing

flash noseband   (flash nōz' band) a cross between a cavesson and a figure eight noseband

flashy   (flash' ē) 1. when the legs and feet move in lateral pairs, as in a pace 2. a flashy hound or a flashy pack is one that is unsteady, wild, and apt to overrun the scent 3. brightly marked so as to stand out 4. outstanding performer

flat   (flat) 1. a class without jumping 2. a horse moving with very little bend in his front knees

flat canter   insufficient suspension between the canter strides

flat feet   flat sole and soft keratin; when the angle of the foot is noticeably less than 45 degrees; a low, weak heel

flat race   a race without jumps

flat saddle   slang for the English saddle

flat sided   lacking spring in the ribs

flatulence   (flach' ə lens) pertaining to excessive amounts of air or gases in the stomach or intestines expelled through the anus

flax   (flaks) see *cyanide*

flaxen   (flak' sən) a light-colored mane or tail

flaxen chestnut   (ches' nut) coat color; chestnut with blond/cream mane and tail

flea-bitten   (flē bit' ən) a white horse covered with small, brown marks; any "mangy-looking" animal

flea-bitten gray   (flē bit' ən grā) coat color; gray with flecks of dark color all over the body

flecked   (flekd') coat marking; white hairs distributed in small patches over the body; can be classified as heavy or light flecked

flehmen response   (flā' mən ri späns') a behavior in reaction to a smell in which the horse raises his head and curls back his upper lip; often a stallion's response to a mare in heat

a=fat; ā=ape; ä=car; â=bare; e=ten; ē=even; i=is; ī=bite; ō=go; ô=horn; ōō=tool; ŏŏ=look; u=up; ᵾ=fur; ŋ=ring; ə=sofa

flesh marks   (flesh märks) coat marking; areas on the skin where there is no pigment

flexion   (flek' shən) **1.** the relaxation of the lower jaw, with head correctly bent at the poll, in response to the bit; a characteristic of a supple and collected horse **2.** the folding of a joint

flexion tests   (flek' shen tests) forcibly flexing a joint for thirty to sixty seconds, then jogging the horse; occurrence or increase of lameness suggests that inflammation and/or degeneration are present in or around the joint

flexor   (flek' sər) any muscle that flexes a joint; opposite of *extensor*

flexor muscles   a group of muscles that cause flexion of a joint

flexor tendons   tendons that bend a joint; see *points of the horse* (illus.)

flexural deformity   (flek' sher əl dē fôrm' it ē) when the affected joints are flexed and cannot be manually straightened; can be congenital or acquired; also called *contracted tendons*

flighty   (flīt' ē) undependable and changeable hounds and scent in a hunt

fling   (fliŋ) hounds that drive or are driven to the right and left at the first indication of a check

float   (flōt) the rasp used to file a horse's teeth or hooves

floating   (flōt' iŋ) removing sharp edges from the teeth with a rasp; often necessary for older horses

Florida Cracker Horse Association   FCHA; a registry in which horses must be from registered stock or supply proof of heritage and pass evaluation by a team of FCHA evaluators

fluke   (flōōk) a trematode flatworm parasite of humans, animals, and birds; a common parasite of domestic livestock is the liver fluke; may live in the bloodstream, intestines, or lungs

fluoroscein   (flōōr' rō sīn) fluorescent dye that, if applied to the surface of the eye, is retained in areas where the cornea is damaged

fluorosis   (flōō' rō sis) a condition in which the teeth deteriorate because of an excess of flouride

flute bit   (flūt bit) a bit's mouthpiece that has a series of holes in it; when the horse gulps in air, this mouthpiece blocks the air flow and the horse receives no satisfaction from the practice

flutter   (flut' ər) **1.** rapid heartbeats **2.** slang for a small bet

fly a jump   a horse jumping a fence in a fast and satisfactory manner; may be spoken in a derogative sense to describe a horse that jumped in a rushed and unsatisfactory manner

flying change of leads   the horse changes leads at the moment of suspension without breaking from the canter

flying fence   a jumping obstacle consisting of a small bank that does not have to be jumped on and off; any fence that can be taken and jumped at a very fast speed

fly jump   a horse jumping over instead of on and off a bank

fly net a series of strings that attach to the brow band of the headstall and fall over the face and the eyes to protect the horse from annoyance by flies

fly-shaker muscle specialized muscle layer that contracts to produce twitchlike wrinkling of the skin; used by the horse to shake off flies, dust and other irritants

foal (fōl) a young horse of either sex; less than twelve months of age

foal ataxia (ə' taks' ē ə) a foal that is unable to walk; usually dies in eight to fourteen days

foal creep (crēp) a feeder designed to give the foal access to grain while on pasture with his dam; designed so that the foals can enter, but the mares cannot

foal heat (hēt) the first heat of the mare after foaling; usually about nine days after a mare has foaled

foaling percentage (fōl' iŋ pər sen' tij) the number of foals born in one season related to the number of mares mated in the past season; generally 50–60 percent

foaling slip (slip) a foal head collar made of lightweight leather or tubular webbing; adjustable to fit around nose, throat, and head, with a leading tag at the back

foil (foil) 1. when the quarry returns over its own tracks 2. the scent of another animal that might obliterate the scent of the fox

follicle (fäl' i kəl) a bubblelike structure on the ovary that contains an egg; a small sac or cavity

follicle-stimulating hormone (stim' yə lāt' iŋ hôr' mōn) a hormone that is produced in the pituitary gland and causes ovarian follicle growth

follow the movement (fäl' ō thē mōōv' mənt) the ability of a rider to keep his seat in contact with the seat of the saddle during the trot and canter; also called *stick to the saddle* and *deep seat*

fomentation (fō' mən tā' shən) warm and moist applications

footlock (fŏŏt' lok) long hair that grows in back of the fetlock; also known as *feather*

forage (fôr' ij) plant material high in fiber; includes pasture, hay, chaff, straw, and silage

forage poisoning (poi' zə niŋ) may be caused by feeding moldy hay or grain contaminated by vermin; also called *botulism*

foramina (fô rā' min ə) natural openings or passages in the body

forceps (fôr' səps) an instrument used for compressing or grasping tissues in surgery or for handling sterile dressings and surgical supplies

forearm (fôr' ärm) the upper part of the front leg; extends from the horse's elbow to the knee; see *points of the horse* (illus.)

forebow (fôr' bō) see *fork*

forehand (fôr' hand) the front of the

---

a=fat; ā=ape; ä=car; â=bare; e=ten; ē=even; i=is; ī=bite; ō=go; ô=horn; ōō=tool; ŏŏ=look; u=up; ʉ=fur; ŋ=ring; ə=sofa

horse; including the head, neck, shoulders, and front legs; the portion of the horse that is in front of the rider

forehead   (fôr' hed) the upper part of the face; extends down to the canthus of each eye and upward to the forelock and the base of the ears; see *points of the horse* (illus.)

foreleg   (fôr' leg') either of the front two legs

forelimb   (fôr' lim') either of the front two legs; hoof, pastern and shoulder angle should be parallel

forelock   (fôr' läk) the hair that covers the forehead and grows from the poll area; the part of the mane that

hangs down over the face; see *points of the horse* (illus.)

foretop   (fôr' täp) see *forelock*

forewale   (fôr' wāl) the lower portion of the padded harness collar; see *harness parts* (illus.)

forfeit   (fôr' fit) 1. the sum of money that is part or all of the entry fee that is not returnable to the owner or nominator of the horse if the horse is withdrawn or cannot compete 2. to scratch or withdraw a horse from an event

forge   (fôrj) 1. to heat steel or shoes in preparation for shaping them for the horse being shod   2. to lunge ahead

forging   (fôrj' iŋ) as a horse travels (at the trot or walk primarily), when the toe of the hind shoe contacts the toe or heel of the forefoot on the same side

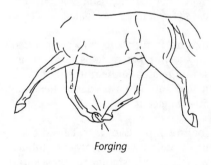

Forging

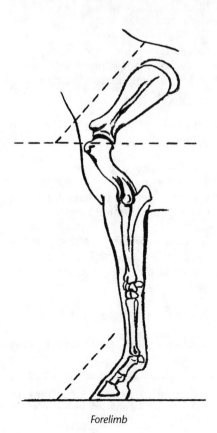

Forelimb

fork   (fôrk) part of the swells of a saddle that makes up the gullet; upright piece that is attached to the front of the saddle at the front end of the base; the saddle horn is attached to the top center of the fork; see *western saddle forks* (illus.)

fork binding   (fôrk bīn' diŋ) roll binding that ties together the fork cover and the gullet cover; if not used, the fork cover is pulled under the gullet in front and nailed with tacks

form (fôrm) 1. the past performance of a racehorse; often a table giving details relating to a horse's past performance 2. the style in which the horse or rider performs

form-fitter saddle (fôrm fit' ər sad' əl) a bronc-riding saddle with the outside lower rear part of the fork cut out to conform to the rider's thighs

Forssell's operation (fōr' selz op' ər rā' shən) surgical removal of the muscles from the underside of the neck between the jawbone and breastbone to prevent cribbing

fortnight (fôrt' nīt) two weeks

forward (fôr' ward) the direction in which the huntsman often directs his hounds

forward schooling (skōōl' iŋ) a form of schooling or education of the horse in which the animal is initially taught voice commands on the longe; the next major step is to teach the ridden horse the effect of soft contact between the rider's hands and the bit, followed by the use of aids

forward seat saddle (sēt' sad' əl) a saddle constructed so that the rider is able to move his body forward and backward to stay over the horse's center of gravity; has a flat seat; hunt seat

fossa (fäs' ə) a hollow or depressed area

foster (fä' stər) to raise a foal other than by his natural mother; if a foal is rejected by his mother, he may be raised by a foster mother or hand fed

foul (foul) any action by any jockey that tends to hinder another jockey or any horse in the proper running of the race

Foundation for the Preservation and Protection of the Przewalski Horse an organization dedicated to the continued survival of the Przewalski Horse; the Przewalski Horse existed only in zoos until 1992, when a few were re-introduced to their natural habitat

foundation gait (foun dā' shən gāt) the walk

foundation stock (foun dā' shən stäk) the original horses used in a breeding program

founder (foun' dər) chronic inflammation of the laminae of the hoof, causing lameness; may be caused by concussion, overeating, retained placenta, overexertion, or exhaustion; the coffin bone may rotate in the hoof capsule due to simultaneous detachment from the hoof wall and pull from the deep flexor tendon

founder rings (riŋz) growth rings that are close together at the front of the hoof and are widely separated at the heels; caused by founder

founder stance the typical stance of a horse with founder in which the animal will try to take as much weight as possible off the affected feet; for example, if the forefeet are affected, the horse will bring them forward in front of his body and move his hind feet up under his body

---

a=fat; ā=ape; ä=car; â=bare; e=ten; ē=even; i=is; ī=bite; ō=go; ô=horn; ōō=tool; ŏŏ=look; u=up; ʉ=fur; ŋ=ring; ə=sofa

four-in-hand   a hitch of four horses, consisting of two pairs, with one pair in front of the other

four-string seat   a seat that has no saddle strings at the base of the fork or the base of the cantle, but instead has a screw-and-ferrule or a screw-and-concho arrangement

four time   (fōr tīm) when the footfalls at the canter are all separate, making it a four-beat gait rather than a three-beat gait; the extended canter (gallop) is naturally a four-beat gait

fox-trot   (fäks trät) a slow, short, broken type of trot in which the head usually nods; in executing the foxtrot, the horse brings each hind foot to the ground an instant before the diagonal forefoot

fox hunt   a hunt with hounds, staged on horseback, after a live fox; the fox may have been released from captivity or tracked and flushed out of hiding by the hounds

foxtail   any of several grasses with brushlike spikes resembling the tail of a fox

fracture   (frak' chər) the breaking of a part, especially a bone

Franches-Montagnes   a breed from Switzerland that dates back to the end of the last century; a versatile agricultural horse; color: bay and chestnut

Frederiksborg   (fred' ər iks bôrg) the oldest Danish Breed; these horses were commonly used as school horses, carriage horses, and for use in military parades; the breed is one of Europe's most popular riding horses because of its powerful gait and elegance; color: chestnut

free choice   (frē chois) when feed and/or water is always available to the horse

freedom of movement   the ability of the horse to take long, relaxed strides without any sign of stiffness or lameness

free fatty acid   group of complex organic chemicals that are the building blocks of fat; provide energy

free-for-all   horses that have won considerable money and must race in fast classes; free for all to enter and open to all horses, regardless of earnings

free going   a horse's gaits executed in a smooth, relaxed manner; action is not excessive or labored

free-legged pacer   a pacer that races without hobbles

free radicals   (rad' i kəlz) reactive molecules that steal or share other molecules' electrons, leading to cellular destruction

free walk   walk on a loose rein to allow the horse to stretch his neck and lower his head

freeze brand   (frēz brand) a relatively painless form of branding; utilizes intense cold and results in the growth of unpigmented hair

French Anglo-Arab   (french aŋ' glō ar' əb) Thoroughbred and Arabian cross; solidly built with good conformation, an energetic but quiet disposition, and an aptitude for jumping; color: bay, brown, and chestnut, with frequent white markings

French Saddle Pony   a recent breed

derived by crossing native ponies with Arabs, Connemaras, and Welsh; a strong animal with exceptional qualities; excels in jumping and dressage events

French trotter   a breed used as a racing trotter; known for speed and endurance

fresh   (fresh) spirited; excitable due to lack of exercise

freshen   (fresh' ən) to trim the edges of a wound before suturing

Friesian   (frē' zhən) a breed originating in Northern Holland; used for a war-horse, it was a popular mount for nobility; a compactly built horse with a distinctive, flowing trot; color: black with feathering on the legs and no white markings; all-around working horse, circus horse; may be spelled *Frisian*

Friesian Society   a registry in which approved, purebred parentage is required for registration; fifty-day stallion testing is mandatory

frog   (fräg) a triangular, rubber-like structure in the sole of the horse's foot; acts as a cushion for the foot; see *hoof* (illus.)

frog support bandage   (fräg sə pōrt' band' ij) foot bandages that put pressure on the frog of the foot; often used for treatment of laminitis

frontal bone   (frun' təl bōn) the bone in front of the head that creates the surface for the forehead

front end   (frunt end) the front legs, chest, shoulders, head, and neck of the horse

front-horn rigging strap   (frunt hôrn rig' iŋ strap) a strap that circles the horn and attaches at the lower end to the front rigging ring

frost   (fräst) white flecks on a dark coat

full   (fŏŏl) ungelded

full bridle   another term for either a Weymouth or show bridle; a headstall that will accommodate dual reins and both curb and snaffle bits

full brothers   male horses having the same sire and the same dam

full cry   the chorus that arises when the pack is hunting

full extended seat   a seat entirely covered with leather

full horse   any male horse that has not had his testicles removed; also called *entire*

full mouth   when the horse has a complete set of permanent incisors; five to six years of age

full pass   the horse moves sideways only, not forward; side pass

full sisters   female horses having the same sire and the same dam

full stamped saddle   a saddle covered with stamped designs

full stocking   white extending from the hoof up to the knee; see *markings, leg* (illus.)

---

a=f<u>a</u>t; ā=<u>a</u>pe; ä=c<u>a</u>r; â=b<u>a</u>re; e=t<u>e</u>n; ē=<u>e</u>ven; i=<u>i</u>s; ī=b<u>i</u>te; ō=g<u>o</u>; ô=h<u>o</u>rn; ōō=t<u>oo</u>l; ŏŏ=l<u>oo</u>k; u=<u>u</u>p; ʉ=f<u>u</u>r; ŋ=ri<u>ng</u>; ə=sof<u>a</u>

fundus   (fun′ dəs) the interior part of the eye exposed to view through the ophthalmoscope

funeral procession horse   (fyōō′ nər əl prə seṣh′ ən hôrs) U.S. armed service horse used in funeral processions, either in a team to draw caisson or as a riderless horse

fungi   (fun′ gī) certain organisms; includes molds, mushrooms, toadstools, and yeasts

fungicides   (fun′ gə sīdz) agents that destroy fungi

fungistatic   (fun′ gə stat′ ik) pertaining to agents that retard the growth and development of fungi

fungus   (fuŋ′ gəs) a general term used to designate a group of microscopic or larger plants that do not contain chlorophyll and that reproduce by forming spores; may be found in hay and straw; cause bronchitis and pulmonary emphysema

Furioso-North Star   the origins of this breed can be traced back to local mares in Hungary being bred to two stallions imported from England; an attractive horse with good stamina and endurance; an excellent saddle horse

furlong   (fʉr′ lôŋ) a racing distance of 0.125 miles, 40 rods, 220 yards, or 201.17 meters

furniture   (fʉr′ ni ᴄẖər) any item of harness or saddlery put on a horse

fusion   (fyōō′ ẕẖən) the abnormal coherence of adjoining parts of the body

futchell   the part of the carriage hitch to which the roller bolt is connected; see *carriage parts* (illus.)

futurity   (fyōō tōōr′ i tē) a competition for horses of a certain age (usually less than four years) for which entries are made well in advance of the event; usually, portions of the total nomination money are called for at specific times

fuzztail running   (fuz′ tāl run′ iŋ) the act of herding and catching wild horses

G

gad (gad) another name for spur

gag bit (gag bit) a snaffle gag bit has holes in the top and bottom of the rings; cheek pieces of the headstall pass through the holes and are connected directly to the reins; a dangerous, severe bit; should always be used with a separate set of regular reins

gag bridle (gag brīd′ əl) cheek pieces are made of rounded leather and pass through holes at the top and bottom of the bit rings; the reins attach directly to the cheek pieces, which causes the bit to be drawn up into the horse's mouth and pressure is applied at the poll when the reins are pulled; a severe bridle/bit combination

gait (gāt) sequence of foot movements such as walk or trot; a particular way of going, either natural or acquired, that is characterized by a distinctive rhythmic movement of the feet and legs

gait defect any deviation in the natural stride and rhythm of a gait, includes forging, paddling, etc.

gaited horse 1. a prominent class of American show horse; these horses have five gaits, the two extra ones being the stepping pace and the rack, both of which are cultivated artificially; however, there is some hereditary ability involved 2. the term for the American Saddle Horse that has been taught to perform the rack, single foot, and slow pace 3. animated horses such as the Arabian, American Saddlebred, Morgan, or Tennessee Walking Horse with flashy gaits

gaiting strap a strap strung inside the shafts of a sulky to keep the horse from swinging the rear end to the right and left and traveling sideways on his gait

Galiceno (gal′ ə sē nō) a breed thought to have descended from the Garrano Pony in Mexico; it has a solid, compact build and is a good riding pony for children; height: 12–13.2 hands

Galician and Asturian Pony three main types of this breed existed, only one has avoided extinction; associations have now been formed to protect and conserve the breed; height: 11.3–13.1 hands; color: black and brown, a white star on the forehead is admitted

gallop (gal′ əp) a four-beat gait resembling the canter, but the diagonal pair breaks, creating four beats; a more ground-covering gait than the canter

galloping boot (gal′ əp′ iŋ bōōt) a protective leg support put on the front legs; covers the tendon, cannon bone, and upper portion of the ankle joint

Galloway (gal′ ə wā) an Australian show ring category based on an animal's height; height: 14–15 hands

galls (gôlz) sores caused by the rubbing of a saddle or harness; untreated galls may result in white hair spots

Galvayne's groove (gal′ vāns grōōv) a longitudinal depression at the gum line on upper corner incisors at nine to ten years; Galvayne's groove extends halfway down the corner incisor

---

a=f**a**t; ā=**a**pe; ä=c**a**r; â=b**a**re; e=t**e**n; ē=**e**ven; i=**i**s; ī=b**i**te; ō=g**o**; ô=h**o**rn; ōō=t**oo**l; ŏŏ=l**oo**k; u=**u**p; ʉ=f**u**r; ŋ=ri**ng**; ə=sof**a**

117

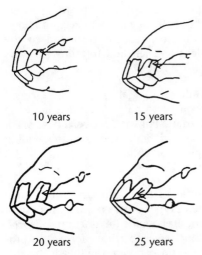

10 years   15 years

20 years   25 years

Galvayne's Groove

teeth at approximately fifteen years of age and extends to the end of the tooth at twenty years; see illustration

gamete   (gam' ēt) a mature sex cell; sperm or egg

gamma ray therapy   (gam' ə rā t͟her' əp ē) a type of radiation therapy using gamma rays to treat such conditions as cancer; photons released spontaneously by a radioactive substance

gangrene   (gaŋ' grēn) death of tissue; usually due to loss of blood supply

Garrano   (gär' an ō) a native pony breed from Portugal; height: 11 hands; often used as a pack pony

Garrison finish   (gär' ə sən fin' is͟h) a fast and furious finish to a race; named for a jockey who was renowned for energetic riding at the finish of every race

Garron   (gär' ən) any native pony of Scotland or Ireland

gaseous   (gas' ē əs) of the nature of a gas

gaskin   (gas' kin) the muscular part of the hind leg above the hock; most easily visualized from the rear as the muscle mass on the inside and outside of the area just above the hock; see *points of the horse* (illus.)

Gasterophilus   (gas' ter ō' fil' əs) another name for stomach botflies

gastric   (gas' trik) pertaining to the stomach

gastric dilatation   (dil' ə tā s͟hən) excessive distension of the stomach; can be a cause of colic

gastric impaction   (im pak' s͟hən) when the stomach is full of feed material that is unable to pass on along the intestinal tract due to some form of blockage; can be a cause of colic

gastric lipase   (lī' pās) an enzyme that helps digest fats into constituent fatty acids and glycerol

gastric tympany   (tim' pə nē) distension of the stomach with gas

gastritis   (gas trīt' is) inflammation of the stomach

gastroenteritis   (gas' trō en' tə rīt' is) inflammation of the stomach and intestinal wall

gastrointestinal   (gas' trō in tes' tə nəl) pertaining to the stomach and intestines

gastrorrhagia   (gas' trō rā' jē ə) hemorrhage from the stomach

gate   (gāt') 1. frequently used as an upright obstacle in show-jumping competitions and trail classes 2. when a horse is excused from the show ring, he is said to "get the gate"

gaucho (gou′ chō) a South American cowboy; a term used in the Pampas area of Argentina; the world's finest roughrider

Gayoe Pony a native pony of Indonesia

gear (gēr) the equipment and accessories used by a working cowboy and in harness driving, polo playing, and other riding activities; see *tack*

gee (jē) the teamster's term signaling a turn to the right

gelatin (jel′ ət ən) a product of bones and other animal tissue; used as a food

geld (geld) to castrate a male horse

Gelderland (gel′ dər land′) a breed that originated in Holland; distinctive in its elegant flow of action; a useful and versatile horse

gelding (geld′ iŋ) a male horse that has had his testicles removed

gelding smacker (geld′ iŋ smak′ ər) cowboy slang for saddle

gene (jēn) the self-reproducing biological unit of heredity located on a chromosome; complex chemical compounds that are carriers of inheritance

gene pool (jēn pōōl) the entire body of available genes in a breeding population

general anesthetic (jen′ ər əl an′ əs thet′ ik) drug used for surgery to produce complete unconsciousness and to abolish pain sensation

generalized (jen′ ər ə līzd′) having spread throughout the body; not local

generation interval (jen′ ə rā′ shən in′ tər vəl) the length of time that the progeny take to replace the parents; in horses, the average generation interval is about three years

generous (jen′ ər əs) a horse that responds well to any aid for increased speed

genetics (jen′ ət iks) the study of how characteristics are passed from parents to offspring

genitalia (jen′ ə tāl′ yə) the external or internal organs of the reproductive system

genotype (jen′ ə tīp′) the genetic makeup of an individual

genotypic selection (jen′ ə tip′ ik si lek′ shən) selection of breeding stock not necessarily from appearance, but according to genetic makeup or pedigree

gentamicin (jen′ tə mi′ sin) commonly used antibiotic; used in combination with penicillin in serious infections

gentling (jent′ liŋ) to handle a young foal in a calm and quiet manner to get him accustomed to humans

genus (jē′ nəs) divided into subordinate species and having certain common attributes

germ (jɐrm) a pathogenic organism; includes bacteria, viruses, and fungi

---

a=fat; ā=ape; ä=car; â=bare; e=ten; ē=even; i=is; ī=bite; ō=go; ô=horn; ōō=tool; ŏŏ=look; u=up; ɐ=fur; ŋ=ring; ə=sofa

German martingale (jʉr' mən mar' tin gāl) a combination of the snaffle rein and the draw rein; the draw rein passes through the ring of the snaffle bit and then attaches to Ds on the snaffle rein; when the rein is pulled, snaffle action engages first, followed by the downward pull of the draw rein

German Martingale

German snaffle bit (jʉr' mən snaf' əl bit) a bit with a hollow, jointed mouthpiece that is light and thick; commonly used on young warmblood horses because it is comfortable for horses with large mouths and works well on tender mouths

gestation (jes tā' shən) the length of time for the development of the foal from the time of breeding to the time of foaling; usually about eleven months

get (get) the progeny of a stallion

get the weight off a racehorse that runs at less than his ability to achieve a lower weight allowance to be carried in upcoming races

get up the command to go, proceed, or move forward

Gidran Arabian a breed originated in Hungary; a balanced, athletic horse

prized as a saddle horse; color: chestnut

gig (gig) a two-wheeled vehicle designed for country use; usually used for attending fox hunts in the old days

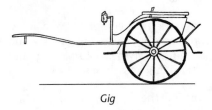

Gig

gingival (jin jī' vəl) the gums of the mouth

ginglymus (jin' gli mus) a type of synovial joint that allows movement in only one plane, forward and backward, as the hinge of a door

Girls Rodeo Association closely patterned after the Professional Rodeo Cowboys Association; organized in 1948

girth (gʉrth) **1.** a measure of the circumference of the barrel at a point behind the withers and in front of the back **2.** a leather, canvas, or corded band that buckles to and holds the saddle in place; see illustration; *harness parts A* (illus.)

girth place (gʉrth plās) a depression in the underline just in back of the front legs that marks the place for the girth

give you his head (giv yōō hiz hed) a horse willing to perform and yield to bit pressure

glanders (glan' dərz) an acute or chronic infectious disease caused by *Malleomyces mallei,* a bacterium; characterized by fever, cough, nasal dis-

English Girths

  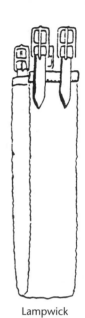

Atherstone   Balding   Lampwick

Western Cinches

Roping   Double Layer   Felt and Nylon   Straight

charge, ulcers, rapidly spreading nodules, and purulent inflammation of the mucous membranes

glands (glandz) aggregation of cells specialized to secrete and excrete materials needed in normal metabolic processes

glass eye (glas ī) an eye without pigment; often present in horses with white face; blue or whitish eye

glaucoma (glô kō′ mə) eye disease marked by an increase in pressure inside the eye that causes changes in the optic disk and vision

glomerulonephritis (glä mer′ yŏŏ lō′ nef rīt′ is) an inflammation of the capillary loops of the glomeruli of the kidneys

glossitis (glä sīt′ is) inflamed tongue

glucose (glōō′ kōs) a sugar that is a principal source of energy; one of the simple sugars; the chief form in which carbohydrates are assimilated in the body

glucosuria (glŏŏ′ kō sū′ rē ə) presence of glucose in the urine; usually due to diabetes mellitus

gluteal muscles (glōō tē′ əl mus′ əlz) three muscles that extend the hip and form the croup; muscles of or near the buttocks; see *muscular system* (illus.)

glycerin (glis′ ər in) when mixed with water, can be used as an enema for a foal

glycogen (glī′ kə jen) chief form in which carbohydrates are stored in the body

gnats (nats) a small, winged insect

that can sting; may be attracted to the horses' ears; insects that suck blood and may cause irritation and tissue damage

goer a horse that performs consistently all the time

goes well into the bridle a horse that willingly accepts the bit

going (gō′ iŋ) the condition of a racetrack or other ground over which a horse travels; used to describe the various states of the ground

goiter (goit′ ər) an enlargement of the thyroid gland; caused by a deficiency of iodine

go large to perform a circle and then proceed around the arena on the rail

Golden American Saddlebred Horse Association a registry for Palomino horses registered with the American Saddlebred Horse Association

golden bay (gōl′ dən bā) similar coloration to bay, but with gold as the primary coat color

golden chestnut (gōl′ dən ches′ nut) chestnut with a primary coat color of reddish brown; body coat a bright yellowish brown

gonad (gō′ nad) an organ that produces sex cells; ovaries or testes

gone away (gän ə wā′) the familiar call when the fox has been routed out of his lair; hounds are running in full cry and the field settles itself down for a bit of hard riding

gone to ground (gän tōō ground) when the fox takes refuge in an earth, drain, or other shelter

gonitis (gō′ nī′ tis) inflammation of the stifle joint; can be an acute or chronic condition predisposed by external trauma, wounds, and strain

good doer (gŏŏd dōō′ ər) a horse that thrives and keeps in good condition even when not well fed or in the best conditions; also known as *good keeper* or *easy keeper*

good form in hunter classes, showing smooth movement and relaxed transitions

good keeper see *good doer*

good minded a horse that is able to concentrate and has a desire to please

good mouth said of an animal six to ten years of age; a horse with a soft, sensitive mouth

goose grass see *arrow grass*

goose rumped (gŏŏs rumpt) having a narrow, drooping rump; having a short, steep croup that narrows at the point of the buttocks

go-round one heat or elimination portion in a class or event with a large number of entries or multiple segments; that portion of a competition in which all eligible contestants have performed and either a winner or a group of further contestants is selected

go short to take short steps; indicative of lameness

Gotland (gät′ lənd) a breed of pony that originated on Gotland Island, Sweden; intelligent, but often stubborn; hardy and attractive

gourd horn (gôrd hôrn) the standard wooden horn on a Mexican sad-

dle; shaped much like a small gourd, flattened diagonally on one side

go with the horse when the rider correctly follows the movements of the horse and is in balance with the horse

graafian follicle (grä′ fē ən fäl′ ə kəl) a small follicle in the ovary of a mammal in which an ovum matures

grab (grab) the thin protrusion of metal on the toe of a horseshoe; used primarily on training and racing plates to give increased forward grip and traction

grade (grād) a measure of a horse's performance; horses start off in the weakest competition or the lowest grade, generally D grade, and advance up through the grades as the horse's performance and results improve

grade horse (grād hôrs) not a purebred; a horse of mixed origin that does not possess purebred registration papers

grain (grān) harvested cereals or other edible seeds including oats, corn, milo, barley, etc.

grain overload (grān ō′ vər lōd) ingestion of abnormally large amounts of grain; often results in diarrhea, colic or laminitis

gram stain (gram stān) stain used to distinguish different types of bacteria microscopically

grand (grand) the champion overall

---

a=f<u>a</u>t; ā=<u>a</u>pe; ä=c<u>a</u>r; â=b<u>a</u>re; e=t<u>e</u>n; ē=<u>e</u>ven; i=<u>i</u>s; ī=b<u>i</u>te; ō=g<u>o</u>; ô=h<u>o</u>rn; ōō=t<u>oo</u>l; ŏŏ=l<u>oo</u>k; u=<u>u</u>p; ᵾ=f<u>u</u>r; ŋ=ri<u>ng</u>; ə=sof<u>a</u>

grand dam (gran' dam) sometimes called the second dam; in human terms, the grandmother of a particular horse

grand mal (gran' mal') epilepsy in which a sudden loss of consciousness is immediately followed by convulsions

grand prix (grand prē) top-caliber classes in dressage and show jumping; often offers large cash prizes

grand sire (grand sīr) sometimes called the second sire; in human terms, the grandfather of a particular horse

granulation (gran' yə lā' s͟hən) the formation of small, rounded masses of tissue in wounds; composed of capillaries and connective tissue cells; a natural step in the healing process

granules (gran' yōōlz) small particles or grains

granuloma (gran' yə lō' mə) a mass consisting of an accumulation of modified macrophages

gravel (grav' əl) an infection in the hoof resulting from the penetration of the white line that drains at the coronet

gray (grā) 1. a horse born black that keeps getting whiter with age 2. coat color is dark, the eyes are pigmented, and the body hair is a mixture of white and colored hairs; the white hairs become more predominant with each change of coat

gray matter (grā mat' ər) the outer layer of the brain and spinal cord

gray ticked (grā tikt) isolated white hairs sparsely distributed throughout the coat on any part of the body

greasewood (grēs wŏŏd) a perennial, two to five feet tall, with small, whitish, light-green flowers; has many thorns with narrow, green leaves and smooth, white bark; a range shrub that livestock can consume safely in small amounts; large amounts can cause death

grease heel (grēs hēl) a low-grade infection affecting the hair follicles and skin at the base of the fetlock joint, most frequently the hind legs; a dermatitis of the skin at the back of the pastern and between the heels

green (grēn) inexperienced horse or rider

greenbroke (grēn brōk) a horse that has been ridden only a few times and is not yet trustworthy

green horn (grēn hôrn) inexperienced rider

green horse (grēn hôrs) 1. a horse that has just started his training; a horse that is young and inexperienced 2. a trotter or pacer that has not been raced against the clock or in public

green osselet (grēn äs' ə let) inflammation of the joint capsule of the fetlock joint

green working hunter (wʉrk' iŋ hunt' ər) 1. horses in their first year of showing in approved AQHA shows in green working hunter, working hunter, or jumping 2. horses that have been shown in previous years but have not accumulated more than a certain number of points, depending on the association

gregarious (grə ger' ē əs) social; living in herds

grinding teeth (grīnd' iŋ tēt͟h) clenching teeth together; may indicate excitement, agitation, pain, or it may be a means of evading or resisting the bit

griseofulvin (gris' ē ō ful' vin) systemic antifungal drug

gristle on heel (gris' əl on hēl) having one or more side bones

Groningen (grō' niŋ ən) a breed originating in Holland; a cross between the Friesian and the Oldenburg; used as a carriage horse; unfortunately, the breed is now almost extinct

groom (grōōm) 1. any person who is responsible for looking after a horse 2. to clean the coat and feet of a horse

grooming (grōōm' iŋ) brushing a horse and/or cleaning out his hooves; acts to improve coat quality, improve muscle tone, and helps to tame the horse

grooming cloth (klôth) a flannel or terry cloth used for a final body polish

grooming kit the brushes and other items of equipment used to groom a horse

grooming tools (tōōlz) the important grooming tools are curry, body brush, dandy brush, mane brush, comb, hoof pick, rub rag, and scraper

ground to let the reins touch the ground after dismounting so that the horse will stand without having to be tied up; also called *ground tie*

ground driving the western version of long reining

ground money in a rodeo, the entry fee and purse money split equally among all the contestants when there is no outright winner

ground seat layers of leather on top of the tree between the tree and the seat; used to form the seat into the desired shape with the strainer

ground tie having a horse stand still when the lead rope or reins are dropped on the ground

ground training working the horse from the ground, rather than being mounted; includes in-hand work, barn manners, longeing, and ground driving

grow on (grō än) to grow and develop

growth plate (grōt͟h plāt) a layer of cartilage near the ends of the long leg bones, at which lengthening of the bone occurs

growth rings (grōt͟h riŋz) rings that remain the same distance apart all the way around the hoof

growthy (grōt͟h' ē) a horse that is large and well developed for his age

gruel (grōō' əl) a semiliquid food made from cereal grain

grullo (grōō' lō) a mouse-colored coat usually with black points and black mane and tail

gullet (gul' ət) area under the fork, swells, or pommel of the saddle; the

---

a=f<u>a</u>t; ā=<u>a</u>pe; ä=c<u>a</u>r; â=b<u>a</u>re; e=t<u>e</u>n; ē=<u>e</u>ven; i=<u>i</u>s; ī=b<u>i</u>te; ō=g<u>o</u>; ô=h<u>o</u>rn; ōō=t<u>oo</u>l; ŏŏ=l<u>oo</u>k; u=<u>u</u>p; ʉ=f<u>u</u>r; ŋ=ri<u>ng</u>; ə=sof<u>a</u>

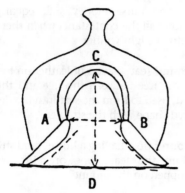

Width is measured from A to B
Height is measured from C to D

Gullet

opening through the fork and above the bars that sits over the horse's withers; see illustration; *English saddle; western saddle* (illus.)

gullet roll   (gul′ it rōl) see *fork binding*

gummy legged   (gum′ ē leg′ id) having legs in which the tendons lack definition or do not stand out clearly

gut stasis   (gut stā′ sis) when normal passage of the intestinal contents is impaired by lack of peristaltic movement

guttural pouches   (gut′ er əl pouch′ əz) two sacs connected to the eustachian tube between the horse's ears and throat; opening into the throat; thought to function as pressure regulators in the airway; a large mucus sac near the base of the skull that is an outpocketing of the eustachian tube

gymkhana   (jim kä′ nə) a program of competitive games on horseback; events are usually based on speed of completion

H

habit (hab' it) the dress worn by a woman riding sidesaddle; consists of a jacket and matching long skirt or shaped panel that is worn over the breeches and boots

True Hackamore

habitat (hab' ə tat') the place where a person or animal lives

habituation (hə bich' ōō ā' shən) when repeated exposure to a stimulus diminishes a horse's response to it

habronema (hab' rō nē' mə) a small parasite that inhabits a horse's stomach; as adults, the parasites can migrate and cause summer sores

Mechanical Hackamore

hacienda (hä' sē en' də) an Argentinean ranch or cattle property

hack (hak) a horse ridden to a hunt meet; a pleasure ride; a riding horse for hire

hackamore (hak' ə môr') a bitless bridle of Spanish origin; because there is no mouthpiece, control is achieved through pressure on the nose and jawbones; there are two types of hackamores: a jaquima (Spanish for hackamore), the true hackamore used to start colts in training, where pressure is applied to the nose and jawbones, and the mechanical hackamore, which works in a manner similar to the true hackamore; however, it has metal shanks so leverage pressure is exerted on the nose and the chin groove via a curb strap or chain

Hack Class (hak klas) a flat class

hacking (hak' iŋ) riding out; pleasure riding; trail riding

Hackney (hak' nē) a breed originating in Great Britain; a descendent of the Norfolk trotter; an elegant, light harness horse with exaggerated, high-stepping, trotting action

Hackney Pony (hak' nē pō' nē) a breed that is a small version of the Hackney; registered in the Hackney Studbook; a dynamic pony that is fast and has good jumping abilities

Haflinger Association of America a registry in which sire and dam must be purebred Haflingers, tracing lineage to Folie

Haflinger Registry of North America a registry in which breeding stallions must be licensed; foals must be registered in the calendar year of birth

---

a=f<u>a</u>t; ā=<u>a</u>pe; ä=c<u>a</u>r; â=b<u>a</u>re; e=t<u>e</u>n; ē=<u>e</u>ven; i=<u>i</u>s; ī=b<u>i</u>te; ō=g<u>o</u>; ô=h<u>o</u>rn; ōō=t<u>oo</u>l; ŏŏ=l<u>oo</u>k; u=<u>u</u>p; ʉ=f<u>u</u>r; ŋ=ri<u>ng</u>; ə=sof<u>a</u>

ha-ha (hä hä) a jumping obstacle consisting of any wall, fence, or hedge set well down in a ditch so as to not obstruct the horse's view

hair (hâr) a slender outgrowth of the epidermis that performs a thermoregulatory function

hair colors five basic coat colors: bay, black, brown, chestnut, and white; additionally, there are five major variations of these colors: dun, gray, palomino, pinto and roan

hair follicle (fäl ik' əl) a flasklike depression from which a hair grows

hairworm (hâr' wʉrm) an uncommon internal parasite that lives in the horse's stomach and intestines; may be harmful in conjunction with other parasites

halfbred a horse with one parent registered; the other parent may be grade, unregistered, or registered as another breed

half breed a western billet; see *billet*

half halt (haf hôlt) 1. a movement that changes the horse's balance by a shift of the weight of the horse from the forehand to the quarters or hindquarters 2. a slight check in pace to collect a horse together before applying the necessary aids for a change in pace or movement

half markers denoted by the letters B and E; used to indicate half of the length of the arena in dressage patterns and riding exercises; see *arena markers; dressage ring*

half pass a dressage term; a two-track exercise in which the horse moves forward and sideways at the same time;

can be performed at the walk, trot, and canter, the head being flexed toward the direction of movement

half pastern a leg marking that includes only half the pastern above the coronet; see *markings, leg* (illus.)

half-rigged saddle a saddle with only a triangle of leather tacked to the tree for a seat

half stocking a leg marking in which white extends from the coronet to the middle of the cannon; see *markings, leg* (illus.)

half twist a method of lacing the stirrup leathers together so that the stirrup automatically faces forward

halitosis (hal' ə tō' sis) bad breath

halothane (hal' ō thān) anesthetic gas used commonly on horses

halt (hôlt) dressage term meaning to stop the horse

halt early or late a horse that halts before or after the marker in a riding pattern

halter (hôl' tər) a headpiece; used for leading a horse when he is not wearing a bridle; used for tying up the horse; used with a lead rope

halter broke a horse that will accept the halter and knows how to yield to the cues of the handler

Halter Class a horse show class in which the horses are shown at halter and are judged on type, conformation, quality, substance, and soundness; sometimes color can be a minor or major factor

haltering the act of putting a halter on a horse

halter pulling a tied horse that pulls back on his halter rope

halter shank a lead rope, strap, or chain that attaches by means of a snap to the halter ring

halter squares brass rectangles at the lower sides of the bars on the Mc-Clellan saddle quarter strap

hames (hāmz) the steel arms fitted to the horse's collar; the reins pass on to the horse's mouth through an eye on each side at the top of the hames; see *harness parts B* (illus.)

hammerhead (ham' ər hed) a horse with a large, unsightly head; a coarse-headed animal

hammers (ham' ərz) used by a farrier to shape shoes; two main types are rounding and driving

hamstring (ham' striŋ) the large tendon above and behind the horse's hock

hamstrung (ham' strung) disabled by an injury to the tendon above the hock

hand (hand) the unit by which the height of a horse is measured; equals four inches; height is measured from the withers to the ground

hand canter a semiextended canter; midway between a promenade canter and a gallop

hand gallop an extended canter, but the horse remains collected, unlike the gallop or run when the horse's gait becomes four-beat

hand hole the rear hole of the gullet on the back side of the fork; the seat may have a semicircle cut out of the front side to leave the hole more open

handicap (han' dē kap') a race in which chances of winning are equalized by assigned weights; the heaviest weights are given to the best horses and lightest weights go to the poorest performers

handle (han' dəl) the aggregate amount of money passing in and out of the pari-mutuel machines for a given period, a race, a day, a meeting, or a season

hands, fixed a rider whose hands stay in one place; if the horse yields to the bit, the reins slacken

hands, good a rider who does not apply excessive pressure to the reins; a rider who does not use the reins to maintain his balance; hands follow the horse's mouth

handy (han' dē) a horse that is prompt and athletic in response to the rider; a horse that moves quickly and willingly, always in control of his movements in a balanced, rhythmic, and alert manner

hang the knees (hang the nēz) when a jumping horse fails to fold up his knees sufficiently

Hanoverian (han' ō vir' ē ən) an old German breed with an aptitude for trotting and jumping; height: usually more than 16 hands; frequently used in show jumping, dressage, and horse shows

a=f<u>a</u>t; ā=<u>a</u>pe; ä=c<u>a</u>r; â=b<u>a</u>re; e=t<u>e</u>n; ē=<u>e</u>ven; i=<u>i</u>s; ī=b<u>i</u>te; ō=g<u>o</u>; ô=h<u>o</u>rn; ōō=t<u>oo</u>l; ŏŏ=l<u>oo</u>k; u=<u>u</u>p; ʉ=f<u>u</u>r; ŋ=ri<u>ng</u>; ə=sof<u>a</u>

hansom cab (han' səm kab) a low, two-wheeled carriage with the coachman's seat placed be-

Hansom Cab

hind the passenger seat; the body is enclosed by windows at the front; usually drawn by one horse

haploid number (hap' loid num' bər) half the number of chromosomes that are usually present in the nucleus; occurs during division

hard mouthed (hard mouthd) describes the membrane of the bars of the mouth where the bit rests, which has become toughened and the nerves deadened because of the continued pressure of the bit; unresponsive to the bit

hard on heel (härd on hēl) having one or more side bones

hardy (här' dē) a tool placed in the anvil hole for cutting steel

hark forward (härk fôr' wərd) in fox hunting, the phrase of the huntsman to cheer his hounds into a covert or encourage them on the scent

harness, parts of (här' nis pärts uv) see illustrations

harness racing (här' nis rās iŋ) racing with Standardbred horses that either trot or pace in harness pulling a driver riding a sulky

harrier (har' ē ər) a medium-size hound used to hunt hares

hat rack (hät rak) an emaciated animal

hauling (hôl' iŋ) see *trailering*

haunches (hônch' ez) hindquarters

haunches in a suppling exercise wherein the horse carries his haunches toward the center of the circle

haunches out a suppling exercise wherein the horse carries his haunches toward the outside of the circle he is describing

haute école (ōt ā kôl) the classical art of equitation

haw (hô) 1. a third eyelid or membrane in front of the eye that removes foreign bodies from the eye 2. a teamster's term signaling a turn to the left

hay (hā) forage cut and dried at a particular time of the year; two main types are legume and grass hay

hay belly having a distended barrel due to excessive feeding of bulky rations such as hay, straw, or grass

hay hook a hook with a handle attached designed to aid in the handling of hay and straw

Hay Hook

hay net a large, knotted bag designed to be tied on a stall or trailer and used for a hay feeder

Hay Net

hazer (hāz' ər) the cowboy in steer wrestling who rides on one side of the steer opposite the wrestler to keep the steer from running from the steer wrestler's horse

hazing (hāz' iŋ) to herd a horse; to direct a horse by irritating or scaring it

Full Harness

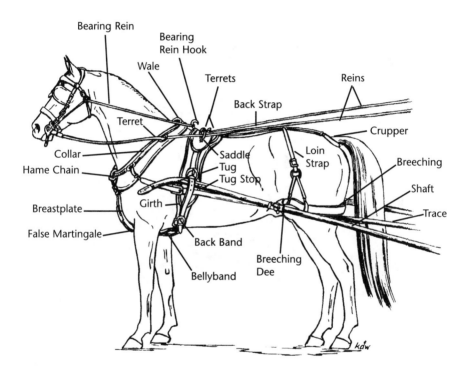

Bearing Rein

Bearing
Rein Hook

Wale

Terrets

Reins

Back Strap

Terret

Crupper

Collar

Saddle

Loin
Strap

Breeching

Hame Chain

Tug
Tug Stop

Shaft

Breastplate

Girth

Trace

False Martingale

Back Band

Breeching
Dee

Bellyband

Harness Parts (A)

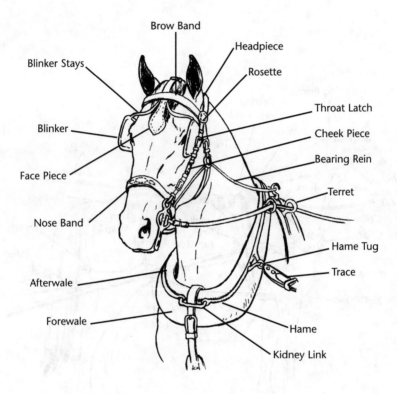

Blinder

Brow Band

Headpiece

Blinker Stays

Rosette

Throat Latch

Blinker

Cheek Piece

Bearing Rein

Face Piece

Terret

Nose Band

Hame Tug

Trace

Afterwale

Forewale

Hame

Kidney Link

Harness Parts (B)

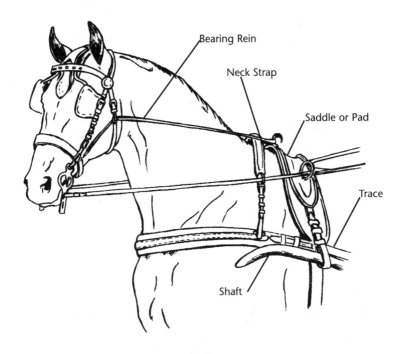

Bearing Rein

Neck Strap

Saddle or Pad

Trace

Shaft

Breast Collar

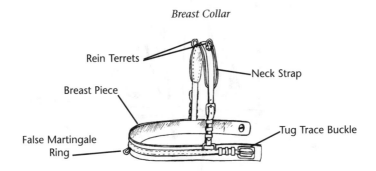

Rein Terrets

Neck Strap

Breast Piece

Tug Trace Buckle

False Martingale
Ring

Harness Parts (C)

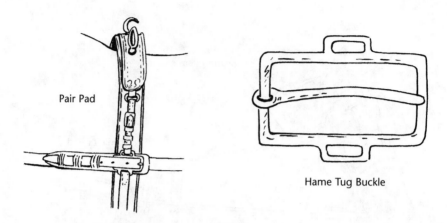

Pair Pad

Pair Pad Showing the Tug Buckle

Hame Tug Buckle

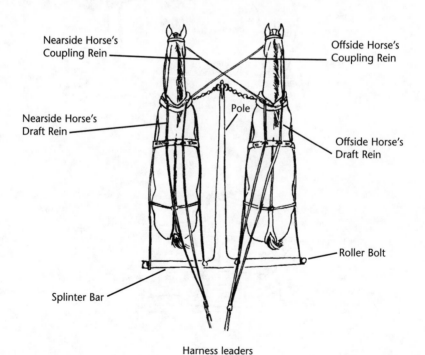

Nearside Horse's
Coupling Rein

Offside Horse's
Coupling Rein

Nearside Horse's
Draft Rein

Pole

Offside Horse's
Draft Rein

Roller Bolt

Splinter Bar

Harness leaders

Harness Parts (D)

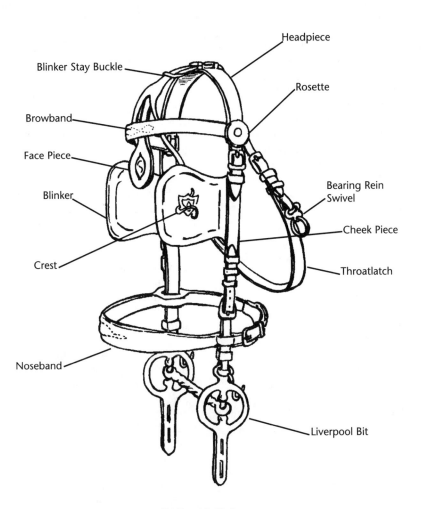

Headpiece

Blinker Stay Buckle

Rosette

Browband

Face Piece

Blinker

Bearing Rein Swivel

Crest

Cheek Piece

Throatlatch

Noseband

Liverpool Bit

Bridle with Blinkers
(sometimes called blinders)

Harness Parts (E)

Hb   see *hemoglobin*

HCl   see *hydrochloric acid*

head   (hed) **1.** one of the measurements of distance by which a horse may be said to have won a race; the length of a horse's head **2.** looking at the horse in profile, we may regard the head as being divided from the neck by a line proceeding from the back of the ear **3.** part of the English saddle tree **4.** in rodeo, a term used in team roping to mean roping the horns of a steer and pulling him around so a partner can rope the heels

head bumper a sturdy protective covering that attaches to the halter and fits between the ears to protect the top of a horse's head; generally used when trailering

Head Bumper

head carriage   the position of the horse's head and neck while the horse is in motion

head collar   halter; a bitless headpiece and noseband, usually of leather or nylon, used to lead a horse that is not wearing a bridle or to tie up a horse in a stable

head joint   the front portion of the carriage hood that allows extension; see *carriage parts* (illus.)

headpiece   headstall; see *harness parts B and E* (illus.)

head pole   a cue fastened alongside a horse's head and neck to keep his head straight

head shy   a horse that is afraid of having his head touched or of quick movements about his head

headstall   the bridle crownpiece, cheek pieces, and browband; does not include the noseband, bit, or reins

head tossing   a horse that frequently throws his head up and his nose out; usually done in fear or to resist handling aids

head up   a momentary lifting of the head to evade the bit; may be as serious as head tossing or as slight as a nod as the horse moves into a canter

health certificate   (helth sər tif' ə kit) a certificate from a veterinarian stating that a horse was sound and free from any contagious disease at the time of examination

heart   the desire and ability to continue running or working even when tired; in modern sports it is often called *second effort*

heart block   (härt bläk) impairment of conduction in heart excitation; results in late or missed heartbeats

heart failure   failure of the heart to pump blood at normal pressure, with resulting problems such as exercise intolerance and fluid accumulation in the lungs and other tissues

heart sounds   sounds heard using a stethoscope during each contraction of the heart; there usually are two heart sounds during each contraction

heat   (hēt) **1.** one round in a race that will be decided by winning two or more trials **2.** a common term for estrus

heat exhaustion (ig zôst′ chən) hyperthermia; circulatory collapse and shock caused by high environmental temperature, high humidity, and poor ventilation

heat period the period in which a mare can be bred; usually recurs at twenty-one-day intervals and averages 5–7 days in length

heat stroke hyperthermia; caused by the same situations as heat exhaustion, but is more serious; sweating usually stops; heat stroke is often fatal

heave line (hēv līn) the line along the abdomen on both sides; found on horses with moderate to severe heaves

heaves (hēvs) a respiratory ailment; characterized by forced expiration and difficulty breathing; resulting from the rupture of alveoli in the lungs; caused by such things as allergies and dust

heavy hands (hev′ ē handz) a rider who has no sensibility in his hands; one who rides by force

heavy horse any horse belonging to one of the breeds of large draft horses such as Clydesdale, Percheron, Shire, or Suffolk Punch

heavy on the front end a horse that moves and turns with too much weight on the front legs; may be caused by a conformational problem or training errors

heel (hēl) 1. the back of the pastern to the hoof; seen as two bulbs; see *hoof* (illus.) 2. a coat marking in which white covers one or both bulbs of the heel

heel crack (krak) a crack located on the heel of the hoof that can involve the sensitive lamina

height (hīt) 1. measured in a perpendicular line from the highest part of the withers to the ground 2. the amount of foot elevation in the stride

helmet (hel′ mit) lightweight, ventilated headgear designed to protect the rider in case of a fall

helminth (hel′ minth) category of intestinal parasite (worm)

hematinic an agent that improves the quality of the blood, increasing the hemoglobin level and the number of red blood cells

hematocrit (hē mat′ ō krit) the fraction of the total blood volume that is occupied by red blood cells

hematology (hē′ mə täl′ ə jē) the study of blood and blood-forming organs

hematoma (hē′ ma tō′ mə) 1. an accumulation of blood in body tissues due to a blood vessel injury 2. a localized collection of blood, usually clotted, in an organ, space, or tissue

hematopoietic (hem′ ə tō poi ē′ tik) affecting the formation of red blood cells

hematuria (hē′ mə tŏŏr′ ē ə) blood in the urine

hemiparesis (hem′ ē pə rē′ sis) weakness on one side of the body

hemiplegia (hem′ i plē′ jē ə) paralysis on one side of the body

---

a=f<u>a</u>t; ā=<u>a</u>pe; ä=c<u>a</u>r; â=b<u>a</u>re; e=t<u>e</u>n; ē=<u>e</u>ven;
i=<u>i</u>s; ī=b<u>i</u>te; ō=g<u>o</u>; ô=h<u>o</u>rn; ōō=t<u>oo</u>l;
ŏŏ=l<u>oo</u>k; u=<u>u</u>p; ʉ=f<u>u</u>r; ŋ=ri<u>ng</u>; ə=sof<u>a</u>

hemlock (hem′ läk) poison hemlock and water hemlock are among the most poisonous plants; has white flowers that grow in small clusters and may grow from four to ten feet; the stem is hollow and usually marked with small, purple spots; has a bitter taste and is extremely poisonous to both livestock and humans

hemoconcentration (hē′ mō kän′ sən trā′ s̲h̲ən) an increase in blood concentration due to a decrease in the fluid volume

hemodynamic (hē′ mə dī nam′ ik) pertaining to blood circulation

hemoglobin (hē′ mə glō′ bin) the oxygen-carrying pigment of the red blood cells

hemoglobinuria (hē′ mō glō′ bi nōō′ rē ə) the presence of free hemoglobin in the urine usually due to the breakdown of red blood cells

hemolymphatic system (hē′ mə lim fat′ ik sis′ təm) the body system that consists of the blood, its cells, the bone marrow, lymph glands, and lymph vessels

hemolysin (hi mäl′ ə sin) a naturally occurring substance that destroys red blood cells

hemolysis (hi mäl′ ə sis) the release of hemoglobin due to the destruction of red blood cells

hemolytic anemia (hē′ mō lit′ ik ə nē′ mē ə) condition of a newborn foal caused by incompatibility between blood types of dam and foal; the antibodies transmitted to the foal through colostrum destroy some of the foal's oxygen-carrying red blood cells; also called *neonatal isoerytherolysis*

hemophilia (hē′ mə fil′ ē ə) a hereditary deficiency of a clotting factor in the blood; causing excessive bleeding

hemoptysis (hi mäp′ tə sis) the coughing up of blood or blood-stained sputum

hemorrhage (hem′ ər ij) the escape of blood from the vessels; bleeding

hemorrhagic (hem′ ō raj′ ik) pertaining to blood loss

hemorrhagic inflammation (hem′ o raj′ ik in′ flə mā s̲h̲ən) an inflammation characterized by an exudate containing large numbers of red blood cells

hemospermia (hē′ mō sper′ mē ə) the presence of blood in the sperm

hemostatic agent (hē′ mə stat′ ik ā′ jent) a substance that checks or stops the flow of blood

hemothorax (hē′ mō thor′ aks) a collection of blood in the space between the lungs and rib cage

heparin (hep′ ər in) a naturally derived substance that prevents blood clotting

hepatic (hi pat′ ik) pertaining to the liver

hepatitis (hep′ ə tīt′ is) inflammation of the liver

herbivore (hʉr′ bə vôr′) plant eater

herbivorous (hʉr biv′ ər əs) feeding on plants

herd bound (hʉrd bound) a horse that refuses to leave a group of other horses herd holders (hōld' ərz) the two mounted riders who, during a cutting competition, hold the herd behind the cutter after the cutter has selected a cow to cut

herding instinct (hʉrd iŋ in' stiŋkt) the natural ability of the horse to stay in groups to protect themselves

heredity (hə red' ə tē) characteristics transmitted to offspring from parents and other ancestors

hermaphrodite (hər maf' rə dīt) an animal with both male and female reproductive organs

hernia (hʉr' nē ə) the protrusion of any internal organ through the wall of its containing cavity; usually means the passage of a portion of the intestine through an opening in the abdominal muscle

herpes virus (hʉr' pēz) a virus that causes rhinopneumonitis, abortion, and possibly other diseases in horses

heterochromia (het' ər ō krō mē ə) a diversity of color in a part or parts that should normally be of one color

heterozygous dominant (het' ər ə zī' gəs däm' ə nənt) a dominant character that produces two kinds of gametes; one carries the dominant gene, while the other carries the recessive gene

hidebound (hīd' bound) a tight hide over the body

high (hī) spirited

high-backed saddle an old-fashioned western saddle with a five- or six-inch-high cantle

higher white markings the extent of the marking should be described, for instance white to the hock, white to halfway up the cannon

Highland (hī' lənd) a breed of strong, sturdy ponies originated in Scotland; particularly well suited to mountainous regions; eel stripes are common

high school the highest form of specialized training of riding horses

high school horse a highly trained horse; schooled in specific maneuvers often based on dressage

hill topper (hil top' ər) a rider who follows the hunt by observing from the hilltops where he guesses the hounds will run and where the kill will take place

hilus (hī' ləs) the structure that allows the nerves and the blood vessels to enter the ovaries

hind bow (hīnd' bō) see *cantle*

hind gut (hīnd gut) distal portion of the alimentary canal; that portion of the digestive system closest to the anus

hind limb either of the rear two legs

hindquarters (hīnd' kwôr' tərz) the rear end of the horse including croup, rump, haunches, gaskin, and hind legs

hind shin guards (hīnd shin gärdz) leather protective guards on the lower

a=fat; ā=ape; ä=car; â=bare; e=ten; ē=even; i=is; ī=bite; ō=go; ô=horn; ōō=tool; ŏŏ=look; u=up; ʉ=fur; ŋ=ring; ə=sofa

hind legs; used to prevent cuts and bruises from the front shoes, which graze the hind legs of some trotters

hind trotting shoe   (hīnd trŏt iŋ shōō) trotting shoe; squared at the toe

hinny   (hin' ē) the resulting offspring of a female donkey being bred to a male horse

hip, point of   (hip point uv) a bony prominence lying just forward of and below the croup

hippodrome   (hip' ə drōm) in ancient Greece and Rome, a course for horse and chariot races surrounded by tiers of seats in an oval

hippology   (hi' päl' ə jē) the study of the horse

hippomane   (hip' ō mān) the large, brown, irregularly shaped, rubbery mass that is passed with the foal at birth

hippophile   (hip' ō fīl) a horse lover

hirsutism   (hur' sōō tiz' əm) abnormally long hair coat; can be caused by a hormone disorder

Hispano   (hi spa' nō) a breed originating in Spain; also known as a *Spanish Anglo-Arab;* resulting from the cross of Arab-Spanish mares with Thoroughbred stallions; known as an excellent jumper with a good temperament

histamine   (his' tə mēn') a chemical compound that dilates capillaries, constricts the smooth muscle of the lungs, and increases secretions of the stomach

hitch   (hich) 1. to fasten or tie a horse; e.g., when hitched to a rail 2. a connection between a vehicle and a horse trailer 3. a defect in gait, noted in the hind legs, which seem to skip at the trot

hitches   1. a system of tying or securing; there are three types of hitches used to secure loads on a pack horse: squaw, box, and one-man 2. the method of attaching a truck to a horse trailer

hitch up   to harness a horse or horses to be driven

hit off the line   hounds recovering the line after a check

hives   (hīvz) small swellings under or within the skin similar to human hives; they appear suddenly over large portions of the body and can be caused by a change in feed or an allergic reaction

hobble   (häb' əl) 1. to restrain the horse by securing his front legs together 2. the restraint used for hobbling; another type of hobble is used on the hind legs of a mare in breeding to prevent her from kicking the stallion

hobble hangers   leather straps encircling the front and hind legs of a pacer on the same side to keep those legs moving in unison and to help the horse maintain gait; the straps run over the horse's back and to the haunches

hobdayed   (hob' dā' əd) when horses with afflictions of their respiratory organs are cured by the hobdaying operation, which consists of removing the paralyzed vocal cords; the only side effect is that the horse can no longer whinny

hock (häk) joint in the hind legs that corresponds to the knee in front legs; permits forward bending of the lower rear leg; also called the *tarsus*; see *points of the horse* (illus.)

hock boot a boot that fits over the hock and is designed to stop a horse from bumping his hocks against the back of the trailer while he travels

hogback see *hog's back*

hogged mane (hägd' mān) a mane entirely clipped off to a length of no more than three inches; less than three inches in length is considered roached

hog's back in show jumping, a spread obstacle in which there are three sets of poles; the first is close to the ground, the second is at the highest point of the obstacle, and the third is slightly lower than the second

hoick (hīk) a cheer to the hounds in a fox hunt

hold hard the warning of the huntsman to the field that they must not override his hounds

hold them forward to take hounds forward in hopes of picking up a lost line

holloa (häl' ō) the cry given by a person out hunting to indicate that he has seen the fox

hollow back (häl' ō bäk) the top line of the horse from the nose to the tail that is concave as opposed to convex

Holstein (hōl' stīn) one of Germany's oldest breeds; dates back to the fourteenth century; distinguished by its free and flowing action at the gallop and for its elegant trot

home (hōm) refers to a position of the rider's foot in the stirrup; the foot of the rider's boot is in the stirrup so that the back of the stirrup tread is touching the front of the boot heel

homeopathic (hō' mē ə pat̲h' ik) treating or preventing disease with very small amounts of the agent or a product of the disease

homeostasis (hō' mē ō stā' sis) a tendency to stability in the normal internal environment of an organism

homeostatic (hō' mē ō stat' ik) possessing a tendency to remain stable

homozygous (hō' mə zī gəs) having like genes in a horse that can represent any of the characteristics of the animal, such as coat color or size

homozygous dominant (hō' mō zī' gəs däm' ə nənt) a dominant character that produces only one kind of gamete

honda (hän' də) the eye of the lariat through which the rope is passed to form a loop

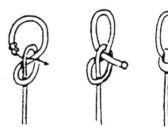

Honda Knot

a=f<u>a</u>t; ā=<u>a</u>pe; ä=c<u>a</u>r; â=b<u>a</u>re; e=t<u>e</u>n; ē=<u>e</u>ven; i=<u>i</u>s; ī=b<u>i</u>te; ō=g<u>o</u>; ô=h<u>o</u>rn; ōō=t<u>oo</u>l; ŏŏ=l<u>oo</u>k; u=<u>u</u>p; ʉ=f<u>u</u>r; ŋ=ri<u>ng</u>; ə=sof<u>a</u>

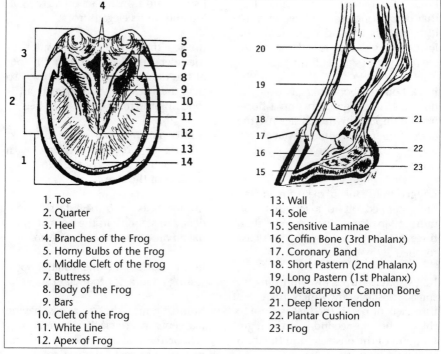

1. Toe
2. Quarter
3. Heel
4. Branches of the Frog
5. Horny Bulbs of the Frog
6. Middle Cleft of the Frog
7. Buttress
8. Body of the Frog
9. Bars
10. Cleft of the Frog
11. White Line
12. Apex of Frog

13. Wall
14. Sole
15. Sensitive Laminae
16. Coffin Bone (3rd Phalanx)
17. Coronary Band
18. Short Pastern (2nd Phalanx)
19. Long Pastern (1st Phalanx)
20. Metacarpus or Cannon Bone
21. Deep Flexor Tendon
22. Plantar Cushion
23. Frog

Hoof

honesty (än' əst ē) a quality in a horse that makes him dependable and predictable

honest hound a trustworthy, dependable dog

honor a line (on' ər ə līn) a hound that speaks on a scent

hood (hŏŏd) **1.** a fabric covering that goes over the horse's head, ears, and part of his neck; usually used in cold weather **2.** a covering used to provide shade and rain protection to carriage drivers; see *carriage parts* (illus.)

hoof (hŏŏf) the horny wall and sole of the foot; see illustration; *points of the horse* (illus.)

hoof boot used to treat a foot by placing medication in a boot; protects the foot from further injury and dirt

hoof gauge used to determine the angle of the hoof relative to the ground surface

hoof growth growth occurs in the hoof on average at a rate of one-quarter to one-half inch per month

hoof horn hard, slightly elastic horny material that forms the protective outer wall of the foot

hoof knife a farrier's tool used to trim excess frog and sole from the hoof; the hook on the end is used to trim the frog and clean between the bar and frog

Hoof Knife

hoof pick a hooked tool used for removing manure, stones and dirt from a horse's foot; should be used in a heel-to-toe motion

Hoof Pick

hoof tester a pincerlike instrument used to gently squeeze the hoof to find sore areas; if the pincher is squeezed in an area of inflammation, the horse will flinch

hormone (hôr' mōn) a chemical substance produced in the body that has a specific effect on the activity or function of a certain organ

hormone assay (ə sā') analysis of hormones in body fluids or tissue samples to determine quantity

horn (hôrn) 1. a prominent projection on the pommel of the western saddle covered with leather and used to hold a lasso or lariat; see *western saddle* (illus.) 2. hard, slightly elastic material that forms the protective outer wall of the hoof

horn cap the enlarged top of the saddle horn; its principal purpose is to keep the lariat from slipping off the top of the horn

horn fly primarily, pests of cattle; sometimes affect horses

horn neck the thin segment between the saddle horn cap and the saddle fork around which the lariat is wrapped by the dally roper

horse (hôrs) 1. the general term for an equine animal, whether he be a stallion, mare, or gelding 2. a stallion or uncastrated horse greater than four years of age

horse length (leŋkth) eight feet; distance between horses in a column

horse liniment (lin' ə mənt) a counter-irritant for providing temporary relief due to overexertion or fatigue, sprains, bruises, and other inflammations; used on muscles and swollen areas

horseman 1. a rider on horseback 2. a person skilled in the training and management of horses 3. a farm laborer who works with horses

horsemanship the art of riding the horse and of understanding his needs

horsepower originally, a measure of the power that a horse exerts in pulling; now, the rate at which work is accomplished when a weight of 33,000 pounds is moved one foot in one minute or 550 pounds is moved one foot in one second

horse pox a mild form of smallpox affecting horses; marked by a pustular eruption of the skin

horseshoe a shaped metal band nailed to the base of riding and harness horse hoofs to protect them and prevent them from splitting

horseshoe borium (bôr' ē əm) pure tungsten carbide particles in a mild steel flux

horse show a meeting at which competitions are held to test or display the qualities and capabilities of horses and their riders

---

a=fat; ā=ape; ä=car; â=bare; e=ten; ē=even; i=is; ī=bite; ō=go; ô=horn; ōō=tool; ŏŏ=look; u=up; ʉ=fur; ŋ=ring; ə=sofa

horse tailing taking charge of the band of horses used by drovers when herding cattle or sheep over long distances

host (hōst) an animal or plant that harbors or nourishes another organism

hotblood (hät' blud) of eastern or oriental blood; having ancestors that trace to Thoroughbreds or Arabians; characteristics include fineness of bone, thin skin, fine hair coat, absence of long hair on fetlocks, and higher red blood cell and hemoglobin values

hot nail a shoeing nail that penetrates the sensitive tissue of the foot

hot quit term used in cutting to indicate when horse and rider stop working a cow when the cow is still moving, resulting in a substantial penalty

hot walker 1. a groom or exercise boy who walks a horse after a race or workout 2. a mechanical device to which horses are fastened that rotates and ensures exercise

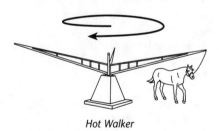

Hot Walker

house fly (hous flī) a nonbiting, nuisance insect

housing, rear (hous' iŋ rēr) decorative covering behind the cantle of the western saddle

hub (hub) the center part of a wheel, which is fastened to the axle; see *carriage parts* (illus.)

hub step a small flat step on the hub of a carriage wheel; see *carriage parts* (illus.)

Hucul a Polish pony with formal breeding that dates back to the nineteenth century; a quiet and docile animal that is powerful and has good endurance

human eye (hyōō' mən ī) visible white sclera around the eye

humerus (hyōō' mər əs) the bone that extends from the shoulder to the elbow; see *skeletal system* (illus.)

Hungarian horse (huŋ gär' ē ən hôrs) a breed originating in Hungary; known for style and beauty with ruggedness; common uses: cow horse, cutting, pleasure, trail riding, hunting, and jumping

Hungarian Horse Association an association formed to record horses and their offspring imported from Hungary after World War II

hunt (hunt) pursuit of game; as used by horsemen, the term usually implies a hunt on horseback with hounds

hunt cap see *hunting cap*

hunter (hunt' ər) a horse used for fox hunting; usually part or full Thoroughbred; type of horse, not a breed, that is suitable for field hunting or show hunting; hunters are defined by the weight carried: light, carry under 165 lb; middle, carry 165–185 lb; heavy, carry 185–205 lb

hunter clip when the coat is

clipped, leaving the legs unclipped; this clip may have a saddle mark, which is an outline of the unclipped saddle area

Hunter Hack   a class in which the horse is required to jump two fences and then is shown at the walk, trot, canter, and hand gallop on the rail

hunter trials   a type of competition held by most hunts and other organizing bodies during the hunting season in which horses are ridden over a course or obstacles built to look natural and similar to those encountered out hunting; the course must be completed within a specified time

hunter under saddle   a class in which the horses are judged on quality of movement and conformation; horses should be obedient, alert, and responsive to the rider

hunting breastplate   used on English saddles; holds the saddle forward on the withers; one end attaches to the girth, runs between front legs, forks at the base of the neck, and attaches to the pommel of the saddle

hunting cap   a velvet-covered protective riding hat

hunting pinks   the scarlet livery of the hunt staff are commonly called *pinks* after a famous British tailor

hunting snaffle   a bridle with reins plaited to prevent them from slipping through the fingers

Hunt Seat Equitation   (hunt sēt ek′ wə tā shən) a performance class in which the rider is judged on basic position in the saddle, legs, seat, and hands in a hunt seat saddle and on the

use of the aids during individual and group work

hunt seat saddle   much like the jump saddle, but with less incline to the cantle and less forward flaps

huntsman   the person who hunts the hounds and is in charge of the kennels

hurdle racing   (hʉr′ dəl rās′ iŋ) horse races over a course of hurdles

hurry   (hʉr′ ē) a horse that moves along without showing any real rhythm or control in the gait

husbandry   (huz′ bən drē) the scientific management of domestic animals

hyaloid vessel   (hī′ ə loid′ ves′ əl) an artery present in the eye of the fetus that is commonly present at birth and usually disintegrates within the first two weeks of life

hyaluronic acid   (hī′ əl yōō rän′ ik as′ id) a component of the thick, lubricating fluid within joints

hybrid   (hī′ brid) the result of crossing two different species; the mule is a good example

hydrocephalus   (hī′ drə sef′ ə ləs) an abnormal amount of fluid beneath the skull, resulting in an enlarged head, brain atrophy, and mental deterioration

hydrochloric acid   (hī′ drə klor′ ik as′ id) substance secreted by the stomach

a=fat; ā=ape; ä=car; â=bare; e=ten; ē=even; i=is; ī=bite; ō=go; ô=horn; ōō=tool; ŏŏ=look; u=up; ʉ=fur; ŋ=ring; ə=sofa

to activate pepsin and break down protein

hydrokinetic (hī' drō ki net' ik) pertaining to moving water, as in a whirlpool bath

hydrolysis (hī drãl' ə sis) the splitting of a compound into fragments by the addition of water

hydrophilic (hī' drə fil' ik) readily absorbing water

hydrotherapy (hī' drə ther' ə pē) 1. the application of water in any form, internally or externally, in treating disease or illness 2. to use the massaging action of water

hydrothermal (hī' drə ther' məl) relating to the temperature effects of water

hydrothorax (hī' drə thôr' aks) a collection of watery fluid in the space between the lungs and rib cage

hygroma (hī' grō mə) a sac distended with fluid

hymen (hī' mən) a fold of mucous membrane that partially or completely covers the opening of the vagina

hyoid bone (hī' oid bōn) a V-shaped bone between the mandible and larynx at the base of the tongue

hypercalcemia (hī' pər kal sē' mē ə) excess calcium in blood

hypercapnia (hī' pər kap' nē ə) an excess of carbon dioxide in the blood

hyperemia (hī' pər ē' mē ə) an excess of blood in a tissue

hyperexcitability (hī' pər ik sīt' ə bil' ə tē) abnormal excitation of the nervous system

hyperextend (hī' pər ik stend') to extend a limb excessively

hyperextension (hī' pər ik stən' shən) extreme or excessive extension of a limb beyond its normal limit; usually due to fatigue, tendon or ligament damage, or excessive forces on the joint during exercise

hyperflexion (hī' pər fləks' shən) forcible overflexion of a limb or part

hyperirritability (hī' pər ir' i tə bil' ə tē) an excessive and abnormal responsiveness to slight stimuli

hyperkalemia (hī' per kal' ē mē ə) an excess of potassium in the blood

hyperkalemia periodic paralysis (hi' pər ka lē mē ə pʉr' ī od' ik pə ral' i sis) HYPP; episodes of muscular weakness due to periods of low potassium levels; found primarily in certain lines of Quarter Horses

hypermotile (hī' pər mō til) increased activity, such as in the intestines

hyperostosis (hī' pər äs tō' sis) abnormal enlargement of bone

hyperparathyroidism (hī' pər par' ə thī' roid izm) abnormally increased activity of the parathyroid gland

hyperpigmentation (hī' pər pig men tā' shən) abnormally increased pigmentation

hyperplasia (hī' pər plā' zhē ə) an abnormal increase in the number of normal cells in a tissue

hyperresonance (hī′ pər rez′ ō nans) an exaggerated resonance; intensification of sound produced by the transmission of vibrations to a cavity

hypersensitivity (hī′ pər sen′ si tiv it ē) a state in which the body reacts with an exaggerated response to a foreign agent

hypertension (hī′ pər ten′ shən) high blood pressure

hyperthermia (hī′ pər thur′ mē ə) heat stroke or heat exhaustion

hyperthyroidism (hī′ pər thī′ roid izm) excessive functional activity of the thyroid gland

hypertonic (hī′ pər tän′ ik) pertaining to a solution that, when bathing cells, causes a flow of water out of the cell

hypertrophy (hī pur′ trə fē) morbid enlargement or overgrowth of an organ or part due to an increase in the size of its cells

hypnotics (hip nät′ iks) drugs that induce sleep

hypocalcemia (hī′ pō kal′ sē′ mē ə) abnormally low levels of blood calcium

hypoflexion (hī′ pō flek shən) decreased flexion in the muscles and tendons of the legs

hypoglycemia (hī′ pō glī sē′ mē ə) an abnormally diminished level of glucose in the body

hypogonadism (hī′ pō gō′ nad izm) abnormally decreased activity of the gonads, resulting in retarded growth and sexual development

hypopigmentations (hī′ pō pig men tā′ shən) abnormally diminished pigmentation

hypoplasia (hī′ pə plā′ zhə) incomplete development of an organ so that it fails to reach adult size

hypopyon (hī pō′ pē än′) an accumulation of pus in the anterior chamber of the eye

hypotension (hī pō ten′ shən) low blood pressure

hypothalamus (hī′ pə thal′ ə məs) the part of the brain that regulates part of the nervous system, hormone activity, and many body functions

hypothermia (hī′ pə thur′ mē ə) temperature below normal

hypothyroid (hī′ pō thī′ roid) pertaining to a condition caused by low output of the hormone thyroxin from the thyroid gland

hypothyroidism (hī′ pō thī′ roid izm) a deficiency of thyroid activity

hypotonic (hī′ pō ton′ ik) pertaining to a solution that, when bathing cells, causes a flow of water into the cell

hypoventilation (hī′ pō ven′ ti lā shən) inadequate exchange of oxygen and carbon dioxide due to inadequate breathing

hypovolemia (hī′ pō vō lē′ mē ə) abnormally decreased circulating blood volume

a=fat; ā=ape; ä=car; â=bare; e=ten; ē=even; i=is; ī=bite; ō=go; ô=horn; ōō=tool; ŏŏ=look; u=up; u=fur; ŋ=ring; ə=sofa

hypoxia (hī päk' sē ə) low oxygen content in inspired air, blood, or tissues

HYPP see *hyperkalemic periodic paralysis*

I

IAHA   see *International Arabian Horse Association*

iatrogenic   (ī at′ rə jen′ ik) symptoms, ailments, or disorders caused by medical treatment

Iberian Warmblood Registry   a registry for horses with 25 percent Andalusian/Lusitano blood

Icelandic Pony   (īs lan′ dik pō′ nē) the only breed originating in Iceland; still exists in relatively large numbers

ichthammol   (ik′ t͟ham mol) ointment made from a coal-tar base that has a soothing, drawing effect; used to treat abscesses and other bacterial infections

icterus   (ik′ tər əs) abnormal accumulation of greenish and yellowish bile pigments in tissues

identity   (ī den′ tə tē) being a specific person, animal or thing

idiopathic   (id′ ē ō path′ ik) arising from an unknown cause

ileum   (il′ ē əm) a distal portion of the small intestine; extending from the jejunum to the cecum

iliopsoas   the muscle on the inside of the loin and pelvis that flexes the hip and/or the lumbosacral joint

ilium   (il′ ē əm) the expansive front portion of the hip bone

immobility insufficient   (im′ mō bil′ i tē in′ sə fish′ ənt) a horse that doesn't completely freeze and wait at atten-

tion after the halt; the horse may have altered the head position, moved a leg, or merely not held a stop long enough

immune   (i myōōn′) protection from a disease because of the presence of antibodies; see *immune cell*

immune cell   (sel) a disease-fighting cell produced by the body

immune system   (sis′ təm) a bodywide group of varying tissues responsible for recognizing and combating foreign material; includes the lymph system, spleen, bone marrow, thymus, intestinal tissues, wandering tissue cells, and other elements

immunity   (i myōōn′ it ē) the manufacture of an individual's own antibodies to combat a disease either from having the disease or from being vaccinated; provides future protection from that disease

immunization   (im′ yōō ni zā′ s͟hən) the process of rendering a subject immune through vaccination

immunodeficiency   (im′ yōō nō de fis͟h′ en se) a deficiency in antibody response; makes the animal more susceptible to infection

immunodiffusion test   (im′ yōō nō di fyōō′ z͟hən) a laboratory test conducted to determine the presence of specific antibodies in the bloodstream; based on the tendency of antibodies and their corresponding antigens to diffuse toward each other when

---

a=f<u>a</u>t; ā=<u>a</u>pe; ä=c<u>a</u>r; â=b<u>a</u>re; e=t<u>e</u>n; ē=<u>e</u>ven; i=<u>i</u>s; ī=b<u>i</u>te; ō=g<u>o</u>; ô=h<u>o</u>rn; ōō=t<u>oo</u>l; ŏŏ=l<u>oo</u>k; u=<u>u</u>p; ᵫ=f<u>u</u>r; ŋ=ri<u>ng</u>; ə=sof<u>a</u>

placed in adjacent chambers of a dish of transparent agar gel

immunofluorescence (im' yōō nō flōō' res' əns) a laboratory test conducted to determine the presence of specific antibodies in the bloodstream by tagging the antibodies with fluorescent dye, then monitoring the pattern they produce when placed with their corresponding antigens

immunoglobulin (im' yōō no gläb' yə lin) a protein functioning as an antibody

immunosorbent (im' yōō nō sor' bent) an insoluble support for antigens used to take up antibodies from a mixture

immunosuppression (im' yŏŏ nō sə prəsh' ən) failure of the immune system to function normally; can be due to disease or medication

impaction (im pak' shən) a type of colic or abdominal pain caused by low gut motility, obstruction or constipation

import (im pôrt) to bring horses from another country; in registering horses from another country in the U.S. studbook of their respective breeds, the certificates of registration issued bear the abbreviation "Imp." and the country of export

impost (im' pōst) weight assessment

imprinting (im print' iŋ) the rapid learning in a young horse's first field of vision that reinforces species behavior; the phenomenon that causes newborn foals to follow any moving object; occurs during first 1–2 hours after birth

impulsion (im pul' shən) the urge, thrust, or inner drive to move forward; a controlled forward impulse; the desire and energy of forward movement

impulsion lacking (im pul' shən lak' iŋ) insufficient energy to keep a horse going forward at a regular speed; almost dropping into a slower pace

inactive (in ak' tiv) when the hind legs of the horse appear lazy and do not come under the horse

in-and-out combination fence

inanition (in' ə nish' ən) a starved condition, with marked weight loss, weakness, and a decreased metabolism; caused by severe malnutrition

inapparent infection (in' ə par' ənt in fek' shən) presence of an infection in a host without occurrence of recognizable clinical signs or symptoms; only identifiable by laboratory means

inattentive (in' ə ten' tiv) a horse that does not heed the aids of his rider

inbreeding (in' brēd' iŋ) breeding of closely related animals; usually done to bring out specific desirable traits

incidence (in' si dens) rate at which a certain event occurs, such as the number of new cases of a specific disease occurring during a certain period

incised (in sīzd') cut into

incision (in' sizh' ən) a cut produced by a surgeon's scalpel

incisors (in sī' zərz) the teeth at the front of the mouth: six top and six bottom; used for cutting rather than grinding; called *pinchers* or *nippers;* the center four are called *centrals;* the next four on each side of the centrals are called *intermediates;* the outside four are called *corners*

incompetence (in käm' pə tens) physical or mental inadequacy or insufficiency; as in cardiac insufficiency

incompetent (in käm' pə tənt) lack of sufficient knowledge or ability

incubation (iŋ' kyə bā' shən) the period of development of an infectious disease from the time the disease-producing organism enters the body until signs of the disease appear

incubation period (pēr' ē əd) time interval between exposure to an infectious agent and appearance of the first sign or symptom of the disease in question

independent seat (in' di pen' dənt sēt) the ability to maintain a firm, balanced position on a horse's back without relying on the reins or stirrups

Indian broke (in' dē ən brōk) horses trained to allow mounting from the off side

Indian pony (po' nē) a small horse of pinto color

Indiana pants (in' dē an' ə pants) the hobbles used on pacers to prevent them from breaking into a trot or gallop

indirect rein (in' di rekt' rān) a rein pressed against the horse's neck on the opposite side to which the rider wants him to move; an opposite or bearing rein

induced parturition (in' dōōsd' pär' tōō rish' ən) starting the birth process by administration of certain drugs

indwelling catheter (in' dwel' iŋ kath' ə tər) a piece of tubing seated in a structure to allow continuous drainage or repeated application of medication; intravenous catheter; urinary catheter

infarction (in färk' shən) the formation of an area of dead tissue resulting from obstruction of circulation to the area

infection (in fek' shən) entry, development and multiplication of an infectious agent in the body

infectious (in' fek shəs) capable of invading and growing in living tissues; used to describe various pathogenic microorganisms such as viruses, bacteria, protozoa and fungi

infectious agent (ā' jənt) an organism that is capable of producing infection or infectious disease; chiefly microorganisms, but includes worms

infertility (in fʉr til' it ē) inability to produce offspring

infestation (in fes tā' shən) large numbers of parasites living in or on the horse

inflammation (in' flə mā' shən) a condition of tissue characterized by pain, heat, redness, swelling, and various exudations as a reaction to injury; serves to eliminate harmful substances and damaged tissue

influenza (in' flōō wen' zə) the flu; a highly contagious viral disease widespread throughout the world; symptoms include high fever, loss of appetite, weakness, and depression; there may also be rapid breathing, a dry cough, and a watery discharge from the eyes and nostrils that changes to a white or yellow discharge

in foal   pregnant

infundibulum   (in' fən dib' yŏŏ ləm) the funnel-shaped membrane that traps the egg when it is released from the follicle of the ovary

infusion   (in fyōō' zhən) the therapeutic introduction of a fluid, such as saline solution, into the body by the force of gravity

ingest   (in jest') to consume; to take into the stomach

ingesta   (in jest' ə) consumed feed and fluids; food and drink taken into the stomach

ingestion   (in jest' shən) the act of taking food, medicines, etc., into the body by mouth

ingestive behavior   (in jest' tiv bi hāv' yər) the process of taking food or water into the digestive track

inguinal hernia   (iŋ' gwe nəl hʉr' nē ə) protrusion of abdominal material through the inguinal ring, usually into the scrotum of the male horse

inhalant   (in hāl' ənt) medication that is inhaled

inhalation   (in' hə lā' shən) the act of drawing air or other substances into the lungs

in hand   a horse shown in halter classes; a horse led with a bridle or hal-

ter; in a show class, indicates unsaddled or without harness, as opposed to a ridden or harness class

In-hand Class   a class in which the horse is led by the exhibitor

inhibitor   (in hib' it ər) an agent that slows or prevents a chemical reaction

injection   (in jek' shən) the act of forcing a liquid into a part, as into the subcutaneous tissues, the blood vessels, or an organ; a substance forced or administered

injury   (in' jər ē) physical harm or damage

innervation   (i nʉr' vā shən) the distribution or supply of nerves to a part; the supply of nerve stimuli sent to a part

innocent murmur   (in' ə sənt mʉr' mər) a heart murmur that does not reflect an abnormality of the heart

inoculate   (i näk' yŏŏ lāt) the introduction of a vaccine or disease-producing organism into the body

insensitive tissue   having no nerves; e.g., insensitive laminae

inside leg or rein   the leg or rein toward the center of a circle being traveled; on the side of the leading leg at the canter; if the horse is bending, the leg or rein on the concave side of the horse

insight learning   a type of learning prevalent in the higher order mammals; the ability to respond correctly the first time that an animal encounters a certain situation or experience

in-skirt rigging rigging in which the rigging rings, Ds, or plates are anchored to the skirt, not the tree; this type of rigging has no rigging leathers

inspiration (in' spə rā' s̲h̲ən) inhaling or drawing air into the lungs

instinct (in' stiŋkt) inborn, intrinsic knowledge and behavior; unlearned form of behavior; particular reaction pattern

instinctual behavior (in' stiŋkt' c̲h̲ōō əl bi hāv' yər) an unlearned form of behavior

insulin (in' sə lin) a hormone secreted by the pancreas to control blood sugar levels and utilization of sugar in the body

integument (in teg' yŏŏ mənt) a covering; the skin

integumentary system (in teg' ye mənt er ē sis' tem) skin and associated structures

intensity (in ten' si tē) a horse that does not eat well or does not digest much of what he does eat

intention (in ten' s̲h̲ən) a determination to do something or to act in a specific way

Intercollegiate Rodeo (in' tər kə lē' jit rō' dē ō) rodeo competitions held between college contestants; the National Intercollegiate Rodeo Association (NIRA) was formed in August 1949

intercostal (in' tər käs' təl) between the ribs

interdental space (in' tər den' təl spās) gum space between the incisors and molars

interfering (in' tər fēr' iŋ) the striking of the inside of one leg with the inside of the hoof or skin of the opposite leg; the impact point may be from the coronary band up to the carpus or hock

intermittent pressure (in' tər mit' ənt pres̲h̲' ər) application and release of an aid

internal (in tɛr' nəl) having to do with the inside

internal blistering (blis' tər iŋ) injection of a counterirritant to increase circulation

International American Albino Association a registry for albino horses, no mottling or gray skin accepted

International Arabian Horse Association a registry for Arabians; half-Arabians: one parent is registered purebred Arabian and the other parent is a breed other than a Thoroughbred or registered Anglo-Arab; Anglo-Arabian: a cross between a registered purebred Arabian and a registered purebred Thoroughbred or a registered Anglo-Arabian

International Buckskin Horse Association incorporated in 1971; a registry for buckskin, dun, red dun, and grullo; the registry was formed to collect, record, and preserve pedigrees of horses duly registered

International Trotting and Pacing Association a registry of the Trotting-

---

a=f<u>a</u>t; ā=<u>a</u>pe; ä=c<u>a</u>r; â=b<u>a</u>re; e=t<u>e</u>n; ē=<u>e</u>ven; i=<u>i</u>s; ī=b<u>i</u>te; ō=g<u>o</u>; ô=h<u>o</u>rn; ōō=t<u>oo</u>l; ŏŏ=l<u>oo</u>k; u=<u>u</u>p; ʉ=f<u>ur</u>; ŋ=ri<u>ng</u>; ə=sof<u>a</u>

bred, which is a harness racehorse with a fifty-one-inch height limit; part Standardbred and raced as a hobby

international units   (in' tər nash' ə nəl yōō' nits) arbitrary units of measurement applying to such variables of time, electric current, temperature, and biological substances, as agreed to by an international committee of scientists

interosseous ligament   (in' ter äs ē əs lig' ə ment) connects the splint bone to the cannon bone

interval training   (in' tər vəl trān' iŋ) a system of conditioning horses to increase their speed and endurance; the program improves respiration, circulation, and removal of waste products by subjecting the horse alternately to the stress of curtailed effort and rest

interventricular septal defect   (in' ter ven trik' yōō lər sep' təl dē' fekt) a condition arising from the failure of the septum to develop completely in the fetus' heart, causing an opening between the ventricles of the heart at birth

intestinal   (in tes' ti nəl) pertaining to the intestines

intestinal flora   (flôr' ə) bacteria and other microorganisms normally residing in the intestine

intestinal incarceration   (in kär' sə rā' shən) a loop of intestine caught behind or around another structure; can be a cause of severe colic

intestinal obstruction   (əb struk' shən) obstruction to movement of feed material in the intestines; can be

caused by hardened fecal material, foreign material, or fecaliths

intestinal stenosis   (sti nō' sis) narrowing of a section of intestine, usually due to scar tissue

intestinal villi   (vil' i) small, fingerlike projections on the inside of the intestines; they increase the surface area of the intestinal wall to increase the absorption of nutrients and water

intestinal volvulus   (vol' vu ləs) twisting of the intestine along its long axis

intestine, lower   (in tes' tin lō' ər) the lower portion of the digestive system; consisting of the cecum, colon, rectum, and anal canal

in the book   accepted for or entered in the general studbook

in the money   in horse racing, placing first, second, or third

intima   (in' tə mə) a general term denoting an innermost structure, such as the inner lining of a blood vessel

intra-articular   (in' trə är tik' yə lər) within a joint

intradermal   (in' trə dɵr' məl) within the skin; an injection given by inserting a very fine needle into the skin

intrathecal   (in' trə thē' kal) within a sheath

intrauterine   (in' trə yōōt' ər in) within the uterus

intravenous   (in' trə vē' nəs) administered directly into the bloodstream through a vein

intravenous outfit (out' fit') the needle, syringe, plastic tubing, and fluid vial used to make a large-volume intravenous injection; if an indwelling catheter is used, plastic tubing is temporarily placed into the vein and the fluid is injected through it

intubation (in' tŏŏ bā' shən) passage of a tube either into the trachea or the esophagus

intussusception (in' tə sə sep' shən) telescoping of one section of the intestine into the lumen of an immediately adjoining part of the intestine

investigative behavior (in ves' tə gā' tiv bi hāv' yər) the act of searching the environment using the five senses; highly developed in horses

involuntary (in väl' ən ter' ē) performed independently of the will; contravolitional, as in an involuntary muscle

iodine (ī' ə dīn') a nonmetallic chemical element; horses require it in minute amounts; a deficiency may cause a goiter

iodoform (ī ō' də fôrm) a light-yellow crystalline compound; used as an antiseptic medicine

Iomud a breed descended from the ancient Turkmene horse in Russia; exceptionally resistant to fatigue and can survive without water longer than most horses; well suited to cross-country races

ipsilateral (ip' sə lat' ər əl) on the same side of the body

iridocyclitis (ir' i dō sī klī' tis) inflamed iris and ciliary body; can be associated with periodic ophthalmia

iris (ī' ris) pigmented membrane of the eye; situated between the cornea and lens; see *eye, horse's* (illus.)

Irish Cob a breed produced by crossing the Connemara, Thoroughbred, and draft horses; stocky, with short limbs and well-developed muscles

Irish Draft a breed that originated in Ireland; a valuable farm horse; a swift coach horse with good endurance and a supple, easy action

Irish Hunter a breed resulting from the cross of the English Thoroughbred and the Irish Draft; surefooted in all kinds of terrain; very good jumpers with good stamina

Irish martingale (mär' tən gāl) a short piece of leather with a ring on either end through which the reins pass; used as a safety device to prevent the reins from flipping to the opposite side during a fall or stumble

iron (ī' ərn) 1. a white, metallic chemical vital to plant and animal life; a deficiency will cause anemia 2. a metal stirrup

iron gray coat color; coat has a blue-gray tint, resembling metal

irons stirrups on an English saddle

irrational (i rash' ən əl) unreasonable; lacking the power to reason

irregular (i reg' yə lər) the gait of the horse when one or more strides are in a different rhythm or are different lengths

---

a=fat; ā=ape; ä=car; â=bare; e=ten; ē=even; i=is; ī=bite; ō=go; ô=horn; ōō=tool; ŏŏ=look; u=up; ʉ=fur; ŋ=ring; ə=sofa

irregular bones bones that protect the central nervous system and the spinal column

irrigation (ir′ ə gā′ shən) see *lavage*

irritant (ir′ i tənt) an agent that causes irritation

ischemia (is kē′ mē ə) a deficiency in the blood supply to a body part; localized tissue anemia in a part of the body due to restricted or blocked blood supply

ischial (is′ kē əl) pertaining to the caudal part of the hip bone

ischium (is′ kē əm) bone that, together with the illium, comprises the hip

isofluorane (ī′ sō flōō′ rān) anesthetic gas commonly used in horses

isoimmune hemolytic jaundice (ī′ sō i myōōn hē mō lit′ ik jôn′ dis) a common form of jaundice found in the newborn foal; the foal's red blood cells are destroyed by antibodies ingested from the mother's colostrum; the foal becomes weak and lethargic, his body temperature drops, and the yellowish discoloration of jaundice appears on the membranes of the mouth and eyes; also called *hemolytic anemia*

isoimmunization (ī′ so im′ myōō ni zā′ shən) development of antibodies against an antigen derived from a genetically dissimilar individual of the same species

isopropyl alcohol (ī′ sə prō′ pil al′ kə häl) a sterilizing agent; may be used to sterilize veterinary tools

isotonic (ī′ sə tän′ ik) a fluid exerting the same osmotic pressure as another; when a solution is compatible with body cells and will not cause shrinking or swelling of cells

isotonic saline solution (sā′ līn sə lōō′ shən) a 0.9 percent sodium chloride (salt) solution

isotope (ī′ sə tōp′) a chemical element having the same atomic number as another, but possessing a different atomic mass

isoxsuprine (ī sok′ sōō prēn) a drug used in the treatment of navicular disease in an attempt to increase circulation to the navicular bone

Italian Heavy Draft a breed that dates back to 1860; active, good natured, hardy, and nimble in relation to size; color: dark-liver chestnut with light mane and tail, chestnut, red roan, and bay; socks and other specific markings may be present

itch (ich) see *mange*

ivermectin (ī′ ver mek′ tin) generic name for a paste form of antiparasitic agent

J

jab (jab) to jerk or pull the reins sharply

jack (jak) a male donkey or ass

jack hare the male hare

jack knife a bucking horse that crosses his forelegs and hind legs or touches them together while bucking

jackpot (jak' pät) entry fees that are pooled and awarded in a predetermined fashion; winners split all or part of the entry fees

Jacksonian epilepsy (jak sō' nē ən ep' ə lep' sē) epilepsy characterized by one-sided movements that start in one group of muscles and spread systematically to adjacent groups

jack spavin see *bone spavin*

jade (jād) an animal that has lost condition, interest, and enthusiasm, possibly due to illness, worm infestation, poor-quality feed, overtraining, or simply old age

jag see *jab*

jagger (jag' ər) 1. a pack horse or a peddler's horse 2. a trail or path used by pack horses

Janus (jan' əs) a Thoroughbred stallion imported into Virginia in 1752; most foundation Quarter Horses trace back to Janus

jaundice (jōn' dis) yellowish discoloration of the mucous membranes and the skin; can signal liver problems

Java (jä' və) a breed of pony originally from Java, one of the largest Indonesian islands; used most commonly to pull two-wheeled taxis on the island

jaw (jô) one of two bony structures in the head that supports the teeth; the lower jaw is formed by mandibular bones and the upper jaw is formed by maxillary bones

jaw, steel dust horses characterized by large, prominent jaw bones; many Quarter Horses still have this feature

jejunum (ji jōō' nəm) the middle portion of the small intestine extending from the duodenum to the ileum

jennet (jen' it) a female ass

jenny (jen' ē) a female donkey

jerk line (jʉrk līn) a single rein; originally used in driving in the western U.S.; it was fastened to the brake handle and ran through the driver's hand to the bit of the lead animal

jib (jib) a refusal by a horse to pass a certain point or object; the horse refuses to go farther and backs away

jibbah (jib' ə) the bulge on the head of an Arabian horse

jiggle (jig' əl) the ordinary gait of a cow horse, averaging about 5 mph

jinete a method of riding similar to the jockey seat; the rider is well forward with short stirrups; introduced into Spain in 711 by the Mohammedan conquest

---

a=f<u>a</u>t; ā=<u>a</u>pe; ä=c<u>a</u>r; â=b<u>a</u>re; e=t<u>e</u>n; ē=<u>e</u>ven; i=<u>i</u>s; ī=b<u>i</u>te; ō=g<u>o</u>; ô=h<u>o</u>rn; ōō=t<u>oo</u>l; ŏŏ=l<u>oo</u>k; u=<u>u</u>p; ʉ=f<u>u</u>r; ŋ=ri<u>ng</u>; ə=sof<u>a</u>

157

jock (jäk) slang for jockey

jockey (jäk' ē) 1. a professional race rider 2. the leather flaps on the side of the saddle 3. formerly a dealer in horses, especially a disreputable one

jockey agent   a person employed by a jockey to secure mounts for him

Jockey Club   registry of Thorough-bred horses

jockey for position   to attempt to find the most favorable position in a race

jockey stick   a stick fastened to the near horse and the bit of the off horse for use in driving with a single rein to prevent crowding

jockey's valet   (jäk' ēz val' ā) a jockey's assistant, whose duty is to take care of the rider's tack, assist him in dressing, carry the tack to and from the scales, and generally help the jockey through a day's racing

jodhpurs (jäd' pərz) 1.   riding breeches cut full at the hips, tapering to the knees, and tight fitting from the knees to the ankles 2. a boot high enough to cover the ankle; usually has an adjustable strap or buckle on the side

jog (jäg) a slow smooth trot in a western class

jog cart   a light, two-wheeled vehicle usually made with a slotted bottom; used for exercising horses; accomodates one or two people facing forward

jogging 1.   a slow warmup or exercise for several miles, with the horse going the wrong way on the track 2. a gait held by excitable horses who refuse to walk or trot properly

Johnson grass (jon' sən gras) sorghum plant species; this plant contains cyanide and causes difficulty breathing, cherry-red blood, and death

joint (joint) an articulation; the place of union or junction between two or more bones of the skeleton

joint block   see blocks

joint fluid   fluid found inside the joint that lubricates and provides nutrition for the joint cartilage

joint ill   inflammation of a joint due to the presence of bacteria or related infective agents

joint mouse   a small chip of bone enclosed in the joint capsule

joint owner   the ownership of a horse in the names of two or more people

judge (juj) a person appointed to determine the winner of an event, competition, or part of a competition

jugging (jug' iŋ) the administration by the jugular vein of a reasonably large quantity of a concentrated mixture generally consisting of amino acids, electrolytes, vitamins, and glucose; this practice is believed by some to allow a horse to perform better; actual results are questionable

jughead 1.   a horse perceived to be lacking intelligence 2. a horse with a large, ugly head

jugular groove (jug' yŏŏ lər grōōv) the groove on each side of the neck just above the windpipe; location of the jugular vein; see points of the horse (illus.)

jugular pulse   the rhythmic expansion of the jugular vein of the neck that may be felt or seen

jugular veins   large veins located on either side of the horse's windpipe in the underside of the neck; carry blood from the head and neck to the chest

jump   (jump) **1.** a pack that has been hunting slowly, but suddenly presses its quarry, is said to have jumped it **2.** an obstacle, either natural or artificial, used in cross-country, hurdles, steeplechase, hunting, and show jumping to test the ability of horse and rider to ride other than on the flat

jumped into canter   when, in transition from trot to canter, the horse makes a stride as though about to jump

jumper   (jum' pər) any horse trained to compete over jumps such as a steeplechaser or show jumper

jump jockey   a jockey who races horses over hurdles or steeplechase fences

jump-off   in the event of a tie, a course may be altered and the two tied horses asked to jump again

jump seat saddle   a saddle with a high cantle that inclines the rider's weight forward to keep in balance with the horse when going over jumps; some may have knee rolls to help maintain balance

junior   (jōōn' yər) **1.** a rider less than eighteen years of age as of January 1 **2.** designation for show horses in performance classes that are five years of age and younger

junior exhibitor   (ig zib' i' tər) any rider in a competitive event seventeen years of age or younger

junior horse   any horse five years old or younger; will vary according to association

junior hunter   a horse of any age ridden by an exhibitor eighteen years or younger

Jutland   (jut' lənd) a medium to heavy breed from Denmark; the heavy type is similar to the Shire, while the medium type is developed from the heavy type by crossing with the Cleveland Bay and the Thoroughbred

a=fat; ā=ape; ä=car; â=bare; e=ten; ē=even; i=is; ī=bite; ō=go; ô=horn; ōō=tool; ŏŏ=look; u=up; ʉ=fur; ŋ=ring; ə=sofa

K

kabakhi   a Russian horse sport comprised of archery at full gallop

Kabardin   (kə bär′ din) a breed that originated in the Caucasus in Russia; well suited to mountainous areas; a goodnatured animal with strength and endurance

kak   cowboy slang for saddle

kallidin   (kal′ i din) factors formed by a group of enzymes produced by the body that maintain dilation of the blood vessels in the inflammatory process

Karabair   a very old breed from the central Asian mountains; used for saddle or harness; gray is the predominant color

Karabakh   a Russian breed that lives in the mountains that separate Azerbaijan from northwest Iran; these horses have adapted very well to the harsh conditions of their environment; average height: 14.1 hands

Karacabey   a breed that originated in Turkey; derived from crosses of local brood mares and imported Nonius stallions; known for good conformation, versatility, and endurance

Kathiawari   a breed that appears to have started when native ponies bred with Arabs that swam ashore from a cargo ship that wrecked off the shore of India; attractive appearance, hardy, and versatile; average height: 14 hands

Kazakh   a breed of ponies that origi-

nate from Russia; average height: 12.2–13.2 hands

keep   (kēp) a grass field used for grazing; also called *pasture*

keeper, free   a piece of leather seamed together at the ends in the shape of a rectangle that encircles two or more straps of leather; its purpose is to keep the straps together neatly and yet allow any movement necessary

keeper, stationary   a keeper is stitched to one strap in a fixed position, the second strap is inserted through the stationary keeper and is held in place

keeping a tight rein   restraining the horse by applying continual and stronger pressure than normal to the bit

keeping the rein   maintaining light contact with the bit through the reins

keg shoes   the most commonly used manufactured or preformed horseshoes

keloid   (kē′ loid) a sharply elevated, irregularly shaped, enlarging scar

Kelso   (kel′ sō) this horse won 1.9 million dollars in the 1950s; selected as Horse of the Year for five years

kennel   (ken′ əl) the fox's lair; also known as *earth* or *den*

Kentucky Oaks   (kən tuk′ ē ōks) a race for three-year-old Thoroughbred fillies

keratin   (ker′ ə tin) an insoluble protein that is the principal constituent of the epidermis, hair, nails, horny tissues, and the enamel of teeth; the sulfur-containing protein comprising the structure of hair and hoof

keratitis (ker′ ə tīt′ is) inflammation of the sensitive transparent cornea

keratoma (ker′ ə tō′ mə) a horny tumor on the inner surface of the wall of a horse's hoof

ketamine (kēt′ ə mēn) injectable drug used for short-duration anesthesia in horses

ketone bodies (kē′ tōn bäd′ ēz) normal metabolic products; acetone, acetoacetic acid, beta-hydroxybutyric acid

keyhole race (kē′ hōl rās) a race run over a course that is laid out with a limed keyhole on the ground

kick (kik) movement by a horse of the back or front leg or legs; intent is to hit a person or other object

kicker (kik′ ər) a horse prone to kicking people and/or other horses; see *stable kicker*

kidney (kid′ nē) one of the main organs involved in the removal of waste products through urine, termed *excretion,* from the body of the horse; a filtering system for the blood

kidney link the metal carrier on the lower portion of the harness collar; used to hold the breastplate in position; see *harness parts B* (illus.)

kidney pad a cowboy's derisive term for an English saddle

kimberwick bit (kim′ bʉr wik bit) a combination of snaffle and very mild curb action bit that does not have curb shanks; the kimberwick bit has loops

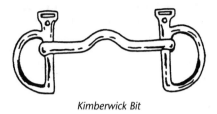

Kimberwick Bit

at the top of the rings for the bridle and curb chain attachment

kimblewick (kim′ bəl wik) see *kimberwick*

Kladruber a breed originating in Czechoslovakia; takes its name from the royal stud at Kladruby; the famous white horse of Czechoslovakia; this breed has remained extremely pure; main use was as a carriage horse; average height: 16.2–17 hands; color: gray or black

knack (nak) an old, worn-out, or useless horse

knacker (nak′ ər) a person who buys and slaughters horses, generally for pet food

knee (nē) the joint between the forearm and the cannon bone; also known as the *carpal joint;* see *points of the horse* (illus.)

knee sprung a condition when the knees protrude too far forward; the horse stands with his knees slightly bent forward

knockdown (nok′ doun) when the rail or the top element of a jump is displaced by the horse during a jump

---

a=f<u>a</u>t; ā=<u>a</u>pe; ä=c<u>a</u>r; â=b<u>a</u>re; e=t<u>e</u>n; ē=<u>e</u>ven; i=<u>i</u>s; ī=b<u>i</u>te; ō=g<u>o</u>; ô=h<u>o</u>rn; ōō=t<u>oo</u>l; ŏŏ=l<u>oo</u>k; u=<u>u</u>p; ʉ=f<u>u</u>r; ŋ=ri<u>ng</u>; ə=sof<u>a</u>

knock-knees (nok′ nēz) in foals, when viewing the horse from the front, the knees bend in toward each other; sometimes due to dietary deficiency; also called *epiphysitis;* see *conformation comparisons, front limb* (illus.)

knowledge bump (näl′ ij bump) the point of the cranium

Konik the Polish name for this breed means "little horse"; this breed has played an important part in the formation of numerous other breeds of Polish and Russian horses and ponies; average height: 12.3–13.3

hands; color: mouse dun and dun with eel stripe, lower limbs dark or black, sometimes with zebra markings

kumiss (kōō′ mis) a drink made from fermented mare's milk that may be distilled to produce a strong alcoholic spirit; common in the Mongolian area of China

kur (kŏŏr) musical freestyle in dressage

Kustanair (kŏŏ stä nər′) a general-purpose Russian breed used for riding and draft work

L

labial (lā′ bē əl) pertaining to the lip

laboratory diagnosis (lab′ rə tōr′ ē dī əg nō′ sis) diagnosis based on the findings of various laboratory tests

labored (lā′ bərd) any gait, pace, or stride of a horse where the horse has to work harder than he should in order to complete the particular action; lack of flow and balance

laceration (las′ ə rā′ shən) a jagged tear or wound

lace strings see *saddle string*

lacking collection (lak′ iŋ kə lek′ shən) when the amount of control and finesse shown by horse and/or rider is insufficient

lacking rhythm (rith′ əm) a gait with irregular, uneven strides

lacrimation (lak′ rə mā′ shən) the secretion and discharge of tears

lactase (lak′ tās) the enzyme in intestinal fluids that breaks down the milk sugar, lactose, to form glucose and galactose, both of which are then absorbed into the blood of the horse for conveyance throughout the horse's body

lactating mare (lak′ tāt iŋ mâr) a mare producing milk

lactation (lak′ tā′ shən) secretion of milk by the mammary gland

lactic acid (lak′ tik as′ id) an organic acid normally present in muscle tissue; produced by anaerobic muscle metabolism or produced in carbohydrate matter, usually by bacterial fermentation

lactic dehydrogenase (lak′ tik dē′ hī droj ən ās) a tissue enzyme; the levels of which are elevated in the blood following either strenuous exercise and/or tissue damage

Lactobacilus acidophilus (lak′ tō bə sil′ lus as′ i dof′ i ləs) milk-digesting bacteria normally found in all young mammals

lad (lad) someone who works in a stable of any kind; also called a *groom*

lair (lâr) where the fox lies in the daytime; den

lamella (lə mel′ ə) a thin plate, as of bone

lameness (lām′ nis) the affected foot is favored when standing or during travel; an abnormality of gait or movement

laminae (lam′ ə nə) interlocking leaves of sensitive and insensitive tissue that connect the hoof wall and the coffin bone

laminar (lam′ ə nər) pertaining to the laminae

laminitis (lam′ ə nīt′ is) inflammation of the sensitive laminae under the horny wall of the hoof; may be a very painful condition; acute laminitis refers to a disturbance with rapid

---

a=fat; ā=ape; ä=car; â=bare; e=ten; ē=even; i=is; ī=bite; ō=go; ô=horn; ōō=tool; ŏŏ=look; u=up; ʉ=fur; ŋ=ring; ə=sofa

163

onset and brief duration; chronic laminitis is a persistent, long-term disturbance; may result in founder

lampas (lam′ pəs) the membranes of the upper hard palate of the mouth, just behind the upper incisor teeth

lamp iron (lamp ī′ ərn) holder for traveling lamplight; see *carriage parts* (illus.)

Landais a breed of pony native to southwestern France; numbers have dropped and some fear it may become extinct

landau (lan′ dou) ˙a four-wheeled carriage drawn by a pair of horses; has two seats, each with folding tops; designed to carry four people

landing side (lan′ diŋ sīd) the far side of an obstacle where a horse lands after making a jump

laparotomy (lap′ ə rät′ ə mē) a surgical incision through the abdominal wall

lapped (lapt) to be one full lap behind another horse during a race

large colon (lärj kō′ lən) extends from the cecum to the small colon

large intestine (in tes′ tin) the lower portion of the digestive system consisting of the cecum, colon, rectum, and anal canal

lariat (lar′ ē it) from the Spanish word meaning rope; a lasso; a twenty-foot rope, usually about one-half inch in diameter with a running noose; used for catching cattle

larking (lärk′ iŋ) jumping fences unnecessarily in fox hunting; a practice often indulged in by the type of hunter who hunts in order to jump

larkspur (lärk′ spur) a plant that grows two to six feet in height; has a hollow stem and spurred blue flowers; often found in thick clusters on hillsides and meadows; all parts of all species are toxic

larva (lär′ və) wormlike form of a newly hatched insect; an early developmental stage

laryngeal hemiplegia (lə rin′ jē al hem′ e plē′ jē ə) paralysis of the larynx; also known as *roaring*

laryngeal ventriculotomy (lə rin′ jē al ven′ trik yōō lot′ ō mē) surgical stripping of the laryngeal ventricles to correct roaring

laryngitis (lar′ ən jī′ tis) inflammation of the larynx; a condition accompanied by dryness and soreness of the throat and coughing

larynx (lar′ iŋks) the structure of muscle and cartilage located at the top of the trachea and below the root of the tongue; centered just behind the lower jaw bones; produces voice

laser (lā′ zər) a device producing a narrow, focused, very intense light beam; used to cut tissue surgically

lash (lash) the end of a stock whip or longeing whip; originally made of hair from a horse's tail; sometimes made of a piece of silk or a synthetic material

lasix (lā′ siks) the trade name for furosemide; a drug having strong, prompt, and short-lived diuretic action; tends to lower blood pressure, especially in the lungs; sometimes used to prevent bleeders in racehorses

late behind   (lāt bi hīnd') rather than completing the flying change in the moment of suspension, the foreleg may come first, followed by the hind leg a stride or half stride later; also called *late change*

late change   (lāt chānj) see *late behind*

latent   (lāt' ənt) concealed; not manifest; potential

latent learning   a type of learning that has been assimilated but has yet to be demonstrated

latent period   the length of time from the administration of an injection and the response to that injection; applicable whether the injection is hormonal, antibiotic, or antibody producing

lateral   (lat' ər əl) of or relating to the side; anatomic term meaning away from the midline; toward the outside as opposed to toward the midline; lateral aids are all applied on one particular side of the horse

lateral aids   (ādz) the rider's aids used on the same side at the same time; hand and leg used on the same side; e.g., left rein, left leg

lateral cartilage   (kär' tə lij) cartilage on the sides of the coffin bone that extends above the coronary band

lateral digital extensor muscles   (dij' i təl ik sten' sər mus' əlz) muscles at the side of the back legs; function to extend and straighten the leg; see *muscular system* (illus.)

lateral flexion   (flek' shən) side-to-side arcing or bending characteristic of a horse doing circular work

lateral gait   (gāt) movement of the legs and feet in lateral pairs, as in a pace

lateral movement   (mōōv' mənt) sideways movement; work in which the horse moves with the forehand and haunches on different tracks; examples include shoulder in, haunches in, haunches out, and half passes

laterals   a second set of incisors located between the central and corner incisors; usually called *intermediates*

lateral suppling   (sup' liŋ) a series of exercises for the horse that consists of circles, serpentines, half turns, turns on the forehand and the quarters; aimed at increasing the flexion and movement in the horse's sides

latigo   (lät' i gō) 1. a cinch strap; a Spanish word meaning the end of every strap that must be passed through a buckle 2. straps that fasten the cinch of the western saddle; very strong, supple type of leather; see *western saddle* (illus.)

Latvian   (lät' vē ən) a Russian breed used for farm work or as a saddle horse; strong with good endurance

lavage   (lə väzh') the washing out of a cavity or wound with a stream of fluid

laxative   (lak' sə tiv) an agent that acts to promote evacuation of the bowel

lay off   (lā ôf) a betting term to hedge or reduce a bet by wagering or betting the other way as the odds change

a=f<u>a</u>t; ā=<u>a</u>pe; ä=c<u>a</u>r; â=b<u>a</u>re; e=t<u>e</u>n; ē=<u>e</u>ven; i=<u>i</u>s; ī=b<u>i</u>te; ō=g<u>o</u>; ô=h<u>o</u>rn; ōō=t<u>oo</u>l; ŏŏ=l<u>oo</u>k; u=<u>u</u>p; ʉ=f<u>u</u>r; ŋ=ri<u>ng</u>; ə=sof<u>a</u>

lead (lēd) a specific footfall pattern at the canter or lope in which the legs on the inside of a circle reach farther forward than the legs on the outside; when cantering to the left in a circle the horse should be on the left lead, his left foreleg reaching beyond the right and his left hind leg reaching farther forward than his right hind

leaders (lē' dərz) the head team of horses in a four-, six-, or eight-horse hitch

leading rein see *opening rein*

lead line 1. a chain, rope, or strap or combination thereof used for leading a horse 2. horse show class in which young riders are mounted and are led by an adult handler

lead pad (led pad) a piece of equipment under the saddle in which thin slabs of lead may be inserted to bring the rider's weight up to that assigned to a horse in a specific race

lead rein the rein that passes from the lead horse of a driving team to the coachman

lead strap a strap or rope attached to the halter for leading; also called *lead line* or *lead rope*

leaning on the bit a horse exerting pressure against the reins; too much weight on the forehand

leaping horn the lower horn on the near side of a sidesaddle

lease (lēs) a legal document that allows one or more persons, other than the owner, to use a horse by the prior payment of an agreed sum of money for a specified period of time as written in the lease

leather-hooded stirrup (leth' ər hŏŏd' id stʉr' əp) a leather stirrup cover extending around the front and sides of the stirrup; protects the rider's boots from brush, grass, cold, etc.; see *tapadera*

leather roll binding (rōl bīnd' iŋ) an early name for the Cheyenne roll

leathers (leth' erz) the straps running from the saddle to the irons on an English saddle; the adjustment straps on a western saddle under the stirrup fenders

leech (lēch) a blood-sucking external parasite that resides in fresh water

left at the post a racehorse jumping from the starting gates later than all the other horses in the same race

left behind a rider who is thrown back in the saddle on a horse while the horse is jumping; the rider has not adjusted his weight and center of gravity with that of the horse by moving forward as the horse takes off to jump

left-hand saddle a saddle with the rope strap on the near side of the fork

left lead when the left front foot and left rear foot lead on the canter

leg brace (leg brās) a soothing liniment or lotion used on the legs to cool and tone up the legs before or after exercise; usually contains water, alcohol, or menthol

leg edema (leg i dē' mə) fluid accumulation in the tissues of the leg, the result of an insufficiency of the muscular activity needed to "pump" excess tissue fluid back into circulation

legging up   progressive workouts designed to stress the weakest systems of the horse without overdoing it; the training sessions are gradually lengthened and intensified until the desired level of fitness is achieved

leg roll   a padded roll on the forward side of the saddle flap on an English saddle on some spring seat saddles

leg swing   an outward swing of the foreleg due to a popped knee or arthritis; because of the pain, the horse swings his leg out and around instead of bending the knee as he walks

legumes   (leg′ yo͞omz) plants such as alfalfa and clover that are higher in protein than grasses; any group of plants of the pea family that store nitrogen in the soil

leg up   to assist a rider into the saddle by someone holding the rider's bent left leg and helping him up as he springs into the saddle

leg wraps   cloth wraps used on the lower legs; protect the legs when the horse is being transported; help reduce swelling and inflammation

leg yielding   exercises designed to teach the horse to move away from leg pressure

length   (leŋkth̲) one of the measurements of distance by which a horse may be said to win a race; the length of a horse's head and body

lengthened   frame   (leŋk′ thənd frām) increased distance from nose to hocks as occurs during the transition from a collected to an extended gait

lengthening   insufficient   (leŋk′ th̲ən′ iŋ in′ sə fish̲′ ənt) any change of pace when the horse does not show enough increase in the length of the stride

lens   (lenz) eye structure that focuses light rays entering through the pupil and forms an image on the retina, the transparent structure in the eye, lying behind the iris; see *eye, horse's* (illus.)

leopard pattern   (lep′ ərd pat′ ərn) dark spots on a white coat; the spots are round or oval

leptospirosis   (lep′ tō spī rō′ sis) infection by *Leptospira* bacteria; systemic disease characterized by red cell destruction, kidney disease, and inflammation of the eye

lesion   (lē′ z̲h̲ən) internal, visible change in the structure, color, or size of an organ or part of the body; area of damaged tissue; any abnormal change in the structure of a part due to injury or disease

lethal   (lē′ th̲əl) a genetic factor that causes death of the animal, either during prenatal life, at birth, or later in life

lethal white   (hwīt) **1.** low fertility first reported in horses of the Frederiksborg breed in Denmark **2.** genetic defect that causes premature death in the fetus or newborn foal; associated with Paints and Pintos

lethargy   (leth̲′ ər jē) condition of drowsiness or indifference

letters   designated points in a dressage ring; see *dressage ring*

---

a=f<u>a</u>t; ā=<u>a</u>pe; ä=c<u>a</u>r; â=b<u>a</u>re; e=t<u>e</u>n; ē=<u>e</u>ven;
i=<u>i</u>s; ī=b<u>i</u>te; ō=g<u>o</u>; ô=h<u>o</u>rn; o͞o=t<u>oo</u>l;
o͝o=l<u>oo</u>k; u=<u>u</u>p; ʉ=f<u>u</u>r; ŋ=ri<u>ng</u>; ə=sof<u>a</u>

leucoderma (lōō′ kə dʉr′ mə) white patches that appear on hairless parts of the horse; an acquired type of localized loss of melanin pigmentation of the skin

leukemia (lōō kē′ mē ə) an increased number of circulating white blood cells, usually due to a form of cancer

leukocytes (lōō′ kə sīts) white blood cells or corpuscles

leukocytosis (lōō′ kə sī tō′ sis) a temporary increase in the number of leukocytes in the blood due to infection, inflammation, etc.

leukopenia (lōō′ kə pē′ nē ə) an abnormally low level of white blood cells

leukosis (lōō kō′ sis) a serious disease of the blood-forming organs; characterized by marked increases in the number of white blood cells in the circulating blood, together with enlargement and quick growth of lymphoid tissue of the spleen, lymph glands, and bone marrow

levade (lə väd′) a dressage movement wherein the horse balances on his haunches while maintaining an immobile position; the horse rears, drawing his forefeet in, while the hind-quarters are deeply bent at the haunches

levelheaded (lev′ əl hed′ id) a horse that is not excited easily; calm and quiet even under unusual situations

liberty horses (lib′ ər tē hôrs′ əs) horses that perform without personal contact from a rider or handler, as in circus acts

libido (li bē′ dō) sex drive

lice (līs) plural of louse; two species infest the horse: bloodsucking and biting; usually transmitted by direct contact

lidocaine (li′ də kān) a local anesthetic; used to numb regions of the body for pain relief or surgical procedures

lift a horse when a rider snatches or pulls at the reins as his horse takes off at a fence in the incorrect belief that the action will assist the horse

ligament (lig′ ə mənt) attaches bone to bone; a band of fibrous tissue that connects bone or cartilage

ligamentum nuchae (lig′ ə men′ tum nŏŏ ka) the ligament running from the poll to the withers; helps to support the horse's head

ligate (lī′ gāt) to tie off a vessel or part with a suture of catgut, steel, silk, etc.

light (līt) 1. a paler shade of a color; not dark 2. not heavy in movement or weight

light bay coat color; same as bay, with a primary body color of light yellow-brown

light horse 1. horses produced to meet the specific purposes of riding or racing; height: 14–17 hands; weight: 900–1,400 pounds; capable of more action and greater speed than draft horses 2. a horse that responds to very light pressure from the legs and reins

light rider a well-balanced rider

limbs (limz) any of the four legs

limbus (lim′ bəs) the border around

the eye where the clear cornea joins the white sclera

lime   (līm) calcium oxide used as a disinfectant

limestone   (līm' stōn) a mineral that may be added to feed to supply calcium

lime water (līm' wô' tər) a mixture of calcium hydroxide and water in the proportion of 1:700; used as an antacid

limited   (lim' i tid) 1. a type of class with entry restrictions for the horse and/or the rider 2. related to prior winnings at specified shows; may be based on the number of blue ribbons or monetary earnings

linea alba   (lin' ē ə al' bə) the tendinous medial line of the ventral abdominal wall between the pairs of abdominal muscles

linear dominance hierarchy   (lin' ē ər däm' ə nens hī' ə rär' kē) the process of horses interacting in a group; see *linear hierarchy*

linear hierarchy   (lin' ē ər hī' ə rär' kē) the social order established through fighting for the boss position, second position, and on down the line to the last individual; once the hierarchy is decided, fighting greatly diminishes

linebacker   (līn' bak' ər) an animal having a stripe of distinctive color along the spine

linebreeding   (līn brēd' iŋ) producing offspring from parents having common ancestry

lines   (līnz') 1. leather webbing or

rope attached to the bit or bits; used for control and direction in driving; sometimes called *reins* 2. of a certain family, as in bloodlines

lingual   (liŋ' gwəl) pertaining to the tongue

liniment   (lin' ə mənt) an oily, soapy, or alcoholic liquid preparation used on the skin and applied with friction

linseed   (lin' sēd) the seed of flax generally used in the form of linseed jelly, oil, or tea; used both as a laxative and to improve the condition and gloss of the coat

lipid   (lip' id) an organic substance containing fat; an important component of living cells

lipids   see *fats*

Lipizzan Association of North America   a registry for American and European purebred horses with ancestry traceable to official European stud farms' original and approved breeding stock

Lipizzaner   (lip' it sä' nər) horses that originated in the sixth century; color: gray with a few bays; height: 15 hands; generally known as the breed that performs at the Spanish Riding School

Lipizzaner   melanoma benign tumor found on gray horses' skin

lipoid   (lip' oid) fatlike; resembling fat

lipoma   (li pō' mə) localized fat tissue accumulation; a benign fatty tumor

---

a=f<u>a</u>t; ā=<u>a</u>pe; ä=c<u>a</u>r; â=b<u>a</u>re; e=t<u>e</u>n; ē=<u>e</u>ven; i=<u>i</u>s; ī=b<u>i</u>te; ō=g<u>o</u>; ô=h<u>o</u>rn; ōō=t<u>oo</u>l; ŏŏ=l<u>oo</u>k; u=<u>u</u>p; ʉ=f<u>u</u>r; ŋ=ri<u>ng</u>; ə=sof<u>a</u>

lip strap   a leather strap that runs between the shanks of a curb or pelham and through a ring on the curb chain for the purposes of keeping the chain in the curb groove and discouraging a horse from playing with the sides of the bit with his lower lip

liquefaction   (lik′ wə fak′ shən) the conversion of material into a liquid form

list   (list) coat marking; a dorsal band of black hairs that extends from the withers backward

listeriosis   (lis ter′ ē ō′ sis) infection caused by bacteria of the genus *Listeria*

Lithuanian Heavy Draft   (lith′ ŏŏ ā′ nē ən hev′ ē draft) a breed developed toward the end of the nineteenth century; influenced by Zhmud, a Finnish horse, and Swedish Ardennes; known to be quiet and have an attractive action at the walk and at the trot; color: chestnut with flaxen mane and tail, bay, black, gray, and roan

live foal   (līv fōl) a foal that stands and nurses

liver   (liv′ ər) abdominal organ that is responsible for detoxification, production of bile, metabolism of fats, and filtration of blood

liver chestnut   coat color; chestnut with a primary coat color of very dark reddish brown; a dark chestnut coat with cream-colored mane and tail

Liverpool bit   (liv′ ər pōōl bit) a bit that has a straight bar mouthpiece and shanks; can be used as a snaffle or a curb; used on heavy harness and plow horses; see *harness parts E* (illus.)

livery   (liv′ ər ē) the distinctive dress worn by professional members of the hunt staff

livery stable   (stā′ bəl) an establishment where privately owned horses are kept, exercised, and generally looked after for an agreed fee

lobe   (lōb) a well-defined portion of any organ

lock   (läk) in carts and carriages, the amount of a vehicle's turning ability; depending on the design of the vehicle, the front wheels may or may not turn freely

locking of the hind legs   when the kneecap becomes fixed; locking the stifle in such a position that it prevents flexion of the hind limb

lockjaw   (läk′ jô) a common term for tetanus; a disease in which one symptom is the inability to open the jaws

locoweed   (lō′ kō wēd) a poisonous weed that grows in clumps four to twenty-four inches high; has flowers that resemble sweetpeas; blossoms may be blue, purple, yellow, or white; all parts of the plant are poisonous and the plant is dangerous throughout the year, even when it is dried

loin   (loin) the portion of the spinal column devoid of ribs, between the back and the croup; the muscular area that lies between the back and the croup; the weakest part of the topline; see *points of the horse* (illus.)

loin strap   the harness strap running from the backstrap at the loin area to the breeching strap; see *harness parts A* (illus.)

Lokai   a breed that originated in Russia; serves well as a saddle horse and a pack horse; height: up to 14.2 hands

long   (lôŋ) relates to the latter part of the year from birth; a long yearling would be close to his second year; a term used only with young horses

long coupled   too much space between the last rib and the point of the hip

long-day breeder   the mare's reproductive efficiency is best when there are long days; late spring and early summer are the best breeding times

longe   (lunj) to work a horse in a circle on a longe line around the trainer

Longeing

longe line (lunj līn) a web line, about twenty to thirty feet, used in training and exercising a horse; a handler stands in the center of a circle and the horse travels around the circumference at the walk, trot, and canter

longeing cavesson (lunj' iŋ kav' i sən) a leather or nylon headstall with a weighted noseband with metal rings for attachment of the longe line

longeing whip   typically has a stock about four feet long and a lash six to eight feet long; used when exercising the horse in longeing

long horse   a horse bred to run a mile or more, such as the Thoroughbred

longissimus dorsi   (län jis i məs dôr sī) longest muscle of the back, paralleling and next to the backbone

longitudinal flexion   (lon' ji tōōd' ən əl flek' shən) bending that takes place in the vertical plane as opposed to lateral flexion, which takes place in the horizontal plane

long lines   webbing reins about forty feet long attached to the bridle; enables the horse to be schooled or exercised in circles around the user without actually being ridden

long pastern bone   first phalanx; see *hoof* (illus.)

long reining   the English term for ground driving; working the bridled horse on a pair of long lines in front of and around the handler

long slow distance   a three- to six-month phase of aerobic conditioning over increasing distances; improves oxygen interchange in the lungs and in the cells, also strengthens bones, joints, tendons, ligaments, and cartilage

long trot   moving a horse at a trot lengthened, free, extended trot

long yearling   (yēr' ling) a horse more than one year old but not yet two years old

loop seat   (lōōp sēt) a full seat; common in the early 1900s; has squares or

a=fat; ā=ape; ä=car; â=bare; e=ten; ē=even; i=is; ī=bite; ō=go; ô=horn; ōō=tool; ŏŏ=look; u=up; ʉ=fur; ŋ=ring; ə=sofa

rectangles of leather cut out of the seat just over the area where the stirrup leathers fit over the tree in the stirrup leather grooves

loops not equal   in a riding pattern with several loops intended to be equal, the horse and rider execute the pattern with loops of varying size

lope   (lōp) a slow to medium-fast collected canter exhibited in western classes; a three-beat gait with an initiating hind leg followed by a diagonal pair (including the leading hind leg) and finally by the leading foreleg

lopped ears   (läpd' ērs) ears that are carried in a loose, inattentive, sluggish manner

lordosis   (lôr dō' sis) excessive swayback of the horse

lorimer   (lôr' ə mər) a person who makes the metal parts of saddlery and harness such as bits, curb chains, and stirrup irons

lost rhythm   (lôst rith' əm) a break in the rhythmic stride of a gait

lugger   (lug' ər) a horse that leans on the bit and tries to go faster than the rider wishes

lugging in or out   a horse that is pulling to the inside or the outside of the rider's intended course

lumbar vertebrae   (lum' bär vʉr tə brā) pertaining to the loins; the part of the back between the thorax and pelvis; see *skeletal system* (illus.)

lumen   (lōō' mən) the cavity or channel within a tube or tubular organ; inner open space of an intestine

lung   (luŋ) one of the two respiratory organs in the thorax; oxygenates the blood and removes carbon dioxide

lunge line   (lunj līn) see *longe line*

lungworms   (lung' wʉrmz) slender roundworm parasites that spend the final phase of their life cycle in the air passages of the horse's lungs; cause bronchi to become inflamed and irritated; rare in the U.S.

Lusitano   a breed famous for its role in Portuguese bullfights; present in declining numbers; color: gray, chestnut, and brown

lutalyse   (lōōt' ə līs) a hormone used to regulate reproductive functions in the mare

luteinizing hormone   (lōōt' ē in īz' iŋ hôr' mōn) a hormone that comes from the pituitary and regulates the corpus luteum in the female and testosterone secretion in the male

luxation   (luk' sā shən) dislocation

Lyme disease   (līm di zēz') bacterial infection spread by deer ticks; infects humans as well as domesticated animals, including horses; symptoms include lethargy, fever, swollen joints, shifting leg lameness, and sensitive skin

lymph   (limf) a transparent yellowish liquid containing mostly white blood cells and derived from tissue fluids; the fluid content of the lymphatic system

lymphangitis   (lim' fən jīt' əs) a bacterial infection of the lymph system causing swelling of the legs

lymph glands (limf glandz) cellular filters along the lymph vessels in which immune cells interact with foreign material

lymph nodes (nōdz) cellular filters along the lymph vessels that collect fluids from between the cells and return them to circulation

lymphocytes (lim' fə sīts') blood cells that produce proteins that result in immunity

lymphosarcoma (lim' fō sar kō' mə) a general term applied to malignant neoplastic disorders of lymphoid tissue

lymph system (sis' təm) a network of thin-walled tubes that collects fluids from between the cells and returns them to the bloodstream, near the heart; important in fighting infections and maintaining the body's fluid balance

lysine (lī' sēn) an amino acid necessary for growth and milk production

---

a=fat; ā=ape; ä=car; â=bare; e=ten; ē=even;
i=is; ī=bite; ō=go; ô=horn; ōō=tool;
ŏŏ=look; u=up; ʉ=fur; ŋ=ring; ə=sofa

M

macrophage (mak' rə fāj) a cell that devours foreign particles and the debris with which it comes in contact

maggot (mag' ət) the soft-bodied, grublike larvae of the fly

magnesium (mag nē' zē əm) a mineral essential for normal skeletal development

maiden (mād' ən) 1. a mare that has never been bred 2. a racehorse that has never won a recognized race

maiden race a race in which only horses that have never won a race may be entered

mail coach (māl kōch) a large, closed vehicle with four wheels and two facing seats used for carrying both mail and travelers; drawn by two or four horses

Mail Coach

maintenance ration (mān' tə nəns rash' ən) a ration that provides an animal with all necessary food components when that animal is at rest or not doing any work; designed to keep the horse in the same physical condition, not allowing weight gain or loss

make a book to to wager or bet on a number of horses in a race; to lay a fixed sum of money against all the runners in a race so that no matter what the race result, the bettor will receive more money than he bet

make the weight when a rider or jockey weighs in at the correct weight for the race or event

malabsorption (mal' əb zôrp' shən) impaired intestinal absorption of nutrients

Malapolski a Polish breed; varies in type according to the region in which the horse is bred; light, calm, and balanced; an excellent jumper

malignant (mə lig' nənt) tending to become progressively worse and usually results in death

mallenders (mal' en derz) an eczemalike condition of the skin caused by a protozoan parasite; there is some evidence that susceptibility to the parasite is inherited

malnutrition (mal' nōō trish' ən) a nutritional disorder caused by either an imbalanced or insufficient diet; may be due to poor absorption and utilization of nutrients

malocclusion (mal' ə klōō' zhən) when the teeth of the upper jaw don't meet the lower jaw in position, resulting in uneven wear of the teeth

mammary gland (mam' ər ē gland) a gland that secretes milk

mammillary (ma mil' ər ē) pertaining to or resembling a nipple

mandible (man' də bəl) the hinged lower jaw; see *skeletal system* (illus.)

mane (mān) the long hair growing on the top of the neck from the poll to the withers

mane and tail comb a small, long-toothed comb used for straightening

or pulling the mane and tail

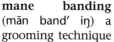

mane banding (mān band' iŋ) a grooming technique

Mane and Tail Comb

using tiny rubber bands to make thirty or forty little pony tails out of the mane

manege (ma nezh') a riding hall used to school a horse and rider

mane hogged when most of the mane has been cut off; sometimes done by performance riders to keep the reins from getting tangled in the mane; also tends to make a thick neck look thinner

mane tamer a cover put over the mane; wrapped around the horse's neck to train the mane to lie neatly to one side

Mane Tamer

manganese (maŋ' gə nēs) a mineral required in very small amounts for the formation of cartilage; symptoms of deficiency include bent bones, deafness, and deformed foals

mange (mānj) communicable dermatitis of humans and animals caused by minute mites that burrow into the skin to feed, live, and reproduce

manger tie (mānj' ər tī) a basic knot used to tie a horse safely; designed so the horse cannot pull free, but one pull on the loose end of the lead rope frees the horse

mania (mā' nē ə) a mental disorder characterized by an expansive emotional state and increased motor activity

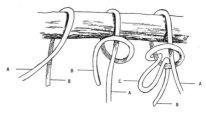
Manger Tie

Manipuri (mun' i pŏŏr' ē) an ancient breed of pony commonly used for polo in India; well-balanced features, fast with good endurance; height: 11–13 hands

man killer a dangerous, vicious, and nasty horse with no respect for man

man-made material fence a fence made of newly developed materials such as rubber and plastic; care should be taken to ensure that if any of the material is ingested by a horse it will not cause damage

manners (man' ərz) the energetic yet cooperative attitude of a horse

marathon (mar' ə thon') an organized, competitive drive over a set course at a standard time for all; chiefly a test of fitness and suitability

march fracture (märch frak' chər) fracture of a bone of the lower extremity; developed after repeated stress

mare (mâr) a mature female four years or older; in Thoroughbreds, five years or older

Maremmana a breed that originated in Italy as a mount for cattle

a=fat; ā=ape; ä=car; â=bare; e=ten; ē=even; i=is; ī=bite; ō=go; ô=horn; ōō=tool; ŏŏ=look; u=up; ʉ=fur; ŋ=ring; ə=sofa

herdsmen; able to handle rough terrain and poor weather conditions

mark (märk) a horse's best winning time

markings (märk' iɳz) any visual change from the predominant coat color of the horse; markings are generally classified as congenital (i.e., present at birth) and acquired (generated after birth) and are permanent in nature; see illustration

marrow (mar' ō) soft red or yellow substance found in the cavities within bones; consists of fat, blood vessels, and blood-containing spaces

martingale, running (mär' tən gāl') a Y-shaped strap with metal rings on the ends through which the reins pass; the other end runs between the horse's front legs and attaches to the girth; helps prevent the horse from tossing and raising his head

mascot (mas' kät) a companion for the horse; the most common mascots are ponies, goats, dogs, and cats

mask (mask) the fox's head

massage (mə säzh') the therapeutic rubbing and kneading of the body tissues to loosen adhesion and relax tense muscles, etc.

masseter muscle (ma sē' tər mus' əl) large muscle in the angle of the lower jaw; it raises the jaw in chewing; see *muscular system* (illus.)

mastication (mas' tə kā' shən) the process of chewing food

mastitis (mas tīt' is) bacterial infection of a mammary gland; causes swelling, pain, and infected milk

mastocytosis (mas' tō sī tō' sis) an accumulation, either local or systemic, of mast cells in the tissue; characterized by the appearance of nodules under the skin

match race (mach rās) a race between two horses owned by different parties on terms agreed to with no money added

mate (māt) to allow a stallion and mare to perform the act of copulation

matrix (mā' triks) the basic material from which a structure develops; the substance between cells

matron (mā' trən) a mare that has produced a foal

maturities (me tŏŏr' ə tēz) 1. events for aged horses, five and older 2. nominating events in which the horses have competed previously; usually for three-year-olds and older; age criteria is specified by event

maverick (mav' ər ik) an unbranded stray

maxilla (mak sil' ə) the upper jaw bone; see *skeletal system* (illus.)

maxillary artery (mak' sə ler' ē) the artery found in the angle of the horse's jaw; commonly used to take the horse's pulse

McClellan saddle a saddletree used by the U.S. Cavalry

mealy mouthed (mēl' ē mouthd') a horse that exhibits faded color around the mouth

measurements (mezh' ər mənts) four common measurements are bone, girth, height and weight

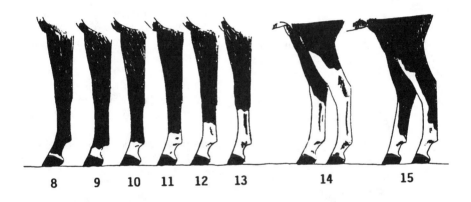

1. Star and Snip	10. Pastern
2. Strip	11. Ankle (Fetlock)
3. Blaze	12. Sock
4. Star and Disconnected Strip and Snip	13. Stocking
	14. High Stocking
5. Small Star	15. High Stocking
6. Race (Star, Strip and Snip)	16. Half Coronet
7. Bald	17. White Spot on Coronet
8. Coronet	18. Inside Heel
9. Half Pastern	19. White Spot on Both Heels

Markings

measuring certificate (mezh′ ər iŋ sər tif′ ə kit) a certificate documenting the height of a horse

measuring stick (stik) the stick used to measure a horse in either hands or in the metric system

mecate (mə′ kä′ tā) a long combination lead rope and reins attached to the heel of a bosal; traditionally a twenty-one-foot horsehair rope used with a bosal and tied to form the reins and a lead rope of the jaquima (hackamore)

Mecklenburg (mek′ lən bʉrg) a breed revived in East Germany after World War II; these horses have a fairly compact physical structure marked by well-developed hindquarters; height: 15.2–16.3 hands; color: bay, brown, black, and chestnut

meconium (mi′ kō′ nē əm) a dark-green or black tar-like material in the intestine of the full-term fetus; a mixture of the secretions of the intestinal glands and some amniotic fluid; first feces passed after birth

medial (mē′ dē əl) pertaining to the middle or inner surface; a position closer to the midline of the body or of a structure

mediastinum (mē′ dē as tī′ nəm) area in the chest cavity that contains the heart, the windpipe, and the esophagus

medicine (med′ ə sin) any drug, compound or substance used to suppress or heal an illness or disease

medium (mē′ dē əm) any preparation or substance used to support the growth of microorganisms; a culture

medium gait (gāt) between a collected and extended gait

medulla (mə dōo′ lə) the white matter of the brain; the brain stem and spinal cord as well as the central part of the adrenal gland

megrim (mē′ grəm) similar to fainting in humans; loss of balance; can be due to defective circulation, worms, digestion, or brain problems; also known as *staggers*

meiosis (mī′ ō′ sis) division of the sex cells; each horse cell contains 64 chromosomes, while each sex cell contains 32 chromosomes (haploid number)

melanin (mel′ ə nin) the dark pigment of the body found in skin, hair, and certain parts of the eye and brain

melanocytes (mel′ ə nō sīts′) cells responsible for the production of melanin

melanoma (mel′ ə nō′ mə) a tumor comprised of melanin-pigmented cells

melanosis (mel′ ə nō′ sis) a condition characterized by the deposition or accumulation of abnormally large amounts of melanin

melena (me lē′ nə) presence of digested blood in the stool making it appear black in color

melioidosis (mē′ lē oi dō′ sis) a bacterial infection occurring mainly in tropical countries; transmitted by rodents; the bacteria live in the soil and infect the horse through skin abrasions, inhalation, or insect bite

membrane (mem′ brān) a thin layer

of tissue that covers a surface, lines a cavity, or divides a space or organ

menace reflex (men′ is rē′ fleks) automatic closing of the eye when the hand is moved toward the eye

meninges (mə nin′ jēz) the three membranes that envelop the brain and spinal cord

meningitis (men′ in jīt′ is) inflammation of the meninges; usually a complication of a preexisting disease

meniscus (mi nis′ kəs) a crescent-shaped disk; part of the stifle joint

Merens a pony breed originating in France; strong and energetic; well suited to mountainous regions

mesentery (mez′ ən ter′ ē) a fold or membranous sheet attaching various organs to the body wall

mesothelium (mes′ ə thē′ lē əm) the layer of flat cells, derived from the mesoderm, that lines the body cavity of the embryo

metabolic (met′ ə bäl′ ik) pertaining to the chemical maintenance processes of the body

metabolism (mə tab′ ə liz′ əm) the sum of physical and chemical activities of an animal

metacarpal (met′ ə kär′ pəl) pertaining to the cannon; the area between the knee and fetlock joint of the foreleg; see *skeletal system* (illus.)

metacarpus (met′ ə kär′ pəs) the bone of the front leg between the carpus and first phalanx or fetlock joint; see *hoof* (illus.)

metal curry (met′ əl kʉr′ ē) a type of brush made of metal; mainly used to remove mud and excess hair during the shedding season; too harsh for use on the body during summer and on the legs at any time; best for cleaning other brushes

Metal Curry

metal fence different types include piping, mesh wire, and cable; this type of fence may be more desirable and expensive than wood

metamorphosis (met′ ə môr′ fə sis) change in structure; the changing of an adult fly from a maggot or a butterfly from a caterpillar

Metamucil (met′ ə mu′ sil) fiber supplement; used to prevent and treat sand impactions

metastasis (mə tas′ tə sis) the transfer of disease from one organ or part of the body to another not directly connected to it

metatarsus (mə ta tär′ səs) the three bones of the cannon on the hind limb; see *skeletal system* (illus.)

metestrus (met′ es′ trus) the period of the estrous cycle in female mammals that follows ovulation and is characterized by the formation of the corpus luteum; 1–2 day average

methionine (mə thī′ ə nēn′) an essential amino acid in proteins; may be prepared synthetically and added to feed

---

a=f<u>a</u>t; ā=<u>a</u>pe; ä=c<u>a</u>r; â=b<u>a</u>re; e=t<u>e</u>n; ē=<u>e</u>ven; i=<u>i</u>s; ī=b<u>i</u>te; ō=g<u>o</u>; ô=h<u>o</u>rn; ōō=t<u>oo</u>l; ŏŏ=l<u>oo</u>k; u=<u>u</u>p; ʉ=f<u>ur</u>; ŋ=ri<u>ng</u>; ə=sof<u>a</u>

Metis Trotter   (mā tēs trät′ ər) a breed resulting from the introduction of American blood with the express purpose of improving the performance of the Russian Orlov; this breeding program led to the official recognition of the breed in 1949; the Metis Trotter is smaller and less solid than the Orlov, but is faster and performs well in trotting races

Mexican saddle   (mek′ sə kən sad′ əl) a saddle characterized by a hide-covered tree with no leather covering except at the rear of the seat and slightly up the cantle

MFH   master of foxhounds

microbial flora   (mī′ krōb′ ē əl flôr′ ə) population of microorganisms found in a location

microchip   (mī′ krō chip′) an electronic device used to permanently identify horses; the electronic signal is read by a scanning device; microchips are generally implanted below the skin in the neck

microcornea   (mī′ krō côrn ē ə) a congenital condition characterized by an abnormally small cornea

microorganisms   (mī′ krō ôr′ gə niz′ əmz) minute, microscopic organisms such as bacteria, viruses, molds, yeasts, and protozoa

microphthalmia   (mī′ krof thal′ mē ə) congenital condition characterized by the presence of an abnormally small eyeball

midges   (mij′ əs) see *gnats*

miler   (mīl′ ər) a horse capable of running a mile and no further

milk fever   (milk fē′ vər) also known as *postparturient hypocalcemia*; due to sudden demand on calcium reserves immediately after foaling, the mare may be unsteady on her feet and show depression, seizures or coma

milk replacer   commercial substance used in place of mare's milk to raise a foal

milk teeth   deciduous teeth that are whiter, smaller, and have a distinct neck; shed by age five

mimicry behavior   (mim′ ik rē bi hāv′ yər) repeating the behavior or act of another horse; known as *modeling* or *contagious* or *infectious behavior*

mineral deposit   (min′ ər əl di päz′ it) extraneous inorganic matter collected in the tissues or in a cavity

mineralization   (min′ ər əl ə zā′ shən) the process of being impregnated with minerals

mineral oil   (oil) lubricant for boluses and capsules, used to treat some cases of colic

minerals   (min′ ər elz) inorganic elements necessary for growth and for functions of the blood and soft body tissues

mineral supplement   (sup′ lə mənt) the most common dietary supplements to provide minerals are steamed bone meal, dicalcium phosphate, and monocalcium phosphate

Miniature Horse   (min′ ē ə chər hôrs) a breed originating in the U.S.; to qualify, horses must stand no more than 32 in tall; common uses: pets and show

minute volume   (min′ it′ väl′ yōōm) the amount of blood that goes through the heart in a minute's time

miosis (mī' ō sis) contraction of the pupil; opposite of mydriasis

miotic (mī' ot ik) any drug that causes the pupil to contract

Missouri Foxtrotter (mi zŏŏr' ē fäks' trät' ər) a breed originated in the states of Arkansas and Missouri; best distinguished by its "fox-trot" gait in which the horse performs a brisk walk with front legs and trots with back legs; reliable and enduring, capable of traveling long distances at an average speed of 5–10 mph

Missouri Foxtrotting Horse Breed Association MFTHBA, a registry in which both sire and dam of a foal must be registered with MFTHBA in order to register the foal

mitbah the angle at which the head and neck meet

mites (mīts') very small parasites that cause mange; infest both animals and plants

mitral valve (mī' trəl valv) the mitral bicuspid or left arteriovenous valve of the heart

mixed color (mixt kul' ər) a marking consisting of the general color mixed with many white or lighter colored hairs

mixed gaited said of a horse that will not adhere to any one true gait at a time

mixed meeting a race meeting at which both flat and steeplechase or hurdle races are held on the same day

mixed stable a racing stable where both flat race and National Hunt horses are kept

mochila (mō chē' lə) an early, one-piece removable leather covering made to fit over the saddle tree and cover the entire saddle from in front of the horn to behind the cantle

model hunter (mäd' əl hun' tər) judged 100 percent on conformation, but horse must be shown over fences in the same show in order for points to count toward a championship

modeling (mäd' əl iŋ) observational learning or mimicry

modified live virus (mäd' ə fīd līv vī' rəs) a virus that has been taken from its natural state and raised in a laboratory; the virus does not have the disease-causing abilities that make it valuable as a vaccine

moist rale (moist ral) an abnormal respiratory sound; occurring with fluid in the air passages; heard through auscultation

molars (mō' lərz) rear teeth used for grinding; generally not used for determining age; a mature horse has twenty-four molars

molasses (mə las' is) usually a by-product of sucrose refined from sugarcane or sugar beet; most horses enjoy the flavor of molasses; it is used to coat grain in sweet feeds

Monday morning sickness (mun' dā môr' niŋ sik' nəs) a condition associated with forced exercise after a period of rest during which feed has not been reduced; characterized by painful movement and tying up; also known as *azoturia*

a=fat; ā=ape; ä=car; â=bare; e=ten; ē=even; i=is; ī=bite; ō=go; ô=horn; ŏŏ=tool; ŏŏ=look; u=up; u=fur; ŋ=ring; ə=sofa

Mongolian (mong gō′ lē ən) a pony breed originating in Mongolia; used for riding, pack, and light draft; one of the oldest breeds; tolerant and hardy

monkshood (muŋks′ hŏŏd) a poisonous perennial plant; its dried leaves and roots yield aconite; also called *wolfsbane*

monocular vision (mə näk′ yə lər viz′ ən) the ability to see independently with each eye; this allows the horse to see separate objects with each eye at the same time

monocytes (män′ ə sīts) white blood cells active in fighting subacute infections

monorchid (män′ ôr kid) individual with only one testicle

montura 1. a riding horse 2. a saddle

moon blindness (mŏŏn blīnd′ nis) an eye disease that causes a cloudy or inflamed condition of the eyes; may lead to blindness; also known as *periodic ophthalmia*

mope (mōp) to cover the eyes of the horse so that he is only able to see downward

morbid (môr′ bid) pertaining to or affected by a disease

morbidity rate (môr bid′ ə tē rāt) number of individuals in a group that become ill during a specified time

Morgan (môr′ gən) a breed of horse descended from the sire Justin Morgan in the U.S.; sturdy with a short, broad back and deep chest; generally elegant and spirited, yet easily managed; color: bay, chestnut, and black, with white markings common; primary uses: all-around riding, and show ring under saddle and harness

moribund (môr′ ə bund) in a dying state; near death

morning glory (môr′ niŋ glôr′ ē) a horse that performs well in morning workouts, but fails to race to his potential in the afternoon

morning line (līn) the approximate odds usually printed in the program and posted on the board prior to any betting; a forecast of how it is believed the betting will go on a particular race

morphology (môr′ fäl′ ə jē) the form and structure of living beings

mortality rate (môr′ tal′ ə tē rāt) the number of individuals that die from a disease during a specified time, usually one year

mortise (môr′ tis) a slot through the cantle or pommel of a McClellan saddle; leather straps passed through the mortises were used to anchor the cavalryman's equipment

mosquito (mə skēt′ ō) a small, biting insect; may transmit equine infectious anemia and equine encephalomyelitis

mother hubbard saddle (muth′ ər hub′ ərd sad′ əl) a mochilalike, covered saddle on which the mochila is permanently attached to the tree

motility (mō′ til′ i tē) the ability to move; may refer to peristalsis in the intestines; may also refer to activity of sperm in a semen sample

mottled (mät′ əld) marked with spots of different colors; dappled; spotted; freckled skin as in Appaloosas with light and dark pigment

mount   (mount) 1. a horse used for riding 2. to get up on the back of a horse

Mountain Pleasure Horse Association MPHA; registry open to offspring of registered parents; must be videotaped, bloodtyped and approved by the MPHA Board of Directors

mounting   the procedure for climbing into the saddle

mounting handle   a handle designed to assist passengers entering a carriage; see *carriage parts* (illus.)

mount money   the money paid in a rodeo to a performer who is riding, roping, or bulldogging in exhibition but not in competition

mouth   (mou‌t‌h) the first part of the digestive system; contains the teeth and the tongue

mouthing   1. determining the approximate age of a horse by examining the teeth 2. a horse playing with the bit

mouthy   a hound that is noisy

moved at halt   see *immobility insufficient*

muck out   (muk out) to clean out a box or stall in which a horse has been stabled, removing the droppings and soiled bedding

mucocutaneous junction   (myōō' kō kyōō tā' nē əs jungk' shən) an area where the mucous membranes join the skin at the lips, nostrils, prepuce, vagina, and rectum

mucoid   (myōōk' oid) resembling mucus

mucopurulent   (myōō kō pyŏŏr' yə lənt) containing both mucus and pus

mucous membranes   (myōō' kəs mem' brānz) membranes that line cavities of the body that are exposed to air; lining of the intestinal tract

mucus   (myōō' kəs) the free slime of the mucous membrane; composed of secretion of the glands

mudder   (mud' ər) a horse that runs well on a track that is wet, sloppy, or heavy; a racehorse that performs well on a muddy track

mud fever   (mud fē' vər) scratches occurring on the pastern due to mud and moisture; an inflammation of the upper layer of skin caused by subjection to wet conditions

mule   (myōōl) a hybrid; the result of mating a mare with a jack; originated in Spain; the mule is seldom fertile; common uses: all-around riding, driving, and pack animals

mule ears   ears that are abnormally long

muley saddle   a western saddle without a horn or with the horn removed

mullen mouth pelham   a half-moon solid bar mouthpiece in a bit; this type of mouthpiece lies flat across the mouth and rests on the bars at either side and is cushioned by the tongue in the center

Mullen Mouth

---

a=f**a**t; ā=**a**pe; ä=c**a**r; â=b**a**re; e=t**e**n; ē=**e**ven; i=**i**s; ī=b**i**te; ō=g**o**; ô=h**o**rn; ōō=t**oo**l; ŏŏ=l**oo**k; u=**u**p; ʉ=f**u**r; ŋ=ri**ng**; ə=sof**a**

Murakoz a draft breed originating in Hungary, also raised in Poland and Yugoslavia; has a compact, powerful build and is sturdy and robust; color: chestnut (mane, tail, and feather on the legs tending to flaxen), bay, brown, black, and gray

Murgese a breed that dates back to the days of Spanish rule in Italy; influenced by Barb and Arab bloodlines; bred in a wild state in a fairly tough environment

murmur (mʉr' mər) an abnormal periodic sound of short duration of cardiac or vascular origin

muscle (mus' əl) an organ that, by contraction, produces the movements of an animal

muscle relaxant an agent that specifically aids in reducing muscle tension

muscle tremor an involuntary trembling or quivering of a muscle

muscular system the network of organs responsible for movement; made up of skeletal muscle, cardiac muscle, and smooth muscle; see illustration

musculoskeletal system (mus' kyə lō skel' ə təl sis' təm) consists of muscles, tendons, joints, and bones

music (myōō' zik) the cry of the pack

Mustang (mus' taŋ) a wild horse found on the western plains of North America; height: 13.2–15 hands; known for physical toughness; common uses: cow horse, general riding, and rodeo

mutation (myōō tā' shən) 1. a sud-

den variation that is later passed on through inheritance and that results from changes in a gene or genes 2. change in position of the fetus in the uterus

mute (myōōt) hounds are said to run mute when they fail to give tongue when following the line

mutton withered (mut' ən with' ərd) being low in the withers with heavy shoulder muscling; having very little bone definition at the withers

mutuel pool (myōō' chŏŏ wəl pōōl) the total amount bet on any race, on any day, or at any meeting

muzzle (muz' əl) 1. the lower end of the nose which includes the nostrils, lips, and chin; see *points of the horse* (illus.) 2. a device that is fastened over the mouth to prevent biting or eating

mycosis (mī' kō' sis) any disease caused by a fungus

mycotic (mī' kät ik) fungal; caused by a fungus

mycotoxic (mī' kō täk' sik) pertaining to toxins produced by fungi

mydriatic (mid' rē at' ik) any drug that dilates the pupil

myelin sheath (mī' ə lin shēth) the lipid substance that forms around certain nerve fibers

myelitis (mī' ə līt' is) inflammation of the spinal cord

myelography (mī' ə läg raf' ē) the act of radiographing the spinal cord after a dye is injected into the space

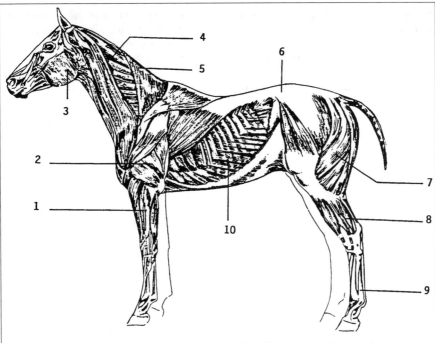

1. Digital Extensor Muscle
2. Triceps Muscle
3. Masseter Muscle
4. Splenius Muscle
5. Trapezius Muscle
6. Gluteal Fascia

7. Biceps Femoris Muscles
8. Digital Extensor Muscles
9. Digital Flexor Tendons
10. External Abdominal Oblique Muscle

Muscular System

between the spinal cord and the vertebral column

mylord (mī' lôrd) an elegant, four-wheeled carriage with a folding top; designed to carry two people plus a coachman

Mylord Carriage

myocarditis (mī' ō kär dīt' is) inflammation of the muscular walls of the heart

myocardium (mī' ō kär' dē əm) heart muscles; the middle and thickest layer of the heart wall; composed of cardiac muscle

myoglobin (mī' ə glō' bin) a ferrous complex pigment that gives muscle its characteristic color and acts as a store of oxygen; the substance released from the damaged cells in tying up disease; turns the urine a coffee color

a=fat; ā=ape; ä=car; â=bare; e=ten; ē=even;
i=is; ī=bite; ō=go; ô=horn; ōō=tool;
ŏŏ=look; u=up; u=fur; ŋ=ring; ə=sofa

myopathy   (mī äp′ ə t͟hē) any disease of a muscle

myopia   (mī ō′ pē ə) nearsighted

myositis   (mī′ ō sī′ tis) inflammation of a voluntary muscle

myotonia   (mī′ ə tō′ nē ə) increased muscular irritation and contraction with decreased power of relaxation; spasm of muscle

N

nag (nag) a derogatory term for a horse; may refer to a horse that is not well bred or is unregistered

nail pricks (nāl priks) a shoeing nail placed incorrectly on the inside of the white line or when driven crosses the white line and penetrates the sensitive tissue of the foot

nails (nālz) horseshoe specialized nails that hold shoes in place on a horse's foot; assorted sizes and styles are available for different types of horseshoes

nap (nap) 1. a horse that fails to obey properly applied aids, as in refusing to go forward or to pass a certain point 2. in racing, a good tip

narcolepsy (när' kə lep' sē) recurrent, uncontrollable brief episodes of sleep

narcosis (när kō' sis) a reversible state of stupor

narcotics (när kät' iks) drugs that induce sleep and relieve pain at the same time

nares (när' ez) external openings of the nasal passages

Narragansett Pacer (nar' ə gan' sit pās' ər) a fast type of pacer; descended from the indigenous horse of the Narragansett Bay area of Rhode Island

narrow fork (nar' ō fôrk) a fork on a saddle tree with sides that do not extend outward beyond their outside attachment point to the bar

narrow spectrum antibiotic (nar' ō spek' trəm an' ti bī ät' ik) an agent that is effective against only a limited number of organisms or a specific organism; the range of certain antibiotics

nasal cavity (nā' zəl kav' ə tē) the passageway for the respiratory system

nasal turbinates (nā' zəl tɥr' bə nātz) passageways from the nostrils to the lungs

nasolacrimal (nā' sō lak' ri mal) pertaining to the nasal opening of the tear-producing apparatus

National Cutting Horse Association a nonprofit organization dedicated to the cause of the cutting horse

National Federation the governing body of equestrian affairs in any country affiliated with the FEI

National Intercollegiate Rodeo Association NIRA; an organization developed to promote intercollegiate rodeo on a national scale; establishes and maintains operating codes to encourage prospective college students to enroll in institutions of higher education represented in the membership of the NIRA

National Pinto Horse Registry a registry for bi- or tri-colored horses of any lineage

National Reining Horse Association a nonprofit organization dedicated to the promotion of the reining horse

---

a=f<u>a</u>t; ā=<u>a</u>pe; ä=c<u>a</u>r; â=b<u>a</u>re; e=t<u>e</u>n; ē=<u>e</u>ven; i=<u>i</u>s; ī=b<u>i</u>te; ō=g<u>o</u>; ô=h<u>o</u>rn; ōō=t<u>oo</u>l; ŏŏ=l<u>oo</u>k; u=<u>u</u>p; ɥ=f<u>u</u>r; ŋ=ri<u>ng</u>; ə=sof<u>a</u>

National Show Horse   a breed originating in the U.S.; Saddlebred/Arabian cross; known for refinement, stamina, and high-stepping action; common uses: show ring under saddle and halter

National Show Horse Registry NSHR; created to meet a growing need within the equine industry for beautiful show horses with athletic ability; horses registered are Arabian/Saddlebred cross

Native Mexican Horse   a breed originated from the animals introduced by the conquistadores in the sixteenth century; predominantly Andalusian with some Arab and Criollo blood

natural aids   (nach' ər əl ādz) the upper body, seat, weight, body, hands, legs, and voice as used by the rider to give instruction to the horse

natural gaits   walk, trot, and canter; in some horses, pace and running walk are included

natural mane and tail   full-length mane and tail such as seen on Arabians, Morgans, and some Quarter Horses and Andalusians

navel cord   (nā' vəl côrd) connects the fetus to the placenta

navel infection   (in fek' shən) an infectious disease of newborn animals caused by several kinds of bacteria; dunking the foal's umbilical cord in iodine helps to prevent infection

navicular bone (nə vik' yə lər bōn) a small, boat-shaped bone between the coffin bone and the short

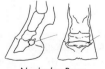

Navicular Bone Location

pastern bone in the foot of the horse; also called *distal sesamoid, distal phalanx,* or *shuttlebone*

navicular bursitis   (bʉr sī' tis) inflammation of the bursa between the navicular bone and the flexor tendon

navicular disease   (di zēz') a chronic inflammation involving the navicular bone and other sensitive structures within the hoof; sometimes caused by excessively straight pasterns and small feet; may involve the deep flexor tendon; difficult to diagnose

NBRA   National Barrel Racing Association

NCHA   National Cutting Horse Association

near side   (nēr sīd) the left side of the horse; the side from which a horse is generally mounted; some say this custom originated from the days of horsemen when they wore swords on their left sides; the swords interfered with the rider if they tried to mount from the right side

neat's foot oil   (nēts fŏŏt oil) oil used to soften, condition, and preserve leather; continued use darkens the leather permanently

neck   (nek) **1.** one of the measurements of distance by which a horse may be said to win a race; the length of a horse's head and neck **2.** separated from the shoulders by a line that passes from the dip that is just in front of the withers to the depression that is made by the union of the neck and breast; see *points of the horse* (illus.)

neck cradle   a wooden collar used as a restraint to prevent the horse from bending his neck

neck of tooth   part of the tooth between crown and root located at the surface of the gums

neck rein   to guide or direct a horse by pressure of the indirect rein on the neck; the horse turns away from the side on which the rein is laid; the rider holds both reins in one hand

neck strap   a strap that supports the breast collar on a harness; see *harness parts C* (illus.)

neck too short   the rider draws in the front of the horse by hand aids and does not collect the hindquarters up under the horse in the proper manner

necropsy   (nek' räp sē) examination of an animal's body after death; an autopsy

necrosis   (ne krō' sis) death of a cell or group of cells that is in contact with living tissue

negative reinforcement   removing a negative stimulus when the horse shows correct response

neigh   (nā) the loud, prolonged call of a horse

nematode   (nem' ə tōd') a class of roundworm that is an internal parasite; has a slender, unsegmented body that tapers at each end; includes hookworms, ascarids, and strongyles

nematodosis   (ne' mə tōd' ō sis) a nervous disorder characterized by uncoordination; caused by one of the nematodes; also known as *kumri*

neonatal   (nē' ō nāt' əl) pertaining to the first month after birth

neonatal isoerythrolysis   anemic condition of newborn foals; caused by incompatibility between blood types of dam and foal; often called *foal jaundice*

neonatal maladjustment syndrome (mal' ə just mənt sin' drōm) a group of brain disorders usually appearing within the first day of a foal's life

neonate   (nē' ə nāt') a newborn foal

neoplasm   (nē' ə plaz' əm) a new and abnormal growth of tissue in which the growth is uncontrolled and progressive; a tumor

neostigmine   (nē' ō stig' mēn) the generic name for a drug used to stimulate smooth muscle contractions and promote muscle tone

nephritis   (ne frīt' əs) inflammation of the kidneys

nephrons   (nef' ränz) the anatomic and functional units of the kidneys

nephrosis   (ne frō' sis) any disease of the kidneys

nephrosplenic entrapment   (nef' ro sple' nik en trap' mənt) entrapment of a loop of intestine behind the ligament that connects the left kidney with the spleen; cause of severe colic

nerve block   (nʉrv bläk) anesthetization of a nerve to remove feeling from the body part it supplies

nerves   (nʉrvz) cordlike structures, visible to the naked eye, comprising a

---

a=f<u>a</u>t; ā=<u>a</u>pe; ä=c<u>a</u>r; â=b<u>a</u>re; e=t<u>e</u>n; ē=<u>e</u>ven; i=<u>i</u>s; ī=b<u>i</u>te; ō=g<u>o</u>; ô=h<u>o</u>rn; ōō=t<u>oo</u>l; ŏŏ=l<u>oo</u>k; u=<u>u</u>p; ʉ=f<u>u</u>r; ŋ=ri<u>ng</u>; ə=sof<u>a</u>

collection of nerve fibers that convey impulses between a part of the central nervous system and some other region of the body

nerving (nᵘrv′ iŋ) cutting a nerve to eliminate pain reception from the body part it supplies

nervous system (nᵘr′ vəs sis′ təm) a system of nerves and sensory organs; includes the central nervous system, peripheral nervous system, and specialized sensory organs

nettlerash (net′ əl rash) hives

neural (nŏŏr′ əl) pertaining to a nerve or to the nerves

neural motor response (nŏŏr əl mō′ tər ri spons′) the specific action triggered by certain nerves

neurectomy (nŏŏ rek′ tə mē) surgical removal of a portion of a nerve to eliminate pain reception from the body part it supplies

neuroglia (nŏŏ räg′ lē ə) the supporting structure of nervous tissue

neuroma (nŏŏ rō′ mə) a tumor or new growth largely made up of nerve cells and nerve fibers; a tumor growing from a nerve

neuron (nŏŏr′ än) nerve cells; any of the conducting cells of the nervous system

neuropsychological (nŏŏ′ rō sī kə läj′ i′ kəl) relating to the science that combines observations on behavior and the mind with examination of the brain and nervous system

neurotoxic (nŏŏr′ ō täk′ sik) poisonous or destructive to nerve tissue

neutralize (nŏŏ′ trə līz′) to make a substance neither an acid nor a base

neutrophil (nŏŏ′ trō fil) a type of white blood cell that fights bacterial infection

neutrophilia (nŏŏ′ trō fil′ ē ə) an increase in the number of neutrophils in the blood; a sign of infection

New Forest Pony an English breed of pony named for New Forest, an area in the county of Hampshire; these ponies live in the wild in their surroundings; the population numbers approximately 2,000; sturdy, well built, ideally suited as riding ponies; height: 12.2–14.2 hands

New Forest Pony Association a registry for progeny of pure New Forest Pony stock

nicks (niks) a slang term used by breeders to describe mare/stallion matches that produce especially good offspring

Nigerian Horse (nī jē′ rē ən hôrs) a Nigerian breed having plain looks but good character and a remarkably hardy constitution; height: 14–14.2 hands

nipper (nip′ ər) a farrier's tool used to cut off excess growth from the hoof

nitrofurazone (nī′ trō fu′ rə zōn) topical antibiotic ointment frequently used for wound care

Nipper

nodular necrobiosis (näj′ ə lər nek′ rō bī ō′ sis) also called *equine collagenolytic granuloma*; common skin disease of horses characterized by multiple nodules in the skin

nomadic (nō mad′ ik) wandering or roaming

nomination (näm′ ə nā′ shǝn) 1. the naming of a horse for a stakes race on a specific date well in advance of the race; a set fee is paid on the nomination of a horse and other fees are paid at stated intervals 2. naming of a horse or offspring so he is eligible for an event

Nonius (nän′ ē əs) a breed that descends from a French stallion called Nonius; this stallion sired a number of excellent sons in Hungary, where he was crossed with Andalusian, Lipizzaner, Kladruber, Arab, and Norman

nonpro (nän prō) a nonprofessional by specific definition from each association such as the NRHA, NCHA, and ASHA; may replace "amateur," a person who does not earn a living or is not paid for training and/or showing horses

nonruminant (nän rōō′ mə nənt) an animal with a simple stomach

nonsteroidal (non ster′ oid əl) containing no steroids; natural or synthetic hormones that control inflammation

nonvascular (nän vas′ kyə lər) not supplied with blood vessels

norepinephrine (nôr′ ep′ ə nef′ rin) a hormone secreted by neurons that acts as a transmitter; substance of the peripheral sympathetic nerve endings

Noriker a draft breed originating in Austria; developed by the Romans in the province of Noricum; calm and

docile; used for heavy draft and farm work

normal horse serum (nôr′ məl hôrs sēr′ əm) the fluid portion of blood taken from healthy horses that have been immunized against common infectious agents; sterilized and packaged for use in treating antibody deficiencies

Norman (nôr′ man) a breed that originated in Normandy, France; a well-built animal with a graceful and balanced appearance; color: bay, chestnut, and gray (rare)

North American Bay Horse Club registry for horses that are true bay

North American District of the Belgian Warmblood Breeding Association all registered mares may be eligible for the main studbook; stallions by approved European warmblood sires standing in the book of their breed, who are out of warmblood dams, are also eligible

North American Draft Cross Association a registry for all one-half and three-fourths draft horse crosses with light horses

North American Exmoors a registry for purebred Exmoor foals

North American Mustang Association and Registry a registry for any Bureau of Land Management Mustang; Mustangs registered with another registry or the offspring of said Mustangs are eligible for registration

---

a=f<u>a</u>t; ā=<u>a</u>pe; ä=c<u>a</u>r; â=b<u>a</u>re; e=t<u>e</u>n; ē=<u>e</u>ven; i=<u>i</u>s; ī=b<u>i</u>te; ō=g<u>o</u>; ô=h<u>o</u>rn; ōō=t<u>oo</u>l; ŏŏ=l<u>oo</u>k; u=<u>u</u>p; ʉ=f<u>u</u>r; ŋ=ri<u>ng</u>; ə=sof<u>a</u>

North American Shagya Society purebreds must have pedigrees that can be traced to the Austro-Hungarian state stud farms of Babolna and Radautz

North American Trakehner Association registration is based on bloodlines

Northlands (nôrth landz) a Norwegian pony that can be traced back to the Mongolian wild horse and the Tarpan

North Swedish Horse a breed believed to have originated in Sweden; good for agricultural draft work; has a docile temperament

Norwegian Fjord Association of North America a registry for dun horses with a full dorsal stripe from the forelock through the mane, back, and down the tail

Norwegian Fjord Pony (nôr wē' jen fyôrd pō' nē) originated in Norway and Sweden; also known as the *Swedish Ardennes;* commonly used for draft work

nose (nōz) 1. the shortest measurement of distance by which it is possible for a horse to win a race 2. down from the forehead to the nostrils; see *points of the horse* (illus.) 3. the scenting ability of the hound

noseband the part of the bridle that encircles the horse's nose; consists of a leather band on an independent headpiece, which is worn below the cheek bones and above the bit; also known as a *cavesson;* other types of nosebands include: flash, dropped, Figure 8; see *harness parts B and E* (illus.)

nose botfly see *botfly*

nose net a light cord muzzle designed to give greater control on a hard-pulling horse with little or no mouth; the net is placed over the nose and fastened tightly to the noseband; it does not inflict great pain, but the nose is sensitive to the added pressure; used primarily by polo players

nose twitch to subdue a horse by applying pressure to his upper lip, which in turn releases endorphins

not accepting hand a horse that is resisting the hand aids of the rider; includes opening the mouth, tongue hanging out, coming above the bit, leaning on the bit, tossing the head, etc.

not between hand and leg overall lack of control; the rider's hand and leg aids are not coordinated, so the horse will be inclined to wander

not enough angle the rider has not indicated that the forehand come sufficiently off the track; also called *shoulder in*

not enough collection collected paces are inadequate in one way or another; includes hind legs that are not engaged enough; the steps are too long; the forehand of the horse is too low; etc.

not enough difference when an alteration within a pace is required, for example, in a conversion from a trot to an extended trot, the difference in the length of stride is not sufficiently shown

not enough extension when a horse is not showing enough length of stride for an extended gait

not enough from behind when the hind legs take a rather shallow step and are not enough under the horse

not forward enough when the horse is not working with enough energy and is lacking in length of stride and impulsion

no time when a contestant in a rodeo has not caught or thrown the animal properly he receives no time on that animal in that go-round; he is still entitled to compete in the next go-round

not lowering enough the walk on a long or free rein; when the rider gives the rein and the horse doesn't stretch his neck out and down

not overtracking in medium and extended gaits, the hoofprint of the rear hooves don't go beyond the prints of the front hooves; may be due to the rider holding the horse on too tight a rein

not square when the four feet do not stop with a leg at each corner of a rectangle; the hind feet should be directly behind the front feet so that from the front, only the forelegs are seen

not tracking up when the hind legs of the horse are moving with too little action; they do not reach the imprint left by the foreleg except in the collected paces

novice (näv′ is) an inexperienced horseman; a division for horse or rider who has not yet won a specified amount at specific shows

Novokirghiz a Soviet breed; a well-built horse with a balanced appearance; tough, useful for pack, saddle, or light draft work

noxious (nok′ shəs) unpleasant; disagreeable

nucleus (nōō′ klē əs) the center of a cell that contains the genetic material

numbered studbook see *American Quarter Horse Studbook*

numnah a pad placed under the saddle to prevent undue pressure on the horse's back; cut to the shape of the saddle, only slightly larger; made of felt, sheepskin, or cloth-covered foam rubber

nutrients (nōō′ trē ənts) the six main types of nutrients are: fats, proteins, vitamins, minerals, carbohydrates, and water; are the building blocks of body structures, assist in the functions of metabolism, or provide energy

nutrition (nōō trish′ ən) the science or study of a proper, balanced diet to promote health

nystagmus (nis tag′ məs) involuntary, rapid, rhythmic movements of the eyeball

---

a=fat; ā=ape; ä=car; â=bare; e=ten; ē=even; i=is; ī=bite; ō=go; ô=horn; ōō=tool; ŏŏ=look; u=up; ʉ=fur; ŋ=ring; ə=sofa

O

oakum (ōk′ əm) hemp or jute fiber often impregnated with tar and used as a hoof packing

oats (ōts) a cereal crop used as part of a horse's feed; given either whole, bruised, boiled, or rolled; more difficult to overfeed than other grains; contains the most protein

obedience (ō bē′ dē əns) the desire of a horse to please, to perform, and to respond willingly

obesity (o bē′ si tē) the condition of being very fat and overweight; fairly common in ponies; generally due to excess feed and inadequate exercise

objection (əb jek′ shən) in racing, an objection may be made against any of the placed horses and must be heard by the stewards at the meeting where it was raised

obligatory loss (ə blig′ ə tôr′ ē lôs) the amount of feed nutrient that will not be absorbed in the gastrointestinal tract and is unavoidably excreted in the urine and/or feces; it is of no nutritional value to the horse

obstetrical (əb stet′ rik əl) relating to birth

occipital crest (äk sip′ i təl krest) the bony prominence at the top of the head that rises between the ears; see *points of the horse* (illus.)

occlude (ə klōōd′) to fit close together; to obstruct or close off

occlusion (ə klōō′ zhən) bite; the relationship between the biting surfaces of the maxillary and mandibular teeth when they are in contact

occult (ä kult′) refers to diseases that have no outwardly visible symptoms and are difficult to detect with the naked eye; many cancers and other internal medical disorders are categorized as occult illnesses

occult blood blood in the stool that cannot be seen with the naked eye

occult spavin typical spavin lameness without external signs

odd colored (äd kul′ erd) coat color in Pintos and Paints; white with various colored patches; the patches merge into one another and cannot be classified under skewbald or piebald

odds (ädz) the betting quotation on a horse in a particular race

odds on betting odds of less-than-even money

off billet a billet on the off side of the horse; see *western saddle* (illus.)

official (ə fish′ əl) in racing, the designation given to the result of a race by the stewards when nothing has happened that, in their judgment, would revise the actual order of the finish

offset cannons (ôf′ set′ kan′ ənz) looking at the front of the horse's legs, the cannon bone is outside the direct line through the radius to the ground; also called *bench knees*; see *conformation comparisons, front limb* (illus.)

off side the right side of the horse; also known as the *far side*

off strap   a leather strap doubled over the off-side front rigging ring to which the cinch buckle is buckled; the front off billet; half-breed

off the bit   when a horse has altered his head position for a moment due to a loss of balance or resistance to aids

oil   (oil) fat that has a melting point below normal temperatures

Oldenburg   (ōl′ dən bʉrg) a breed originating in West Germany; influenced by Fresian, Anglo-Arab, and Thoroughbred; a well-rounded saddle horse

Older Horse Registry   a registry for horses fifteen years of age or older

old shoe inspection   (ōld shoō in spek′ s̠hən) competent farriers always inspect old horseshoes removed from horses to determine whether the previous method of shoeing produced even wear of the shoes and, if not, correct the method of shoeing to ensure even wear

olecranon   (ō lek′ rə nän) the point of the elbow formed by the bony projection of the ulna

olfactory   (ōl fak′ tər ē) pertaining to the sense of smell

o m n i b u s (äm′ nə bus′) another name for a horse-drawn tram; a covered, four-wheeled public

Omnibus

coach drawn by two or more horses; the body is long, with the seating arranged lengthwise; there is a rear entrance

one-day event   a combined training competition consisting of dressage, show-jumping, and cross-country phases, and is completed in one day

on its toes   a horse eager and keen to move on

onchocerca   (oŋ′ kō ser′ kə) a roundworm parasite found chiefly in the eyes, the skin, and the connective tissues under the skin

onchocerciasis   (on′ kō ser sī′ ə sis) a general term applied to several disorders that involve the larvae of a parasitic nematode; characterized by redness, swelling, and eventual drying of the skin; also called *summer sores*

on terms   hounds able to keep hunting steadily because there is a strong scent

on the bit   when a horse has accepted contact with the bit and reacts to aids with a quiet yet responsive manner

on the forehand   when the weight of the horse is not evenly distributed over all four legs and more weight is borne by the front legs

on the hand   a horse that leans into the bit

on the line   in dressage, when the horse is following the exact line as specified in the dressage test

on the pull   when a jockey holds a horse back in a race and doesn't let him run at his ability

---

a=f<u>a</u>t; ā=<u>a</u>pe; ä=c<u>a</u>r; â=b<u>a</u>re; e=t<u>e</u>n; ē=<u>e</u>ven; i=<u>i</u>s; ī=b<u>i</u>te; ō=g<u>o</u>; ô=h<u>o</u>rn; oō=t<u>oo</u>l; ŏŏ=l<u>oo</u>k; u=<u>u</u>p; ʉ=f<u>u</u>r; ŋ=ri<u>ng</u>; ə=sof<u>a</u>

on-tree rigging   a type of rigging in which the leathers are anchored to the saddletree; as opposed to in-skirt rigging

on two tracks   when the hind legs don't follow the tracks of the front legs

opacity   (ō pas′ ə tē) an area, as in the eye, that does not allow light to pass through

open   (ō′ pən) **1.** competition available for professionals, nonpros, amateurs, and youths; anyone can enter **2.** a mare that is not in foal

open a shoulder   to turn the horse's head slightly toward the wall or rail during schooling, forcing the hindquarters outward and freeing the shoulder

open behind   when the hocks are far apart and the feet are close together

open bridle   a bridle without blinders or blinkers covering the eyes; some bridles are rigged with blinders that shut off vision to the rear and side

Open Class   **1.** a class in which any horse of a specified breed is eligible to compete **2.** may also refer to contestants

open hocked   when the horse is wide apart at the hocks with the feet close together; also called *open behind*

opening rein   an outward pull on a rein

open joint   a wound in the vicinity of a joint; exposes some of the bones in the joint

open knee   a condition, usually the result of a mineral imbalance, wherein the profile of the knee is irregular due to the enlarged epiphysis of the lower end of the radius and the carpal bone is deviated toward the back

open meet   the first meet of the regular hunting season

open stirrup   a stirrup with no leather hood or tapadera

ophthalmia   (äf′ thal′ mē ə) severe inflammation of the eye or conjunctiva; due to infection or to a blow

ophthalmology   (äf′ thal mäl′ ə jē) the branch of medicine dealing with the eye, and its anatomy and physiology

ophthalmoscope   (äf′ thal′ mō skōp) an instrument containing a perforated mirror and lenses used to examine the interior of the eye

opiate   (ō′ pē ət) a preparation of opium; induces rest and quiets uneasiness

opposition rein   (äp′ ə zish′ ən rān) in neck reining, the rein on the side of the horse opposite to that side to which the rider wishes to proceed; used by gently pressing the opposition rein against the horse's neck; in a turn to the right, the left rein is the opposition rein

optic   (äp′ tik) pertaining to the eye

optic nerve   (nʉrv) the nerve that transmits electrical impulses from the light-sensitive retina of the eye to the brain; see *eye, horse's* (illus.)

optic neuritis   (nŏŏ rī′ tis) inflammation of the nerve that enters the back of the eye; can result in blindness

oral   (ôr' əl) by mouth; pertaining to the mouth

oral electrolytes   (i lek' trə lītz') salt solution to be given by mouth

orbit   (ôr' bit) eye socket; see *skeletal system* (illus.)

orbital cavity   (ôr' bit əl kav' i tē) the bony socket that surrounds and protects the eye

orbital cellulitis   (sel' yə lī' tis) inflammation of the tissue surrounding the eyeball

orchitis   (ôr' kī' tis) inflammation of the testes

organ   (ôr' gan) a somewhat independent part of the body that performs a special function or functions

organic   (ôr gan' ik) any substance or compound containing carbon and hydrogen in its structure; most feed and substances in a horse's body are organic, with the exception of minerals

organoleptic   (ôr' gə nō lep' tik) making an impression on or stimulating any of the senses: sight, smell, taste, and touch

organophosphate   (ôr gan' ō fäs' fāt) a phosphorus-containing organic pesticide

oriental   (ôr' ē en' təl) see *eastern*

orifice   (ôr' ə fis) the entrance or outlet of any cavity in the body

Orlov Trotter   a breed of horse originating in Russia in the eighteenth century; used for light work, pleasure driving, and riding; exhibited at fairs in various forms of competition including dressage and harness racing

orphan foal   (ôr' fen fōl) a foal that is being raised without his dam

orthopedic   (ôr' thə pē' dik) pertaining to the correction of bone disorders

osmosis   (äs mō' sis) diffusion through a semipermeable membrane, as of a living cell; typically separating a solvent and a solution that tends to equalize their concentrations

osselet   (äs' let) a bony growth on the inner aspect of a horse's knee or on the lateral aspect of the fetlock

ossify   (äs' ə fī) to change or develop into bone

osteitis   (äs' tē īt' əs) inflammation of a bone

osteoarthritis   (äs' tē ō är thrīt' is) degeneration and inflammation of one or more joints due to excessive wear or joint weakness

osteochondrosis   (äs' tē ō kon drō' sis) disease of a growth center in a bone or cartilage; often causes lameness in young horses

osteodystrophy   (äs' tē ō dis' trō fē) defective bone formation

osteomalacia   (äs' tē ō mə lā' shə) a condition characterized by softening of the bones; usually due to a calcium/phosphorus deficiency

osteomyelitis   (äs' tē ō mī' ə līt' is) inflammation of bone caused by a pyogenic (pus-producing) organism

---

a=f<u>a</u>t; ā=<u>a</u>pe; ä=c<u>a</u>r; â=b<u>a</u>re; e=t<u>e</u>n; ē=<u>e</u>ven;
i=<u>i</u>s; ī=b<u>i</u>te; ō=g<u>o</u>; ô=h<u>o</u>rn; ōō=t<u>oo</u>l;
ŏŏ=l<u>oo</u>k; u=<u>u</u>p; ʉ=f<u>u</u>r; ŋ=ri<u>ng</u>; ə=sof<u>a</u>

osteopetrosis (äs′ tē ō pē trō′ sis) abnormal condition of the bone characterized by increased size, density, and brittleness

osteoporosis (äs′ tē ō pô rō′ sis) abnormal thinning of the bone, making it weaker

otitis (ō′ tīt′ əs) inflammation of the ear

otoscope (ōt′ ə skōp) an instrument for examination of the ears

outcross (out′ kräs) the offspring of two unrelated or distantly related horses; the infusion of new blood in linebreeding

outfit (out′ fit) 1. a ranch with all its equipment and employees 2. the personal equipment of a cowboy

outlaw (out′ lô) a horse that cannot be broken; a horse that is particularly vicious and unable to be tamed

outline not maintained when the position of the horse's head and neck, the roundness of the back, and the engagement of the hindquarters do not maintain a correct position

out of signifying the female parent of a horse

out of the money when a racehorse fails to gain any one of the places in a race that pays prize money; usually, the first three places are paid; in some races, payment is made for the first five places

out on a limb when a harness racing horse is on the outside of the field as far away from the running rail as possible

outrider (out′ rīd ər) 1. the mounted racetrack employee whose duties include keeping the horses in order during the parade from paddock to post before a race, catching runaways, and assisting jockeys thrown from their mounts 2. the mounted horseman who rode on the outside of a coach or wagon as protection against armed robbers

outsider (out′ sīd′ ər) a racehorse that is given long odds in the betting, as he is thought to have little chance of winning the race

ovariectomy (ō vər′ ē ek′ tə mē) surgical removal of an ovary

ovary (ō′ vər ē) the female organ that produces eggs; there are two ovaries, which are connected to the uterus by the fallopian tubes

over at the knee conformational fault; when a horse stands with knees permanently bent forward; also called *buck kneed* or *knee sprung*; see *conformation comparisons, front limb, front and side view* (illus.)

overbent (ō′ vər bənt′) when a horse is bent too much at the poll and the nose is behind the vertical

overbite (ō′ vər bīt′) see *parrot mouth*

overface to ask a horse to jump an obstacle that is beyond his capabilities

overfeeding feeding too much protein and energy; may lead to handling problems, founder, colic, and tying up

overflexion flexing the neck between the second and third vertebrae to a point where the poll is no longer the highest point of the neck

overhorsing   refers to a small person on a big horse where the horse appears to be too big for the rider and/or the proposed use

overlay   in wagering parlance, when the odds are greater than those estimated by the track's official morning line maker

overmounted   a rider who doesn't have enough experience to control a particular horse

overnight   a race for which entries close seventy-two hours or less before the post time for the race

overo   (ō′ ver ō) coat color in Pintos and Paints; white patches are more dense on the stomach and extend up the body, as if white paint were splashed on the horse from underneath

overreach   indicates injury to the lower forelegs caused by the horse striking himself with his hind hooves; the limbs can be protected by the use of overreach boots

override   to ride too closely to the hounds

overrun   when the hounds shoot past the line when the scent has been diverted by a change of course or foil

overshot jaw   when the upper jaw protrudes beyond the lower jaw; also called *parrot mouth*

overtrack   when the hind foot hits the ground at a point ahead of where the forefoot did; noted at the walk and trot

overweight   depending on the con-

ditions of a race, each horse carries an assigned weight; when the jockey cannot make weight, overweight is allowed up to five pounds

oviduct   (ō′ vi dukt) tubes through which the egg passes from the ovary to the uterus

ovoid   (ō′ void) egg shaped

ovulation   (äv′ yə lā′ sh̲ən) the time when the follicle bursts and the egg is released; usually occurs in the last two days of the mare's heat period (estrus)

ovum   (ō′ vəm) unfertilized egg

owlhead   (oul hed) a horse that is impossible to train

own   (ōn) to own the line is to speak to it or to honor it

owner   (ō′ nər) the person in whose name a racehorse runs, irrespective of whether that person is the sole owner of the horse or is a member of a syndicate

oxbow stirrup   (äks′ bō stᵾr′ əp) a type of western stirrup with a rounded, narrow tread that allows the rider's foot to ride home in the stirrup rather than on the ball

oxer   (äks′ ər) a hedge with a ditch and a guardrail; a ditch and guardrail on both sides makes it a double oxer; common in hunt courses in England

oxidant   (äk′ sə dənt) a substance that combines another substance with oxygen

---

a=f<u>a</u>t; ā=<u>a</u>pe; ä=c<u>a</u>r; â=b<u>a</u>re; e=t<u>e</u>n; ē=<u>e</u>ven; i=<u>i</u>s; ī=b<u>i</u>te; ō=g<u>o</u>; ô=h<u>o</u>rn; ōō=t<u>oo</u>l; o̅o̅=l<u>oo</u>k; u=<u>u</u>p; ᵾ=f<u>u</u>r; ŋ=ri<u>ng</u>; ə=sof<u>a</u>

oxygen   (äk′ si jən) a colorless, odorless, tasteless, gaseous chemical element; essential in the respiration process; comprises 20 percent of air content

oxygenated   (äk′ si je nāt′ əd) saturated with oxygen

oxyhemoglobin   (äk′ si hē′ mə glō′ bin) a compound formed from hemoglobin on exposure to the atmosphere

oxytocin   (äk′ si tō′ sin) a hormone that stimulates labor contractions and the release of milk

Oxyuris equi   (ok′ sē yōō′ ris e′ kwə) pinworms

P

pace (pās) a two-beat lateral gait in which the front and hind feet on the same side start and stop simultaneously; all four feet are off the ground for a split second and the horse appears to float forward

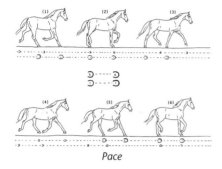

Pace

pacemaker in racing, the horse that takes the lead and sets the speed for the race

pace not true a gait that is not in the correct rhythm; the walk should be a four-beat gait; the trot should be a two-beat gait; the canter should be a three-beat gait

pacer (pās′ ər) **1.** a Standardbred horse that races in a lateral two-beat gait—both left legs in unison, then both right legs **2.** a horse that continuously walks in his stall; often an unhappy horse's reaction to confinement

pack (pak) a number of hounds hunted together regularly

pack sense (pak sens) the trait in hounds of working well together as a pack, honoring each other, and running in a mass

pad (pad′) **1.** the small, lightweight "saddle" used with pair and team harnesses; the pad can be much lighter and less sturdy than the saddle used for a single-horse harness, because no weight is born directly on the horses' backs **2.** the term used for English saddle blankets **3.** a piece of material installed between the shoe and the hoof for various reasons: protect the sole, balance the hoof, absorb shock, and prevent snow buildup

padded seat, inlaid a seat on which the seat leather is cut out underneath the padded area and the pad covering at its joint is flush with the remaining portion of the seat

padded seat, overlaid a seat on which the padding rests on the seat leather and the pad covering is stitched to the seat leather

paddling (pad′ əl iŋ) throwing the front feet out to the side during the stride; this defect is common in pigeon-toed horses; also called *winging out*

paddock (pad′ ek) **1.** the area where the horses are saddled and viewed prior to the race **2.** a grassy enclosure near a stable or house in which horses can be turned out

paddock boot (bo͞ot) a style of boot that is slightly above ankle height, has a small heel, and laces or zips up the front

paddock judge (juj) a racetrack offi-

---

a=fat; ā=ape; ä=car; â=bare; e=ten; ē=even; i=is; ī=bite; ō=go; ô=horn; o͞o=tool; o͝o=look; u=up; ʉ=fur; ŋ=ring; ə=sofa

cial whose duty is to get the jockeys or drivers and their horses to the racing strip on time

pad groom   the groom who slowly rides the hunter to the meet and brings back the covert hack ridden there by the owner

pad saddle   a pad with stirrups and a cinch; used for exercising the horse

Pahlavan   a Persian breed bred until recently by the Shah of Iran; a cross of the Thoroughbred, Plateau Persian, and the Arab; bred in the 1960s to combine the soundness and grace of the Plateau Persian and the Arab, with the height and jumping abilities of the Thoroughbred

pain   (pān) an annoying or hurting sensation occurring as a direct result of some external influence on the specialized nerve endings; horses exhibit pain by lameness, sweating, pawing the ground, rolling over, loss of appetite, etc.

pain receptors   (pān ri sep' tərz) nerve ends that respond to painful stimuli of various kinds

paint   (pānt) **1.** coat color; a coat pattern of both white and colored patches **2.** a breed, Paint; breeding aimed at producing coat color; to be registered a horse must have a paint coat pattern and at least one parent registered as a Paint; the other must be a Quarter Horse or Thoroughbred; pattern types include overo, tobiano, tovero, and piebald

pair   (pâr) two horses hitched abreast; also used in reference to two horses ridden side by side

palatable   (pal' it ə bəl) agreeable and pleasing to the taste

palate   (pal' it) the partition separating the mouth and nasal cavities

palisade worms   (pal' ə sād wʉrmz) see *strongyle*

palliative treatment   (pal' ē āt' iv trēt' mənt) care that is designed to relieve pain and distress; does not attempt a cure

pallor   (pal' ər) paleness; absence of skin coloration

palmar   (pal' mər) pertaining to the flexor surface of the foreleg

Palomino   (pal' ə mē' nō) a color, breed, or type of horse in which the coat color is yellow to golden and the mane and tail are white to cream; a dilution of the chestnut color

Palomino Horse Association   a color registry; ideally, coat color should be the same as a freshly minted gold coin with a white mane and tail

Palomino Horse Breeders of America   an organization formed in 1941 to collect, record, preserve the purity of blood, and improve the breeding of Palomino horses; a color registry with pedigree is a secondary requirement

Palomino Ponies of America   ponies the color of a U.S. gold coin with a white mane and tail

palpable   (pal' pə bəl) perceptible by touch

palpation   (pal' pā shən) the act of feeling with the hand

palpebral   (pal' pə brəl) refers to eyelid

pancake   (pan' kāk) an English riding saddle

pancreas (pan' krē əs) a small gland in the abdomen that produces pancreatic juice and insulin; also called the *pancreatic gland*

panels (pan' əlz) heavy coverings for the underneath side of the bars of the saddle; a cushion on the underneath surface of the bars; gives clearance of the horse's backbone, between the horse's back and the saddletree; see *English saddle* (illus.)

panic snap (pan' ik snap) a snap with a quick-release collar; often used in horse trailers in order to release the rope while the horse is pulling on it

panniculus carnosus (pə nik' yōō lus cärn' ō sus) the sheet of skeletal muscle that separates the rest of the body tissue from the skin

panniculus muscle (pə nik' yōō lus mus' əl) the muscle that underlies the skin of the horse and is capable of shaking off a fly

panniculus reflex (ri fleks') twitching of the thin sheet of muscle under the skin of the chest and flank in response to gentle stimulation of the skin along the topline; generally a horse's response to any touch that feels as if an insect lit on the skin

panniers (pan' yərz) large boxes, either of wood and fiberglass or canvas, that fit on either side of the pack saddle; used to hold equipment and food

papilla (pə pil' ə) a small, nipple-shaped projection

papilloma (pap' ə lō' mə) a growth of epithelial tissue; see *warts*

parabola (pə rab' ə lə) the arc made by a horse from the point of takeoff to the point of landing as he jumps an obstacle

paracentesis (par' ə sen tē' sis) the surgical puncture of a cavity for aspiration of a fluid

parade (pə rād') a halt in dressage

parade horse (pə rād hôrs) a horse of special refinement with graceful movement

parahormone (par' ə hôr' mōn) hormone secreted by the parathyroid glands; instrumental in maintaining proper calcium levels in the body

parallel bars (par' ə lel bärs) a type of spread fence used in show jumping and cross-country courses; consists of two sets of posts and rails

paralysis (pə ral' ə sis) loss or impairment of motor function in a part due to nerve damage or disease

paralytic myoglobinuria (par' ə lit' ik mī ō gläb' in yōōr ē ə) overexertion of a muscle without adequate conditioning; depletes muscle stores of glycogen; related to azoturia

paraparesis (par' ə pə rē sis) weakness of the back legs

paraphimosis (par' ə fī mō' sis) retraction of phimotic foreskin, causing a painful swelling of the tip of the penis that, if severe, may cause dry gangrene unless corrected

paraplegia (par' ə plē' jē ə) paralysis of both back legs

a=fạt; ā=ạpe; ä=cạr; â=bạre; e=tẹn; ē=ẹven; i=ịs; ī=bịte; ō=gọ; ô=họrn; ōō=tọọl; ŏŏ=lọọk; u=ụp; ʉ=fụr; ŋ=riŋg; ə=sofạ

Parascaris equorum (par' əs' kär is e' kwôr əm) common intestinal parasite; can be passed from dam to foal before birth; also called *ascarids, intestinal worms, large roundworms, white worms*

parasite (par' ə sīt') a plant or animal that lives on or within another living organism, at its expense, to obtain some advantage; any insect or other organism that lives on the skin of the horse or in one or more of the internal organs

parasitic infection (par' ə sit ik in fek' shən) a state of infestation by parasites; symptoms sometimes include a rough coat, weakness, distended abdomen, tucked-up flanks, pale membranes in the eyes and mouth, and frequent colic or diarrhea

parasympathetic (par' ə sim' pə thet' ik) a part of the nervous system that soothes and is constantly active when the animal is at rest

parathyroid gland (par' ə thī' roid gland) small glands located at or near the thyroid gland in the region of the throatlatch; the main function of these glands is to prevent decrease in blood calcium levels

parenchymal (pə ren' ki məl) the essential elements of an organ; used as a general term to designate the functional elements of an organ

parenteral (pa ren' tər əl) administration of medication through some other route than the gastrointestinal tract, such as subcutaneous and intramuscular

parenteral nutrition (pa ren' ter əl nōō trish' ən) supplying nutrients not through the intestinal tract but by an alternate route, such as intravenously

parents (pär' ənts) the stallion (sire) and the mare (dam) responsible for the genetic material imparted to a foal

paresis (pə rē' sis) partial paralysis or weakness

pari-mutuel betting (par' ə myōō' chŏŏ wəl bet' tiŋ) a form of betting in which the total amount wagered, after a deduction of a percentage for costs, is divided among the holders of the winning and place tickets

paring (pâr' ing) cutting away at the sole of the horse's hoof

parked out 1. in racing, when a horse is forced to leave the inside rail to pass other horses; a horse parked out usually has farther to go and usually tires out and falls back 2. stance of some show horses, such as Saddlebreds, where the front and hind legs are extended in a stretched position

park horse (pärk hôrs) a horse with a brilliant performance, style, presence, finish, balance, and cadence

park paling (pärk pā' liŋ) a jumping obstacle that consists of a fence of narrow, pointed strips of wood or metal set vertically on crosspieces; the picket fence

parotid salivary gland (pə rät' id) the largest of the three pairs of salivary glands; located below the ear

parrot mouth (par' ət mouth) when the upper incisors overhang the lower incisors, causing uneven wear; a congenital defect of imperfectly meshed teeth; an extreme overbite; also called *overshot jaw*

partial lethals (pär' shəl lē' thəlz) inherited genetic condition that rarely causes the death of a foal or horse after birth, but can have such an effect on the horse as to restrict either its potential use or reduce the length of life

particulate   (pər tik' yə lit) composed of separate particles

parturient paresis   (par tōō' rē ent pə rē' sis) partial paralysis to young mares beginning lactation that occurs at or near the time of giving birth; commonly called *milk fever*

parturition   (pär' tŏŏ riṣḫ' ən) the act or process of giving birth; also called *foaling*

Paso Fino   (pä' sō fē' nō) a breed known as a strong and willing riding horse; descended from horses taken to America by the Spanish conquistadores; now prominent in certain parts of the U.S.; derived from the Peruvian Paso Horse; walking and trotting gait is very smooth and comfortable; common uses: pleasure, parade, and endurance

Paso Fino Horse Association   an association designed to protect and promote the characteristics and heritage of the Paso Fino horse

passage   (pas' ij) a dressage movement in which the horse trots in a very cadenced, floating manner with a marked period of suspension

passenger   (pas' ən jər) one who rides a horse without control, letting the horse go as he wishes

passive immunity   (pas' iv i myōōn' ə tē) acquired immunity produced by administration of preformed antibodies, as in a foal getting antibodies through the dam's milk or through administration by a veterinarian

passive transfer   (pas' iv trans fʉr') transfer of existing antibodies from one animal to another; the transfer of a mare's antibodies through colostrum to her newborn foal

pass out   (pas out) when a horse goes through the auction ring but does not sell

pastern   (pas' tərn) 1. the area between the fetlock joint and the coronary band; see *points of the horse* (illus.) 2. coat marking in which the white covers the entire pastern; see *markings, leg* (illus.); see illustration

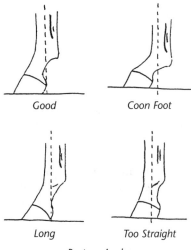

Good   *Coon Foot*

Long   *Too Straight*

Pastern Angle

pasteurization   (pas' cḫər i zā' ṣḫən) process of heating a food material, usually a liquid, to a specific temperature for a specific length of time; a heating process that destroys some bacteria and significantly delays development of others

---

a=fạt; ā=ạpe; ä=cạr; â=bạre; e=tẹn; ē=ẹven; i=ịs; ī=bịte; ō=gọ; ô=họrn; ōō=tọol; ŏŏ=lọok; u=ụp; ʉ=fʉr; ŋ=ring; ə=sofạ

past the mark (past thə märk) the "mark" is a depression in the wearing surface of the horse's incisors; when the depression is no longer present the horse is at least seven years old

pasture (pas' chər) a fenced section of land designed to allow horses to run free safely within its boundaries

pasture breeding (pas' chər brēd' iŋ) releasing mare and stallion into the same pasture, where mating takes place without human intervention

patch (pach) coat marking; an irregularly shaped area on the coat that is a different color than the primary coat color

pate (pāt) the fox's mask

patella (pə tel' ə) a small triangular bone situated at the front of the stifle; also called the *kneecap*; see *skeletal system* (illus.)

patent urachus (pat' ənt u' rə kəs) a relatively common condition in which urine drips from the stump of the navel cord; the flow increases when the foal strains to urinate

pathogen (path' ə jən) any microorganism or material able to cause disease

pathogenic (path' ə jən' ik) capable of producing disease or developing pathology

pathological (path' ə läj' i kəl) a diseased condition

pathological fracture (path' ə läj' i kəl frak' chər) a fracture due to some disease

pathology (pə thäl' ə jē) the scientific study of causes, processes, development, and consequences of disease

patrol judge (pə trōl' juj) a racing association official who watches a race from a certain part of a racetrack and reports what he has seen to the stewards; there are usually three or four patrol judges

pattern (pat' ərn) prescribed order of maneuvers in the individual work of a particular horse show class, such as reining or trail

paunchy (pônch' ē) an undesirable extension of the stomach; usually due to unhealthy conditions caused by worms, disease, malnutrition, etc.

pawing (pô' iŋ) when the horse digs at the ground with one of his front feet; usually an expression of frustration, impatience, or anger, but can be a symptom of colic; can be a vice

pay out when permission has been given by the persons in charge of a race meeting for bets to be paid after the result of the race has been announced

pay up time the nominated time when all entry fees for horses entered in a race are required to be paid

PCV see *packed cell volume*

peacock (pē' käk) a horse that really attracts onlookers' attention; a horse possessing style, color, carriage, and presence

peat moss (pēt môs) an absorbent material that usually consists of decaying plant matter; may be used for bedding

Pechorsky (pe chô' rä' skē) a very hardy and active heavy horse from the valley of the Pechora River in Russia

peck at a jump when a horse jumps slowly, to the extent of almost falling

pecking order the common name for the dominance hierarchy exhibited by a group of horses; the social rank

pectoral (pek' tər əl) pertaining to the chest

pedal bone (ped' əl bōn) also called the *third phalanx* or the *coffin bone;* bone encased in the hoof

pedal osteitis (ped' əl äs' tī tis) inflammation of the pedal bone; associated with demineralization of the pedal bone and formation of a roughness on its outer edge

pediculosis (pi dik' yə lō' sis) infestation with lice

pedigree (ped' ə grē) a form showing the line of ancestors and their performance for an individual horse

pedigree breeding (ped' ə grē brēd' iŋ) selection on the combined basis of the merits of the individual and the average merits of his ancestry

pedunculated (pi duŋ' kyə lāt' əd) growing on a stalk

Pegasus (peg' ə səs) a winged horse of Greek mythology

pelham bit (pel' əm bit) a bit that combines snaffle and curb bits in one mouthpiece; a one-piece bit equipped to handle four reins: two are snaffle reins, used for guiding the horse and

lifting the head, and two are curb reins, used for control and collection

Pelham Bit

pelican horn (pel' i kən hôrn) an early horn on which the top of the cap was flat and the underneath side was shaped like the under side of a pelican's bill

pellets (pel' ətz) compressed feed, usually cylindrical in shape; generally reduces dust; can be supplemented with vitamins and minerals; easy to store

pelvis (pel' vis) the hoop of bones connecting the spine to the hind legs and anchoring the muscles that facilitate hind leg motion; the rear portion of the trunk of the body bounded by the hip bones

penalty (pen' əl tē) in racing, an additional weight handicap carried by a horse; usually imposed when he has won a race since the weights for the race in which the penalty is given were published

pendular (pen' jŏŏ lər) having a pendulumlike movement

Peneia a pleasing, well-balanced breed of pony with oriental origins; a willing worker still used in the province of Peneia in the Peloponnese region of Greece

penicillin (pen' ə sil in) antibiotic commonly used to fight infection in horses

a=fat; ā=ape; ä=car; â=bare; e=ten; ē=even;
i=is; ī=bite; ō=go; ô=horn; ōō=tool;
ŏŏ=look; u=up; ʉ=fur; ŋ=ring; ə=sofa

penis (pē' nis) the male sex organ

pepsin (pep' sin) an enzyme of the stomach that breaks down most proteins to polypeptides, aiding in digestion

perch (pʉrch) in carriages, the connection between the front and rear axle serving as a foundation around which the undercarriage of many vehicles is built

Percheron (pʉr' chə rän') a draft breed native to France; thought to have an infusion of Arab and Barb ancestry; sometimes referred to as the breed of blacks and grays; stands 15.2–17 hands; powerful, with stamina and endurance, fine head, and graceful movement

Percheron Horse Association of America a registry for foals of registered parents

percussion (pər kush' ən) the act of striking a part with short, sharp blows as an aid in diagnosing the condition of the parts beneath by the sound obtained

perennial (pə ren' ē əl) refers to a plant that remains green and active throughout the year; plants that revegitate each spring without being replanted

perfecta (pʉr' fek' tə) a type of wagering in which the bettor must select the first and second place finishers without regard to the actual order in which they pass the post

performance (pər fôr' məns) exhibition of gaits or other required routines

Performance Only Class a class in which the horse is judged on his ability to perform the required exercises; conformation and manners are not considered

pergamino parchment-thin leather rawhide used by Mexican saddlemakers for many years

periarticular (per' ə är tik' yōō lər) situated around a joint

pericardiocentesis (per' i kär' dē ō sen tē' sis) puncture of the saclike structure around the heart for the aspiration of fluid

pericarditis (per' ə kär dīt' is) inflammation of the pericardium

pericardium (per' ē kär' dē əm) the thin, tough, connective tissue membrane that encloses the heart in a saclike structure

perilymph (per' i limf) the fluid contained within the space separating the membranous from the osseous labyrinth of the ear

perinatal (per' ə nāt' əl) occurring shortly before or immediately after birth

perineal (per' i nē' əl) pertaining to the pelvic floor and the structures of the pelvic outlet

periodic ophthalmia (pēr' ē od' ik of thal' mē ə) an inflammatory disease of the eye which is the most common cause of blindness in the horse; also called *moon blindness*

periople (per' ē ō' pəl) the narrow strip below the coronary band that functions somewhat like the human cuticle; it produces the varnishlike substance that covers the outer surface of the wall and seals it from excess drying

perioplic corium (per' ē äp lik kō' rē əm) the sensitive tissue that feeds the periople

periosteal (per' i äs' tē əl) pertaining to the periosteum

periosteum (per' i äs' tē əm) a specialized connective tissue covering all bones of the body and is capable of forming bone; covers bones throughout the body except at points of articulation (joints)

periostitis (per' i äs tīt' əs) inflammation of the periosteum

peripheral (pə rif' ər əl) the part of the circulatory system that carries blood to the outer parts of the body such as the legs; the part of the nervous system that provides a network of communication between the internal or external environment and the central nervous system

peripheral nervous system (nur' vəs sis' təm) consists of the nerves after they exit the spinal cord or the brain stem

peristalsis (per' ə stôl' sis) wavelike contractions that move food down the esophagus and along the muscular walls of the intestine

peritoneum (per' it ən ē' əm) the serous membrane lining the walls of the abdominal and pelvic cavities and surrounding the internal organs

peritonitis (per' it ən īt' is) inflammation of the lining of the abdominal cavity; marked by severe abdominal pain

perivascular (per' i vas' kyōō lər) situated around a vessel

perlino a pearl-colored horse that is off-white, often with rust-colored legs, tips of tail, muzzle, and mane; not a true albino, but often referred to as a *type B albino*

permanent teeth (pʉr' mə nənt tēth) the teeth that erupt, some displacing the deciduous (baby) teeth; permanent teeth begin to erupt at 9–12 months of age (1st molars)

permeability (pʉr' mē ə bil' ət ē) ability to be penetrated

permeate (pʉr' mē āt) to spread throughout or penetrate

permit to drive authorization for Standardbred drivers that allows them to gain experience by driving on the training track and in trials in order to gain their license to drive in races

permit to ride authorization given to apprentice jockeys that allows them to ride track work and exercise, and to ride in trials so that they can gain sufficient experience to gain a license to ride in races

Persian Arab (pʉr' zhən ar' əb) a breed with its origins in Iran; more robust in shape and structure than other Arabians; known as a spirited, athletic riding horse

Peruvian Part-Blood Registry a registry open to horses, mules, and ponies who are at least 50 percent Peruvian Paso

Peruvian Paso (pe' rōō vē ən pä' sō) developed some 300 years ago in Peru

---

a=f<u>a</u>t; ā=<u>a</u>pe; ä=c<u>a</u>r; â=b<u>a</u>re; e=t<u>e</u>n; ē=<u>e</u>ven; i=<u>i</u>s; ī=b<u>i</u>te; ō=g<u>o</u>; ô=h<u>o</u>rn; ōō=t<u>oo</u>l; ŏŏ=l<u>oo</u>k; u=<u>u</u>p; ʉ=f<u>u</u>r; ŋ=ri<u>ng</u>; ə=sof<u>a</u>

from the Barb and the Andalusian; possesses the Paso gait, a distinct sideways or lateral movement of the legs that can be maintained at the one pace for considerable periods of time; known for long hind legs, long pasterns, and unusual and extreme flexibility of the joints; also called *Peruvian Stepping Horse*

Peruvian Paso Horse Registry of North America   a registry for horses that are purebred and qualify for a closed studbook

Peruvian Stepping Horse   see *Peruvian Paso*

pervious urachus   (pɜr' vē əs u' rə kəs) a condition that develops when the urachus, a small ureterlike structure within the umbilical cord, fails to close when the umbilical cord is severed

pesade   (pə sād) a maneuver in which the horse is made to rear

pessary   (pes' ər ē) an instrument placed in the vagina to support the uterus or rectum; used as a contraceptive device

petechia   (pə tē' kē ə) a small, round, purplish red spot caused by hemorrhage that later turns blue or yellow

petrissage   (pə' tri säz̲h) massage in which the muscles are kneaded and pressed

pH   a symbol for the measurement of alkalinity and acidity; pH 7 is neutral, greater than 7 is alkaline, less than 7 is acidic; normal body pH is 7.4

phaeton   (fā' i tən) a country carriage with four wheels, a high front seat, and a low rear seat; only the front seat is protected by a hood; drawn by a pair of horses

Phaeton Carriage

p h a g o c y t e   (fag' ə sīt') any cell that ingests microorganisms or other cells and foreign particles

phagocytosis   (fag' ō sī tō' sis) the engulfing of microorganisms and foreign particles by a phagocyte

phalanx   (fā' laŋks) any of the three bones below the fetlock; the long pastern bone, the short pastern bone, and coffin bone

pharmacology   (fär' mə käl' ə jē) the science that deals with drugs, their sources, appearance, chemistry, actions, and uses

pharyngeal   (fār' in jē' əl) pertaining to the pharynx

pharyngitis   (far' in jīt' əs) inflammation of the pharynx

pharynx   (far' iŋks) the section of the alimentary canal between the mouth and the esophagus; also serves, except during swallowing, to connect the nasal passages with the windpipe

phenobarbital   (fē' nō bär' bi tal') a crystalline barbituate commonly used as a sedative

phenothiazine   (fēn' ō t̲h̲ī' ə zēn) generic name for a commercial chemical widely used in deworming medicines; the parent compound for many other drugs, including the tranquilizers acetylpromazine and promazine hydrochloride

phenotype (fē' nə tīp') the physical makeup of an animal; traits that are visible

phenylbutazone (fen' əl bu' tə zōn) generic name for an odorless, white, anti-inflammatory powder used in the treatment of joint, bone, and muscle injuries or disorders, as well as wounds

pheromone (fer' ə mōn) any substance or hormone secreted by one animal that alters the behavior of another; substances that are present in the mare's urine when she is in heat and excites the stallion

phlebitis (fli bīt' is) inflammation of the veins

phlegmon (fleg' män) inflammation of the connective tissues

phosphorus (fäs' fər əs) one of the important minerals in the horse's body; in combination with calcium, phosphorus is responsible for bone formation, growth, and maintenance

photodynamic agent (fō' tō dī nam' ik ā' jənt) an agent that reacts with sunlight

photo finish (fō' to fin' ish) the result of a race photographed by a camera with a very narrow field of vision situated at the winning post on a racecourse

photoperiod (fō' tə pēr' ē əd) the period of time an animal is exposed to sunlight over the course of one day

photophobia (fōt' ə fō' bē ə) an abnormal aversion to light

photosensitivity (fō' tə sen' sə tiv' it ē)

a reaction of unpigmented areas of the skin to sunlight; inflammation and sunburn are symptoms

phycomycosis (fī' kō mī' kō' sis) an infection caused by any of several fungi in the class phycomycetes; the first signs of the infection may be swellings on the skin that discharge clear fluid

physical (fiz' ik əl) referring to the body rather than the mind

physiological (fiz' ē ə läj' i kəl) of or relating to normal body, organ, or tissue function

physiology (fiz' ē äl' ə jē) the branch of biology that deals with the normal functions and activities of life or living matter (cells, organs, tissues), and with the chemical and physical phenomena involved

phytotoxin (fīt' ə täk' sin) any toxic substance of plant origin

piaffe (pyaf) a high, collected trot in place, with a prolonged period of suspension

pica (pī' kə) a horse with a depraved appetite, prone to eat dirt, wood, hair, bones, etc.

pickup man in rodeo, a mounted cowboy who helps the rider off a bronc when a ride is completed; the pickup man pulls off the flank strap from the bronc and removes the bronc from the arena

picnic races meetings held in Aus-

a=fat; ā=ape; ä=car; â=bare; e=ten; ē=even; i=is; ī=bite; ō=go; ô=horn; ōō=tool; ŏŏ=look; u=up; ʉ=fur; ŋ=ring; ə=sofa

tralia's Outback; amateur riders and their mounts compete against each other for small prizes on primitive racetracks

Piebald (pī' bôld) a color term for a black and white horse; coat color in Paints and Pintos; patches of black and white

pied (pīd) refers to certain colors and markings of hounds

pigeon-toed (pij' ən tōd) the toes of the front legs point in rather than straight ahead; horses with this condition will usually paddle or wing out; see *conformation comparisons, front limb* (illus.)

pig-eyed (pig īd) having small, narrow, squinty eyes, set back in the head; also having thick eyelids

piggin' string (pig' in striŋ) the six-foot length of rope used to tie the three legs of a calf in calf-roping events

pigment (pig' mənt) any coloring matter of the body; the material that imparts color to the eyes, hair, or skin

pillion (pil' yən) a small pad behind the saddle on which a second rider or pack is carried

pilot (pī' lət) a rider who knows the country well and who can act as a guide to a less-experienced rider

pimple (pim' pəl) a cowboy's derisive term for an English saddle

Pindos a very old Greek breed, influenced by oriental blood; bred in the mountainous regions of Thessaly and Epirus; strong and hardy, especially well suited to farm work in hilly, upland areas; also used as a riding pony

pineal gland (pin' ē əl gland) an appendage of the floor of the brain that functions, in part, as the body's time-measuring system or biological clock

pin firing (pin fī' ər iŋ) a method of using an electric needle to insert into an injured area to induce healing at the site; burning the skin over a minor internal leg injury with a hot iron to produce scar tissue and aid in healing

Pinkafelder a medium-weight draft or heavy horse from Belgium

pink eye (pink ī) an acute, contagious form of conjunctivitis in which the eyeball and the lining of the eyelid become red and inflamed

pinna (pin' ə) the part of the ear outside the skull; the external ear

Pintabian Horse Registry a registry for horses possessing more than 99 percent Arabian blood with tobiano markings

pinto (pin' tō) 1. coat color; a horse with large colored and white patches on his body 2. a breed (Pinto) based on the pinto color pattern; a horse registered with the Pinto Horse Association of America

Pinto Horse Association of America a breed registry and association for pinto-colored horses of various crosses and types

pinworms (pin' wɥrmz') parasites that infect the horse and may cause intense itching in the rectal area, resulting in tail rubbing; two species of pinworms, or rectal worms, are frequently found in horses; these worms mature in the large intestine and lay their eggs on the hairs around the anus

piperazine   (pip' ər ə zīn) the generic name for a common dewormer used against roundworms

pique   (pēk) a calvary term for a high pommel arch

piroplasmosis   (pī' rō plas mō' sis) a protozoal disease transmitted by blood-sucking ticks; also called *Texas fever*

pirouette   (pir' ōō et') a two-track movement performed at the walk or canter; the forehand moves around the haunches in a small circle with a radius equal to the length of the horse

pit   (pit) the imprint retained by a soft swelling after pressure has been applied and released

pitch   (pich) 1. A cavalry term used to describe a loose seat covering 2. a bucking motion

pitting edema   (pit' iŋ i' dē mə) accumulation of fluid under the skin that leaves an indentation after firm finger pressure

pituitary gland   (pi tōō' ə ter' ē gland) a gland at the base of the brain that secretes and stores hormones that regulate most of the basic body functions

pivot   (piv' ət) 1. a crisp, prompt 90° or 180° turn on the hindquarters 2. a movement in reining in which the horse pivots around his hindquarters, holding the inside hind leg more or less in place while stepping around it with the other hind foot

pivoted   a turn on the hindquarters in which the inside hind leg stays in place and is not picked up

place   (plās) to finish second in a race

placebo   (plə sē' bō) preparation containing no medication; administered in order to simulate treatment

placenta   (plə sen' tə) saclike membrane connecting the unborn fetus to the lining of the mother's uterus; serves to nourish the fetus and transport waste material through contact with the mother's uterus; expelled from the uterus shortly after delivery

placentitis   (plə' sen tī' tis) inflammation of the placenta; can be a cause of abortion, prematurity, or unhealthy foals

placing judge   (plās' iŋ juj) a racing association official who, with the other placing judges, decides the placement of the horses in their order of finish

plain ankles   (plān aŋ' kəlz) puffed around the ankles

plain scrole   the metal support below a rumble seat; see *carriage parts* (illus.)

plaiting   (plāt' iŋ) 1. when the horse places one forefoot directly in front of the other; interference and stumbling usually result; also called *rope walking* 2. braiding mane and tail hair for show

plaits   (plāts) braids

planks   (plaŋks) a show-jumping obstacle made up of one-foot-wide painted planks

---

a=f<u>a</u>t; ā=<u>a</u>pe; ä=c<u>a</u>r; â=b<u>a</u>re; e=t<u>e</u>n; ē=<u>e</u>ven;
i=<u>i</u>s; ī=b<u>i</u>te; ō=g<u>o</u>; ô=h<u>o</u>rn; ōō=t<u>oo</u>l;
ŏŏ=l<u>oo</u>k; u=<u>u</u>p; ʉ=f<u>u</u>r; ŋ=ri<u>ng</u>; ə=sof<u>a</u>

plantar (plan′ tər) pertaining to the sole of the foot; see *hoof* (illus.)

Plantation Horse Tennessee Walking Horse

plaque (plak) any patch or flat area

plasma (plaz′ mə) the clear, yellowish fluid portion of blood in which the various blood cells are suspended

plasma extenders (ik sten′ derz) substances that can be transfused to maintain plasma volume of the blood

plasma volume (vol′ yo͞om) proportion of the circulating blood that is fluid

plate (plāt) part of the English saddle tree; see *English saddle tree* (illus.)

platelets (plāt′ lits) disk-shaped structures found in the blood of all mammals and chiefly known for their role in blood coagulation; also called *blood platelets* and *thrombocytes*

Pleasure Class a popular English or western class in which the horses are ridden on the rail at the walk, trot, and canter or lope; the performance of the horse is judged based on the smoothness and consistency of his gaits

Pleasure Driving a class in which horses are harnessed to a pleasure-type, two-wheeled, single-horse cart

pleasure horse 1. a well-mannered, obedient horse, having easy gaits and no serious vices 2. a horse shown in the Pleasure Class 3. a horse used for recreational riding

pleura (plo͝or′ ə) the thin, serous membrane located in the chest cavity; the parietal pleura lines the inside surface of the rib cage; the visceral pleura covers the outer surface of the lungs

pleurisy (plo͝or′ ə sē) inflammation of the membranous covering of the lungs; usually caused by bacterial infection; the symptoms are sweating, fever, and signs of pain

pleuropneumonia (plo͝or′ ō no͞o mōn′ yə) acute and often fatal combined inflammation of the lungs and the pleura

Pleven (plev′ ən) a recently developed breed that takes its name from the state-owned agricultural establishment near Pleven in Bulgaria; intelligent, good natured, used as a saddle horse and for light farm work and jumping; color: chestnut

pleximeter (plek′ sə mēt′ ər) a veterinary instrument used to perform percussion

plexus (plek′ səs) a network of lymphatic vessels, nerves, veins, or arteries

pliohippus (plī′ ō hip′ əs) the ancestor of equus that is thought to have migrated across the land bridge that existed in the area of the Bering Sea

plow reining (plou rān′ iŋ) another name for direct reining

pluck (pluk) courage and ability

plug (plug) a horse of common breeding and poor conformation; any slow or broken-down horse

PMSG see *pregnant mare serum gonadotropin*

pneumonia (no͝o mōn′ yə) inflammation of the lungs, usually involving one or more lobes; causes consolidation of lung tissue and usually a generalized toxemia

pneumonitis (nŏŏ′ mō nī′ tis) condition of localized, acute inflammation of the lung without generalized toxemia

pneumothorax (nŏŏ′ mə thôr′ aks) presence of air between the chest wall and the lungs, resulting in difficulty breathing

pneumovagina (nŏŏ′ mō və jī nə) the presence of air in the vagina, often resulting in infection; the single most common cause of female infertility

POA see *Pony of the Americas*

point (point) the team in back of the leaders in an eight-horse hitch

pointing standing with one foreleg extended more than normal; a sign of pain in the leg

point of hock the bulblike protrusion that points back from the stifle joint of the hind legs

points 1. coloring of the legs, mane, and tail 2. the part of the pommel arch on an English saddle that extends below the bars to reduce rolling or sideways movement of the saddle; in western saddles, the long-pointed lower parts of a tapadera 3. assigned values for winning or placing at approved shows

point-to-point originally a type of race in which the contestants might choose their own courses; required to go from one designated point, such as a church steeple, to another; modern point-to-points held by many hunt clubs are usually flagged and require riders to follow a definite course

points of the horse see illustration

poisonous plants (poi′ zə nəs plants) some examples of plants poisonous to horses include wild cherry, nightshade, yew bush, mountain laurel, water hemlock, bracken fern, goldenrod, and jack-in-the-pulpit

Poitevin a French breed that descends from the Netherlands; developed in the French region of Poitier on marshy terrain; used for heavy draft and farm work

pole (pōl) in harness driving, a length of wood with metal fittings to which horses, for pair driving, are hitched on either side; used to prevent the horse from bearing to one side, a tendency that can be dangerous; hooked between the bridle and the saddle; keeps the horse moving straight

pole bending a timed event in which the horse must travel a pattern around six poles; if the horse knocks down a pole, he is disqualified or is given a time penalty

poling a cruel practice of striking the underpart of a horse as he goes over a jump with any number of devices, from a bamboo pole to a heavy bar wrapped with barbed wire; a practice used by inefficient trainers

poll (pōl) the bony prominence lying between the ears; the junction of the vertebrae with the skull; an area of great sensitivity and flexion; see *points of the horse* (illus.)

a=fat; ā=ape; ä=car; â=bare; e=ten; ē=even; i=is; ī=bite; ō=go; ô=horn; ōō=tool; ŏŏ=look; u=up; ʉ=fur; ŋ=ring; ə=sofa

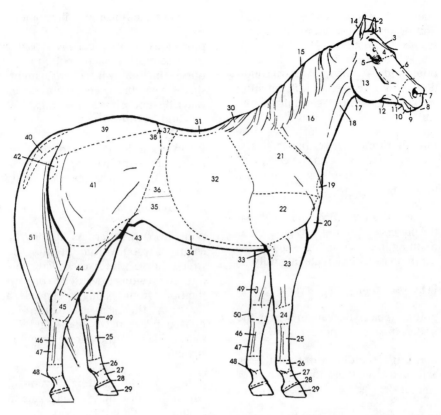

1. Occipital Crest
2. Ear
3. Forelock
4. Forehead
5. Eye
6. Bridge of Nose
7. Nostril
8. Muzzle
9. Lower Lip
10. Chin
11. Chin Groove
12. Branches of Jaw
13. Jowl or Cheek
14. Poll
15. Crest
16. Neck
17. Throatlatch
18. Jugular Groove
19. Point of Shoulder
20. Chest
21. Shoulder
22. Upper Arm
23. Forearm
24. Knee
25. Cannon
26. Fetlock Joint (Ankle)
27. Pastern
28. Coronet
29. Hoof
30. Withers
31. Back
32. Ribs
33. Elbow
34. Belly
35. Flank
36. Coupling
37. Loin
38. Point of Hip
39. Croup
40. Dock
41. Thigh
42. Point of Buttock
43. Stifle
44. Gaskin
45. Hock
46. Suspensory Ligament
47. Flexor Tendon
48. Ergot
49. Chestnut
50. Accessory Carpal Bone
51. Tail

Points of the Horse

poll evil an inflamed condition in the region of the poll; usually caused by bruising the top of the head

polo (pō′ lō) a mounted game, bearing a resemblance to hockey; played between two teams of four on a team

polo chain (pō′ lō c͟hān) a chin chain of flat, large links

polo crosse a game based on polo and lacrosse; particularly popular in Australia

polo pony a saddle horse usually with some pony breeding used for the sport of polo; possessed of stamina, brains, and quick maneuverability; trained to carry a rider with almost no guidance through the mazes of the game; most often bred from Thoroughbreds or Quarter Horses

polyarthritis (päl′ ē är t͟hrī′ tis) an inflammation of several joints at the same time

polycythemia (päl′ i sī thē′ mē ə) an increase in the total red blood cell mass of the body

polydactylism (päl′ ē dak′ təl izm) a rare occurrence in horses; the development of a second toe on one foot

polydipsia (päl′ ē dip′ sē ə) persistent and excessive thirst

polyestrus (päl′ ē es′ trus) a term given to a mare that cycles continuously throughout the breeding season in absence of conception

polyp (päl′ ip) a benign, narrow-based tumor growing from the membrane lining a body cavity

polyuria (päl′ i yŏŏr′ ē ə) passage of an abnormally large volume of urine in a given period; characterized by frequent urination

pommel (päm′ əl) the horn and swells on a western saddle; the front portion of the English saddle; see *English saddle; western saddle* (illus.)

poncho (pän′ chō) a cape-type garment, normally rain proof, designed to cover a person's body from head to toe

pony (pō′ nē) a horse of any small breed that stands 14.2 hands or less at maturity

pony boy 1. the rider of a horse who accompanies and aids the jockey in controlling his mount in the post parade 2. the rider of a horse who leads a riderless horse in a workout

pony horse the horse used to accompany racehorses on the track to help keep them calm

ponying leading a horse while riding another horse

Pony of the Americas an American breed of pony known for its distinctive spotted coat like the Appaloosa; an excellent trotting pony and a good jumper; often used by younger riders for long distance and flat racing; height: 11.2–13 hands; color: same as Appaloosa

Pony of the Americas Club an organization for ponies with a height of 46–56 in, with Appaloosa coloration and characteristics

---

a=f<u>a</u>t; ā=<u>a</u>pe; ä=c<u>a</u>r; â=b<u>a</u>re; e=t<u>e</u>n; ē=<u>e</u>ven; i=<u>i</u>s; ī=b<u>i</u>te; ō=g<u>o</u>; ô=h<u>o</u>rn; ōō=t<u>oo</u>l; ŏŏ=l<u>oo</u>k; u=<u>u</u>p; ʉ=f<u>u</u>r; ŋ=ri<u>ng</u>; ə=sof<u>a</u>

pony speed test   the racing of ponies ridden by light boy riders around the quarter-mile circuit at show grounds in Australia

pool   (pōōl) total money bet on horses in a race

pop-eyed   (päp īd) **1.** a horse that has eyes that are generally more prominent or bulge out a little more than normal **2.** a horse that is "spooky" or attempts to see everything that goes on

popped knee   (päpt nē) a general term describing inflammatory conditions affecting the knees, so named because of the sudden swelling that accompanies it; see *blemishes and unsoundnesses* (illus.)

port   (pôrt) the part of the mouthpiece of a bit curving up over the tongue

portable corral   (pōr' tə bəl kə ral') plastic pipe or metal panels that can be fastened to the side of the trailer for transport; on arrival they can be easily assembled into a corral; allows horses to move about freely, making them less likely to stiffen up after a rigorous workout

positioning insufficient   (pə zish' ən iŋ in' sə fish' ənt) failure of a rider to prepare the horse for a movement; i.e., by putting him into a position where he will not be able to perform the exercise easily

positive reinforcement   (päz' i tiv rē in fōrs' mənt) a reward; giving something pleasant to encourage the behavior it follows

post   (pōst) **1.** the starting point for the race; either the starting or winning position in racing **2.** to rise from the saddle at the trot

postage stamp   (pō' stij stamp) a cowboy's derisive term for an English saddle

post and rail   an obstacle used in cross-country and show jumping consisting of upright posts separated by a number of horizontal rails

postanesthetic   myoneuropathy (pōst' an es thet' ik mī' ō nōō räp ə thē) muscular weakness and/or neurological deficits after anesthesia due to poor circulation in large muscle groups of the horse

post entry   a horse entered after the official entries have closed; double or triple fee is usually charged

posterior   (pä stēr' ē ər) situated in the back of a structure; toward the rear end of the body

posterior synechia   (pä stēr ē ər si nek' ē ə) adhesion of the iris to the lens

Postier   Breton   originating in France, this variety of Breton is of medium size; used originally as a fast, medium-size draft horse

posting   the rising and descending of a rider with the rhythm of the trot

post legged   too little angle at the hock

post mortem   after death

post parade   the time before the race when the horses leave the paddock, come on the racetrack, and walk in front of the stands

postpartum (pōst′ pär′ təm) occurring after delivery, with reference to the mother

postpartum metritis (pōst′ pär′ təm met rī′ tis) inflammation of the lining of the uterus after giving birth; can be a cause of laminitis

postparturient (pōst′ pär tōō rē ənt) occurring after delivery

postparturient hypocalcemia see *milk fever*

post position a horse's position in the starting gate from the inside rail outward; determined by a drawing at the close of entries

post time the official time set by the stewards at which a race will start and at which the horses are required to be at the post and ready to start

potable (pōt′ ə bəl) suitable for drinking; used to describe water supplies that have been tested and determined to meet or exceed the appropriate health authority standards for drinking water

potassium (pə tas′ ē əm) scientific abbreviation: K; an electrolyte that is closely related to muscle contractability

Potomac horse fever (pə tō′ mək hôrs fē′ vər) acute onset of severe diarrhea, fever, and laminitis that can be fatal; caused by *Ehrlichia risticii;* named after the Potomac River Valley, where it was first recognized in 1979

pottering (pät′ ər iŋ) a short stride, generally on the front legs, with a tendency for the horse to throw weight on the heels; may be the result of an injury or a conformational defect

poultice (pōl′ tis) a moist, mealy mass applied hot to a sore or inflamed part of the body; creates moist local heat or counterirritation

pounding (pound′ iŋ) striking the ground hard; making unduly heavy contact with the ground at the completion of the stride

poverty line (päv′ ər tē līn) a line or depression that appears in the muscles on the hindquarters of a horse; a sign that the horse could be better muscled or carrying more muscle; may be due to underfeeding, poor conformation, or an internal parasitic infestation

power of association (pou′ ər uv a sō′ sē ā′ shən) the ability to link an action and a reaction; a stimulus and a response; the key to training horses, since they will try to avoid mistakes and earn a reward

prad (prəd) an old-fashioned term for horses

PRCA Professional Rodeo Cowboys Association

Preakness (prēk′ nes) the second race of the Triple Crown

precipitate (pri sip′ ə tāt) to cause a substance in a solution to settle as solid particles

predators (pred′ ə tərz) animals that kill and feed on other animals

prednisone (pred′ ni sōn) generic name of a steroidal anti-inflammatory agent

a=fat; ā=ape; ä=car; â=bare; e=ten; ē=even; i=is; ī=bite; ō=go; ô=horn; ōō=tool; ŏŏ=look; u=up; ʉ=fur; ŋ=ring; ə=sofa

pregnancy   (preg′ nən sē) the physi-ological state of the female carrying a fetus or unborn foal

pregnant mare serum gonadotropin (preg′ nənt mâr sēr′ em gō nad′ ə trō′ pin) may be detected in a blood test after forty-five days of pregnancy

prehension   (pri hen′ shən) the act of seizing or grasping, as when the horse grasps food with the lips

prematurity   (prē′ mə tŏŏr′ i tē) un-derdevelopment; the condition of a premature foal

premaxilla   (prē′ mak sil′ ə) either of two bones in the upper jaw

prenatal   (prē nāt′ əl) occurring be-fore birth

preparation insufficient   (prep′ ə rā′ shən in′ sə fish′ ənt) the rider has not warned the horse early enough what is coming next and was probably unbal-anced

prepotency   (prē pōt′ ən sē) ability to pass outstanding characteristics to off-spring; breeding power, as measured by the degree in which parent likeness is transmitted to offspring

prepuce   (prē′ pyōōs) the sheath of the male penis

presence   (prez′ əns) personality; charisma

presentation   (prez′ ən tā′ shən) a driving competition in which contes-tants are judged on the driver, the grooms, the horse or horses, the vehi-cle, and general appearance

presumptive diagnosis   (pri zump′ tiv dī′ əg nō′ sis) expected diagnosis

prevalence   (prev′ ə ləns) number of cases of disease in a specific group at a particular time

price   (prīs) the odds quoted by a bookmaker at a race meeting for a par-ticular horse

primary treatment   (prī′ mer′ ē trēt′ mənt) first treatment in order of devel-opment; the principal treatment

prince of ponies   (prins uv pō′ nēz) the Hackney pony is sometimes re-ferred to as the prince of ponies be-cause of his elegance and friskiness

Prix des Nations   an international team show-jumping competition held at an official international horse show; four members compete in each team, jumping the course twice; the three best scores of the team are counted in each round

prize money   (prīz mun′ ē) money paid to the winners of the various events in a rodeo

procaine   (prō′ kān) generic name for a local anesthetic

produce   (prō′ dōōs) the progeny of a dam

proestrus   (prō es′ trus) the period of rapid follicle growth in the estrous cycle just prior to "heat" or estrus

professional   (prə fesh′ ən əl) a per-son older than eighteen who engages in any of the following activities for pay: riding, driving, showing at halter, training, boarding, instructing, con-ducting seminars or clinics; employed as groom or farrier; a person who uses his name or photo in connection with advertisement and for accepting prize money in classes; will vary according to the association

progenitor (prō jen' ə tər) one that originates or precedes

progeny (präj' ə nē) offspring or descendants of one or both parents

progesterone (prō jes' tə rōn) female hormone secreted by the corpus luteum of the ovary, beginning prior to the implantation of the fertilized egg; maintains pregnancy by stopping the estrous cycle

prognathism (präg' nə t̪hiz əm) marked protrusion of the lower jaw

prognosis (präg nō' sis) the prospect of recovery from a disease or injury

progressive (prə gres' iv) advancing in severity; going from bad to worse

prolactin (prō lak' tin) the hormone produced in the anterior pituitary gland; initiates lactation or milk production

proliferate (prō lif' ə rāt') to multiply; to grow by reproducing similar cells

prophet's thumb (präf' its t̪hum) a muscular depression of unknown origin; often seen on the neck, but also seen on the quarters and shoulder

prophylactic (prō' fə lak' tik) an agent that acts to prevent disease

proppy action (präp' ē ak' s̪hən) when a horse is lame in the two front or two back legs; stilted action

proprioceptive sense (prō' prē ə sep' tiv sens) a horse's awareness of his body parts in relation to each other and in movement

propulsion (prə pul' s̪hən) a driving force; moving ahead with vigor; the tendency to fall forward in walking

prostaglandins (präs' tə glan' dins) a group of hormonelike fatty acid substances that are active in many physiological processes, including inflammation, reproduction, and the lowering of blood pressure

prostate (präs' tāt) accessory sex gland; produces fluid that nourishes sperm; see *urethra*

prosthesis (präs' t̪hə sis) an artificial substitute for a missing part of the body

protective behavior (prə tek' tiv bi hāv' yer) any act of a horse to preserve itself; either seeking shelter from weather elements or fleeing when he feels threatened

proteinaceous (prō' tē nā s̪həs) pertaining to the nature of protein

proteins (prō' tēns) any of a group of complex compounds that contain nitrogen and are composed of amino acids

proteinuria (prō tēn yōō' rē ə) presence of protein in the urine; usually due to kidney disease

proteolytic (prō' tē ə lit' ik) used to describe substances, usually enzymes, that attack or digest complex proteins, resulting in simpler proteins or amino acids

prothrombin (prō t̪hräm' bin) precursor of the clotting protein present in plasma

---

a=fat; ā=ape; ä=car; â=bare; e=ten; ē=even;
i=is; ī=bite; ō=go; ô=horn; ōō=tool;
ŏŏ=look; u=up; ʉ=fur; ŋ=ring; ə=sofa

protozoa (prōt' ə zō' ə) single-celled microscopic animal living chiefly in water; the simplest, most primitive form of animal life

proud flesh (proud flesh) unhealthy tissue that sometimes forms around a wound; excess granulation tissue rising out of and above the edges of a wound

proximal (präk' sə məl) nearest or closer to a particular point of reference

pruritus (prŏŏ rīt' əs) intense itching

Przewalski's horse a rare species of horse; subspecies of *Equus caballus*; efforts are being made to reintroduce this horse to the wild

Pseudomonas (sōō' dō mō' nas) a bacterial organism that flourishes in open wounds

psoroptic mange (sō' rop' tik mānj) mange caused by a mite of the genus *Psoroptes;* occurs mainly on sheltered parts of the body and areas covered with long hair

psychogenic (si' kō gen' ik) originating in the mind

psychology (sī' käl ə jē) the science of human and animal behavior

PtHA Pinto Horse Association of America

ptyalin (tī' ə lin) the enzyme that transforms starch into maltose in the mouth of the horse

puberty (pyōō' bər tē) the state of being capable of siring or bearing offspring; point of sexual maturity; mares generally reach the age of puberty at fifteen to twenty-four months of age

pudgy (puj' ē) short and thickset

pueblo saddle (pweb' lō sad' əl) a type of saddle popularized by the Texas trail-driving cowboys; the design came from the Pueblo, Colorado, saddlemakers in the late 1800s

puffs (pufs) windgalls, bog spavins, or thoroughpins

pug (pug) a fox

pulled a leader when the tendon or ligament behind the cannon is pulled or sprained; also referred to as a *bowed tendon*

pulling leather hanging on to the saddle to maintain balance; when a saddled bronc rider touches any part of the saddle with a free hand, he or she is said to be pulling leather and is disqualified

pulling record, world the world's record in a pulling contest was established at the 1965 Hillsdale County Fair, in Michigan: 56,493 lbs or more than 28 tons on a wagon

pulling the mane or tail thinning the hair in the mane or tail by pulling part of the hair out

pulmonary (pul' mə ner' ē) pertaining to the lungs

pulmonary artery (är' tər ē) the artery that carries blood from the heart to the lungs

pulmonary edema (i dē' mə) accumulation of fluid in the lungs, impairing the absorption of oxygen by the blood

pulmonary emphysema (pul' mə ner' ē em' fə sē' mə) also known as *broken wind;* a condition of abnormal distention and inability to empty the lungs of air; caused by the rupture of some alveoli

pulp (pulp) the soft substance at the center of a horse's teeth

pulse (puls) rhythmic throbbing of an artery that may be felt with the finger; caused by blood forced through the vessel by contractions of the heart; normal adult resting heart rate varies among horses, but is usually forty beats per minute; a horse's pulse may be taken on the inner side of the jaw, inside the elbow of the foreleg, or at the back of the fetlock joint

puncture (puŋk' chər) a wound that is deeper than it is wide

punishment (pun' ish mənt) administering something unpleasant to discourage the behavior it follows

punter (punt' ər) a person who bets regularly on horses

pupa (pyōō' pə) an inactive stage in development of some insects following the larval stage and before the adult form

pupil (pyōō' pəl) the black, circular aperture in the center of the iris

pupillary light reflex (pyōō' pə ler' ē līt rē' fleks) automatic closing of the pupil when a bright light is shone in the eye

purpura hemorrhagic (pʉr' pyōō rə hem' ə räj' ik) a disease of the horse characterized by extensive collections of fluid and blood in tissues beneath the skin; occurring primarily on the head and legs

purebred (pyōōr' bred) a horse with

parents that are both recorded in the same registry

purgative (pʉr' gə tiv) an agent that causes a cleansing or evacuation of the bowels

purse (pʉrs) race prize money to which the owners of horses in the race do not contribute

pursuit (pər sōōt') to chase in order to capture and kill; a term generally used in fox hunting

purulent (pyŏŏr' ə lənt) full of, containing, forming, or discharging pus

purulent inflammation (in' flə mā' shən) an inflammation associated with the formation of pus

pus (pus) a liquid product of inflammation composed of dead white blood cells (leukocytes) and cellular fluids; the yellow-red-colored substance containing bacteria-containing cells and fluid produced as a result of a wound or infection

push corn (pŏŏsh côrn) blood-colored spot at the angle of the sole resulting from bleeding in the angle of the sole or its adjacent white line; caused by overloading the heel of the hoof

puss (pŏŏs) English expression for hare

pustules (pus' chōōlz) visible collections of pus within or beneath the skin

---

a=fat; ā=ape; ä=car; â=bare; e=ten; ē=even; i=is; ī=bite; ō=go; ô=horn; ōō=tool; ŏŏ=look; u=up; ʉ=fur; ŋ=ring; ə=sofa

put down   put to death; euthanize

putrid   (pyōō′ trid) rotten or decomposed

putting to   attaching the harnessed horse or horses to the vehicle

PVC fencing   fencing made of polyvinyl chloride; resembles very hard plastic and requires little maintenance

pylorus   (pī lôr′ əs) the part of the stomach that joins with the small intestine

pyometra   (pī′ ō mē′ trə) an accumulation of pus within the uterus

pyramidal   (pir′ ə mid əl) shaped like a pyramid; cone shaped

pyramidal disease   (di zēz′) a form of low ringbone; a new abnormal bone growth that may be due to fracture, periostitis, or osteitis of the extensor process of the coffin bone; also known as *buttress foot*

pyrantel   (pī′ ran til) a dewormer commonly used in horses

pyrethrin   (pī′ re thrin) insecticide commonly used in fly sprays

pyridoxine   (pir′ ə däk′ sēn) another name for vitamin B6

pyrogen   (pī′ rə jən) a fever-producing substance

Q

quadrem (kwäd′ rəm) four horses harnessed one in front of the other

quadrille (kwä dril′) ballet on horseback; performed by teams in multiples of four; the horses and riders perform various movements of dressage and high school riding to music

quality (kwäl′ ə tē) refinement and breed character; generally a horse that shows all the characteristics and features of the ideal horse; to some extent, it is a matter of opinion

quarantine (kwôr′ ən tēn) the period during which a horse must be isolated from other horses to determine whether the horse has a particular disease or to prevent the spread of any disease to other horses

quarry (kwôr′ ē) the hunted animal

quarter (kwôr′ tər) **1.** the hindquarters; that area of the horse's body that covers the croup, rump, and down the sides of the body to the gaskins **2.** the portion of the hoof wall between the toe and the heel

quarter blanket attached to the girth; a covering for the horse's loin and quarters to keep the horse warm while warming up and cooling down; used in dress parades and to keep horses warm in the saddling enclosure prior to a race; also known as *exercise rug*

quarter crack a crack in the side of the hoof that may extend to the coronary band; may or may not be a cause of lameness; should be treated by a farrier; see *blemishes and unsoundnesses* (illus.)

Quarter Horse a popular American breed of horse originally bred to race at the quarter mile; many colors with restricted white markings; well muscled and powerful with small, alert ears; common uses: cow horse, racing, pleasure hunters, jumpers, cutting, reining, roping, and barrel racing

American Quarter Horse

quarter mark patterns placed or combed into the coat over the hindquarters of a horse; normally used to draw the judge's attention to the horse

quarter markers those points around an arena between the center and half markers; denoted by F, K, H, and M; used to define dressage riding patterns and exercises; see *dressage ring*

quarters in instead of following the tracks of the front legs, the hind legs travel on the inside track

quarters leading the execution of the half pass where the horse should travel forward and sideways with the body remaining largely parallel to the side of the arena

---

a=f<u>a</u>t; ā=<u>a</u>pe; ä=c<u>a</u>r; â=b<u>are</u>; e=t<u>e</u>n; ē=<u>e</u>ven;
i=<u>i</u>s; ī=b<u>i</u>te; ō=g<u>o</u>; ô=h<u>o</u>rn; ōō=t<u>oo</u>l;
ŏŏ=l<u>oo</u>k; u=<u>u</u>p; ʉ=f<u>u</u>r; ŋ=ri<u>ng</u>; ə=sof<u>a</u>

quarters not engaged the hind legs of the horse are placed too far behind the hindquarters, with insufficient flexion in the joints of the hind legs; insufficient power is delivered to the hindquarters

quarters out instead of following the tracks of the front legs, the hind legs swing outside the circle

Quarter Sport Horse Registry a registry for Quarter Horses and all sport horse breeds

quarters swinging the horse is not accepting any pressure from the rider's legs; the horse swings his hindquarters slightly away from the rider's leg as a form of evasion

question (kwes' chǝn) as in to *ask the question;* to ask a horse to perform to the best of his ability; to require a horse to go to the limits of his capabilities

quick (kwik) a series of membranes containing a large number of very small blood vessels; covers the pedal bone

quicked (kwikt) when a horseshoe nail penetrates the sensitive tissues; may result in an abscess

quickened rather than extended rather than a horse lengthening his stride for an extended gait, he increases the frequency of his strides

quickset (kwik set) relates to the use of growing plant or hedge material in the construction of jumps cut down or removed from its natural surroundings

quittor (kwit' ǝr) a wound of the heel or rear quarter of the hoof that discharges pus above the coronet

R

rabies (rā′ bēz) an acute, infectious, viral disease of the central nervous system; fatal in all mammalian species

race (rās) a competition between horses where the result is determined by speed

race apprentice (ə pren′ tis) any race in which only apprentice jockeys may ride

race bridle the American type is usually doubled or lined and stitched leather; has a slip-type headstall with a throatlatch; the reins are always finished with rubber hand parts to allow a firmer grip

race card the printed program of a race meeting giving information including the name and time of each race, and the names of all horses, their owners, trainers, and the weights to be carried

race, claiming a flat race in which every horse, including the winner, may be claimed (purchased) for a previously stated price

racecourse a racetrack properly constructed for flat and/or steeplechasing and hurdle racing; together with all the relevant facilities such as grandstands, paddock, stables, office buildings, etc.; administered by appointed officials

race free-for-all a harness race open to any horse; all horses start off scratch

race futurity a race for two-year-old horses

racehorse a horse trained and used for running under the saddle either on the flat or over hurdles or steeplechase obstacles; such horses are usually Thoroughbreds

race meeting the period of days during which races are run at any specified racetrack

race post a flat race in which a person may, by paying one entry fee, enter two or more horses and run any or all of them

racetrack the place where races are run; the racing strip; America's first racetrack was New Market on Long Island, New York

rachitic (ra kit′ ik) pertaining to or affected with rickets

racing chemist an analytical chemist whose duty is to analyze saliva, urine, and blood samples of horses that have just completed a race to ensure that such samples are free from forbidden substances such as narcotics and stimulants

racing colors the Jockey Club assigns colors to racing stables; jockeys must wear the colors assigned to the stable

racing commission a state-appointed body charged with regulating and supervising the conduct of racing in its jurisdiction

racing plate a thin, very lightweight horseshoe used on racehorses

---

a=fat; ā=ape; ä=car; â=bare; e=ten; ē=even;
i=is; ī=bite; ō=go; ô=horn; ōō=tool;
ŏŏ=look; u=up; ʉ=fur; ŋ=ring; ə=sofa

227

racing saddle a saddle designed for use on racehorses; ranges from the very light type of less than 1 kg (2 lb), used for flat racing, to the heavier more solid type, used for hurdling and steeplechasing

racing secretary the official who writes the conditions for the races and assigns the weights for handicap races

racing sulky the light, strong vehicle pulled by horses involved in harness racing

rack (rak) one of the gaits of the five-gaited saddle horse; a fast, four-beat gait in which each foot comes down separately and in turn

Racking Horse Breeders Association of America a registry for horses with the ability to rack or perform a natural, bilateral, four-beat gait; neither a pace nor a trot

radial paralysis (rā′ dē əl pə ral′ i sis) injury to the radial nerve, which innervates the extensors of the elbow, knee, and ankle joints; the animal is unable to put weight on the leg; prognosis is usually favorable, although uncertainty of movement may persist for ten days to several months

radiation (rā′ dē ā′ shən) particulate rays, such as alpha, beta and gamma rays

radiation therapy (ther′ ə pē) treatment using X rays, beta rays, and gamma rays to destroy or retard the growth of tumors

radiational irritant (ir′ i tənt) an agent that is used in radiation therapy to cause counterirritation

radiograph (rā′ dē ō graf′) a film of internal structures of the body produced by the action of X rays or gamma rays on a specially sensitized film

radiology (rā′ dē äl′ ə jē) the medical science that uses radiant energy in the treatment of disease or as an imaging technique

radiolucent (rā′ dē ō lōō′ sənt) transparent to X rays; shows as a dark area on a radiograph

radiopaque (rā′ dē ō pāk′) opaque to X rays; shows as a white area on a radiograph

radius (rā′ dē əs) the large, principal bone of the forearm; located between the elbow joint and the knee; see *skeletal system* (illus.)

rail (rāl) **1.** western term for group work in a flat class such as Pleasure **2.** the fence surrounding an arena or racetrack

rain rot (rān′ rät) crusted, infectious skin inflammation that lifts the hair and removes it at its roots; results in slipping away of affected areas of the hair coat; triggered when small amounts of moisture fall on a dirty, neglected coat

rain scald (rān skäld) a skin irritation caused by a fungal infection; developed in horses exposed to the environment without shelter or protection

rales (rālz) any abnormal respiratory sound

ramped retina (ramp′ əd ret′ ə nə) thought to be a selective advantage that allows horses to eat and watch for predators at the same time

random (ran′ dəm) three horses hitched in single file usually to a dogcart

range horse (rānj hôrs) a horse that is born and brought up on the range and is never handled until he is brought in to be broken

rangy (rānj′ ē) elongated, lean, muscular; of slight build; long limbed and long backed

rapping (rap′ iŋ) when the top pole is raised by hand at the last moment as a horse jumps it so that the horse hits the pole and therefore needs to jump higher to avoid being hurt; this practice is not permitted under the rules of most show-jumping organizations

rarefaction (rer′ ə fak′ shən) becoming less dense; a decrease in density and weight, but not in volume

rasp (rasp) **1.** to level the hoof after trimming **2.** a barlike filing tool that is coarse on one side and fine on the other

rasper (ras′ pər) a large, untrimmed hunting fence

Rasp

rasping (ras′ piŋ) **1.** filing hooves **2.** filing teeth with a rasp to provide dental care; also called *floating*

rat catcher (rat kach′ ər) the informal dress worn during the cub-hunting season; especially a tweed jacket and tan breeches

rate (rāt) **1.** to establish a horse's gait and speed in order to arrive at a destination at a preselected time **2.** in steer roping or steer wrestling, when the horse stays in the correct position relative to the steer to allow the cowboy to perform **3.** when a master or huntsman punishes his hounds with a thong or a sharp word

rating (rā′ tiŋ) **1.** a means of classifying the size of a show; sometimes done beforehand according to prizes offered and sometimes done after according to the number of entries **2.** monitoring the rhythm and speed of a horse's pace

ration (rash′ ən) generally refers to all feed available for the horse, including the nutrients and feed components that are of little nutritional value

rat tail a horse having few long hairs in his tail

rattlers (rat′ lərz) **1.** weights of some type on a cord or strap placed around the coronet, usually only on the front feet; encourages the horse to increase his action and step higher at the trot **2.** rattlesnakes

rattles (rat′ əls) a common name for pneumonia; name is derived from the rattling sound in the chest that accompanies breathing

rawhide (rô hīd) material much like parchment but made from split cattle hide that has been dehaired and dressed, but not tanned

ray (rā) a dorsal stripe

RBC see *red blood cells*

reactor (rē ak′ tər) an animal that has reacted positively to a test for an

---

a=fat; ā=ape; ä=car; â=bare; e=ten; ē=even; i=is; ī=bite; ō=go; ô=horn; ōō=tool; ŏŏ=look; u=up; ᴜ=fur; ŋ=ring; ə=sofa

infectious disease such as tuberculosis or brucellosis

rear cinch   see *flank cinch*

rearing   (rēr' iŋ) a bad habit in a horse of rising up on his hind legs when he is being led or ridden; an extremely dangerous habit that should be dealt with by a professional only

rear jockey   see *back jockey*

rear step   step to the rumble seat of a carriage; see *carriage parts* (illus.)

reata   (rē ä' tə) Spanish for *lasso* or *lariat*

recessive   (ri ses' iv) tending to recede; not exerting a ruling or controlling influence; a recessive gene in genetics is not dominant

recessive character   (kar' ik tər) a characteristic that appears only when both members of a pair of genes are alike; opposite of dominant

reciprocal action   (ri sip' rə kəl ak' shən) the complementary interaction of two distant entities

reciprocal apparatus   (ri sip' rə kəl ap' ə rat' əs) when the stifle and hock function in unison

recover   (rē' kuv' ər) when the scent is picked up again after a check

rectal palpation   (rek' təl pal pā' shən) a procedure to test for pregnancy; a diagnostic aid in colic and other abdominal diseases

rectum   (rek' təm) last section of the large intestine

recumbent   (ri kum' bənt) a prone position

recurrent   (ri kʉr' ənt) returning after remission

recurrent uveitis   (yōō' vē ī' tis) periodic ophthalmia or moon blindness

red bay   (red bā) coat color; bay with a primary color of reddish brown

red blood cells   oxygen-carrying blood cells produced in bone marrow; also called *erythrocytes* or *RBCs*

red chestnut   coat color; chestnut with a primary color of reddish brown

red dun   a form of dun with a body color that is yellowish or flesh colored; mane and tail are red or flaxen, white or mixed; has red dorsal strip and usually red zebra stripes on legs and transverse stripe over withers

red flag   a marker used in equestrian sports to denote the right-hand extremity of any obstacle; also used to mark a set track and must always be passed on the left-hand side

red ribbon on tail   a sign that a horse kicks

red roan   coat color; chestnut base with an equal mixture of white hairs, giving a red tint to the coat; the legs and head are usually darker

red worms   see *strongyle*

reefing   (rēf' iŋ) when a horse continually throws his head up and down, attempting to pull the reins from the rider's hands

refinement   (ri fīn' mənt) quality appearance; indicating good breeding

reflex arc   (rē' fleks ärk) the nerve arc used in a reflex action

refusal (ri fyōō′ zəl) in racing, the failure of a horse to attempt to jump a hurdle or steeplechase fence; in show jumping and combined training, either the act of passing an obstacle that is to be jumped or stopping in front of it

refuse (ri fyōōz′) when a horse stops in front of a jump

regeneration (ri jen′ ə rā′ shən) the natural renewal of a structure; as of a tissue or part

registered (rej′ is tərd) a horse with purebred parents that have numbered certificates with a particular breed organization

registration (rej′ i strā′ shən) entering a horse into the registry of the breed association if he meets the qualifications stipulated by the organization

registry (rej′ is trē) pedigree record kept by associations of recognized breeds of horses

regular (reg′ yə lər) the evenness with which the horse puts his feet to the ground; each step should be at a regular speed, rhythm, and of an even length

rehabilitation (rē′ hə bil ə tā′ shən) the restoration of normal form and function after injury or illness

rein back (rān bak) when the horse moves backward with the diagonal legs raised and put down simultaneously

rein back crooked when, as the horse is reining back, the hindquarters swing to one side rather than maintaining a straight line

rein, bearing in neck reining, the rein pushed against the neck in the direction of the turn

rein, draw loops at the end of the reins are fastened to the girth; the reins are then passed through the rings of the snaffle bit and returned along the horse's neck to the rider's hands

reinforcement (rē′ in fôrs′ mənt) strengthening an association with primary reinforcers, such as feed or rest, or using secondary reinforcers such as praise or a pat

reining western event to demonstrate a high degree of a horse's responsiveness to his rider based on riding patterns

rein, neck see *neck rein*

rein rail upper section of the carriage dash; see *carriage parts* (illus.)

reins (rānz) leather, webbing, or rope fastened to the bit or noseband; used by the rider to steer, guide, and communicate with the horse; see *harness parts A; western bridle* (illus.)

relapse (rē′ laps) the return of a disease after it has apparently ceased

remittent (ri mit′ ənt) abating for a while, at intervals, and then returning

remouthing the act of attempting to correct mouthing problems that occurred in the initial mouthing process; a very difficult process

---

a=fat; ā=ape; ä=car; â=bare; e=ten; ē=even;
i=is; ī=bite; ō=go; ô=horn; ōō=tool;
ŏŏ=look; u=up; ʉ=fur; ŋ=ring; ə=sofa

remuda (rə mōō′ də) a collection of saddle horses at a roundup from which the ones to be used for the day are chosen; a group of horses kept together on a ranch; each cowboy's horses

renal (rē′ nəl) pertaining to the kidney

renvers a dressage movement on two tracks in which the horse moves at an angle of not more than 30 degrees along the long side of the arena with the hind legs on the outer track and the forelegs on the inner track; the horse looks in the direction he is going and bends slightly around the inside leg of the rider

rep (rep) a cowboy employed to search for and round up cattle that have strayed from the ranch of his employer

reprimand (rep′ rə mand′) to discipline severely

reproductive cycle (rē prə duk′ tiv sī′ kəl) 1. cycle of approximately twenty-one days between each heat 2. the cycle of lack of heat in the winter and heat in the summer

reproductive system (rē′ prə duk′ tiv sis′ təm) the biological system responsible for the production of offspring; refers to males or females

repulsion (ri pul′ shən) the pushing back of the fetus into the uterus; usually done before any correction of incorrect birthing position is attempted

reride (rē rīd′) when another ride is given to a bronc or bull rider in the same go-round when the first ride was unsatisfactory for any of several reasons

resection (ri sek′ shən) surgical removal of part of a structure and reconstruction of the remaining structure

Reserve Champion (ri zʉrv′ cham′ pē ən) second place or runner-up in a particular division

reset shoes (rē′ set shōōz) to remove shoes, trim the hoof, and reapply the old shoes

resilient (ri zil′ yənt) elastic; returning to its former shape after distortion

resistance (ri zis′ təns) 1. the act of refusing to go forward; stopping, running back, or rearing 2. sum total of body mechanisms that interpose barriers to the progress of invasion or multiplication of infectious agents or to damage by their toxic products

resisting (ri zis′ tiŋ) any desire from the horse to evade his rider's aids

resolution (rez′ ə lōō′ shən) the subsidence of an inflammation; the softening and disappearance of a swelling

resonance (rez′ ə nəns) the prolongation and intensification of sound produced by the transmission of its vibrations to a cavity; especially a sound elicited by percussion; a vocal sound, as heard in auscultation

respiration (res′ pə rā′ shən) breathing; the exchange of oxygen and carbon dioxide between the atmosphere and the cells of the body; normal adult respiration varies among horses, but is usually twelve to fifteen breaths per minute

respiratory distress (res′ pər ə tôr′ ē di stres′) difficulty breathing

respiratory system (sis′ təm) supplies oxygen and removes carbon dioxide; the organs of the respiratory system are the nasal cavity, pharynx, larynx, trachea, bronchi, and lungs

resting leg (res′ tiŋ leg) applies to the halt where the horse should be taking an even weight on all four legs; in this instance, he may be resting one leg and only standing on three

restrain (ri strān′) preventing a horse from moving, acting, or advancing by psychological, mechanical, or chemical means

restricted (ri strik′ tid) being limited or confined; when a rider has held the pace back so that it is too slow; when a rider uses psychological, chemical, or physical means to limit a horse's movement

retained placenta (ri tānd plə sen′ tə) part of or entire placenta not having been passed after birth; may be the cause of postpartum metritis

retention (ri ten′ shən) a process of keeping a fluid or secretion in the body that is normally excreted

retina (ret′ ən ə) the sensory membrane lining the back surface of the eye's interior; the lens focuses an image on the retina, which in turn transmits it to the optic nerve; see *eye, horse's* (illus.)

retinal detachment (ret′ ə nəl di tach′ mənt) a condition associated with periodic ophthalmia or injuries that may affect the eye; may cause blindness

Rhineland Heavy Draft (rīn′ land hev′ ē draft) a West German breed established in 1876; used for heavy draft work in transport and agriculture;

height: 16–17 hands; color: chestnut, red roan, and bay

rhinitis (rī nīt′ əs) inflammation of the mucous membranes lining the nasal passages

rhinopneumonitis (rī′ nō nōō mō nī′ tis) inflammation of the nasal and pulmonary mucous membranes; a viral upper respiratory infection of young horses that can also cause paralysis and abortion in pregnant mares

rhinosporidiosis (rī′ nō spō rid′ ē ō′ sis) a nonfatal fungal infection characterized by growths on the mucous membrane of the nasal cavity

rhinovirus (rī′ nō vī′ rəs) a group of viruses that cause colds and other upper respiratory tract ailments

rhythm (rith′ əm) the order and spacing of footfalls; the beat of the horse's gait as defined by the sound of his hoofbeats

riata (rē ä′ tə) see *reata*

ribbed up when the back ribs are well arched and incline well backward, bringing the ends closer to the point of the hip and making the horse shorter in coupling

ribbons (rib′ əns) generally ribbon colors are: first place, blue; second place, red; third place, yellow; fourth place, white; fifth place, pink; sixth place, green; seventh place, purple; eighth place, brown

a=f<u>a</u>t; ā=<u>a</u>pe; ä=c<u>a</u>r; â=b<u>a</u>re; e=t<u>e</u>n; ē=<u>e</u>ven; i=<u>i</u>s; ī=b<u>i</u>te; ō=g<u>o</u>; ô=h<u>o</u>rn; ōō=t<u>oo</u>l; ŏŏ=l<u>oo</u>k; u=<u>u</u>p; ʉ=f<u>u</u>r; ŋ=ri<u>ng</u>; ə=sof<u>a</u>

ribs (ribz) area of the chest bound by flanks behind and shoulders in front; see *points of the horse* (illus.)

ricin (rīs' in) a poisonous substance found in the seeds of the castor oil plant

rickets (rik' its) a disease caused by lack of vitamin D, calcium, or phosphorus

rickettsia (ri ket' sē ə) tiny round microorganisms, a genus of which has been found to be the cause of Potomac horse fever

ridden to the death when a bucking horse is ridden to the stage when he has stopped bucking and the rider is still mounted

ride (rīd) 1. a lane cut through a forest; a path through a covert 2. being carried on horseback

ride a fence to ride along the perimeter of a ranch or property to inspect and repair the fencing

ride for a fall to ride carelessly and recklessly, without consideration or good judgment

ride hard to ride straight to hounds or to push the horse to his limit, at the same time being aware of the limits of both horse and rider

ride into the ground to ride a horse to his absolute limit so that he is exhausted and unable to go any further

ride off in polo, to push one's pony against that of another player in order to prevent him from playing the ball

ride straight the person who takes his fences as they come, riding "as the crow flies"

ridgling (rij' liŋ) a stallion in which one or both testicles have not descended into the scrotum or where only one testicle has been removed

riding school 1. an establishment where people are taught to ride and horses can be hired for riding 2. a livery

rig (rig) 1. a male horse with one or both testicles retained in the abdomen; an operation can enable it or them to descend; after this, the animal should be gelded, as the tendency can be hereditary 2. slang for truck, trailer 3. to fix the outcome of an event

rigging (rig' giŋ) style and configuration of the front and rear cinches on a western saddle

right lead (rīt lēd) right front foot and right rear foot lead in the canter

rigor mortis (rig' ər môr' tis) stiffness or rigidity that occurs soon after death as a result of coagulation of cell proteins

rimfire full (rim' fīr) a saddle with the rigging ring in the full position; a full double-rigged saddle

ring an English riding area; see *dressage ring*

ringbone (riŋ bōn) a bony enlargement occurring in the region of the pastern bone on the first, second, or third phalanx; occurs more frequently in the front legs than in the hind legs; caused by strain on ligaments of the coffin and pastern joints; see *blemishes and unsoundnesses* (illus.)

ring, cinch the circular metal ring at each end of the cinch; if the ring has a tongue, it is called a cinch buckle

ringer (riŋ′ ər) a horse passed off under false identity, with the idea of entering him in a race below his class where he is almost certain to win; with the development of lip tattoos, freeze branding, and microchips, ringers are a thing of the past

Ringer's solution (riŋ′ ərs sə lōō′ sh̲ən) a physiological salt solution that contains chloride, sodium, potassium, calcium, bicarbonate, and phosphate ions

ring sour (riŋ sour) poor attitude in a horse that does not enjoy working in an arena and looks for ways to leave the arena or quit working

rings, rigging metal rings of varying diameters and shapes at the lower end of the rigging leathers to which the cinch straps, billets, or flank cinch billets are attached

ringworm (riŋ′ wʉrm) a contagious infection of the outer layers of skin caused by an infestation of microscopic fungi; characterized by itching and ring-shaped, discolored patches covered with scales; also called *trichophytosis* or *barn itch*

rise to the trot see *posting*

rising scent (riz′ iŋ sent) a scent that is weak at ground level but can be smelled by a mounted rider

roached (rōc̲hd′) a mane or tail that has been clipped close to the skin; the mane will usually stand upright

roached back thin, sharp, arched back; a conformation fault in which the back is arched and convex; predisposes a horse to forging and shortens the gait of the animal

road founder (rōd found′ ər) mechanical failure of the hooves caused by extreme concussion, resulting in separation of the sensitive and insensitive laminae

road hunter a hound that can follow a line along a road

road puffs soft, puffy swellings about the size of a hickory nut located on or above the fetlocks on either forelegs or hind legs; may also be called *windgalls* or *wind puffs*

roadster (rōd′ stər) a type of driving horse originally bred in England

roan (rōn) coat color; white hairs are interspersed with colored ones in an even mixture; if the base color is bay, the horse is a bay roan; chestnut, red roan; sorrel, strawberry roan; black, blue roan

roarer (rôr′ ər) an animal that makes a loud noise when drawing air into the lungs; see *roaring*

roaring (rôr iŋ) loud unnatural noise made while breathing; caused by paralysis of the muscles of the larynx

Robert Jones bandage dense, thick, multilayered bandage incorporating wood or metal splints to restrain and support an injured leg

Rocky Mountain Horse a breed originating in eastern Kentucky; height: 14.2–16 hands; natural, ambling, four-beat gait; all solid colors, no white above the knee or hock; common uses: pleasure, trail riding, endurance riding, and working cattle

---

a=f<u>a</u>t; ā=<u>a</u>pe; ä=c<u>a</u>r; â=b<u>a</u>re; e=t<u>e</u>n; ē=<u>e</u>ven; i=<u>i</u>s; ī=b<u>i</u>te; ō=g<u>o</u>; ô=h<u>o</u>rn; ōō=t<u>oo</u>l; ŏŏ=l<u>oo</u>k; u=<u>u</u>p; ʉ=f<u>u</u>r; ŋ=ri<u>ng</u>; ə=sof<u>a</u>

Rocky Mountain Horse Association
a registry for horses born to registered
parents certified before breeding

rodeo   (rō′ dē ō) an event or contest
with horses and livestock; events include roping, bulldogging, bronc riding, bull riding, barrel racing, etc.

rollback   (rōl′ bak) a movement in
western riding where a galloping
horse stops, lifts his forelegs, swings
around 180 degrees and starts again at
a gallop in the direction from which
he came

rolled heels   (rōld hēlz) a hoof abnormality in which low heels or too small
shoes cause the wall to bend under at
the heel

roller bolt   (rōl′ ər bōlt) part of a carriage hitch; see *carriage parts; harness
parts D* (illus.)

rollers   (rōl′ ərz) wooden balls on a
cord encircling a horse's pastern to
give the horse more action

rolling   (rol′ liŋ) side motion of the
forehand; excessive lateral shoulder
motion characteristic of horses with
protruding shoulders

romal   (rō′ məl) a long, flexible rein
extension that can be used as a quirt;
attached to closed reins

Roman   nose   (rō′
mən nōz) a large nose
that curves outward
and downward; an un-
desirable trait in most
breeds

Roman Nose

Roman   nosed   a
horse having a profile that is convex
from poll to muzzle

roof seat   (rōōf sēt) a seat on top of
the roof of a driving vehicle

roping horse   (rōp′ iŋ hôrs) any horse
that is especially trained and used for
roping cattle

roping saddle   a style of western saddle popular with
ropers   today;
characterized by
a flat seat and a
high dally horn
with a flat, hori-
zontal horn cap,
square   Texas-
style skirts, and
cinches   spread
as far apart as
possible

Roping Saddle

rosadero   see *fenders*

rosettes   (rōz′ ets) **1.** one, two, or
three decorative leather or silver but-
tons, each with two slits; used as a fastening device on a western saddle
through which the saddle strings pass
on a saddle; decorative flower-shaped
adornments on tack, clothing, and the
upper portion of some show ribbons;
see *harness parts B and E* (illus.)

rostral   (rōs′ trəl) toward the nose

rotation   (rō tā′ s̲h̲ən) the process of
turning around an axis

rough   (ruf) when the hock is flexed
noticeably; when the body is lifted
high and the knees are folded with
forearms nearly horizontal; also called
hard gaited

roughage   (ruf′ ij) the indigestible
fiber in the diet needed to give bulk
and to keep the digestive system functioning properly

roughout   (ruf' out) leather with hair side roughed up by machine; affords some added security to saddles

rough stock events   the bucking events of a rodeo; bareback riding, saddle bronc riding, and bull riding

round hock   see *curb*

rounding   (roun' diŋ) engagement of the muscles; characterized by an arched back, a dropped croup, hind legs well under the body, flexed abdominals and an elevated head and neck

roundworms   (round' wʉrmz) nematode parasites including lungworms, stomach worms, red worms, white worms, and pinworms

route   (rōōt or rout) a distance race; usually one and one-eighth miles or longer

route of treatment   the path in or part of the body through which a medication is administered

router   (rout' ər) a horse at his best over a distance of ground more than a mile

rowels   (rou' əlz) the toothed wheels on spurs

rubber curry comb   (rub' ər cʉr ē kōm) a grooming tool used in a circular motion to loosen dirt on a horse's body

Rubber Curry Comb

rubber curry mitt   (mit) a glove made of rubber with small raised bumps to help massage the horse's skin

rubberneck   (rub' ər' nek) a horse with a very flexible neck; hard to rein; neck may bend but body doesn't follow

rubber weed, bitter   (rub' ər wēd bit' tər) a yellow-flowered weed that ranges from a few inches to two feet tall; an irritant to the digestive tract

rubdown   (rub' doun) a rubbing of the body with a rough towel; usually given after exercise to promote circulation and remove fatigue

rubefacient   (rōō' bə fā' shənt) an agent that reddens the skin and produces mild irritation to improve circulation

rug   (rug) a throw used by some drivers instead of an apron; should be wide enough to cover the user's lap and long enough to reach from the waist to the floor

rumble seat   (rum' bəl sēt) an open seat in the rear part of a carriage; see *carriage parts* (illus.)

rumen   (rōō' min) first division of the stomach in ruminant animals

rumensin   (rōō' men sən) feed additive used to increase the rate of weight gain in cattle; highly toxic to horses

ruminant   (rōō' min ənt) an animal such as cattle, sheep, and goats that has a stomach divided into four compartments

run   (run) a fast, four-beat gait during which the two diagonal legs of the

a=fat; ā=ape; ä=car; â=bare; e=ten; ē=even; i=is; ī=bite; ō=go; ô=horn; ōō=tool; ŏŏ=look; u=up; ʉ=fʉr; ŋ=ring; ə=sofa

canter are broken and strike the ground separately between the successive beats of the other two unpaired legs; also called *extended gallop*

running　when a horse dashes along too fast on the forehand, with no balance or rhythm and very little suspension in the stride

running martingale　(run' iŋ mär' tən gāl') a type of martingale with rings through which to run the reins; designed to train a horse to maintain the proper flexion at the poll and keep the horse from throwing his head

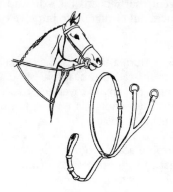

Running Martingale

running out　**1.** a stallion turned out to grass with mares who are to mate with him **2.** in show jumping, to avoid an obstacle that is to be jumped by running to one side of it **3.** in racing, to avoid an obstacle that is to be jumped or to pass on the wrong side of a marker flag

running walk　a four-beat gait intermediate in speed between the walk and the rack; the hind foot oversteps the front foot from a few to as many as eighteen inches giving the motion a smooth gliding effect; gait common to Tennessee Walkers

rupture　(rup' chər) breaking or tearing of tissue

rushing　(rush' iŋ) the pace is hurried and there is a lack of balance and rhythm

Russian Heavy Draft　a breed developed in Russia over the past hundred years; local mares were crossed with Ardennes, the Belgian Heavy Draft, and the Percheron

S

Sable Island Pony (sā′ bəl ī land pō′ nē) this pony is bred and reared in the wild state on Sable Island, which lies about 200 miles off the coast of Nova Scotia; small and wiry in appearance; 300 ponies are currently in existence

sacral vertebrae (sā′ krəl vʉr′ tə brā) lowest part of the spinal column that extends into the rump area; see *skeletal system* (illus.)

saddle (sad′ əl) the seat designed to fit both rider and horse to make the act of riding more comfortable; may be English or western, see *English saddle; western saddle* (illus.)

saddle blanket a pad or blanket used underneath the saddle to cushion the horse's back

saddle horn a prominent projection on the pommel of the western saddle; common to western saddles and some Australian stock saddles

saddle horse a wooden or metal stand or frame that can attach to a wall; saddles are placed on it when not in use

saddle mark any mark on a horse generally due to a poorly fitting saddle

saddle pad a thick, soft cushioning placed under the saddle; may be made of cotton or sheepskin; sometimes called *saddle blanket*

saddle strings sometimes located below the swells and behind the cantle of western saddles; used for tying coats, etc., to the saddle; see *western saddle* (illus.)

saddle tree see *western saddle tree; English saddle tree; tree*

Salerno (sə lʉr′ nō) an Italian breed; revived in the twentieth century; first a carriage horse, but later a saddle horse; height: 16.1–17 hands; color: bay, chestnut, black, and gray

saline (sā′ lēn or sā′ līn) salt solution similar in composition to serum; can be used as an intravenous fluid or to flush wounds

saliva (sə lī′ və) fluid produced in the mouth; moistens food for easier swallowing and also aids in digestion; moistens the mouth for better contact with the bit

Salmonella (sal′ mə nel′ ə) intestinal bacteria that can cause diarrhea, food poisoning, and gastrointestinal inflammation; sometimes severe enough to result in death

salt (sält) a cation necessary for the transfer of nutrients and waste to and from the cells; associated with muscle contractions; necessary to produce bile

Sandalwood (san′ dəl wŏŏd) an Indonesian breed of pony native to the Sumba and Sumbawa islands; named for the country's principal export

sand colic abdominal pain due to sand collecting in the large intestine and causing a partial or complete obstruction

sand cracks a crack in the wall of

---

a=fat; ā=ape; ä=car; â=bare; e=ten; ē=even; i=is; ī=bite; ō=go; ô=horn; ōō=tool; ŏŏ=look; u=up; ʉ=fur; ŋ=ring; ə=sofa

239

the hoof that extends from the coronary band part or all the way down the wall; the severity of the problem correlates with the depth of the crack

sand fly   an insect known to cause Queensland itch or skin itch

San Fratello   an Italian breed reared in the wild in Sicily; a strong horse with a powerful body and outstanding resistance

sarcoid   (sär' koid) a common skin condition that can resemble ulcerated warts; may be caused by a virus

sarcoma   (sär' cō mə) a usually malignant tumor made up of a substance similar to embryonic connective tissue

Sardinian   (sär din' ē ən) an Italian breed with uncertain origins; a hardy pony that lives in Sardinia

Sardinian Anglo-Arab   a hardy, well-balanced riding breed of Italian origin; known as a good jumper

scalping   (skalp' iŋ) occurs when the hairline at the top of the hind foot hits the toe of the front foot on the same side as the horse strides forward

scapula   (skap' yŏŏ lə) shoulder blade; see *skeletal system* (illus.)

scar   (skär) a permanent mark on the horse as a result of injury or damage, such as a wire cut or veterinary operation

Schleswig Heavy Draft   a West German draft breed that can be traced back to Denmark's Jutland horse; formerly used for farm tasks and drawing omnibuses; currently the breed is in decline

sclera   (sklir' ə) outer white fibrous membrane covering the eyeball, except the area covered by the cornea; see *eye, horse's* (illus.)

scope   (skōp) the athletic ability required in good jumping horses

scours   (skou' ərs) diarrhea; may be caused by stress or improper diet

scowling   (skoul' iŋ) the act of a horse laying back his ears in a threatening manner

scratch   (skrach) 1. vigorous use of the spurs 2. to withdraw a horse from an equestrian event after he had been officially entered

scratches   a scabby and/or oozing skin inflammation in the back of the pastern above the heels

scratching   the act of declaring a horse as being withdrawn from a race or event after entries have closed for that particular race or event

scrotum   (skrōt' əm) the fold or sac containing the testes

scurry   (skɥr' ē) a show-jumping contest where refusals do not count and the whole event is judged on time and faults; the horse completing the course in the fastest time, with the least faults, is the winner

seasonal anestrus   (sē' zə nəl an es' trəs) failure of a mare to come into heat in the winter

seat   (sēt) 1. the position of the rider in the saddle, including the manner in which the rider holds his arms and legs; a correct seat should combine the weight and position of the rider with the weight and position of the horse, so that the two perform together as one **2.** the part of the saddle just in front of the cantle; see *English saddle; western saddle* (illus.)

seat and hands the ability of a rider to balance in the saddle and control the mount without excessive pressure on the reins

seat jockey part of the western saddle located just below the seat area; see *western saddle* (illus.)

seat rail bars on sides of the rumble seat of a carriage; see *carriage parts* (illus.)

sebaceous glands (sə bā shəs glandz) skin glands that have a greasy, lubricating secretion (sebum) that helps to improve the condition of the coat

seborrhea (seb′ ə rē′ ə) skin condition resulting from malfunction of the oil-forming glands; characterized by dry, waxy, or excessively oily accumulations on the skin

sebum (sē′ bəm) a fatty secretion from certain glands in the skin; contributes to a healthy coat

sedatives (sed′ ə tivz) drugs that reduce the activity of the brain and, as a result, reduce excitement levels

seedy toe (sēd′ ē tō) the separation of the inner and outer walls of the hoof or the insensitive laminae from the sensitive laminae

selenium (sə lē′ nē əm) a mineral in horse nutrition; in combination with vitamin E, acts to prevent muscle destruction

selenium poisoning (poi′ zə niŋ)

horses may ingest high levels of selenium by eating certain plants; symptoms include loss of hair from mane and tail, rough coat, weight loss, reduced eyesight, inability to swallow, etc.; acute poisoning may result in death

self carriage (self kar′ ij) a horse that naturally holds his head up without any prompting from the rider

Selle Francais a European breed originating in France; a natural descendant of the ancient Norman breed; known as a quiet riding horse

semen (sē′ mən) the thick, white-colored secretion produced by the testes and accessory glands of the stallion; contains spermatozoa

seminal vesicle (sem′ ən əl ves′ i kəl) present only in the male; consists of two long sacs lying on either side of the top of the bladder and opening into the urethra

senior horse (sēn′ yər hôrs) a class for horses six years of age or older; will vary according to the association

sense (sens) any sensation conveyed to the brain; includes heat, cold, and pain

sensitive laminae (sen′ sə tiv lam′ ə nā) blood-rich leaves of tissue on the surface of the coffin bone that interlock with the insensitive laminae that line the hoof capsule; see *hoof* (illus.)

sepsis (sep′ sis) presence of microorganisms and their toxins in the blood

---

a=f<u>a</u>t; ā=<u>a</u>pe; ä=c<u>a</u>r; â=b<u>a</u>re; e=t<u>e</u>n; ē=<u>e</u>ven; i=<u>i</u>s; ī=b<u>i</u>te; ō=g<u>o</u>; ô=h<u>o</u>rn; ōō=t<u>oo</u>l; ŏŏ=l<u>oo</u>k; u=<u>u</u>p; ʉ=f<u>u</u>r; ŋ=ri<u>ng</u>; ə=sof<u>a</u>

septic (sep' tik) decomposition of tissue as a result of microorganic activity

septic arthritis (är t͟hrīt' is) inflammation of a joint due to the introduction of bacteria into the joint

sequestrum (si kwes' trəm) a piece of dead bone that has become separated from the remaining healthy bone

serology (si räl' ə jē) use of reactions to determine the presence and amount of specific antibodies in the blood

serpentine (sʉr' pən tēn') 1. a schooling movement in which the horse moves across the arena performing a series of connected half circles so that the top of the half circle touches the long side of the arena and at the same time the horse is moving down the arena toward the opposite end 2. in western riding, a movement requiring the horse to weave in and out of obstacles placed in a set pattern

serum (sir' əm) the liquid portion of blood that remains after blood has clotted

service fee (sʉr' vis fē) the money paid to the owner of a stallion for the use of that stallion to breed a mare

sesamoid bones (ses' ə moid bōnz) small bones at the rear of the fetlock joint; absorb pressure from the tendons; see skeletal system (illus.)

sesamoiditis (ses' ə moid ī' tis) inflammation of the soft tissue surrounding the sesamoid bones; may be due to strain, nutritional imbalance, or some type of injury

set fair (set fâr) the final and finishing touches made to a horse's bedding before the horse is put away for the night

sex (seks) the distinction between male and female

shackle (s͟hak' əl) a fastener located between the back wheels of a carriage; see carriage parts (illus.)

shadow roll (shad' ō rōl) a large sheepskin-type roll worn just above a horse's nose and just below his eyes; cuts off the horse's view of the track so that he will not shy at shadows, pieces of paper or other objects

shaft (s͟haft) 1. the long middle section of the long bones between the top and bottom articular cartilage 2. the wooden poles or attachments on harness vehicles between which the horse are placed and coupled; see harness parts A and C (illus.)

Shagya Arabian a breed developed in Syria; gray; height: 15 hands; has typical Arabian characteristics; common uses: all-purpose riding and harness

shaker foal syndrome (s͟hā' kər fōl sin' drōm) often fatal; progressive weakness of the newborn that has recently been ascribed to botulism infection of the intestines

shamateurism (s͟ham' ə tər' ism) some forms of horse sports where the rules prevent the rider from being a professional by paying the horse or a representative of the horse the prize money

shank (s͟haŋk) 1. the part of the leg that is situated between the knee and fetlock; often called the *cannon bone* **2.** that portion of the cheek of the bit from the mouthpiece down **3.** a long strap or rope used for leading a horse

shaping   (shāp' iŋ) the progressive development of the form of a movement; the reinforcement of successive approximations to a desired behavior

sheared heel   (shērd hēl) the structural breakdown between the heel bulbs caused by more pressure on one heel

sheath   (shēth) another name for the prepuce in a male horse; a tubular structure enclosing or surrounding an organ or part

shed row   (shed rō) the stables

sheep hurdle   (shēp hʉr dəl) a jumping obstacle consisting of stout twigs or small branches joined together in a fashion similar to the fences used to hold sheep

sheepskin lining   (shēp' skin līn' iŋ) the lining on the underneath side of the skirt of the western saddle used to cushion the rider's weight on the horse's back; primarily used to prevent the saddle from slipping

sheet   (shēt) a light cotton or similar material; may also be called a *fly sheet* or a *summer sheet*

shelly feet   (shel' ē fēt) feet with thin soles and/or walls that are brittle and tend to break easily; horses with these types of feet need to be carefully managed; may be an inherited condition

Shetland Pony   (shet' lənd pō' nē) a small type of pony originating in the Shetland Islands; maximum allowable

height is 10.2 hands; common uses: pack, driving, and mount for children

shigellosis   (shi' gə lō' sis) an acute, highly fatal septicemia; also called *navel ill, joint ill,* and *sleepy foal disease;* symptoms include sudden fever, diarrhea, rapid respiration, and lethargy

shin   (shin) the front portion of the cannon bone

shin boot   a well-padded boot; used to protect the shins against scuffs and bruises

shin buck   inflammation of the bone covering the front side of the cannon bone; often seen in young horses that have been strenuously exercised

shipping boots   (ship' piŋ bōōts) thick wraps to guard against injury to the lower legs; generally used when transporting horses

shipping fever   (fē' vər) an illness that can arise when adrenal glands are overworked in reaction to prolonged physical stress; as a result, bacterial or other types of infections develop

Shire   (shīr) an English breed most likely descended from the famous charger used in the Middle Ages for jousts and tourneys; characterized by full feathering on the legs; average height: 16.2–17.3 hands

shivering   (shiv' ər iŋ) the spasmodic, involuntary muscle contraction that produces heat to help maintain body temperature

---

a=fat; ā=ape; ä=car; â=bare; e=ten; ē=even; i=is; ī=bite; ō=go; ô=horn; ōō=tool; ŏŏ=look; u=up; ʉ=fur; ŋ=ring; ə=sofa

shock (shäk) a condition of partial blood circulation failure due to injury, blood loss, infection, allergy, reaction to drugs, etc.; symptoms include pale mucous membranes, cold and clammy skin, decreased blood pressure, and slow breathing

shod (shäd) past tense of the verb "to shoe"

shoe (shoō) 1. the act of nailing a metal or plastic rim to the bottom of the horse's foot to protect the hoof from excessive wear 2. the metal or plastic rim used as a horseshoe

shoe bar a horseshoe made with a bar across it to provide additional protection to the hoof in cases of cracks, tendon problems, thrush, and other abnormal conditions

shoe boil a soft, flabby swelling over the point of the elbow; also called *capped elbow;* see *blemishes and unsoundnesses* (illus.)

shoe, cross fire a shoe that is heavier on one side to help counteract the problem of cross firing

shoe, diamond toe designed to offset the effects of forging; both sides of the toe are beveled or sloping down and back

shoe, egg bar a normal shoe with the heels connected by a curved piece of metal so that, in effect, the shoe is a complete circle; this type of shoe may be used on horses affected with navicular disease

shoe, eventing the normal shoe that has been modified to withstand the stress of cross-country competition

shoe, heart bar a type of shoe used for the treatment of founder; the toe is rolled to ease the strain on the pedal bone and tendons; the heart bar on the rear of the shoe should be shaped to touch but not apply pressure to the tip of the frog

shoeing the act of putting shoes on a horse

shoe pad placed between the hoof and the shoe and held by nails that hold the shoe to the hoof; full pads, which cover the hoof completely, may be used for working in snow or to provide protection to the hoof sole

shoe, racing plates a lightweight shoe made of aluminum; used on Thoroughbred racing horses

short (shôrt) 1. a Thoroughbred not advanced enough in his conditioning to run the complete distance of a race at his fastest 2. racing Quarter Horses that run 400 yards or less

shortened frame (shôr' tənd frām) decreased distance from the nose to the hock; exhibited by a horse performing a collected gait

shoulder (shōl' dər) that part of the horse's body to which the forearm is attached; formed by the shoulder blade; see *points of the horse* (illus.)

shoulder in a schooling exercise to help a horse become supple, balanced, and obedient; there are three tracks in a shoulder-in: the outside hind, the inside hind with the outside fore, and the inside fore. The horse's forehand is 30–35° in and the horse moves actively forward

shoulders falling out when the rider has lost control of the forehand and is allowing the shoulders of the horse to break the true line of the curve or the straight line

shoulder slip atrophy of the shoulder muscle; usually due to injury

show (shō) 1. to compete in a horse show 2. to finish third in a race

show bridle (brī′ dəl) one in which the leather is cut finer

showmanship classes (shō′ mən ship′ klas əz) the horse is shown in hand and the horse's grooming and presentation and the skill of the handler are evaluated rather than the conformation of the horse

shut off (shut ôf) the situation that exists when a horse is forced back by another horse pulling over in front of him

shuttle bone (shut′ əl bōn) the navicular bone

shut up when a horse ceases to perform to the best of his ability in a race

shy (shī) when a horse swerves away suddenly in fear (or high spirits) from an object or sound

Sicilian (si sil′ ē ən) a spirited Italian breed known for having good stamina

sickle hocks (sik′ əl häks) deviations in the angle of the hock as seen from the side; the cannon slopes forward due to excessive angulation of the hock

side bones (sīd bōnz) when one or both of the lateral cartilages in the foot turn to bone; since the lateral car-

tilages normally act as a shock-absorbing apparatus, they can no longer function properly; see *blemishes and unsoundnesses* (illus.)

side pass moving the horse sideways, with no forward movement; the horse should step with both the forequarters and hindquarters moving together

side reins part of training equipment; attached to the horse from the bit to the surcingle or saddle

side saddle a saddle on which the rider sits facing forward with both legs on one side; usually the near side of the horse

side spring the spring between the rear wheels to absorb shock; see *carriage parts* (illus.)

side wheeler a pacer that rolls his body sideways as he paces

sight zones (sīt zōns) the regions in the perimeter of the horse's vision in which he has the ability to see; in monocular vision, the sight zones are on the sides of the horse; in binocular vision, the sight zone is in front of the horse

sign (sīn) any objective evidence of a disease

silage (sī′ lij) a form of livestock feed fermented and preserved in a silo or other structure

silks (silks) the peaked cap and silk blouse worn by a jockey in racing; the colors of the owner

a=fat; ā=ape; ä=car; â=bare; e=ten; ē=even; i=is; ī=bite; ō=go; ô=horn; ōō=tool; ŏŏ=look; u=up; ʉ=fur; ŋ=ring; ə=sofa

silla (sē′ yə) the Spanish word for saddle

silver (sil′ vər) a horse tail that is white with a few black hairs in it

simple (sim′ pəl) the point at which hairs converge from various directions

simple change of leads when the horse is brought down from the canter to a walk or trot for, ideally, one stride and is restarted into the canter on the opposite lead

simple lead change change from one lead to another with at least one stride at the walk or trot, or a halt in between

single foot (siŋ′ gəl fŏŏt) now called a rack; see *rack*

single-jointed eggbutt snaffle bit a mild bit that cannot pinch; the disadvantage is that it allows for very little movement of the mouthpiece

single rig see *center fire*

sinking vagina (singk′ iŋ və jī′ nə) a condition in which the cervix has dropped down and becomes filled with urine; particularly found in older mares

sinuous (sin′ yŏŏ əs) when hairs from two directions meet along an irregular curving line

sinus (sī′ nəs) a cavity or hollow space

sinusitis (sī′ nə sī′ tis) inflammation of a sinus; marked by discharge of pus from one or both nostrils

sire (sīr) the male parent of a horse

sit fast (sit′ fast) an area of dry, dead skin on the neck or back; caused by pressure that stops the blood supply to the area

sitting trot (sit′ tiŋ trät) in English riding events, the judge may call for the riders to trot their horses and sit the trot rather than post

six bar (siks bär) a show-jumping competition in which the fences are identical in type, placed in a straight line, and increase in height from the first to the last obstacle

six-string seat (siks striŋ sēt) a saddle with six saddle strings instead of eight; the two strings at the base of the fork are replaced with a screw-and-ferrule arrangement

skate (skāt) a horse of poor quality

skeleton (skel′ ə tən) gives the body form; supports soft parts and protects vital organs; the horse's skeleton is made up of 205 bones; see illustration

skeleton-rigged saddle an early saddle consisting of only a rawhide-covered tree and rawhide rigging for the rigging ring

skewbald (skyŏŏ′ bôld) a white horse splashed with any solid color other than black

skid boots (skid bŏŏts) protective leg boots that cover the rear portion of the fetlocks to prevent abrasion and burns when the horse is performing sliding stops; often used on roping and reining horses

skin pinch test (skin pinch test) a method of testing for dehydration; begin by grasping a fold of skin and pull it away from the horse's neck,

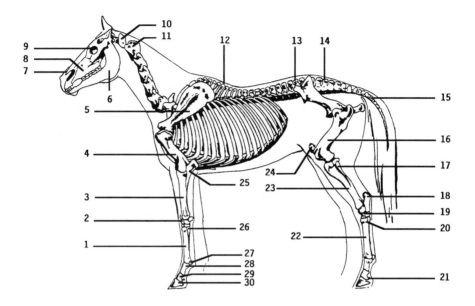

1. Metacarpal (cannon)	16. Femur
2. Carpus	17. Fibula
3. Radius	18. Fibula Tarsal (point of the hock)
4. Humerus	19. Tarsus
5. Scapula	20. Small Metatarsal (splint)
6. Mandible	21. Distal Sesamoid (navicular bone)
7. Nasal Bone	22. Metatarsus
8. Maxillary Bone	23. Tibia
9. Orbit (eye)	24. Patella (stifle)
10. Atlas	25. Ulna
11. Axis	26. Metacarpal (splint)
12. Thoracic Vertebrae	27. Sesamoid
13. Lumbar Vertebrae	28. 1st Phalanx
14. Sacral Vertebrae	29. 2nd Phalanx
15. Coccygeal Vertebrae	30. 3rd Phalanx

Skeletal System

then release it; if the horse is well hydrated, the skin will return to its original shape immediately; if the horse is dehydrated, the fold will remain standing or lower very slowly

skip   (skip) a container such as a bucket or basket used to remove stained and used bedding and straw from a stable

skirts   (skᵤrts) small flaps on either side of the seat covering the stirrup bars; see *English saddle; western saddle* (illus.)

skirt wear leathers   (skᵤrt wâr le<u>th</u>′ ərz) a leather strap or leather plate on top of the skirt to prevent wear of the skirt by the rigging and stirrup leathers

skull   (skul) the 37 bones comprising the structure of the head; see illustration

skull cap   (skul kap) the protective headgear worn by riders; with race jockeys, it is generally covered with the owner's racing colors

Skyros   (skī′ ros) a primitive breed of pony from the island of Skyros, Greece; known as being quiet and trustworthy

slab sided   (slab sīdəd) a flat-ribbed horse

sleeper   (slēp′ ər) a horse that unexpectedly wins a race having previously shown poor form

sleeping sickness   (slē′ piŋ sik′ nis) there are three types: eastern, western, and Venezuelan; inflammation of the white matter in the brain and spinal cord often caused by a virus; see *encephalomyelitis*

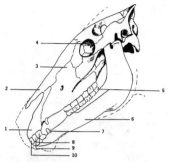

1. Incisive bone
2. Nasal bone
3. Maxilla
4. Orbital
5. Molars
6. Mandible
7. Canine tooth
8. Incisor
9. Incisor
10. Incisor

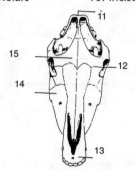

11. Occipital bone
12. Orbital bone
13. Incisive bone
14. Maxilla
15. Frontal bone

Skull

sleepy foal disease   (slēp′ ē fōl di zēz′) see *shigellosis*

slicker   (slik′ ər) a raincoat made of oiled canvas or other water-resistant fabrics

sliding plates   (slīd′ iŋ plāts) wide, flat-surfaced horseshoes used on the hind feet of reining horses

slip head   (slip hed) another variation of the English bridle; a simple strap attached to a snaffle bit adjusted under the headstall and used with a Weymouth or full bridle

slit braid tie (slit brād tī) two straps held together by means of a slit in each strap

sloping shoulders (slōp' iŋ s̲h̲ōl' dərz) shoulders properly angulated

slot (slät) the channel through the center of the bar where the stirrup leathers are anchored

slough (sluf) dead tissue in the process of separating from the body

slow gait (slō gāt) a slow, animated, four-beat gait, similar to the rack; one of the gaits of the five-gaited American Saddle Horse; it is a true prancing action in which each foot in turn is raised and then held momentarily in midair before being brought down

slow lopers (slō lōp' ərz) slang term for western pleasure horses

slow pace (slō pās) see *stepping pace*

small colon (smôl kō' lən) the part of the large intestine extending from the cecum to the rectum where digestive fluid is absorbed and solid food residue is formed into balls of dung; measures three to four inches in diameter and ten to twelve feet in length

small intestine (smôl in tes' tin) the primary site of protein digestion; consists of the duodenum, jejunum, and ileum

small strongyles (smôl strän' jil əs) any of forty species of strongyles that commonly infect the horse; thought to be less harmful than large strongyles; their larval migrations are limited to the intestinal walls

smegma (smeg' mə) the secretion of sebaceous glands, especially the cheesy secretion

smoky eye (smōk' ē ī) a whitish, clouded eye; see *wall eyed*

smooth (smōōt̲h̲) unshod; barefoot

smooth coat (smōōt̲h̲ cōt) short, hard, close-fitting coat of hair

smooth mouth (smōōt̲h̲ mout̲h̲) the smooth biting surface of the upper and lower incisors after the cups have disappeared; indicates a horse that is older than twelve years

snaffle bit (snaf' əl bit) the oldest and simplest form of bit available; comes in a variety of types; consists chiefly of a mouthpiece with a ring at each end to which one pair of reins is attached; the snaffle is a nonleverage bit; the action of the snaffle is on the corners of the lips; some have a straight bar, some are slightly curved, and some are single- or double-jointed; snaffle bit control requires two hands on the reins; the term *snaffle* is sometimes mistakenly used to describe any bit with a jointed mouthpiece; see *English bridle* (illus.)

Snaffle Bit

snaffle bridle (brī' dəl) the bridle used in conjunction with a snaffle bit

a=f<u>a</u>t; ā=<u>a</u>pe; ä=c<u>a</u>r; â=b<u>a</u>re; e=t<u>e</u>n; ē=<u>e</u>ven; i=<u>i</u>s; ī=b<u>i</u>te; ō=g<u>o</u>; ô=h<u>o</u>rn; ōō=t<u>oo</u>l; o͝o=l<u>oo</u>k; u=<u>u</u>p; ʉ=f<u>u</u>r; ŋ=ri<u>ng</u>; ə=sof<u>a</u>

snaffle key bit   (kē bit) a snaffle with small metal pieces dangling from the center; used in training young horses to the bit

snip   (snip) face marking; white area between nostrils; size and shape vary and should be noted for purposes of identification; see *markings, face* (illus.)

snort   (snôrt) a warning signal used to alert a group of horses of impending danger; the sound is made by blowing air out through the nostrils; a horse will snort when he sees something that frightens him

snorter   (snôr' tər) an excitable horse

snowflake   (snō flāk) spotting all over the body, but may be dominant over the hips; small white or frostlike spots on a dark base coat

sock   (säk) coat marking; a white area on the leg, usually extending from the coronet up to the middle of the cannon bone

soft   (sôft) easily fatigued

soft palate   (sôft pal' it) flexible rear part of the partition separating the mouth from the nasal passages; forced up by the tongue during swallowing to keep food out of the nose

Sokolsky   a Polish draft breed influenced by the Norfolk, the Belgian Ardennes, and the Anglo-Norman; generally chestnut in color, but bay and brown are also found

sole   (sōl) the portion of the ground surface of the hoof between wall, bars, and frog; see *hoof* (illus.)

solid color   (säl' id ku' lər) having no white markings

solution   (sə lōō' shən) the homogeneous mixture of one or more substances dispersed in a sufficient quantity of dissolving medium

soporific   (sop' ə rif' ik) any drug or compound that induces or causes sleep

sored   (sôrd) having physical evidence of inhumane training practices

sorghum   (sôr' gəm) a grain that has a very hard outer seed coat that can slow digestion; not a preferred feed for horses; also called *milo*

Sorraia   a pony from Portugal; thought to be one of the first breeds of horses to be domesticated by man; height: 12–13 hands; extremely hardy; if domesticated, becomes a good riding and pack pony; distinguished by its zebra markings and eel stripe

sorrel   (sôr' əl or sär' əl) a body color of red or copper red; mane and tail are usually the same color as the body, but may be flaxen

sound   free from any abnormal deviation in structure or function that interferes with the usefulness of the horse; physically fit and shows no signs of weakness or illness

soup plate feet   (sōōp plāt fēt) large, round feet, much bigger than normal; common in horses having spent a considerable period of time (usually in excess of six months) walking in wet, swampy, and/or marshy conditions; the feet usually return to normal when the horse is moved to dry ground

sour   when a horse becomes sullen in his work performance or performs far below his ability; often a result of overtraining or overschooling

Soviet Heavy Draft (sō′ vē et′ hev′ ē draft) a breed developed when draft mares were crossed with Belgian and Percheron stallions; the most common breed in Russia

Spanish Mustang Registry a registry in which the parents must be registered or pass inspection

spares (spārz) a term used in English racing stables for horses that are being prepared for racing, but are not up to the standard of those horses actually racing

spasm (spaz′ əm) a sudden, involuntary contraction of a muscle or constriction of a passage

spastic (spas′ tik) pertaining to or affected by spasm

spasticity (spas tis′ i tē) an increase in the normal muscle tone

spavin (spav′ in) a disease affecting the bones of the hock joint; usually appears as a bony enlargement on the inner and lower parts of the hock

spavin test (spav′ in test) a test in which the affected leg is held acutely flexed for about two minutes, then released immediately before the horse is trotted; the test is considered positive for bone spavin if lameness is markedly increased for the horse's first few steps

specific gravity (spi sif′ ik grav′ i tē) the ratio of the weight or mass of a given volume of a substance to that of an equal volume of another substance used as the standard

speculum (spek′ yə ləm) an instrument for showing the interior of a passageway or cavity of the body; may be used to keep the horse's mouth open while the teeth are being floated

speed index (spēd in′ deks) a method of rating racehorses; determined by both the horse's speed and distance covered

speed of horses approximate speed of normal gaits; walk, 4 mph; trot, 9 mph; gallop, 12 mph

speedy cutting any type of limb interference at the fast gaits

spermatozoa (spər mat′ ə zō′ ä) mature male germ cells capable of fertilizing the ovum; the specific output of the testes; sperm

sphincter (sfiŋk′ tər) a ringlike band of muscle fibers that constricts a passage or closes an opening

spider (spī′ dər) a second, reinforcing rigging strap over the fan of the tree attaching at each end of the rear rigging ring; reinforces the flank cinch rigging for heavy holding, like steer roping

spike team (spīk tēm) a team of three horses, two abreast immediately in front of the vehicle and one horse out in the lead; used to enable a four-horse team to continue its journey if one horse goes lame

spinal column (spīn′ əl käl′ əm) has five regions: cervical (neck), thoracic (back), lumbar (loin), sacral (croup), and coccygeal (tail)

spinal cord the thick trunk of nerve

---

a=f<u>a</u>t; ā=<u>a</u>pe; ä=c<u>a</u>r; â=b<u>a</u>re; e=t<u>e</u>n; ē=<u>e</u>ven; i=<u>i</u>s; ī=b<u>i</u>te; ō=g<u>o</u>; ô=h<u>o</u>rn; ōō=t<u>oo</u>l; ŏŏ=l<u>oo</u>k; u=<u>u</u>p; ʉ=f<u>u</u>r; ŋ=ri<u>ng</u>; ə=sof<u>a</u>

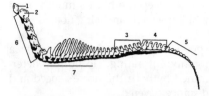

1. C1 (Atlas)	5. Coccygeal
2. C2 (Axis)	6. Cervical
3. Lumbar	7. Thoracic
4. Sacral	

Spinal Column

tissue that extends down the spinal canal from the base of the brain to the pelvic region

spinal tap   the removal of fluid from around the spinal cord for analysis

Spiti   a breed of pony originated in the Himalayas; used as a pack animal; a sturdy, vigorous mountain pony

spiv   (spiv) a groom without permanent employment, but who is prepared to do odd jobs for anyone on a casual basis

splashboard   (splash' bōrd') a barrier designed to keep water from splashing up onto the passengers in a carriage; see *carriage parts* (illus.)

splay footed   (splā fŏŏt' ed) a condition in which the feet turn outward because the legs turn out through their entire length

spleen   (splēn) highly vascular, ductless, visceral organ in the upper left abdomen near or across the surface of the stomach; stores blood cells, breaks down old red blood cells, and produces some of the infection-fighting white blood cells

splenius muscles   (splē' nē əs mus' əlz) large flat muscles of the neck; see *muscular system* (illus.)

splint   (splint) bony enlargements occurring on the cannon or splint bones; characterized by swelling, heat, and sometimes lameness; most common in young, strenuously worked horses; see *blemishes and unsoundnesses* (illus.)

splint boots   protective coverings worn around the cannons of the front legs to prevent injury

splinter bar   the stiff bar attached to the front of the carriage; the bar by which the vehicle is drawn; see *harness parts D* (illus.)

splinting   1. immobilizing a limb using a rigid material bandaged onto the leg 2. tensing the abdominal muscles in response to pain

split hide   (split hīd) the outer, or grain, layer of a hide from which the under, or flesh, side has been removed

spoke   (spōk) a brace or bar extending between the hub and rim of the carriage wheel; see *carriage parts* (illus.)

spongy bone   (spun' jē bōn) see *cancellous*

spooky   (spōō' kē) nervous and prone to shy

spoon   (spōōn) 1. a spoon-shaped protrusion from the upper side of the cantle or pommel of a cavalry saddle; there is a slot in the center of the spoon, used to attach the crupper or equipment 2. spoon-shaped metal extension on a spade or half-breed bit

spore   (spōr) 1. seed of microscopic plants, such as fungi 2. inactive or resting form of certain bacteria

sporotrichosis (spō′ rō trī kō′ sis) a mildly contagious disease causing nodules in the subcutaneous lymph nodes; a chronic fungal infection

sport horse (spôrt hôrs) purebred or crossbred horse suitable for dressage, jumping, eventing, and endurance

spots (späts) **1.** coat marking; small areas on the coat that are a different color than the primary coat color; small, rounded collections of hairs differing in color from the rest of the body **2.** a small white patch of hair located on the forehead; see *markings, face* (illus.)

sprain (sprān) any abnormal or unusual stretching of any ligament, tendon, muscle, or joint capsule; often associated with heat, swelling, and pain

spread (spred) **1.** to stretch or pose **2.** the type of fence that requires jumping the width from front to rear

spread eagle (ē′ gəl) to be thrown from the horse

spread fence an obstacle in show jumping or cross-country that is wide rather than high; examples include water jumps and parallel bars

spread himself when a horse jumps very wide and flat

springing (sprin′ in) methods of carriage suspension

spring-seat saddle (sprin sēt sad′ əl) a saddle with a heavily padded seat and a large, soft, round cantle and pommel roll

sprint a race of short distance

sprinter (sprint′ ər) a horse that is able to move at great speed over a short distance, but is seldom able to maintain the pace over a long distance; runs best at distances under a mile

spur (spʉr) a pointed device strapped on to the heel of a rider's boot and used to urge the horse onwards

squamous cell carcinoma (skwā′ məs sel kär′ sə nō′ mə) lumpy, irregular cancer of the superficial cells of the skin

square (skwār) when a horse is standing in a balanced way so that each foot is at one corner of a rectangle (not a trapezoid); weight is equally distributed on all four feet

squatter's rights (skwät′ ərz rīts) a western expression used when a rider falls off his horse

squaw roll (skwô rōl) a large, soft, protective roll across the back of the fork on a western spring-seat saddle

squeal (skwēl) a sound of anger; most often heard when horses are fighting

stable (stā′ bəl) **1.** a building in which one or more horses are kept **2.** a collection of horses belonging to one person, such as a racehorse owner or riding school proprietor

stable cough see *rhinopneumonitis*

stable fly a fly similar to the house fly, but with a painful bite

---

a=f<u>a</u>t; ā=<u>a</u>pe; ä=c<u>a</u>r; â=b<u>a</u>re; e=t<u>e</u>n; ē=<u>e</u>ven; i=<u>i</u>s; ī=b<u>i</u>te; ō=g<u>o</u>; ô=h<u>o</u>rn; ōō=t<u>oo</u>l; ŏŏ=l<u>oo</u>k; u=<u>u</u>p; ʉ=f<u>u</u>r; ŋ=ri<u>ng</u>; ə=sof<u>a</u>

stable kicker   a horse that kicks frequently at the walls and doors of his stable; apparently kicks just for the satisfaction of striking something with his hind feet

stable management   the ability and expertise to attend correctly to all the necessary details of stabled horses

stage coach (stāj kōch) a large, four-wheeled coach drawn by as many as eight horses

Stage Coach

stain   (stān) any horse that appears to be well bred, but is not registered

stakes class   (stāks klas) money-earning class

stakes race   (stāks rās) a race in which the owners nominate their horse for participation and pay subscription, entrance, and starting fees, whether money or any added prize is added or not; usually stakes races are classified into grades

stakes winner   (stāks win′ ər) a horse that has won a stakes race; denoted by black type on his sales catalog entry

stallion   (stal′ yən) a mature male horse that has not been castrated; may be used for breeding

stall walker   (stôl wäl kər) a horse that constantly paces or circles in the stall; can be a symptom of a horse being too confined

Standardbred   (stan′ dərd brəd) a breed of light horses originating in the U.S.; known for good stamina; used for driving and racing

standing back   (stan′ diŋ bak) a jumping horse that takes off too far away from the obstacle

standing heat   the mare's heat cycle, when a mare will stand for a stallion to breed her

standing martingale   a piece of training equipment that attaches to the noseband, preventing the horse from raising his head

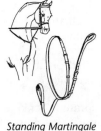

standing under description of a limb that is placed too far beneath the horse when viewed from the side

Standing Martingale

stanhope   (stan′ hōp) a light, open carriage with one seat

star   (stär) a white mark of varied size on the forehead; the size and shape should be noted; see *markings, face* (illus.)

stargazer   (stär gāz′ ər) a horse that holds his head too high and thrusts his nose out and upward

starter   (stärt′ ər) the racetrack official whose duty is to get the horses off to a fair start in a race

stay apparatus   (stā ap′ ə rat′ əs) a system of muscles, tendons, and ligaments in the body and legs that has the following three functions: helps support the horse while standing, acts to reduce concussion during movement, and prevents overextension; also known as the ligamentous structure that locks the leg so the horse can sleep while standing

stayer (stā′ yər) a horse that has great strength, power of endurance, and is therefore likely to be successful over a long distance

steel pipe fence steel pipe is often used for fencing and panels due to safety factors and easy maintenance

steeplechase (stē′ pəl chās) a race over natural or artificial obstacles, such as fences, hedges, and water jumps; the name stems from the fact that in the late 1700s, the races often went from one church to another

steeplechase jockey (jäk′ ē) a professional or amateur jockey who rides in steeplechases, often at heavier weights than normally carried by horses that race on the flat

steer wrestling (stēr res′ liŋ) a standard rodeo event; the contestant rides alongside a running steer and jumps from the saddle onto the head and neck of the steer; the object is to stop the steer, twist it to the ground, and hold it there with the head and all four feet facing in the same direction; the contestant that achieves this in the shortest amount of time is the winner; also called *bulldogging*

stenosis (stə nō′ sis) narrowing or stricture of a duct or canal

step (step) **1.** a single beat of a gait; it can involve one or more limbs **2.** a jumping obstacle that consists of a series of steps that can be negotiated up or down; commonly used in cross-country events

step mouth abrupt change in height of the molars; often occurs between the third and fourth cheek teeth

stepping pace a modified pace in which the rolling motion of the true pace is eliminated because the two feet on each side do not move together exactly

stepping short a symptom of lameness; the length of stride may be shorter in the lame leg

sterile (ster′ əl) **1.** completely free of living organisms **2.** a stallion or mare that is infertile

sterilization (ster′ ə li zā′ shən) any procedure by which an individual is made incapable of reproduction, as by castration

sternum (stʉr′ nəm) thin structure of bone and cartilage that forms the ventral surface of the rib cage; serves as an attachment for the distal ends of the ribs; the breastbone

steroid (ster′ oid) artificially produced drug that is similar to the natural hormone that controls inflammation; sometimes used illegally to promote muscle development

stethoscope (steth′ ə skōp) an instrument for listening to the sounds produced in the heart, lungs and gastrointestinal tract

steward (stōō′ ərd) an official at a race meeting appointed to see that the meeting is conducted according to the rules

sticker (stik′ ər) a thin, rectangular, metal wedge placed on the ground surface of the heel of a horseshoe; used to provide better traction

a=fat; ā=ape; ä=car; â=bare; e=ten; ē=even; i=is; ī=bite; ō=go; ô=horn; ōō=tool; ŏŏ=look; u=up; ʉ=fur; ŋ=ring; ə=sofa

sticky (stik' ē) a horse that is most uncertain when attempting to jump any obstacle

stiff (stif) a horse that moves without bend or even flexion

stiff-necked fox a fox that runs in a straight line

stifle (stī' fəl) the joint between the hip and the hock; corresponds to the knee of humans; see *points of the horse* (illus.)

stifling (stī' fliŋ) upward fixation of the patella; occurs when the stifle joint is fully extended; if permanent it is a serious unsoundness

stile (stīl) a jumping obstacle that consists of a portion of a fence or wall where steps allow people to cross, but deny access to livestock

stillbirth (stil' burth') the delivery of a dead foal that occurs after 300 days from the date of conception; any birth of a dead foal prior to 300 days after conception is usually termed an *abortion*

stimulant (stim' yə lənt) any agent, medicine, or drug that produces a feeling of well being or increased energy or alertness

stint (stint) the right to graze or pasture one or more horses on common land

stirrup (stur' əp) a flat-based loop hung from either side of a saddle to support the rider's foot while riding and mounting; English or flat saddle stirrups are made of metal and vary according to tread, weight, and style; western-style stirrups are usually wooden or metal and may be covered with leather; bronc riding stirrups are

rounded, decreasing the danger of a foot being caught; see *English saddle; western saddle* (illus.)

stirrup bar projections on the English saddle tree of either metal or fiberglass to which the stirrup leathers attach; see *English saddle* (illus.)

stirrup bolt a bolt through the upper part of the stirrup, used to suspend it from the stirrup leather; also known as the cross bar at the upper end of the stirrup; the stirrup's point of suspension in the stirrup leather

stirrup iron the metal, D-shaped device on the saddle through which the leather runs and on which the foot rests; see *English saddle* (illus.)

stirrup leathers long leather straps that support the stirrups; see *English saddle; western saddle* (illus.)

stirrup, open a stirrup without a front leather hood, shield, or tapadera

stirrup wear leathers a leather cover over the stirrup tread to reduce wear; laced or stitched on the underneath side of the tread

stock (stäk) **1.** a hunting necktie that can be used as a bandage for horse or rider should an emergency arise **2.** the handle of a whip **3.** livestock; refers to any animal such as cattle, horses, sheep, goats, etc.

stock horse a short-coupled, deep-bodied horse; a western-style horse of the Quarter Horse type, includes Quarter Horses, Appaloosas, Paints, etc.; a horse suitable for working livestock

stocking coat marking; a white area on the leg, usually extending from the coronet up to the knee or hock; see *markings, leg* (illus.)

stock saddle   a western-style saddle

stock seat equitation   a western class in which the rider is judged on his horsemanship, style and abilty, and effectiveness at applying aids

stock up   swelling of the horse's lower leg with edema due to restricted exercise

stomach   (stum' ək) initial part of the gastrointestinal tract where food is mixed with stomach acid and some nutrient absorption takes place

stomatitis   (stō' mə tīt' əs) inflammation of the mucous membranes lining the mouth

stone boat   (stōn bōt) in pulling competitions, the stone weight that is pulled

stones   (stōns) masses of extremely hard and unyielding material

stopper   (stäp' ər) any drug that slows down a horse or prevents him from performing to the best of his ability

straight action   (strāt ak' shən) when a horse moves his forelegs straight and true from the shoulder; the feet remain in line and the hind legs follow the line

straight behind   excessively straight legs as viewed from the side

straight shoulder   a shoulder lacking sufficient angulation; see *conformation comparisons* (illus.)

strain   (strān) an overstretching or overexertion of some part of the musculature

strangles   (straŋ' gəlz) an acute infectious disease of the lymph glands caused by bacteria; symptoms include nasal discharge, elevated temperature, and swelling of the lymph glands; if the swelling of the lymph glands is severe, it can restrict the horse's breathing (strangled), hence the name; also called *distemper*

strangulated   (strang' gyə lāt' id) overloaded with blood due to constriction

strangulating lipoma   (straŋ' gyə lāt' iŋ lip' ō mə) a small fatty tumor that is suspended by a stringlike structure and can encircle a piece of intestine, causing an obstruction and lack of circulation to that segment of intestine

strangury   (straŋ' gyə rē) slow and painful urination; caused by urethra and bladder spasm

strawberry roan   (strä' ber' ē rōn) coat color; chestnut or sorrel with an equal mixture of white hairs, giving the coat a pink tint; solid chestnut may be seen on the lower legs

stress fractures   (stres frak' chərz) also called *fatigue fractures;* most commonly seen in young horses training at high speeds on dirt surfaces; incomplete microfractures usually on the front surface of the cannon bone

stretch call   (strech käl) the demand on the racehorse by the jockey for the final effort just prior to the finish of the race

---

a=fat; ā=ape; ä=car; â=bare; e=ten; ē=even; i=is; ī=bite; ō=go; ô=horn; ōō=tool; ŏŏ=look; u=up; ʉ=fur; ŋ=ring; ə=sofa

stride   (strīd) an entire sequence of steps in a particular gait; length of stride measured from where one hoof has left the ground to the spot where the same hoof again hits the ground; see *step*

strike off late or early   when the canter does not start at the marker

striking   (strīk' iŋ) 1. a horse that strikes one leg with the toe or side of another leg 2. a dangerous vice in which the horse strikes out with his forelegs

string   (striŋ) a number of horses under the control of one person or outfit

stringhalt   (striŋ' hôlt) a nerve and muscle disorder characterized by the sudden, irregular, violent jerking up or flexing of the hock when the horse is moving

strip   (strip) a narrow, white marking from the horse's forehead to his nose; see *markings, face* (illus.)

stroke volume   (strōk vol' yōōm) the amount of blood the heart pumps with each beat

strongyle   (strän' jil) various parasitic roundworms commonly called *bloodworms;* any of various nematode worms of the family *strongylidae;* approximately fifty-four species; parasitic worms found in the gastrointestinal tract of horses

stud   1. an establishment at which horses are kept for breeding purposes 2. a stallion

stud fees   (stud fēz) fees that the owner of the stallion collects from the owner of the mare when she is bred; see *service fee*

stumor   (stōō' mər) a worthless horse or one that is not trying

style   (stīl) usually relates to a way of going; distinct personal flair of an individual horse; involves presence and charisma

subcutaneous   (sub' kyōō tā' nē əs) beneath the skin

subcuticular   (sub' kyōō tik' yŏŏ lər) beneath the epidermis

sublingual   (sub' liŋ' gwəl) the salivary gland located beneath the tongue

submaxillary salivary gland   (sub' mak' sə ler' ē) the salivary gland located between the jaws

submucous   (sub' myōō' kəs) beneath the mucous membrane

subscapular   (sub' skap' yə lər) beneath the scapula

substance   (sub' stəns) 1. strength and density of bone, muscle, and tendons 2. an indication of large body size; a horse with conformation that gives the impression of stamina and hardiness

substrate   (sub' strāt) substance acted on by a chemical

suckle reflex   (suk' əl re' fleks) automatic suckling when a finger or nipple is placed in a newborn foal's mouth; often used in the assessment of newborn foals

suckling   (suk' liŋ) a foal that is not weaned

Suffolk   (suf' ək) a breed of draft horse that is always chestnut in color

Suffolk Punch (suf′ ək punch) originating in Suffolk County, England, this breed is said to be a descendant of the "Great Horse," which was a medieval charger bred in the Netherlands for military purposes by crossing the largest draft horses with eastern bloodstock; a strong, dependable draft horse; color: all shades of chestnut

sugar eater (shŏŏg′ ər ēt′ ər) a pet horse

suitability (sŏŏt′ ə bil′ it ē) appropriate for a particular purpose or for a type or size of rider

sulci (sul′ kī) grooves, trenches, or furrows

sulfur (sul′ fər) a mineral required by horses; works with nitrogen to form the structure of some amino acids; most common horse feeds have adequate supplies of sulfur

sulky (sul′ kē) a light, two-wheeled racing rig; a small cart with rubber-covered wheels; designed for one person; used for trotting races

sullen (sul′ ən) sulking; resentful; withdrawn

sulphonamide (sul fän′ ə mīd′) a common drug used to control infections; an overdose may cause loss of appetite, weak pulse, diarrhea, and kidney dysfunction

summer sheet (sum′ ər shēt) light, unlined blanket; see *sheet*

summer sores (sōrz) irritated, spreading sores that develop from a wound; may be as small as a dime, but will enlarge rapidly within a week's time; caused by the eggs of the Habronema fly

Sunday horse (sun′ dē hôrs) any horse with comfortable gaits

sunfisher (sun′ fish′ ər) a rodeo horse with good bucking abilities; used in bronc-riding events; a bucking horse that twists his body in the air

superficial flexor tendon (sōō′ pər fish′ əl flek′ sər ten′ dən) outer tendon connecting the muscles of the upper leg to the back of the pastern bones

super saturated solution a solution containing more of the ingredient than can be held in solution permanently; the ingredient will fall to the bottom of the solution if allowed to stand

supple (sup′ əl) flexible; the ability of the horse to bend and flex his entire body

supplement (sup′ lə mənt) addition to a ration in order to increase specific nutrients; to provide more of a substance such as vitamins, minerals, or protein

supportive treatment (sə pôr′ tiv trēt′ mənt) a treatment directed at sustaining the strength of the patient

suppuration (sup′ yə rā′ shən) formation or discharge of pus

surcingle (sur′ siŋ′ gəl) a broad strap about the girth to hold the blanket or saddle in place; can be used in vaulting;

Surcingle

a=fat; ā=ape; ä=car; â=bare; e=ten; ē=even; i=is; ī=bite; ō=go; ô=horn; ōō=tool; ŏŏ=look; u=up; ʉ=fur; ŋ=ring; ə=sofa

for training such as longeing and ground driving, it supplies fasteners for side reins or long lines

surfactant (sʉr fak′ tənt) substance found in foals' lungs to allow the lungs to inflate adequately

surrey (sʉr′ ē) a four-wheeled vehicle with two forward-facing seats

suspension (sə spen′ s͟hən) **1.** a condition of temporary cessation, as of animation, pain, or any vital process **2.** a preparation of a finely divided drug intended to be incorporated in some suitable liquid before it is used

suspensory ligament (sə spen sə rē) a ligament, bone, muscle, sling, or bandage that holds up a part

suspensory apparatus the part of the stay apparatus that supports the fetlocks and keeps them from touching the ground

suture (sōō′ c͟hər) **1.** a stitch used to close a wound **2.** a fibrous, immovable joint in which the edges of the bones are closely united, as in the bones of the skull

swamp cancer (swämp kan′ sər) a disease caused by a fungus; lesions are most commonly found on the legs, abdomen, and chest; large ulcerated or draining nodules

swamp fever (swämp fē′ vər) see *equine infectious anemia*

swan neck (swän nek) the downward arch of the upper and lower sides of the neck

swaybacked (swā bakt′) having a decided dip in the back; also termed *easy backed* and *saddle backed*

sweat glands (swet glandz) glands located all over the horse's body, except the legs

sweat scraper (swet skrāp′ ər) an instrument for removing excess sweat or excess water after bathing a horse

Sweat Scraper

swedged shoe (swedjd′ shōō) a horseshoe with a crease in the bottom surface to provide greater traction and protect the nail heads from wear

Swedish Ardennes (swēd′ dis͟h ar den′) a draft breed developed in the nineteenth century from the Belgian and the French Ardennais; quiet and docile, these horses are still used to transport timber in mountainous regions

Swedish Warm-Blood (wôrm blud) a breed originating in Sweden; the breed goes back to the early seventeenth century when it was derived from crossing several different breeds including the Arab, the Andalusian, the Frisian, and the Hanoverian

Swedish Warm-Blood Association for registry, proof of four generations is required; stallions must be licensed

sweeny (swē′ nē) atrophy or shrinking of the shoulder muscles due to a nerve injury

sweet feed (swēt fēd) a horse feed that is characterized by its sweetness due to the addition of molasses

sweet itch (itc͟h) a skin condition found in horses that are allergic to a particular pasture plant; causes intense irritation; rubbing to relieve the itch leads to loss of hair; generally affects the crest, croup, and withers

swell, swells (swel) on a western saddle, the portion of the fork that bulges on each side from a line perpendicular to the point where the fork attaches to the bars of the tree; see *western saddle; western saddle fork types* (illus.)

swing team (swiŋ tēm) the middle team in a six-horse hitch; the team in front of the wheelers in an eight-horse hitch

swipe (swīp) racetrack slang for a groom, stable hand, or exercise boy

swishing tail (swish' iŋ tāl) tail movement; some horses may swish their tails to express anger or frustration; shows resistance

Swiss Warm-Blood (swis wôrm blud) a breed originating in Switzerland; the main foundation stock is the Einsiedler; used for riding and light draft work

swung round (swuŋ round) a pirouette in walk or canter when the horse makes the turn too quickly and is not under control

symmetrical (si met' ri kəl) proper balance or relationship of all parts

sympathetic (sim' pə thə' tik) existing or operating through an interdependence or mutual association

symptom (simp' təm) evidence of a disease as perceived and described by the handler

syncope (siŋ' kə pē) fainting

syndicate (sin' də kit) a group of people or organizations that forms a legally identifiable organization for the purposes of owning, leasing, and/ or training a horse for a particular purpose

syndrome (sin' drōm) a set of symptoms that occur together, usually indicating a particular type of disease process

synergism (sin' ər jiz' əm) the total effect of combined agents that is greater than the simple sum of their individual effects

synovial fluid (si nō' vē əl flōō' id) a transparent fluid resembling the white of an egg; secreted by the synovial membrane and contained in joint cavities, bursae and tendon sheaths for lubrication

synovitis (sin' ə vīt' əs) inflammation of the membrane lining the joint cavity

synthesis (sin' thə sis) the production or buildup of a substance by combining its elements or compounds

systemic (sis tem' ik) pertaining to the body as a whole

systole (sis' tə lē') the contraction or period of contraction of the heart

---

a=fat; ā=ape; ä=car; â=bare; e=ten; ē=even; i=is; ī=bite; ō=go; ô=horn; ōō=tool; ŏŏ=look; u=up; ʉ=fur; ŋ=ring; ə=sofa

T

table of the tooth (tā' bəl uv the tōōth) grinding surface of the tooth

tachycardia (tak' i kär' dē ə) unusually fast heart rate

tack (tak) riding equipment or gear for the horse, such as saddle, bridle, halter, etc.

tack room (rōōm) a storage room where bridles, saddles, and harnesses are kept

tack up (up) to put on bridle and saddle

tactile hairs (tak' tīl hârz) the hairs on the outside of the nostrils and lips of the horse; help the horse distinguish between good and bad feed

tag (tag) the white tip of the fox's tail

tail (tāl) includes the dock and all the hair

tail bandage see *track bandage*

tail docked the removal of a large quantity of hair from the tail by either cutting or pulling to produce a very short tail; in some cases, a horse's tail used to be severed to permanently shorten it

tail, female the female or bottom line of the pedigree

tail guard a rectangular piece of blanket or leather with three or four straps at the sides and a long strap at the top; fitted over a tail bandage to prevent the horse from rubbing the hair from his tail

tail hounds hounds that run at the rear of the pack

tailing (tāl' iŋ) when the pack of hounds, because of ill-matched age, speed, or ability, tends to straggle out

tail, male the sire line or top line in a pedigree

tail rubbing when a horse rubs his tail against the wall in the stall or against the fence; may be an indication the horse has lice, worms, or a dirty sheath or udder

tail set 1. a crupperlike contrivance with a shaped section for the tail to give it an arch and extremely high carriage; worn most of the time while the horse is in the stable and until a short time before the horse is shown 2. an operation that may be performed on American Saddlebreds to induce high tail carriage

takeoff point when jumping, the point from which the horse leaps to complete the jump; putting the horse in a position to jump from the correct point is the rider's responsibility

take out the total amount deducted from the bet on a race to be paid to the taxing authority and the racetrack

take the horse an expression used when a mare will stand and accept service from the stallion

tallyho (tal' ē hō) the cry of the hunt once the fox is sighted

tamed iodine (tāmd ī' ə dīn') an iodine solution from which the usual burning effect has been removed

tandem (tan' dəm) **1.** two horses hitched one in front of the other **2.** a covered carriage with two large wheels; designed for country use and drawn by two horses, one behind the other; typically used by huntsmen

Tang horse (täŋ hôrs) the war horse of Chinese art; usually depicted with open mouths and tossing heads

tap (tap) to drain fluid from a body cavity using a hypodermic needle

tapadera (tap' ə der' ə) toe fender; leather covering or shields over the front of western stirrups to protect the rider from brush; a decorative covering used in parades

tapeworms (tāp' wʉrms) internal parasites of the small intestine of the horse

tap root (tap rōōt) the direct female line of descent or female line in a pedigree

taps see *tapadera*

Tarbenian a breed of horse from the French region of Tarbes; basically, an Anglo-Arab

Tarpan (tär pan') a hardy dun horse originating in Poland; the breed has been extinct for more than a century; found in the wild and used by farmers for meat and as work animals

tarsus (tär' səs) the region of articulation between the gaskin and lower hind leg; the hock; see *skeletal system* (illus.)

tattoo (ta tōō') an artificial permanent identification; Thoroughbreds are tattooed on the inside of the lips

taxus (tak' səs) poisonous plant

TDN see *total digestible nutrients*

TEAM see *Tellington-Jones Equine Awareness Movement*

team (tēm) generally two, four, or six horses harnessed together and pulling a vehicle; any number of horses pulling together through any number of hitches

team roping (tēm rōp' iŋ) a popular event that is the rodeo version of cattle work, in which a cowboy ropes a steer around the horns and another cowboy then ropes the steer's heels

teaser (tēz' ər) a stallion used to find mares in estrus by observing the mare's behavior toward him

teasing (tēz' iŋ) a method to test mares in estrus for heat; especially useful when the mare exhibits no other visible signs of heat

technical delegate (tek' ni kəl del' ə gāt') the person at an international horse show or three-day event who is responsible for seeing that the competition is run according to international rules; usually from a country other than the host nation

teeth (tēth) bony projections in the upper and lower jaws, used to grasp, pull, and chew food; when fully grown, the male horse has forty teeth; the female has thirty-six teeth and lacks canines; sharp points wear on the inside of the lower teeth and the outside of the upper teeth

teeth, aging the wear, angle of bite,

a=fat; ā=ape; ä=car; â=bare; e=ten; ē=even; i=is; ī=bite; ō=go; ô=horn; ōō=tool; ŏŏ=look; u=up; ʉ=fur; ŋ=ring; ə=sofa

and presence of various features on the teeth allow a horse to be given an approximate age if the exact date of birth is not known

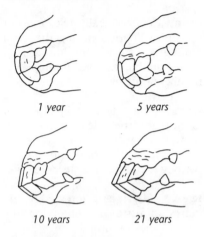

1 year   5 years

10 years   21 years

Estimating Age by Angle of Teeth

teeth, angle of bite   see *angle of bite*

teeth, canine teeth   see *canine teeth*

teeth, caps   see *caps*

teeth, centrals   see *centrals*

teeth, corners   see *corners*

teeth, crown of tooth   see *crown of tooth*

teeth, cups   see *cups*

teeth, deciduous   see *deciduous teeth*

teeth, dental star   see *dental star*

teeth, floating   see *floating*

teeth, full mouth   see *full mouth*

teeth, Galvayne's groove   see *Galvayne's groove*

teeth, interdental space   see *interdental space*

teeth, laterals   see *laterals*

teeth, molars   see *molars*

teeth, neck of tooth   see *neck of tooth*

teeth, smooth mouth   see *smooth mouth*

teeth wear   the amount of wear seen on the biting surface of the incisors

teeth, wolf teeth   see *wolf teeth*

Tellington-Jones Equine Awareness Movement   an alternative approach to working with problem horses

temperament   (tem' pər ə mənt) the general consistency with which the horse behaves; the horse's suitability for the job he is to perform

temperature   (tem' prə chər) normal adult temperature varies among horses, but will usually range from 99.5–100° F

temples   (tem' pəls) an area on each side of the forehead

tempo   (tem' pō) the speed at which the footfalls occur in a gait; increasing the tempo means covering more yards per minute

tendencies   (ten' dən sēs) to move or act in a certain way; e.g., the horse has a tendency to resist stepping into a trailer

tendon   (ten' dən) tough, nonelastic, fibrous connective tissue that connects muscle to bone or cartilaginous structures

tendon boot   boots made of leather

with a thick pad at the back; used to protect tendons from overreach injury

tendon, contracted when a foal grows extremely fast, causing the bones to lengthen faster than the tendons and causing a developmental deformity

tendon, digital extensor a tendon that helps bring the hoof forward and straightens the joint

tendon, digital flexor a tendon that helps draw the hoof up and bend the fetlock joint

tendonitis (ten' də nīt' əs) inflammation of the tendons and tendon-muscle attachments

tendon sheath a tube enveloping a tendon; secretes a lubricant to reduce friction at points of stress

tendosynovitis (ten' dō sin ō vī' tis) inflammation of the tendon sheath

tenectomy (tē nek' tō mē) the cutting out of a lesion of a tendon or a tendon sheath

Tennessee Walking Horse breed of the U.S.; height: 15–16 hands; strong, well built, docile, with a comfortable, four-beat running walk; common uses: show, saddle, harness, and all-around riding

tenosynovitis (ten' ō sin' ō vī' tis) inflammation of the tendon sheath

tenotomy (te nät' ə mē) the cutting of a tendon

tense (tens) the state of the horse mentally and physically; when a horse

is agitated, either by outside distractions or because he has not been taught to relax

tension band plate (ten' shən band plāt) bone repair implant that prevents separation of a fracture

terminal (tur' mə nəl) forming or pertaining to an end or ending; the conclusion

terrets (ter' its) the rings on the surcingle; any harness through which the reins pass; see *harness parts A and B* (illus.)

Tersky a Russian breed; a docile, intelligent horse developed and bred at state-controlled locations for use in the military; now used for sporting events, cross-country, jumping, and dressage

tertiary follicle (tur' shē er' ē fäl' i kəl') see *Graafian follicle*

testes (tes' tēz) see *testicle*

testicle (tes' ti kəl) male reproductive gland that occurs paired in an external skin sac; produces sperm; also called *testes*

testosterone (tes täs' tə rōn') male sex hormone responsible for masculine appearance and behavior of a stallion; secreted by the testicles and adrenal glands

tetanus (tet' ən əs) a rigid paralytic disease that causes death by asphyxiation due to rigidity of the respiratory muscles; caused by a toxin produced by a soil bacterium (*Clostridium tetani*);

---

a=fat; ā=ape; ä=car; â=bare; e=ten; ē=even; i=is; ī=bite; ō=go; ô=horn; ōō=tool; ŏŏ=look; u=up; ʉ=fur; ŋ=ring; ə=sofa

usually due to a contaminated puncture wound

tetanus antitoxin (an' ti täk' sin) antibody used for the purpose of temporarily immunizing against tetanus

tetanus toxoid (täk' soid) vaccine for prolonged protection against tetanus

tetany (tet' ən ē) disorders probably related to the high crude protein content of certain pasturage; a diet lacking in magnesium and calcium is associated with the condition

tetracycline (tet' rə sī' klin) antibiotic used against certain infections; can cause diarrhea in horses

Tevis Cup America's most famous endurance ride; ridden over the old Pony Express route from Lake Tahoe across the Sierra Nevada to Auburn, California

Texas skirt (tek' səs skʉrt) a square skirt so named because of its popularity in early-day Texas

Texas trail saddle (trāl sad' əl) a saddle popular around the 1880s to 1900; characterized by its three-quarter seat, high cantle with a roll, separate side jockey, eight-string seat, and full double rigging; a lightweight and comfortable saddle

therapeutic (ther' ə pyo͞ot' ik) curative

therapeutic index (in' deks) in drug use, the margin between the safe dose of a drug that will effect a cure and the toxic dose that will kill the patient

therapy (ther' ə pē) the treatment of disease

thiabendazole (thī' ə ben' də zōl) see *dewormer*

thick wind (thik wind) difficulty in breathing

thigh (thī) bordered by the stifle, flank, croup, buttock, and gaskin; see *points of the horse* (illus.)

third eyelid (thʉrd ī' lid) membrane that covers the inside corner of the eye underneath the eyelids; in an injured eye, it can cover more of the eyeball

thoracentesis (thō' rə sen tē' sis) surgical puncture of the chest wall for draining fluid

thoracic vertebrae (thô ras' ik vûr' tə brə) part of the spinal column that has ribs attached; forms the chest; see *skeletal system* (illus.)

thorax (thôr' aks) cavity enclosed by the rib cage and the diaphragm; the part of the body between the neck and the diaphragm

Thoroughbred (thʉr' ō bred') product of at least 200 years of breeding; the Darley Arabian, the Byerly Turk, and the Godolphin Arabian are the progenitors of the breed; today's Thoroughbreds usually stand 16–17 hands and are fine in conformation with long, well-muscled legs; their fame lies in racing; also used as saddle horses, polo mounts, and hunters; the term Thoroughbred refers strictly to the breed and should not be used as a synonym for purebred

Thoroughbred Horses for Sport promotes Thoroughbreds in the Olympic disciplines

thoroughpin (thʉr' ō pin') unsoundness or a blemish; soft, puffy swelling

Thoroughbred

that appears on the upper part of the hock, in front of the large tendon; the swelling can be pushed from one side to the other; see *blemishes and unsoundnesses* (illus.)

Three Bars   (thre bärz) a Thoroughbred stallion that became a leading Quarter Horse sire

three-calk pacing shoe   shoe for pacers

three-calk trot shoe   shoe for trotters

three-day event   a combined training competition completed over three consecutive days; consists of a dressage test, a cross-country section, and a show-jumping event

three-gaited saddle horse   often called *walk-trot horses;* horses that have three gaits: walk, trot, and canter

three-quarter rigging   rigging in which the front rigging is placed halfway between the center fire rig and the full double rig

three-quarter seat   a seat on which the leather extends forward to the rear edge of the stirrup leather grooves in the tree; has a separate side jockey; later, when the side jockey and the seat of the saddle became one piece of leather, it was called a *short seat*

three-quarter shoe   a shoe used on horses that brush or those that need to have pressure removed from the heel; it has no inside heel, which leaves that section of the foot unprotected and without support; allows ailments such as corns to be treated easily

three-year-old   a young horse between his third and fourth birthday; for a racehorse, between January 1 and December 31 of his third year

thrifty condition   (thrif′ tē kən dish′ ən) healthy; active; vigorous

throat   (thrōt) the portion of the saddle seat under and just in front of the rider's crotch; also called the *twist*

throat fly   (flī) see *botfly*

throatlatch   (thrōt lach) 1. the narrow strap of the bridle that goes under the horse's throat and is used to secure the bridle; see *English bridle; western bridle; harness parts B and E* (illus.) 2. the point where the horse's neck and head meet; see *points of the horse* (illus.)

thrombocyte   (thräm′ bə sīt) blood platelets; important in blood clotting

thrombosis   (thräm bō′ sis) the formation of a blood clot that remains attached at the point of formation in the blood vessel, causing an obstruction

throng   (thräŋ) the lash of a whip

throw a colt   (thrō ə kōlt) when a mare gives birth to a male

---

a=fat; ā=ape; ä=car; â=bare; e=ten; ē=even; i=is; ī=bite; ō=go; ô=horn; ōō=tool; ŏŏ=look; u=up; ʉ=fur; ŋ=ring; ə=sofa

throw a filly when a mare gives birth to a female

thrown out a horseman or hound that loses his position in the hunt

throw off to cast hounds at the beginning of the meet; derived from the early practice of taking hounds to the covert side coupled together; when the time came to start the hunt, the couples were thrown off

throw up an English expression meaning that the hounds have lost the scent and have given up or thrown up their heads

thrush (thrush) a disease of the foot caused by anaerobic microorganisms characterized by a pungent odor; is caused by wet or unsanitary conditions; thrush causes deterioration of tissues in the cleft of the frog or in the junction between the frog and bars; this disease produces lameness and, if not treated, can be serious

thruster (thrus' tər) a thoughtless, inexperienced rider who makes a nuisance of himself by overriding hounds and larking

thumps (thumps) contractions of the diaphragm in unison with the heartbeat; sometimes called *diaphragmatic flutter*

thyroid gland (thī' roid gland) two-lobed endocrine gland in the neck that controls the rate at which basic body functions proceed; produces the hormone thyroxin

thyroxin (thī räk' sēn) hormone produced by the thyroid gland

Tibetan (ti bet' ən) horse breed of Tibet; possibly descended from Chi-nese and Mongolian ponies; strong; suitable for farm work, packing, or riding; lively and energetic

tibia (tib' ē ə) the larger of the two bones of the gaskin, between the stifle and the hock; see *skeletal system* (illus.)

tice straw brush (tīs strô brush) brush that penetrates hair and lifts out dirt

tick (tik) external parasite; several kinds may be found on horses; the most common are the winter tick (*Dermacentor albipictus*), the lone star tick (*Amblyoma americanum*), and the spinose ear tick (*Otobius megnini*)

tick paralysis (pə ral' ə sis) paralysis due to a toxin secreted in the saliva of certain female ticks

tie (tī) **1.** to attach or fasten by use of halter and shank **2.** hounds are said to "tie to the line" when they hunt in closely and are difficult to lift **3.** when two contestants obtain an identical score and are given the same placement in the results

tied in at the knee a condition that occurs when the flexor tendons appear to be too close to the cannon bone just below the knee

tie-down a strap connecting the noseband on the bridle to the cinch; prevents the horse from throwing his head up; the western version of the standing martingale

tied up suffering from the painful spastic condition of large rump muscle masses; also known as *azoturia*

tie-out chains a controlled outdoor exercise

tie stalls a type of housing for horses that provides stabling for more horses than box stalls and requires less bedding and labor; a manger is usually built into the front of the stall; a provision is made for tying the horse and a tail chain is often put across the back; severely resticts the mobility of the horse, therefore exercise is important

tie strap see *cinch strap holder*

tie strings see *saddle string*

tie weight an iron weight formerly used for ground-tying horses; rounded, but flat on the ground side, or square; usually weighed 8 lbs

tilbury (til' bər ē) a carriage made to seat two persons; has two wheels and is light and elegant; a typical English gig

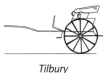

Tilbury

tilbury phaeton (til' bər ē fā' ət' ən) a light and elegant four-wheeled vehicle with a folding top over the front seat and a rear seat for the footman

Tilbury Phaeton Carriage

tilted head see *tipping head*

timber (tim' bər) any jump or obstacle made of wood such as a gate, hurdle or fence

time allowed (tīm ə loud') the prescribed time in which a competitor must complete an event if he is not to incur time faults

timed events calf roping, team roping, and steer wrestling

time limit the prescribed period of time in which a competitor must complete a show-jumping course if he is not to be eliminated

Timor (tē' môr) a small and agile Indonesian pony; residents of the Island of Timor and thus subject to strict isolation.

timothy (tim' ə thē) a nonlegume hay; forage grass common to the midwest

tincture of iodine (tiŋk' chər uv ī' ə dīn) used to treat navel cords of newborn foals, wounds, ringworm, etc.

tipping head (tip' piŋ hed) also called *tilted head;* the face of the horse is not held vertical; from the front, the head is slanted to the right or the left

tips (tips) tip shoes; small, lightweight toe ends of shoes; used on horses at grass to stop their feet from breaking up and, sometimes, because of their light weight, on racehorses during a race

tipster (tip' stər) a person who makes a business of providing information or tips about the chances of a horse in a race

tissue (tish' ōō) an aggregation of similarly specialized cells united in the performance of a particular function

titer (tīt' ər) concentration

tobiano (tō' bē än' ō) coat color in Pintos and Paints; white patches extend from the back down, as if white

---

a=f**a**t; ā=**a**pe; ä=c**a**r; â=b**a**re; e=t**e**n; ē=**e**ven;
i=**i**s; ī=b**i**te; ō=g**o**; ô=h**o**rn; ōō=t**oo**l;
ŏŏ=l**oo**k; u=**u**p; ʉ=f**u**r; ŋ=r**i**ng; ə=sof**a**

paint were splashed on the horse from above; borders between color and white are usually sharper than in the overo; all the legs are white and the face is colored or colored with white facial markings

toe   (tō) the front part of the hoof; see *hoof* (illus.)

toe crack   a crack located specifically at the toe of the horse's foot; see *quarter crack;* also see *blemishes and unsoundnesses* (illus.)

toe grab a thin protrusion of metal on the ground surface of the toe of a horseshoe; used primarily in training and racing plates to give increased grip and action

toes in   base narrow; see *conformation comparisons, front limb* (illus.)

toes out   base wide; see *conformation comparisons, front limb* (illus.)

toe weight   a metal weight fitted to a spur previously placed on the front hoof to induce a change or balance in motion; used extensively in the training and racing of harness horses

Tom Thumb bit   (täm t͟hum bit) a curb bit with short, straight, swivel shanks and a broken mouthpiece; sometimes called a *cowboy snaffle*

tongs   (tän͡z) instrument used to hold hot metal

tongue   (tu͡n) 1. movable muscular structure attached to the floor of the mouth; first point of pressure, regardless of the type of bit used 2. to bay or to cry

tongue grid   a thin, metal serpentine suspended high in the mouth above the bit; the horse is scarcely aware of its presence, but cannot physically bring his tongue high enough to put it over the bit

tongue loller   a horse that lets his tongue hang out

tongue out   placement of a horse's tongue out of the side of the mouth as an evasion of the bit

tongue over the bit   experimentation that can lead to an evasion; the horse puts his tongue over the top of the bit instead of keeping it underneath, thus getting away from the correct influence of the bit

tongue strap   a strap that passes across the tongue, fastening to the lower jaw; quite painful, but is used in flat racing to stop the horse from swallowing his tongue

tonneau   (tu nō′) an open vehicle drawn by one medium-build horse; easy to handle

too low   (tōō lō) when the whole front of the horse is carrying too much weight

tooth rasp   (tōōt͟h rasp) a file with a long handle; used for floating or removing sharp edges from the teeth

top bed   (täp bed) a carriage footrest; see *carriage parts* (illus.)

top boots   boots with contrasting mahogany tops and white garters; originated with the cavaliers in Britain in the 1700s, who used to turn down the tops of their boots to display the colored linings

top hat   formal headwear made from

gossamer or shellac and finished in polished felt; made in various heights, with the highest used by men in scarlet hunting, and the lowest used for dressage and showing; during a fall, the top of the hat may help cushion the head

topical   (täp′ i kəl) pertaining to a particular surface area, as in topical treatment

topical treatment   (tret′ mənt) care affecting a particular spot on the surface of the body directed to the cure of a disease or injury

top line   1. the proportion and curvature of the line from poll to tail 2. the stallion's side of the pedigree or direct line of male descendants

Toric   (tôr′ ik) breed originated in the Soviet Union; known for its quiet disposition; used for light agricultural work

torque   (tôrk) a twisting or turning force

torsion   (tôr′ shən) twisting; as in torsion of the intestines in colic

torticollis   (tôr′ ti käl′ is) a condition marked by contracted neck muscles, producing twisting of the neck and an unnatural position of the head

total digestible nutrients   (tōt′ əl dī jes′ ti bəl nōō′ trē ənts) TDN; in any given feed, the amount of nutrients actually used by the horse's system; concentrate has about 75 percent TDN, roughage has about 50 percent TDN

totalisator   (tōt′ əl i zāt′ ər) an electromechanical device used for a form of betting in which the total amount wagered, after deducting a percentage

for costs, is divided among the holders of winning and placing tickets

tote board   (tōt bôrd) the indicator board of the totalisator on which is flashed all pari-mutuel information before or after a race

tourniquet   (tʉr′ nə kit) an instrument for compressing a blood vessel by applying pressure around an extremity to control the circulation and prevent the flow of blood to or from the distal area

tout   (tout) a low-order con man who peddles tips, betting systems, etc., to the unwary race goer

tovero   (tō′ vär ō) a classification of Paint; those horses that have characteristics of both tobiano and overo coat patterns

toxemia   (täk′ sē′ mē ə) a general intoxication or poisoning sometimes due to the absorption of bacterial products formed at a local source of infection; presence of toxins or poisonous substances in the blood stream

toxic   (täk′ sik) pertaining to or due to the nature of a poison

toxic shock   (shäk) circulatory collapse due to the release of toxins from bacteria in the body

toxin   (täk′ sin) an organic poison; usually a protein produced by a living organism

toxoid   (täk′ soid) a portion of bacterial toxin that has no toxicity, but still

---

a=f<u>a</u>t; ā=<u>a</u>pe; ä=c<u>a</u>r; â=b<u>a</u>re; e=t<u>e</u>n; ē=<u>e</u>ven; i=<u>i</u>s; ī=b<u>i</u>te; ō=g<u>o</u>; ô=h<u>o</u>rn; ōō=t<u>oo</u>l; ŏŏ=l<u>oo</u>k; u=<u>u</u>p; ʉ=f<u>u</u>r; ŋ=ri<u>ng</u>; ə=sof<u>a</u>

retains the ability to stimulate production of antitoxin when injected; used for immunization

trace clip (trās klip) clipping the horse under the neck, along the belly, and above the thigh; essentially the area the traces of a cart would be; the back, neck, legs, and rump are not clipped

trace horse (trās hôrs) the lead horse when horses are driven in front of each other; at the bottom of steep hills, spare horses were often available to be hitched in front of a single horse to help with a heavy load

trace minerals minerals found in small quantities in feed and required in small quantities by the body

traces in driving, the parts of the harness that run from the collar to the single tree; the leather bands by which pressure is to be transferred from the collar to the vehicle; see *harness parts A, B, and C* (illus.)

trachea (trā′ kē ə) the windpipe, which descends from the larynx to the bronchi

tracheal wash (trā kē əl wash) recovery of mucus from the lung by injecting and then withdrawing a sterile solution; done through a long, flexible, fiber-optic endoscope or a small surgical incision

tracheitis (trā′ kē īt′ əs) inflammation of the trachea

tracheotomy (trā′ kē ät′ ə mē) the formation of an artificial opening into the trachea to keep a horse from suffocating in an emergency

track bandage (trak ban′ dij) **1.** a fabric wrap with a slight degree of elasticity used to keep cottons in place on leg wraps; often used on racehorses **2.** a wrap used to control short flyaway hairs in the tail; it may cut off circulation in the tail if wrapped too tightly or left on longer than three hours; also called *tail bandage*

track conditions a description of the racetrack; *fast* indicates a track that is thoroughly dry and at its best; *sloppy* means the horses are running during or immediately after a heavy rain, water has saturated the cushion, and there may be puddles but the base is still firm; *muddy* means that water has soaked into the base and it is soft and wet, and footing is deep and slow; *heavy* indicates a track that is muddy and drying out, footing is heavy and sticky

track left counterclockwise movement in an arena so that the left leg is on the inside

track right clockwise movement in an arena so that the right leg is on the inside

track up when the left hind steps into the left forefoot print, and the right hind foot steps into the right forefoot print; said of the trot and walk; for many horses, tracking up at the trot is a sign of adequate impulsion

tractable (trakt′ ə bəl) easily manageable; docile; trainable

trailer (trāl′ ər) **1.** the horseshoe heel that is extended one-half inch or more beyond the heel of the horse's foot; **2.** vehicle used for transporting horses

trailering (trāl′ ər iŋ) transporting horses in a trailer suited to their large size

trail horse (trāl hôrs) **1.** a horse trained, bred, or used for cross-country rides; **2.** a class in which horses must work on a loose rein through and over obstacles

trail riding (rīd' iŋ) **1.** social, endurance, and competitive trail riding **2.** riding outside an arena

trainer (trān' ər) the person who conditions and prepares horses for racing or other sport

training (trān' iŋ) teaching the horse what actions are expected in response to the cues of the handler

training tracks (traks) concentric tracks inside the racecourse proper at Australian racetracks on which the great majority of Australian racehorses are trained; tracks that are set up for race-training purposes

Trait du Nord French horse breed; hardy, heavy draft breed; remarkably strong and able to withstand harsh winters

Trakehener West German horse breed; developed for Army use; a series of crosses resulting in a solid, sturdy horse with endurance; docile, yet dynamic; used for show jumping, dressage, combined training, etc.

trandem three horses harnessed abreast

tranquilizer (traŋ' kwe lī' zər) an agent that produces a quieting or calming effect without changing the level of consciousness

transfusion (trans fyōō' zhən) the introduction of whole blood or a blood component directly into the bloodstream

transition (tran zish' ən) upward or downward change between gaits, speed, direction, or maneuvers

transition not defined when a horse drifts from one pace to the other

transition rough any resistance to the rider's aids during a transition; gait changes that are not smooth

transmission (trans mish' ən) a transfer of a disease, nerve impulse, or inheritable characteristic

transplacental (trans' plə sen' təl) through the placenta

transudate (tran' sōō dāt) a fluid substance that has passed through a membrane or has been forced out of a tissue as a result of inflammation

transverse (trans' vʉrs) placed crosswise, at right angles to the long axis of a body part

transverse cross (krôs) a dark stripe that runs across the withers

trapezium (trə pē' zē əm) a small, irregularly shaped bone behind the knee joint; see *points of the horse* (illus.)

trapezius muscle (trə pē' zē əs mus' əl) either of a pair of large muscles of the back and neck that draw the head backward and sidewise; see *muscular system* (illus.)

trappy (trap' ē) a course with sharp turns

trappy action (ak' shən) a short, quick turn

---

a=fat; ā=ape; ä=car; â=bare; e=ten; ē=even; i=is; ī=bite; ō=go; ô=horn; ōō=tool; ŏŏ=look; u=up; ʉ=fur; ŋ=ring; ə=sofa

trauma (trô′ mə) a wound or injury that injures and destroys tissue

travel (trav′ əl) the path of flight of each limb during movement

travel a horse an English term; to trailer a horse

travel boots shipping boots; thick, contoured, padded boots held in place by straps; specifically designed to protect the leg during travel

traverse (trav′ ərs) 1. haunches in; the horse is slightly bent around the inside leg of the rider; the horse's outside legs pass and cross in front of the inside legs; the horse is looking in the direction in which he is moving; performed along the wall or on the center line at an angle of about 30 degrees to the direction the horse is moving 2. lateral movement of the animal without forward or backward movement; this step often helps riders in opening or closing gates, lining up horses in the show ring, and taking position in a mounted drill or posse; also called *side step*

TRPB Thoroughbred Racing Protection Bureau

tread (tred) the bottom of the stirrup and support place for the foot when riding; see *English saddle; western saddle* (illus.)

tread worms (tred′ wʉrmz) *Strongylus westeri;* genus of Strongyloides

treble (treb′ əl) a combination obstacle consisting of three separate jumps

tree (trē) the wooden, plastic, or fiberglass structure forming the foundation of the saddle, which consists of a fork, two bars, and a cantle; see *English saddle tree; western saddle tree*

trematode (trem′ ə tōd) see *fluke*

trephine (tri fīn) a crown saw for removing a circular area of bone, chiefly from the skull

trial and error (trī′ əl and er′ ər) this is a method by which horses learn; reinforced through the judicious employment of reward and punishment

triceps (trī′ seps) the muscle that has three heads or parts; part of the forearm; heavy, three-branched muscle behind the shoulder and above the elbow; see *muscular system* (illus.)

trichoglyphs (trī′ kō glifs) swirls of hair coat; cowlicks; hair whorls

trichomoniasis (trik′ ə mō nī′ ə sis) an infectious intestinal disease characterized by sudden, severe diarrhea

trichostrongylus (trik′ ō stroŋ jil′ əs) the cause of a skin condition called summer sores

tricuspid valve (trī kus′ pid valv) having three cusps; referring to the left atrial ventricular valve of the heart

triglyceride (trī glis′ ər īd′) intermediate form of fat circulating in the body for chemical transport or nutrition

triple bar (trip′ əl bär) ascending staircase jump consisting of three bars that add spread and increase in height

Triple Crown (croun) the Thoroughbred race series that consists of three races: the Kentucky Derby, the Preakness Stakes, and the Belmont

Stakes; famous winners include Sir Barton, Gallant Fox, Omaha, Whirlaway, Count Fleet, Assault, Citation, and Secretariat

tripped (tripd) loss of or lack of balance; during a movement, when the horse trips in one or more strides

trochar (trō′ kär) a sharp, hollow-pointed instrument for piercing the wall of a body cavity

troika a Russian word meaning *trio* or *three;* a three-horse combination team hitched to a vehicle such as a carriage, wagon, sleigh, or sled

trot (trät) a natural, two-beat diagonal gait in which the front foot and the opposite hind foot take off together and strike the ground together; a natural gait in which the tracks of the hind legs fall directly in the tracks of the forefeet

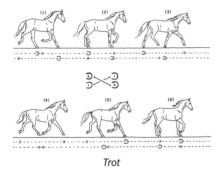

Trot

trotter a Standardbred horse that races with a diagonal gait; slowest racehorse gait

trotting gene a dominant gene that determines whether a horse will be a trotter or a pacer

Trotting Horse Association makes the rules for harness horses

trotting shoes flat shoes worn in front and swedged shoes worn behind to give more traction; sometimes removable toe weights are used on the front feet of trotters

Truckle Feature (truk′ əl fē tʉr) a Quarter Horse that set the quarter-mile record at 21.02 seconds in 1969

true lethals (trōō lē′ thəls) an inherited condition in horses that causes death of the foal just prior to or shortly after birth

true osselet (os′ ə let) the chronic, abnormal growth of new bone in the fetlock joint

trypanosomiasis (trip′ ə nō′ sō mī′ ə sis) a general term for the diseases nagana, surra, mal de caderas, and murrina, all caused by various trypanosomes

tryptophane (trip′ tə fān′) an essential amino acid

tuberculosis (tŏŏ bʉr′ kyə lō′ sis) any of the infectious diseases of man and animals caused by a species of mycobacteria and characterized by the formation of tubercles and caseous necrosis in the tissues

tuberosity (tōō′ bə räs′ ə tē) a large prominence on a bone, usually for the attachment of muscles or ligaments

tubule (tōōb′ yŏŏl) a small tube

tucked up (tukt up) a small-waisted horse; may be a temporary condition

---

a=fat; ā=ape; ä=car; â=bare; e=ten; ē=even; i=is; ī=bite; ō=go; ô=horn; ōō=tool; ŏŏ=look; u=up; ʉ=fur; ŋ=ring; ə=sofa

due to hard work, lack of water, lack of bulk in the diet, etc.; also called *gaunted up* or *ganted up*

tufted whorl   (tuft' əd wôrl) a whorl where the hairs pile up into a tuft

tug   (tug) see *billet* or *cinch*

tug   (tug) an oval-shaped band topped with a buckle through which the shafts on a single-horse harness pass; in pair or team driving, the tug is the part of the harness by which the traces are attached to the hames; see *harness parts A and B* (illus.)

tularemia   (tōō' lə rē' mē ə) a highly contagious disease of rodents; resembles plague; transmitted by flies, ticks, fleas, and lice; may be contracted in horses by the bite of a tick

tumor   (tōō' mər) a mass of new tissue that persists and grows independently of its surrounding tissue and that has no useful function

tunica   (tōō' ni kə) a covering; a general term for a membrane or other structure covering or lining a body part or organ

tunnel keeper   (tun' əl kē' pər) see *channel keeper*

turbinate bones   (tur bə nāt bōnz) bones in the nasal passage that filter and warm the air that is inhaled

turbulence   (tur' byə ləns) departure from a smooth flow in a fluid

turf   (turf) 1. any course over which horse racing is conducted 2. in America, turf races are held over grass courses as opposed to dirt tracks 3. the world of horse racing in general

turgid   (tur' jid) swollen and congested

Turkish Pony   (tur' kish pō' nē) a breed of pony not particularly attractive; calm in temperament; endurance makes it a good farm and pack animal

Turkoman   (tur' kə mən) a Russian horse breed; an elegant horse developed from ancient breeds crossed with Akhal-teké bloodlines; noted for speed and endurance

turn away   (turn ə wā') to put a horse out on pasture for a period of time to rest and unwind

turned welt   see *welt*

turning device   a piece of equipment used on horses that refuse to turn to one side or that hang to one side

turn on center   a pirouette when the horse fails to keep the hindquarters on the spot

turn on the forehand   a movement where the horse pivots on the forehand while describing concentric circles with his hind legs

turn on the haunches   a maneuver in which the horse's forehand rotates around his hindquarters; turn on the hindquarters

turnout   overall appearance of a horse and rider

tushes   (tush' əs) canine teeth that erupt in the interdental space; usually only found in mature male horses

twist   (twist) the part of an English

saddle tree that is directly between the rider's thighs where they meet the body; see *English saddle* (illus.)

twitch   (twich) a means of restraint; a nose twitch is a wooden stick with a loop of rope or chain attached or a metal instrument that is used to apply pressure to the sensory nerves of the nose; a shoulder twitch is applied by grabbing skin at the horse's shoulder and rolling it around the knuckles

two-horse man   a rider who always goes to the hunt with a second horse so that he can hunt all day and keep up front without overtiring his mount

two-string saddle   a western saddle on which there are only two saddle strings, one on each back jockey of the saddle

two track   (tōō trak) a movement in which the horse moves forward with his front and back feet making two sets of tracks

two-year-old   a young horse between his second and third birthday; for most registered horses, between January 1 and December 31 of their second year

tying up   (tī' iŋ up) characterized by muscle rigidity and lameness; affecting the muscles of the croup and loin; accompanied by pain, disinclination to move, a variable temperature, and brownish colored urine; commonly seen in fit horses that resume heavy exercise after a few days of rest without any reduction in grain; also called *Monday morning sickness, azoturia,* or *myositis*

tympany   (tim' pə nē) distension due to the presence of gas or air, as in the abdomen or guttural pouch

type   (tīp) an ideal or standard of perfection combining all the characteristics that contribute to the animal's usefulness for a specific purpose; embodying all the breed's characteristics

type A knee   the lower epiphysis of the radius; mature, completely closed

type B knee   the lower epiphysis of the radius; in the process of closing, slightly open

type C knee   the lower epiphysis of the radius; open, immature

types of horses   a classification of the different kinds of horses; one type is the light horse, which is subdivided into driving horses, racing horses, and riding horses; under driving horses, we find harness, heavy harness, ponies, and roadsters; under racing horses, we find harness race, quarter race, and running race horses; under riding horses, we find five-gaited, hunters, jumpers, plantation walking, polo, ponies, stock, and three-gaited horses; the second type is work horses, which is subdivided into draft horses, farm chunks, southerners, and wagon horses

a=f<u>a</u>t; ā=<u>a</u>pe; ä=c<u>a</u>r; â=b<u>a</u>re; e=t<u>e</u>n; ē=<u>e</u>ven; i=<u>i</u>s; ī=b<u>i</u>te; ō=g<u>o</u>; ô=h<u>o</u>rn; ōō=t<u>oo</u>l; ŏŏ=l<u>oo</u>k; u=<u>u</u>p; ʉ=f<u>u</u>r; ŋ=ri<u>ng</u>; ə=sof<u>a</u>

U

udder (ud′ ər) mammary gland; the equine udder consists of two mammary glands; may be called *bag* or *dug*

Ukrainian Riding Horse Russian breed developed recently from selected breeds on state farms; suitable for sports, draft, jumping, and farm work

ulcer (ul′ sər) a hollow space on the surface of an organ or tissue due to the erosion, disintegration, and necrosis of tissues

ulcerated (ul′ sə rāt əd) affected with an ulcer

ulna (ul′ nə) a bone that, fused together with the radius, forms the forearm of the horse; see *skeletal system* (illus.)

ultrasonic (ul′ trə sän′ ik) the use of controlled doses of high-frequency sound for therapeutic treatment; see *ultrasound*

ultrasound (ul′ trə sound) high-frequency sound waves above the range of human hearing **1.** used to break down unwanted tissue, promote healing by stimulating circulation, and aid in accurate diagnosis **2.** a sonogram that uses sound waves bounced off tissues; is often used in diagnosing pregnancy

ultraviolet light (ul′ trə vī′ ə lit līt) light rays beyond the violet end of the spectrum; having powerful chemical properties and used in radiation treatment

umbilical cord (um bil′ i kəl kôrd) a tubelike cord that connects the fetus to the placenta; serves as the transport mechanism of nutrients and oxygen from the mare to the growing fetus; also called *navel cord*

umbilical hernia (hʉr′ nē ə) congenital defect; the protrusion of contents of the abdomen through an opening in the muscle, forming a swelling or lump in the area of the navel

unbalanced (un bal′ ənst) the state of the horse when he has lost his balance temporarily or completely

unconstrained (un′ kən strānd′) in dressage, a horse that is moving freely, yet energetically, with relaxed muscles, as if on free rein

under blanket a liner used to make a blanket heavier and warmer; needed in the winter under the stable blanket; made of heavy wool or synthetic fleece

underface (un′ dər fās) to train a horse to jump an obstacle that is clearly too small and that the horse can accomplish with ease

underlay in wagering parlance, when the odds are less than those estimated by the track's official morning line maker

underline (un′ dər līn) the length and shape of the line from the elbow to the sheath or udder

underpinning the legs and feet of the horse

under saddle (un′ dər sad′ əl) a horse that is being ridden, as opposed to a horse that is led (in hand)

undershot jaw when the lower jaw

is longer than the upper jaw and protrudes

ungulate   (uŋ′ gyŏŏ lāt) a mammal that has digits protected by a hoof, as in horses

unicorn   (yōō′ nə kôrn) **1.** a type of hitch in which two horses are hitched as a pair, with a third in front of them **2.** a mythological horse with a single horn

uniform   (yōō′ nə fôrm) the prescribed dress worn by followers of the hunt

unilateral   (yōō′ nə lat′ ər əl) affecting one side only

united   (yŏŏ nīt′ id) the action, movement, or gait of the horse when the body and leg movements of the horse are coordinated in such a way as to represent the perfect action; generally used when referring to the canter

unlevel   (un lev′ əl) instead of the feet taking even weight as they come to the ground at the walk or trot, one foot may take more weight than the other, giving the appearance of slight lameness

unraced   (un′ rās′ əd) a horse that has not yet taken part in a race

unregistered   (un rej′ is tərd) a horse that is not accepted as a specific breed

unseated   (un sēt′ əd) a rider who has been removed from the saddle by other than intentional methods of dismounting

unsighted   (un sīt′ əd) when a horse or rider is unable to see ahead, particularly in jumping, as the line of sight is temporarily blocked by other horses

unsound   (un sound′) a general term indicating that a horse has some form of body tissue damage, generally affecting bone, muscle, tendon, or ligaments, which can affect the horse's serviceability and performance at one or more gaits

unsoundness   (un sound′ nəs) defects or more serious abnormalities that affect serviceability; for example, blindness, spavin, bowed tendon, calf knees, capped elbow or hock, cocked ankles, contracted feet, corns, curb, fistulous withers, founder, grease heel, heaves, hernia, knee sprung, laminitis, moon blindness, navicular disease, parrot mouth, poll evil, quarter crack, quittor, ring bone, roaring, sand crack, scratches, shoe boil, side bones, splints, stifled, stringhalt, sweeny, thick wind, thoroughpin, thrush, undershot jaw, windgall, and windpuffs

unsteady halt   (un sted′ ē hôlt) when the horse comes to a halt but does not really achieve immobility; he may fidget with his legs or his head, or move off the line

unsteady head   (hed) the lack of steadiness of head carriage due to loss of balance or difficulty in movement; some horses may consistently be unsteady in their head carriage

unthrifty   (un thrif′ tē) a defect in the way the horse looks, grows, behaves, and/or performs, as compared to what one would normally expect

---

a=fat; ā=ape; ä=car; â=bare; e=ten; ē=even;
i=is; ī=bite; ō=go; ô=horn; ōō=tool;
ŏŏ=look; u=up; ʉ=fur; ŋ=ring; ə=sofa

untrack (un trak') to lead or ride the horse a few steps

unwind (un wind') to start bucking

upward transition (up' wərd tran zish' ən) change to a faster pace, as in going from a slow trot to an extended trot, or a walk to a canter

urachus (yŏŏ' rə kəs) the tube connecting the fetal bladder with the placenta

uremia (yŏŏ rē' mē ə) an intoxication caused by the accumulation in the blood of waste materials normally eliminated in the urine; a result of inadequate kidney function

urethra (yŏŏ rē' thrə) the tube that carries urine from the bladder to the exterior of the body; transports semen in the male

urinalysis (yŏŏ' ri nal' i sis) a physical, chemical, or microscopic analysis or examination of the urine

urinary calci (yŏŏ' ri nar' e kal' sē) see *urolithiasis*

urinary system (sis' təm) consists of the kidney, ureters, bladder, and urethra; removes waste materials from the body in the form of urine

urine (yŏŏ' rin) the fluid excreted by the kidneys, passed through the ureters, stored in the bladder, and discharged through the urethra; healthy urine is of a slightly amber color

urolithiasis (yŏŏ' rō li thī' ə sis) the formation of urinary stones and solid masses of mineral substances somewhere in the urinary tract

uroliths (yŏŏr' ə liths) urinary stones

urticaria (ʉr' tə ker' ē ə) an allergic condition characterized by the appearance of welts on the skin surface; also known as *hives*

using horse (yŏŏz iŋ hôrs) a horse that is used regularly for work purposes, generally with livestock; maintained primarily for a purpose other than for show and racing

uterine body (yŏŏt' ər in bäd' e) part of the uterus between the horns and the cervix

uterine horn (hôrn) either of the two upper projections in the Y-shaped uterus of the mare connecting the two oviducts to the body of the uterus

uterus (yŏŏt' ər əs) a hollow, muscular organ in the pelvis of the female, in which the fertilized ovum is implanted and the embryo and fetus are protected and developed; the womb

utility (yŏŏ til' ə tē) the use to which a horse is designated

utility saddle (sad' əl) a saddle that is between the jump seat and the show seat and is designed for general-purpose use, except jumping

uveal tract (yŏŏ' vē əl trakt) the iris, ciliary body, and choroid of the eye

V

vaccinate (vak′ sə nāt) to protect a horse against a likely disease or infection by the administering of a vaccine; also called *inoculate*

vaccine (vak′ sēn) a suspension of attenuated or killed microorganisms administered for the prevention or treatment of infectious diseases; specific in that a separate vaccine must be used for immunization against each disease

vagina (və jī′ nə) the canal that leads from the uterus to the external orifice of the genital canal

vaginitis (vaj′ ə nīt′ əs) inflammation of the vagina marked by pain and a purulent discharge

valet (val′ ā) an employee who takes care of the jockey's equipment; helps the trainer saddle the horse, and helps carry saddle and equipment to and from the paddock

van (van) horse box; horse trailer

vaquero (vä kär′ ō) the Spanish term for cowboy

varicose vein (var′ ə kōs′ vān) blood spavin; located at the inside of the hock

varmint (vär′ mənt) another name for a fox

varnish roan (vär′ nish rōn) an Appaloosa roan pattern with a predominance of white hairs with dark varnishlike patches usually on the head, knees, hocks, and lower limbs

vascular (vas′ kyə lər) pertaining to blood vessels

vascular tissue (tish′ ōō) tissue with a good supply of blood vessels

vas deferens (vas def′ ə renz′) the tube that carries sperm from the epididymis to the urethra in the male

vasectomy (vas ek′ tə mē) removal of part of the vas deferens in the male; this operation causes the sperm to be produced, but prevents the sperm from passing out during ejaculation, thus preventing conception

vasoconstrictor (vas′ ō kən strik′ tər) a muscle that causes constriction of the blood vessels

vasodilation (vas′ ō dī′ lā shən) dilation or enlargement of a vessel; causes increased blood flow to the area

vasopressin (vas′ ō pres′ ən) a hormone produced in the posterior pituitary gland that causes the smooth muscles in the blood vessels to contract

vaulting (vôlt′ iŋ) the art of gymnastics on the moving horse

vaulting surcingle (sʉr′ siŋ′ gəl) a thick leather strap with two handles that is fastened around the horse's barrel just behind the front legs

vector (vek′ tər) a carrier; capable of transmitting a disease; applies to flies, mosquitoes, ticks, etc.

VEE see *Venezuelan equine encephalitis*

---

a=fat; ā=ape; ä=car; â=bare; e=ten; ē=even; i=is; ī=bite; ō=go; ô=horn; ōō=tool; ŏŏ=look; u=up; ʉ=fur; ŋ=ring; ə=sofa

vehicle (vē′ hi kəl) anything that can mechanically carry diseased organisms from one source animal to another, such as clothing, food, water, and dust

vein (vān) vessel through which blood passes from various organs back to the heart

Venezuelan equine encephalitis (ven′ i zwā′ lan ē′ kwīn en sef′ ə līt′ is) a form of viral encephalitis transmitted by insects; see *sleeping sickness*

venom (ven′ əm) a poison; a toxic substance normally secreted by a snake, insect, or other animal

venous (vē′ nəs) pertaining to the veins

ventilation (ven′ tə lā′ shən) ability of air to be exchanged in an enclosed space such as a barn or trailer; generally provided by the doors, windows, and louvered boards of a barn; one of the critical aspects regarding a horse's health when constructing a barn

ventral (ven′ trəl) on or located toward the lower or bottom surface

venule (ven′ yōōl) any of the small vessels that collect blood from the capillaries and join to form veins

verminous (vʉr′ mi nəs) pertaining or due to a worm

verminous aneurysm (an′ yə riz′ əm) localized dilation of the wall of an artery; caused by worm infestation

version (vʉr′ zhən) change of the polarity of the fetus in the uterus in relation to the mare

vertebrae (vʉr′ tə brā) bones that make up the spinal column; extend from the head to the tail

vertical (vʉr′ ti kəl) 1. in the vertical plane, that is, perpendicular to the horizon 2. a straight or upright fence

vertical flexion (flek′ shən) an engagement of the entire body: abdomen, hindquarters, back, neck, and head; often mistakenly associated with head set; also called *longitudinal flexion*

vertigo (vʉr′ ti gō) a feeling of dizziness

vesicants (ves′ i kənts) a counterirritant that produces blistering and scurfing of the skin

vesicle (ves′ i kəl) a small sac containing fluid, such as a blister

vesicular disease (və sik′ yə lər di zēz′) a disease that includes the development of fluid-filled blisters on the outer layer of the skin or mucous membrane; in animals, includes foot-and-mouth disease, swine vesicular disease, and vesicular exanthema

vesicular stomatitis (və sik′ yōō lər stō′ mə tī′ tis) a localized inflammation of the soft tissues of the mouth and the formation of blisters; a contagious disease caused by a virus

vesiculitis (və sik′ yōō lī′ tis) inflammation of a vesicle, especially the seminal vesicle of the male horse

vessel (ves′ əl) any channel for carrying fluid

vestigial (ves tij′ ē əl) pertaining to the remnant of a structure that functioned at an early stage of development; rudimentary

veterinarian (vet′ ər ə ner′ ē ən) one who treats diseases or afflictions of animals medically or surgically; a practitioner of veterinary medicine or surgery

veterinary thermometer (t͟her mom' i tər) used to take rectal temperatures

VFA   see *volatile fatty acids*

viable (vī' ə bəl) alive or capable of living

Viatka   a Russian breed with good conformation and a solid build; suitable for light farm work

Vic   the name of the horse General Custer rode in the Battle of the Little Bighorn

vice (vīs) acquired abnormal behavior that results from confinement or improper management; can affect the horse's usefulness, dependability, and health; examples are cribbing, weaving, and kicking

viceroy (vīs roi) a lightweight, cut under, wire-wheeled show vehicle with a curved dash; used for some heavy harness classes, especially Hackney ponies, Shetlands, and harness show ponies

Victoria (vik tôr' ē ə) a coachman-driven summer vehicle that was much favored by ladies of fashion due to the ease of entering; introduced by the Prince of Wales in 1869; a small, four-

Victoria

wheeled carriage with a low seat and a folding top; designed for two persons plus the coachman; usually drawn by one horse, often used for hire

view halloo (vyōō hal' ōō) a peculiar piercing scream uttered by some huntsmen when the fox is viewed; some hunts use whistles

viewed away (vyōōd ə wā') when a fox is seen to leave the quarry; this occurrence is rare in America, although it is common in the more open country of England

villi (vil' ī) the tiny, fingerlike extensions of the intestine; designed to increase the surface area

viral arteritis (vī' rəl är' tə rīt' əs) a contagious viral disease causing inflammation of the arteries, often leading to abortion

virulent (vir' yŏŏ lənt) an organism with great ability to cause disease; exceedingly pathogenic or noxious

virus (vī' rəs) ultramicroscopic bundle of genetic material capable of multiplying only in living cells; causes a wide range of disease in plants, animals, and humans, such as rabies and measles

vis-a-vis (vē' zə vē) an open, four-wheeled carriage with facing seats for four passengers

Vis-a-Vis

viscera (vis' ər ə) internal organs and glands contained in the thoracic and abdominal cavities

visceral (vis' ər əl) pertaining to the large internal organs, especially those in the abdomen

---

a=fat; ā=ape; ä=car; â=bare; e=ten; ē=even; i=is; ī=bite; ō=go; ô=horn; ōō=tool; ŏŏ=look; u=up; ʉ=fur; ŋ=ring; ə=sofa

viscous (vis′ kəs) sticky; thick; syrupy

vise (vīs) an instrument used by farriers to finish shoes and to hold metal

vision (vizh′ ən) the ability to see; can be blurred, clear, or distorted

vitamin A (vī′ tə min ā) required for normal body cell function, especially in the skin, hair, eyes, and other outer body tissues; deficiency can cause moon blindness or the inability to see properly at night

vitamin B consists of a number of related compounds; B complex vitamins are present in virtually all the metabolic processes that take place in the horse

vitamin C a nonessential vitamin for horses, as they are able to synthesize vitamin C in their digestive tract

vitamin D directly involved in the use of calcium and phosphorus; obtained by most horses from a compound in green plants and hay, which is acted on by sunlight in a reaction inside the horse; a vitamin D deficiency can only occur from inadequate sunlight

vitamin E essential for normal cell structure; lack of vitamin E can cause anemia and white muscle disease

vitamin K responsible for the production of the blood-clotting factor; any deficiency will cause internal bleeding

vitamins nutrients necessary for growth and general health; different vitamins are used for different functions and can be categorized into two main groups: fat soluble (vitamins A, D, E, and K) and water soluble (vitamins C and B complex)

vitiligo (vit′ ə lī′ gō) a condition characterized by the destruction of pigment in small or large circumscribed areas of the skin

vitreous humor (vit′ rē əs hyōō′ mər) the clear, gelatinous substance filling the area behind the lens in the eye

vixen (vik′ sən) a female fox

Vladimir Heavy Draft (vlad ə mir′ hev′ ē draft) a Russian breed produced when local mares were crossed with a variety of draft breeds; a well-built, powerful horse

voice (vois) the bay of a hound

voice commands (kə mandz′) a natural training aid; must be consistent in word used, volume, tone, and inflection

volatile (väl′ ə təl) tending to evaporate very quickly

volatile fatty acids (fat′ ē as′ idz) VFA; breakdown products of fats

volte a full turn on the haunches in dressage; a circle with a radius about the length of the horse; may also describe the smallest circle a horse is able to travel (generally about nineteen feet in diameter)

voluntary (väl′ ən ter′ ē) accomplished in accordance with will

voluntary muscle (mus′ əl) a muscle used in an action the animal can control, such as moving a leg

volvulus (väl′ vyŏŏ ləs) a knotting and twisting of the intestines that causes an obstruction and colic

vulva (vul′ və) the outside opening of a mare's genital tract

vulva winking (wiŋk′ iŋ) the movement of the labia or lips of the vulva when a mare is either in season or urinating; exposes the clitoris

---

a=f<u>a</u>t; ā=<u>a</u>pe; ä=c<u>a</u>r; â=b<u>a</u>re; e=t<u>e</u>n; ē=<u>e</u>ven; i=<u>i</u>s; ī=b<u>i</u>te; ō=g<u>o</u>; ô=h<u>o</u>rn; ōō=t<u>oo</u>l; ŏŏ=l<u>oo</u>k; u=<u>u</u>p; ʉ=f<u>u</u>r; ŋ=ri<u>ng</u>; ə=sof<u>a</u>

W

wagonette (wag′ ə net′) a coach used for public service between towns; has a low body with two lengthwise facing seats and a rear entrance

Wagonette

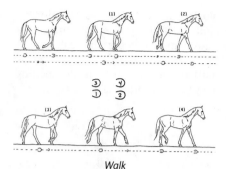

Walk

wagon horses (wag′ ən hôrs əz) horses intermediate in weight and height between the draft and the chunk; weight: 1300–1600 lbs; height: 15.2–16.2 hands; usually have less depth of body and longer legs than draft horses; occasionally still used to make deliveries

waist (wāst) part of the English saddle just forward of the seat; see *English saddle* (illus.)

waiting race (wā′ tiŋ rās) when a jockey holds his horse back at the start and in the early stages of a race to be able to come to the front at the latter stages of the race

Waler (wā′ lər) an Australian horse breed; a docile, courageous horse originally used by the military; the few remaining horses are now being used for jumping, hurdle races, and polo

walk (wôk) a natural, slow gait of four beats in which each foot strikes the ground in separate intervals in the following sequence: near hind, near fore, off hind, off fore; the walk should be free moving, even, and flat footed; see illustration

walker a piece of equipment used to exercise horses; consists of several arms extending from a central pole; horses are tied to the end of the arms and follow it in a circular path; see *hot walker*

Walking Horse also referred to as the *Tennessee Walking Horse;* originally developed for plantation riding; characterized by an easy, running walk

Walking Horse Class any of various competitions held for Tennessee Walking Horses at horse shows

Walking Horse Owners Association an organization designed to promote the Tennessee Walking Horse

walkover a race in which only one horse has been declared a starter; generally, to qualify for the prize money, the horse has to be saddled, paraded before the crowd, and then walked past the winning post

Walk-Trot Class for young, beginning riders (generally less than nine years of age) the walk and trot are the only required gaits

walk-trot horse a show term meaning a saddle horse that only walks, trots, and canters; distinguished from the five-gaited horse

wall (wôl) **1.** an upright show-jumping obstacle made of hollow wooden blocks that are painted and stacked to look like a brick wall **2.** a cross-country obstacle built of brick, concrete blocks, sleepers, or stone; obstacles are usually built as uprights, but dry stone walls may be as wide as a narrow-topped bank

walleyed   used to describe lack of pigment in the iris; the eye is bluish white or gray in color; is not considered a blemish; also referred to as *glass, blue, china,* or *crockery eye*

wall of the hoof   that part of the hoof that is visible when the foot is placed flat on ground; divided into the toe, the quarters (the sides), and the heel; see *hoof* (illus.)

wanderer foal   (wän' dər' ər fōl) a foal suffering from convulsive syndromes caused by a lack of oxygen at birth

wandering   (wän' dər iŋ) when the horse has deviated from a straight line or the circle on which he started

warble   (wôr' bəl) swelling under the horse's skin caused by a parasitic larva of the ox warble fly; in horses, larvae sometimes migrate to the back or flank area where they form abscesses after failing to break through the surface

war bridle   (wôr brīd' əl) an emergency bridle made of rope; used in leading unruly horses by exerting pressure on the poll; also called a *come-along;* often made of stiff lariat rope

ware hole, ware wire   warning given by advance followers in the field to those behind

ware hounds   warning given if a hound comes up from behind, the front, or the side to avoid followers stepping on him

ware riot   the warning to the hounds when they show signs of riot

warmblood   (wôrm blud) **1.** a European term used to describe breeds that have descended from Arab, Barb, and/or Turkmene blood in the original foundation horses **2.** result of crossing heavy horses (coldblood) with Thoroughbreds or Arabians (hotblood); could include any breed of horse except those animals that are 100 percent hot- or coldblood

warming-up   (wôrm' iŋ up) the routine of graduated exercise until the horse is properly conditioned for strenuous effort

warranty   (wôr' ən tē) any description, expression, or statement made concerning any matter relating to the conformation, health, or ability of a horse; given in writing at or prior to a sale; any legal recourse to litigation for recovery of any possible loss or damages by the purchaser can only apply to any matter detailed in the warranty

warren   (wôr' ən) a colony of rabbit burrows

warts   (wôrts) epidermal growths caused by a papilloma virus; usually occur around the heads of young horses up to three years old; they can vary in number from a few to a hundred

wash rack   (wäsh rak) specific area

---

a=f**a**t; ā=**a**pe; ä=c**a**r; â=b**a**re; e=t**e**n; ē=**e**ven; i=**i**s; ī=b**i**te; ō=g**o**; ô=h**o**rn; ōō=t**oo**l; ŏŏ=l**oo**k; u=**u**p; ʉ=f**u**r; ŋ=ri**ng**; ə=sof**a**

for washing horses; must ensure good footing when wet and adequate drainage

water (wät' ər) a nutrient consumed in large volumes; an average adult horse drinks six to ten gallons per day

water brush 1. a brush used to wash the feet and dampen the mane and tail 2. in show jumping, a small sloping brush fence placed in front of a water jump to help the horse take off

water gripes a form of colic resulting from the intake of too much water; can occur if working a horse too soon after drinking or if allowing a hot, stressed horse to drink too much water, especially cold water, before the horse has cooled down

water hemlock a poisonous plant found in moist areas throughout most of the U.S.

water jump a spread show-jumping obstacle consisting of a sunken trough of water with a minimum width of 14 ft and a length of up to 16 ft; a small brush fence is usually placed on the takeoff side

water out to cool a harness horse after a race by walking him about and only allowing him occasional drinks of water

wave mouth (wāv mouth) a condition of uneven teeth wear found mainly in older horses

waxing (waks' iŋ) the collection of a drop of dry colostrum at the end of each teat that occurs eighteen to forty-eight hours before foaling

WBC see *white blood cell count*

weaning (wēn' iŋ) removing the foal from the dam; usually done at four to six months of age by separating foal and dam

weanling (wēn' liŋ) a weaned foal that has not yet turned one year old

wear (wâr) amount of biting surface of the incisors that is ground off in chewing

wear leather a piece of leather on a saddle positioned to reduce wear between leathers and other materials

weaving (wēv' iŋ) a rhythmic swaying of weight from one front foot to the other when confined; this nervous condition or habit can be socially contagious; may be a symptom of a horse under too much confinement

web (web) the width of the horseshoe from the inner to the outer edges

webbed shoe (webd) a type of shoe to protect corns

WEE see *western equine encephalomyelitis*

weed (wēd) refers to a horse that is small, underdeveloped, and lacking in size and muscle when compared to other horses of the same breed

weigh in (wā in) in certain equestrian sports where a specified weight has to be carried, such as show-jumping, combined training and racing, the rider has to be weighed immediately after completion of the race or after his round in the competition to ensure the correct weight was carried throughout the event

weighing room the place on a racecourse where jockeys are weighed

weight aids   when a rider influences the horse by shifting his weight; weight may be shifted to one seat bone, the thighs, or the seat; may also include leaning back or following the movements of the horse more aggressively

weight allowance   in racing, claimed by a jockey or apprentice who has not ridden a certain number of winners

weight cloth   a cloth carried under the saddle on a horse; equipped with pockets in which lead weights may be inserted to achieve the correct weight

weight for age   a method of handicapping horses in a race by their age; older horses carry more weight than the younger horses

weight out   in certain equestrian sports, a specified weight has to be carried, such as racing, combined training, and show jumping; the rider has to be weighed before the race or competition to ensure the correct weight is carried

weights   blocks, normally of lead, placed in the weight cloth and used by the rider who is not heavy enough to make the specified weight for an event

well in hand   (wel in hand) a horse running at a fraction of his best speed

well let down   (wel let doun) the condition of the horse that gives the impression of having a body that appears to be cylindrical or round in shape from the ribs through to the flanks; opposed to a performance horse in training where the flanks are usually tucked up

Welsh Cob   (welsh kob) breed from Wales; a courageous, agile horse bred from the Welsh Mountain Pony, possibly Arab, Spanish breeds, and the Hackney; now used for riding, jumping, trekking, and show jumping

Welsh Mountain Pony   height: less than 12 hands; originated in Wales; section of the Welsh studbook that includes animals less than 12 hands; this pony is smaller and probably the most elegant of the Welsh ponies; resembles the Arab; appearance combined with action makes it a desirable riding and harness pony

Welsh Pony of Cob Type   "C" registers those not exceeding 13.2 hands, but that have an appearance that places them in the cob category; thicker and more short set than others with the same desirable action; good for light draft and endurance or rough terrain riding

Welsh Pony Section B   "B"-registered animals are between 12.2 and 13.2 hands; resembles Welsh Mountain Pony except it shows more Hackney and Thoroughbred; handsome action makes it a good riding or light draft pony

welt   (welt) a piece of leather stitched into the outer seam in the leather covering of swell forks; extends up the sides of the swells; necessary to make the leather fork covering conform to the shape of the fork; there are two types of welts: a single welt is a single piece of leather between the stitched-together pieces of the leather of the seam; a turned welt is a double piece of leather between the stitched-together pieces of leather of the seam

a=fat; ā=ape; ä=car; â=bare; e=ten; ē=even; i=is; ī=bite; ō=go; ô=horn; ōō=tool; ŏŏ=look; u=up; ʉ=fur; ŋ=ring; ə=sofa

western bridle consists of a set of reins, a bit, and a headstall; the type of reins may vary depending on rider's preference and use of the horse

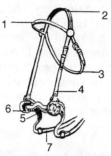

1. Browband
2. Crown Piece
3. Throatlatch
4. Cheek Piece
5. Curb Strap
6. Curb Bit
7. Reins

Western Bridle

Western Division composed of stock, trail, and pleasure horse classes; horses may be of any breed or combination of breeds as long as they are at least 14.1 hands, serviceably sound, and of stock horse type; riders must be dressed as for the stock seat equitation classes and carry a lariat or reata; a rain slicker may be required in trail and pleasure classes

western equine encephalomyelitis (ē' kwīn en sef' ə lō mī ə līt' is) a viral disease of horses and mules that causes inflammation of the brain and spinal cord; observed west of the Mississippi River in the U.S.; also present along the Gulf and Atlantic coasts

Western Horsemanship a class in which the rider is judged on seat, hands, ability to control and show horses; judges may assign an individual riding pattern

Western Pleasure a class in which the western-type horse is ridden in the show ring and judged at a walk, trot, and lope both ways of the ring on a loose rein

western riding 1. a style of riding used by working cowboys in the U.S., Canada, and Central and South America, and for pleasure and endurance riding; the western saddle and the seat position forces the rider to adopt a much more comfortable seat position for long rides 2. a class (cap.) that demonstrates a horse's ability to perform several manuevers, especially a series of controlled, collected flying lead changes

western saddle a common type of saddle distinguished by a large noticeable fork on which there is some form of horn, a high cantle, and large skirts; see illustrations pp. 291, 292

Westfalen Westfalen is the German spelling of *Westphalian*; see *Westphalian*

Westphalian (west fä' lē ən) a horse breed of good size and stature; bred for athletic ability and temperament; used for dressage, combined training, and jumping

Weymouth bridle (wā' meth brīd' əl) a double-bitted, double-reined bridle where the snaffle bit and the curb bit are separated; commonly used on three- and five-gaited horses

Weymouth Bridle

Weymouth curb bridle (kʉrb brīd' əl) a double bridle using the English curb bit and a snaffle bit; used primarily on gaited horses,

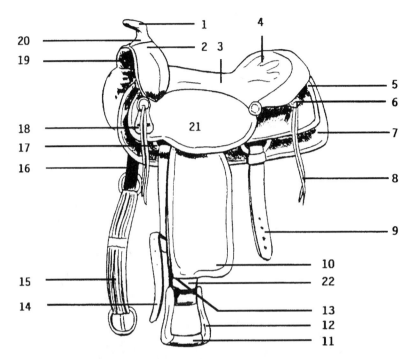

1. Horn
2. Swells
3. Seat
4. Cantle
5. Rear Housing or Back Jockey
6. Concha
7. Skirts
8. Saddle Strings
9. Rear Billet
10. Fender
11. Tread Cover

12. Stirrup
13. Stirrup Leather (inside)
14. Full Latigo
15. Cinch
16. Off Billet
17. Rigging Dee or Ring
18. Latigo Carrier
19. Gullet
20. Pommel
21. Seat Jockey
22. Stirrup Leather Keeper

Western Saddle

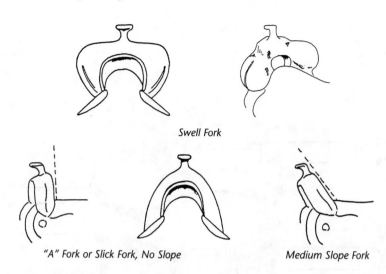

Swell Fork

"A" Fork or Slick Fork, No Slope   *Medium Slope Fork*

Western Saddle Fork Types

but also used for dressage and some-times on hunters; see *English bridle* (illus.)

whang strings   (hwaŋ stringz) see *saddle strings*

wheals   (whēlz) smooth, slightly raised areas of the skin surface that are redder or paler than the surrounding areas

wheel   (hwēl) when a horse turns around suddenly without guidance from his rider

wheelers   (hwē' lərz) the team on the pole or tongue, hitched directly in front of a rig or wagon in a four- (or more) horse hitch

whelp   (hwelp) a very young puppy

Whimpy   (hwim' pē) first horse reg-istered in the American Quarter Horse Association

whinny   (hwin' nē) the horse's sound that denotes happiness, antici-pation, anxiety, etc.

whip   (hwip) **1.** an instrument or device of wood, bone, plastic, leather, fiberglass, metal, or a combination thereof with a loop or cracker of leather or cord at the upper end; used for disciplining or goading an ani-mal; sometimes a required accessory when exhibiting, as in a horse show **2.** one who handles a whip expertly; one who drives a horse in harness other than racing **3.** one who "whips in" or manages the hounds of a hunt club

whipper-in   (hwip' ər in') a member of the hunt staff who assists the huntsman

whiskey   (hwis' kē) a two-person, open carriage with very high wheels

white   (hwīt) coat color; light hair on white skin; this color is rare, as most light horses are gray (light hair on dark skin)

white blanket over back and hips with dark spots Appaloosa coat pat-tern

white blood cell count   the number of white blood cells in a specific volume of blood; used to assess infection

white cells   leukocytes or white blood cells; colorless blood cells active in body defense against infection or other assault; occur in five types: neutrophils, lymphocytes, eosinophils, monocytes, and basophils

white coronet   limb marking; hair immediately above the hoof is white; see *markings, leg* (illus.)

white fetlock   limb marking; white on the fetlock joint in any variation; see *markings, leg* (illus.)

white flag   a marker used in equestrian sports to mark the left-hand extremity of an obstacle; also used to mark a set track and must always be passed on the right

white foal syndrome   an inherited condition in which the foal is born healthy, all white, with blue eyes, but has a constriction in the large intestine; surgical correction is usually unsuccessful

white heel   limb marking; white at the back of the pastern to the hoof; may be one or both heel bulbs; see *markings, leg* (illus.)

white lethal   an inherited, genetic, lethal condition in foals in which the foal receives the gene for albinoism from both parents; the embryo will die in the uterus

white line   the junction of the wall and sole of the hoof where the sensitive and insensitive laminae meet; visible on bottom of hoof; see *hoof* (illus.)

white muscle disease   a disease brought about by a selenium deficiency in the diet that eventually damages muscle

white muzzle   a white marking over both lips up to the region of the nostrils

white pastern   a limb marking; white from the fetlock downward; may be half pastern, three-quarter pastern, etc.; see *markings, leg* (illus.)

white eye   when the sclera around the eye is visible, as in the Appaloosa; see *human eye*

whoa   (hwō) the command to stop or stand; when repeated softly, it means to slow down; may also mean attention

whole colored   (hōl ku' lərd) no hairs of any other color on the body, head, or limbs

whorl   (hwôrl) coat marking; may be a line or a spot where hair that lies in different directions meets; often seen on the neck in a circular pattern

Wielkopolski   a Polish breed; relatively new breed influenced by Arab, Prussian, Hanoverian, and English Thoroughbred bloodlines; used as draft horses and for riding; courageous, calm, and a good mover

wild black cherry   see *cyanide*

Wild Horse of Wyoming   breed of the U.S., originated from Arab, Spanish, Turkmene and Berber lines; introduced by colonists and Cortez; stubborn and resistant

---

a=f<u>a</u>t; ā=<u>a</u>pe; ä=c<u>a</u>r; â=b<u>a</u>re; e=t<u>e</u>n; ē=<u>e</u>ven; i=<u>i</u>s; ī=b<u>i</u>te; ō=g<u>o</u>; ô=h<u>o</u>rn; ōō=t<u>oo</u>l; ŏŏ=l<u>oo</u>k; u=<u>u</u>p; ʉ=f<u>u</u>r; ŋ=ri<u>ng</u>; ə=sof<u>a</u>

Wild Horses of America Registry a registry to give recognition to wild horses and burros of America

Willie Shoemaker a jockey whose mounts won more than $63,000,000 in more than 7,200 races; considered the most successful jockey of all time

wind (wind) the breathing ability of the horse; a horse with good wind is sound and has sufficient capacity

wind and work when an animal has good wind and will work

windgall (wind' gôl') a distention of the synovial sheath between the suspensory ligament and the cannon bone or of the synovial sheath between the long pastern and the middle inferior sesamoid ligament; usually a result of too fast or too hard road work, especially on hard surfaces; also called *wind puffs* or *road puffs*

winding a twisting of the striding leg around in front of the supporting leg so as to walk in the manner of a "rope walking" artist; most often occurs in horses with very wide fronts; also called *rope walking*

wind puffs enlargements of the fluid sacs or bursa around the pastern or fetlock joint on either the front or rear legs; protrusions of joint capsules and/or tendon sheaths caused by stretching due to excessive fluid; see *blemishes and unsoundnesses* (illus.)

wind sucker a horse that cribs; see *cribbing* and *wind sucking*

wind sucking 1. a harmful habit in which a horse draws in and swallows air, causing indigestion 2. term applied to mares with flaccid vulvar labia that results in air being pulled into the vagina

windy an animal that whispers or roars when exerted; also called *windbroken*

wing (wiŋ) one of a pair of upright stands with cups or similar fittings used to support the poles or other suspended parts of a show-jumping obstacle

Wing Commander a Saddle Horse stallion that won the world's five-gaited championship six times

winging in when the hoof swings in when viewing a horse from the front at the walk or trot

winging out an exaggerated paddling; particularly noticeable in high-going horses

win in a canter (win in ə kan' tər) to pass the winning post first at an easy pace; being far ahead of the rest of the field

winkers see *blinkers*

winner's enclosure (win' ərz en klo' zhər) the place on a racecourse reserved for the first three horses in the race and to which their riders have to return mounted immediately after the end of the race

winter horse (win' tər hôrs) a horse that is kept at a home ranch for use during the winter

winter out (win' tər out) when a horse is left out in the field in the winter rather than brought into the stable

wire (wīr) has a wire scar

withers (wit͟h' ərz) the highest point of the horse's shoulders; the bony protrusion between the neck and back; see *points of the horse* (illus.)

Wobbler (wob′ blər) a horse with the condition called Wobbler's disease; seen on young horses usually under two years of age; characterized by uncoordinated movement of the hindquarters; may be due to some form of injury to the spinal cord

wobbles (wob′ əlz) a group of diseases of the spinal column and spinal cord; characterized by various defects of coordination; the wandering or staggering gait of affected horses; also called *ataxia*

wolf teeth (wŏŏlf tēth) small teeth located in the interdental space just in front of the premolars; horses may have up to four wolf teeth

wood chewing (wŏŏd chōō′ iŋ) a vice that generally results from boredom, in which the horses will bite and chew wood; most horses don't swallow the wood

wood fence (fens) fencing constructed from pine, oak, or fir; most wood fences are post and rail, in which wood posts are set in the ground and the rails are run perpendicular to connect them

Working Cow Horse (wʉr′ kiŋ kou hôrs) a class in which a horse is judged on his performance in cattle working and reining exercises

working from the ground the use of longeing and long reining as part of the education process of the horse; consists of some form of training that is performed without a rider on the horse's back

working gaits when a horse goes forward with adequate energy and rhythm; gaits at which most lower level work is done

Working Hunter a class in which the horse is judged on style, form, and his ability to negotiate a course safely

working the rope the action of the roping horse to maintain the tension in the rope attached to the calf at one end and the saddle horn at the other

worm (wʉrm) a jumping obstacle usually consisting of split logs and/or tree trucks and limbs piled on each other in a V-shaped manner

worming (wʉrm′ iŋ) slang for the act of administering medications to help control parasitic infestation; medication may be administered through tubing, paste, in the feed, etc.; more correctly called *deworming*

wrangler (raŋ′ glər) a person who looks after horses

wraps (raps) a turn of reins around the jockey's hands to restrain a horse

wrong bend (rôŋ bend) a dressage term to describe a horse that takes a turn without bending into the turn; the turn is straight, stiff, or even bent in the wrong direction

wrong leg not corrected when a horse picks up a canter with the incorrect lead and the rider does not correct it

wry tail (rī tāl) a tail that is carried to one side rather than being held straight

Wurttemberg (wʉrt′ əm bʉrg) a West German breed; a steady, docile riding horse used for saddle and light draft work

---

a=f<u>a</u>t; ā=<u>a</u>pe; ä=c<u>a</u>r; â=b<u>a</u>re; e=t<u>e</u>n; ē=<u>e</u>ven; i=<u>i</u>s; ī=b<u>i</u>te; ō=g<u>o</u>; ô=h<u>o</u>rn; ōō=t<u>oo</u>l; ŏŏ=l<u>oo</u>k; u=<u>u</u>p; ʉ=f<u>u</u>r; ŋ=ri<u>ng</u>; ə=sof<u>a</u>

X

xylazine (zī′lə zīn) generic name for a tranquilizer or sedative; see *zylazine*

XC finish a type of surface finish on malleable iron stirrups; an extrabright cadmium plating used in place of galvanizing

X rays roentgen rays; used to take radiographs of the body, thus locating fractures, etc.; used because of their tissue-ionizing ability

Y

yawning (yôn' in) a vice in horses when the horse continually opens his mouth and stretches his head down and out so as to attempt to evade any contact with the bit

yearling (yir' lin) a horse between one and two years old; a young horse from January 1 to December 31 of the year following its birth

yearling head collar (hed käl' ər) a halter/head collar that is adjustable at the nosepiece to fit the growing head of a yearling

yeld mare (yeld mâr) a mare that did not produce a foal during the current season

yellow dun (yel' ō dun) coat color; dark skin with a diffuse yellow coat; the mane and tail may be black or chocolate; a withers stripe, list, and zebra markings may be present

yellow star thistle (stär this' əl) poisonous plant found throughout the southern, western, and eastern U.S.

yew (yōō) a poisonous bush, also called *Taxus,* with green needles and red berries; sometimes grown as an ornamental bush; can cause a horse's heart to stop

Yorkshire boot (yôrk' shir bōōt) a rectangle of material, usually felt, with a tape sewn along the center; after the leg is wrapped, the tape is tied just above the fetlock joint and the top of the boot is folded down over it; provides two layers of protection

Yorkshire halter (hôl' tər) a type of halter with a complete, ribbed, hemp headpiece and nosepiece with a string throatlatch and a fitted shank; strong and particularly useful for horses that pull back

young entry (yun en' trē) young hounds and young riders just entered

youth (yōōth) exhibitor less than eighteen years old; additional age divisions are often created to separate children further

Ysabella an offshoot of the American saddle horse; originated in the U.S. on McKinzie Ranch, Williamsport, Indiana; used for pleasure riding and as an exhibition horse

---

a=fat; ā=ape; ä=car; â=bare; e=ten; ē=even; i=is; ī=bite; ō=go; ô=horn; ōō=tool; ŏŏ=look; u=up; ʉ=fur; ŋ=ring; ə=sofa

Z

zebra (zē' brə) a family relative of the horse

zebra marks striping on the limbs, neck, withers, or quarters, as in the zebra-striped legs of a dun

zebrass (zē' bras) the offspring resulting from the mating of a horse and a zebra

zebra stripes dark stripes that run on the neck, withers, body, and limbs

Zemaituka a Russian breed believed to be a descendant of the Asiatic wild horse; survives on poor feed; resistant to cold; may travel forty miles per day

zinc (ziŋk) forms an essential part of many enzymes required by a horse; responsible for growth; a deficiency can cause depressed appetite, skin lesions, and reduced growth

zoonosis (zō än' ə sis) an infection transmissible under natural conditions from animals to humans

zoonotic disease (zō än not' ik di zez') zoonosis

zootoxin (zō' ə täk' sin) a toxic substance of animal origin

zygote (zī' gōt) a fertilized egg

zylazine (zī' lə zīn) a sedative or tranquilizer used commonly in horses; rompun

---

a=fat; ā=ape; ä=car; â=bare; e=ten; ē=even; i=is; ī=bite; ō=go; ô=horn; ōō=tool; ŏŏ=look; u=up; ʉ=fur; ŋ=ring; ə=sofa